INFLATION
AND DISINFLATION

INFLATION
AND DISINFLATION

The Israeli Experiment

Leonardo Leiderman

The University of Chicago Press

Chicago and London

Leonardo Leiderman is professor of economics at Tel Aviv University, and senior advisor for policy and research at the Bank of Israel. He has also served as a consultant to the International Monetary Fund and the World Bank.

The University of Chicago Press, Chicago 60637
The University of Chicago Press, Ltd., London
© 1993 by The University of Chicago
All rights reserved. Published 1993
Printed in the United States of America

02 01 00 99 98 97 96 95 94 93   1 2 3 4 5

ISBN: 0-226-47110-1 (cloth)

To Betty

Contents

Preface

The Israeli economy contains many interesting puzzles, in that some of its developments do not conform well with mainstream models. In addition, several of its institutional features are quite unusual. This is a very open economy in which there is a high degree of indexation of wages, taxes, and financial assets, and a largely accommodative monetary policy and exchange-rate policy.

Consider for example the effects of the inflation-stabilization plan adopted in mid-1985. Standard textbooks in macroeconomics have relatively sharp predictions about the impact of contractionary aggregate demand policy measures, aimed at reducing inflation, on the economy. These measures are typically envisioned to initially result in a drop in output and a rise in unemployment, with relatively little impact on the rate of inflation. Disinflation is produced only a few periods after the adoption of this policy. As time passes, and to the extent that the policy is not reversed, output and unemployment start moving back toward their "natural" levels.

In sharp contrast, the recent Israeli disinflation featured an immediate and abrupt reduction in the rate of inflation which was accompanied, for about three years, by a boom in private consumption spending and in economic activity, and by sizable increases in real wages. The rate of unemployment has risen markedly only since the beginning of the fourth year after the stabilization program, and the previous strong upward trends in private consumption spending and in real wages were no longer observed at that time.

Interestingly, these patterns of disinflation are not unique to Israel. Similar outcomes have been observed in response to various stabilization policies in Argentina, Brazil, Chile, and Mexico. There is reason to suspect that at least some of these phenomena will characterize post-stabilization developments in Eastern European economies.

These considerations stimulated and motivated much of the research work presented in this book. In particular, I have found great intellectual challenge in confronting macroeconomic models with the relatively high-quality time-series data for Israel, and in deriving, when possible, the policy implications of the analysis.

Because of its rapid and successful results, Israeli disinflation in the second half of the 1980s, as well as the high inflation that preceded it, has generated a great deal of attention in the economics profession. This episode is likely to be discussed at length in future editions of macroeconomics textbooks, perhaps along with other famous case studies such as the German hyperinflation. Accordingly, I thought it would be useful to present in a book my own research on the process of inflation and on stabilization policies in Israel. Most of the material in this book is the outcome of joint work with other authors over the last dozen years. In addition to selected articles that were published previously in professional journals, the book contains previously unpublished material. The latter includes a comparison of the economy's structure before and after disinflation (chapter 4), and an update of evidence on the relation between inflation and relative price variability (chapter 17). Two chapters on the relation between inflation, devaluation and money growth are published here in English for the first time (chapters 6 and 8). Additional new material in this book consists of an elaboration of and expansion on basic conclusions and a discussion of controversies and of alternative approaches. Although each chapter has its own motivation and theme, the topics are closely related and they all share my approach that subjecting macroeconomic models to formal empirical analysis—even in the somewhat unusual conditions of Israel—is a prerequisite for both the process of scientific progress and the application of these models to practical and policy issues.

I would like to thank my coauthors for agreeing to publish our papers in this volume. I have been fortunate to work with, and learn from, Alex Cukierman, Zvi Eckstein, Elhanan Helpman, and Assaf Razin from Tel Aviv University, Guillermo A. Calvo from the International Monetary Fund, Nissan Liviatan from Hebrew University, and Elise Brezis, Arie Marom, and Rafi Melnick from the Bank of Israel. The ways in which I approached the research work in this book have been heavily influenced by my teachers at the University of Chicago: Robert E. Lucas, Jr., Jacob A. Frenkel, Robert Barro, and Thomas J. Sargent. I have closely followed their work over the years and have learned much from them. Much of the research in this book was done within the dynamic and stimulating territory of the Department of Economics at Tel Aviv University. In addition to my colleague-coauthors whose names appear above, I have benefitted from numerous discussions with Eitan Berglas, Zvi Hercowitz, Efraim Sadka, and Zvi Sussman. And the research on the Israeli economy by Michael Bruno and Stanley Fischer has certainly influenced my own work. Finally, I would like to thank an anonymous reviewer for useful comments on a previous draft of this book.

Introduction

This book centers around five main controversies on the causes and characteristics of high inflation in Israel and on the factors that produced disinflation in 1985. Basic research can provide useful inputs for attempting to resolve these controversies and for the understanding of similar processes in other countries. Since the economic issues that motivated this research work are not unique to Israel, there is room for learning from comparative cross-country studies. Accordingly, part of the analysis in this book draws on the experience of Latin American countries with inflation and disinflation processes.

The role of fiscal fundamentals for inflation and disinflation has been a first source of controversy. This controversy was influenced by the empirical observation that even in high-inflation countries there is a rather weak statistical association between quarterly or annual movements in the rate of inflation and in the government budget deficit. In many policy discussions, this was taken to imply that the fiscal deficit is not a main source of existing inflationary pressure, and that the latter can be attenuated without a fiscal adjustment. These were certainly influential arguments in the design of disinflation policy attempts in Israel in the early 1980s, in Argentina in the late 1970s, and Brazil in the mid-1980s (see chapters 2 and 8).

This issue motivated much of my work with Elhanan Helpman (see chapter 2). Based on our own research and on work by other authors, Helpman and I advance the argument that the dynamics of inflation and of the budget deficit depend on changing expectations by the public about future fiscal regimes. In particular, it is plausible that in several high-inflation episodes the private sector developed expectations that the existing policies could not be sustained and that therefore a major policy change would occur in the future. These expectations, along with the substantial uncertainty that is likely to exist about the timing and specific form of the policy change, can give rise to a weak contemporaneous relation between the rate of inflation and the budget

deficit, even in cases in which by construction the deficit is the only fundamental source of inflation. The facts that for longer-period averages there is a
link between budget deficits and inflation, and that disinflation policies succeeded in Latin America and in Israel only when accompanied by major fiscal
adjustments, support the notion that fiscal fundamentals play a key dynamic
role on the processes of inflation and disinflation.

A subset of the controversy on the role of fiscal fundamentals in the inflation process involved the claim that government revenue motives were not
responsible for the acceleration of inflation. This claim was often supported
by the empirical observation that there is a weak statistical relation between
government seigniorage and the rate of inflation. Furthermore, it was argued
that in several high-inflation episodes the rate of inflation was higher than the
revenue-maximizing rate so that the authorities could have actually raised
revenue by generating lower inflation. To deal with these issues using formal
methods of modern monetary economics, Zvi Eckstein and I developed and
estimated an intertemporal model of optimal decisions about private consumption and real money holdings (see chapter 12). After implementing the
model on time-series data, the estimated parameters were used in simulations
of the relation between seigniorage and the rate of inflation. Although we
found a positive relation between the rate of inflation and seigniorage, it
turned out that no sizable gains in revenue could be obtained for inflation rates
that exceeded 10 percent per quarter. Accordingly, we concluded that the
revenues from money creation obtained at the inflation rates of the first half
of the 1980s were very close to the maximum possible revenues from this
source. When the authorities' choice of seigniorage and of the rate of the
inflation was endogenized, as in the research work with Guillermo Calvo in
chapter 13, we found some support in the data for Argentina, Brazil, and
Israel for the restrictions implied by an optimization model of the inflation
tax. Specifically, the results indicated that an extension of an intertemporal
tax-smoothing model that takes into account financial liberalization, state-
contingent inflation, and time inconsistency goes a long way in statistically
accounting for fluctuations in the rate of inflation within the framework of
government's revenue motive for inflation.

A second important controversy centered around the issue of inflation inertia. It was argued that during the late 1970s and early 1980s the rate of
inflation developed its own momentum, or inertia, as revealed by its relatively
high and slowly decaying autocorrelations. Under this argument, much of the
acceleration of inflation was related to large devaluations effected by the authorities in response to adverse trade-balance shocks. These one-time devaluations, it was argued, were transformed into permanent rises in inflation
through mechanisms of staggered price setting, of monetary and exchange-
rate accommodation to past price shocks, and of wage indexation. It was then

concluded that anti-inflation policies were not likely to be effective unless they directly broke any existing inflationary inertia.

Research on this issue is presented in parts I and II. In part I, Elhanan Helpman and I show that when these ideas are embedded in a simple wage-price spiral model, they imply an inverse relation between unexpected inflation and real wages and a positive relation between inflation and employment. Yet the evidence pointed to several episodes in which the comovements of these variables sharply differ from these predictions, in that marked increases in inflation were accompanied by steep rises in real wages. Thus, it appeared that inflation and real wage comovements were dominated by factors other than backward-looking inertia. Based on this insight, Helpman and I developed a price-wage spiral framework in which nonsynchronization in the forward-looking behavior of price and wage setters coupled with monetary accommodation gives rise to a positive correlation between movements in the rate of inflation and the real wage, of the type that have been observed in Israel. While by construction there are no elements of inflation inertia in the model, the latter can give rise to a highly autocorrelated time path of the rate of inflation—a path that would be erroneously interpreted as reflecting inertia. In our view, the mere finding that inflation is highly persistent in a time-series sense does not necessarily provide an indication about the degree of inertia, or predetermination, of the price level.

The issue of inflation inertia is further analyzed in part II using model-free time-series methods such as causality tests and vector autoregressions for the period before disinflation. The results revealed the existence of strong feedbacks from exchange-rate depreciation to money growth and inflation. Yet the impulse-reponse functions estimated by Assaf Razin and myself in chapter 9 indicated that exchange-rate shocks have only temporary effects and do not give rise to inflation inertia. In spite of this, the findings that exchange-rate variance accounts for a substantial fraction of inflation forecast error variance, and that a temporary slowdown in exchange-rate depreciation was estimated to generate a temporary slowdown in money growth and inflation provide support to the heterodox notion of using a fixed exchange rate at the start of a stabilization program which also includes major adjustment of fiscal and monetary fundamentals.

Different interpretations of the results of the 1985 inflation-stabilization program were the source for a third set of controversies. Standard macroeconomic models, based on contractual rigidities or imperfect information, imply that both a shift to less accommodative exchange rate and monetary policies and an increase in the relative importance of real shocks are likely to affect the tradeoff between inflation and unemployment, the degree of persistence in the economy, and the comovements of variabilities of relative prices, relative wages and relative outputs across different sectors. Much of the evidence in the quantitative comparison of macro performance before and after stabilization, with Nissan Liviatan in chapter 4, accords with these propositions. Less standard were the immediate and abrupt reduction in the rate of inflation after the program and the timing and form of the impact of disinflation on real variables. The boom in private consumption spending during the first three years of the program and the delayed contractionary responses of output and of the rate of unemployment are especially puzzling in this context. Although research has not generated unambiguous and decisive explanations for these phenomena, chapter 9 discusses how lack of full credibility of government policies coupled with a process of reallocation of resources, or structural adjustment, can combine to provide useful insights.

Fourth, with the advent of high inflation Israel's economy developed ways to live with it. For example, nominal wages, taxes, and assets' returns were indexed to the consumer price level and in some cases to the exchange rate. While it was argued that these institutional adaptations reduced the allocative and welfare costs of inflation, casual observation suggested that high inflation was accompanied by high variability of relative prices. This phenomenon is studied in part IV. With Alex Cukierman, I constructed several indexes of relative price variability and documented their empirical links with the rate of inflation and with the variability of inflation through time. We found that it is the unexpected component of inflation that had strongest effects on relative price variability, though statistically significant effects were also found for expected inflation. Moreover, we found a positive and statistically significant relation between movements in relative price variability and the variability of the rate of inflation over time. Part of our research was devoted to examining the impact of government setting of prices of controlled goods (such as basic food items, gasoline, and public utilities) on relative price variability within the free-goods sector of the economy. We found that the latter was affected not only by aggregate shocks, as in standard models, but also by the extent to which the average price of controlled goods is not synchronized with the nominal money supply. Finally, an update of the evidence to account for the period after 1985 indicated that the abrupt disinflation after the stabilization program was accompanied by sharp decrease in relative price variability and in the variance of inflation over time. Thus, there is reason to believe that disinflation has reduced both an element of noise in relative prices and the degree of inflation uncertainty.

The last part of the book focuses on the controversy about the impact of government budget policies on aggregate demand; that is, on the Ricardian neutrality proposition. Casual empirical evidence indicates that there have been several episodes in Israel in which the saving ratio of the private sector has moved in opposite direction than the saving ratio of the public sector, much as under the predictions of Ricardian neutrality. For example, after the

1985 stabilization program the saving ratio of the public sector increased by about 6 percent of national income and at the same time the private saving ratio decreased by about the same magnitude. Assaf Razin and I formally tested the Ricardian proposition within the context of an intertemporal model of consumers' optimization (see chapter 19), and could not reject the restrictions imposed by this proposition. Thus, the results of this part of the book support the notion that private consumption spending is invariant with respect to changes in the financing of a given stream of government expenditures whether by conventional taxes or public debt.

The book is organized as follows. Part I deals with disinflation and with inflation stabilization policies such as the heterodox program of 1985. I have briefly set out what I believe are the main lessons from this research work on inflation and disinflation in the first chapter of that part. In part II, I present empirical research on the dynamic interactions between inflation, devaluation, and money growth. The analysis is based on time-series methods of vector autoregressions and causality tests. Part III presents empirical studies of money demand and of the relation between the rate of inflation and government seigniorage revenue. The links between inflation and relative price variability are empirically explored in part IV. Part V focuses on the effects of government budget policies on private consumption and on aggregate demand.

Part I: Stopping High Inflation

1

Overview: The Main Lessons

In this chapter, I provide a brief account of the main broad lessons from the research work in this and other parts of the book on the origins and characteristics of high inflation and on the key factors that contributed to disinflation in 1985. The discussion is organized around the main empirical regularities, or stylized facts, of these phenomena that were documented in this and related research. The analysis and interpretation of these regularities can provide useful inputs for attempting to resolve important controversies on the causes of high inflation and on the reasons for the success of the 1985 program at stopping high inflation, and for the understanding of similar phenomena in other countries.

Origins and Characteristics of High Inflation

Israel had annual rates of inflation below 10 percent before the 1970s. During the decade of the 1970s inflation accelerated to double-digit figures. The height of the inflation process was in the first half of the 1980s, when the annual rate of inflation reached triple-digit figures. The benefit of hindsight and the results of extensive research point to the following five main regularities for this period of high and rising inflation.[1]

First, the acceleration of inflation was not accompanied by higher levels of government seigniorage. That is, the evidence does not support the notion that as inflation accelerated, the government was obtaining more real revenues through money creation. Instead, the data indicate that seigniorage remained relatively stable in spite of wide fluctuations in the rate of inflation. This fact is not unique to Israel. A similar finding holds for the European inflations of the 1920s and for Latin American inflations of the 1970s and 1980s, with the exception of the most extreme inflation observations (that is, the peak of hy-

---

1. For a comprehensive historical perspective on the macroeconomic conditions in Israel, see Bruno (1989).

perinflation).[2] Furthermore, calculations presented below indicate that the observed seigniorage figures in Israel of about 2–3 percent of GNP on average for 1960–90 were very close to the maximum possible amounts that could be extracted via this source of government revenue.

Second, high inflation developed in the presence of high government budget deficits. The fiscal stance of balanced budgets in the first half of the 1960s changed into budget deficits of 13 percent of GNP on average in 1967–72 and to 17 percent of GNP on average in 1973–84; see table 1.1. Interestingly, marked increases in the deficit were closely associated with increases in defense expenditures after the wars in June 1967 and October 1973. No major adjustment of fiscal fundamentals was made prior to the 1985 stabilization program.

The relation, or lack thereof, between fluctuations in the budget deficit and movements in the rate of inflation is a controversial theme that appeared repeatedly in discussions in Israel and elsewhere. Theoretical and empirical work on this subject has indicated very clearly that there is a dynamic and complex relation between these two variables. Although there may be a relatively weak degree of comovement between the rate of inflation and fiscal fundamentals on a quarter-to-quarter or even year-to-year basis, the evidence for broad period averages is unambiguous: high inflation developed under high budget deficits.

Third, throughout the period of high and rising budget deficits and inflation there was a sizeable accumulation of internal and external debt. This can be viewed as an implication of large budget deficits that were not financed by money creation, as explained under the two regularities above. Figure 1.1 illustrates the increase in internal public debt from 50 percent of GNP in 1970 to 135 percent on the eve of the 1985 disinflation program, and the accompanying increase in external debt from 40 percent of GNP in 1970 to about 80 percent by mid-1985. Thus, at the peak of the crisis, and right before the stabilization program was implemented, the sum of internal and external debt amounted to more than double the economy's GNP. It is important to stress that most internal public debt was indexed to the consumer price level and that external debt was denominated in foreign currencies. Therefore, in contrast to other economies, there was limited room for the inflation process to erode the real value of these debts. The accumulation of debt until 1985 left an important implication for the government budget thereafter, namely the burden of interest payments on that debt. This burden amounted to 10 percent of GNP during the low-inflation period from 1985 to 1990 (see table 1.1).

An important class of models developed in recent years has emphasized how in a prolonged episode of sizable accumulation of internal and external

---

2. See, e.g., the evidence provided by Sargent and Wallace (1973) on the European hyperinflations.

Table 1.1
Fiscal Fundamentals: The Public Sector Budget

	1960–66	1967–72	1973–84	1985–90
Total expenditures:	36.8	55.3	76.0	61.5
Defense spending	9.7	21.1	25.7	16.0
Interest payments	1.6	2.9	5.7	9.8
Total revenues	35.6	42.7	58.8	61.2
Deficit	1.3	12.6	17.3	1.1

Source: Bruno (1989); and *Annual Report 1990,* Bank of Israel.

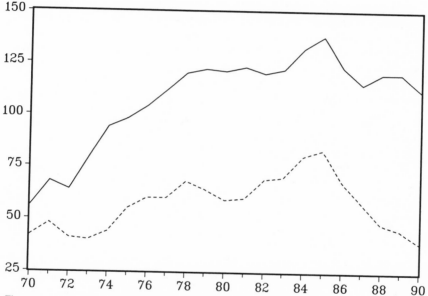

Figure 1.1   Internal and external debt as percentage of GNP (Israel, 1970–90). Source: Annual Reports from the Bank of Israel; and Bruno (1989) (———— = internal; - - - - - = external).

debt the dynamics of inflation may depend on the public's expectations of a change in the fiscal regime in the future. In this context, the time path of the rate of inflation has been shown to depend on expectations about the specific form of fiscal adjustments expected for the future as well as on uncertainty about the date of the policy switch.[3]

Fourth, the evidence indicates that autonomous increases in real wages

3. See, e.g., Sargent and Wallace (1981); and Drazen and Helpman (1990). This class of models is discussed in chapter 2 below.

played a nonnegligible role in the inflation process. Real wages rose by about 20 percent from the early 1970s to the early 1980s, and then by an additional 16 percent until 1984. That both these episodes correspond to marked rises in the rate of inflation seems to be more than pure coincidence (see chapter 3). Although in simple macro models an autonomous rise in the real wage leads to a once-and-for-all jump in the price level, the analytical framework in chapter 3 illustrates how once-and-for-all changes in the real wage can induce permanent changes in the rate of inflation in economies with staggered determination of prices and wages and with monetary accommodation. This issue is related to the next point.

Fifth, beyond fiscal and monetary fundamentals there was a role of institutional adjustments to high inflation in enhancing the economy's capacity to transform one-time nominal shocks into persistent changes in the rate of inflation. The existence of substantial degrees of indexation of nominal wages and of financial assets and the highly accommodative nature of monetary and exchange-rate policies in the high-inflation economy clearly worked in that direction.[4]

Stopping High Inflation

Having discussed the factors that played most important roles in the acceleration of inflation, I turn now to what can be considered as the main ingredients for, and features of, disinflation after 1985.

First, the presence of a sharp adjustment of fiscal and monetary fundamentals in the 1985 stabilization program is the key factor that differentiates this program from earlier attempts to stop inflation. The monetary authority imposed tight controls on credit growth, and fiscal discipline was achieved by a combination of three factors: a reduction in government spending, an increase in taxes, and increase in foreign aid. Consequently there was a rapid decrease in internal and external debt (see figure 1.1), thus reversing previous upward trends in these variables. Most previous anti-inflation plans relied on some form of fixing the exchange rate and on price controls as in the 1985 program. Yet there is evidence to suggest that the earlier programs failed because these measures were not accompanied by any major adjustment of fiscal and monetary fundamentals. In this respect, the experience of Israel is similar to that of several Latin American countries in the late 1970s and in the first half of the 1980s.[5]

Second, the fact that the adjustment of fundamentals was combined with a fixed exchange rate and with temporary wage and price controls, in what

4. These factors have been emphasized in the context of Israel by Bruno and Fischer (1986).

5. See Dornbusch (1990), who stresses the key role of adjustment in fiscal and monetary fundamentals in heterodox programs. For a description of the application of heterodox programs in Latin American countries see Kiguel and Liviatan (1989).

defines the program as heterodox, probably resulted in faster and less costly disinflation than otherwise. It seems that the use of a fixed exchange rate as the nominal anchor along with temporary wage and price norms attenuated the underlying high degree of inflation persistence and thus allowed for a greater impact of the change in fundamentals on the rate of inflation.

Third, for the first two years disinflation was accompanied by a boom in private consumption and in economic activity. Signs of a recession and a slowdown in the rates of growth of private consumption and aggregate output appeared only three years after the start of the program. The pattern observed for the first two years does not conform well with the notion of a short-run tradeoff between inflation and unemployment (i.e., a Phillips curve). Recent research has made progress in producing models that can explain these phenomena. In particular, analytical frameworks have been developed in which lack of full credibility of an exchange-rate-based stabilization program may play a crucial role in accounting for a temporary rise in private consumption spending.[6] The well-known failure of previous stabilization plans and the persistence of high inflation make it plausible that even a program as comprehensive as the one in 1985 was perceived by the public as being of a temporary nature. Lack of full credibility, and hence temporariness, may also account for the rise in the real wage and the real interest rate and the real appreciation of the domestic currency in the first few years after the program.

As far as the delayed response of economic activity to disinflation is concerned, it appears that the economy's real sector started to adjust to the new conditions only after the new policy gained credibility. This adjustment entailed major reallocation of resources among sectors, such as a shift of factors of production from banking and financial activities to nonfinancial sectors. In addition, the reduction in government subsidies to the corporate sector, the high levels of the real wage and the real interest rate, and the prolonged appreciation of the real exchange rate resulted in a drop in corporate profits. All these factors contributed to the stagnation that prevails in the early 1990s. From the standpoint of policy, Israel's disinflation highlights the importance of heterodox stabilization measures in a small open economy. Yet, no clear recipe has emerged on how to disinflate and to ensure at the same time a sustained renewal of economic growth.

References

Bruno, M. 1989. Israel's Crisis and Economic Reform: A Historical Perspective. Working Paper no. 3075, NBER, August.

6. See Calvo and Vegh (1990, 1991).

Bruno, M., and S. Fischer. 1986. The Inflationary Process: Shocks and Accommodation. In *The Israeli Economy: Maturing Through Crisis,* ed. Y. Ben-Porath. Cambridge: Harvard University Press.

Calvo, G. A., and C. A. Vegh. 1990. Credibility and the Dynamics of Stabilization Policy: A Basic Framework. Unpublished manuscript. International Monetary Fund, October.

————. 1991. Exchange-Rate-Based Stabilization Under Imperfect Credibility. Working Paper 91/77. International Monetary Fund, August.

Dornbusch, R. 1990. Experiences with Extreme Monetary Instability. Unpublished manuscript. MIT, March.

Drazen, A., and E. Helpman. 1990. Inflationary Consequences of Anticipated Macroeconomic Policies. *Review of Economic Studies* 57:147–66.

Kiguel, M. A., and N. Liviatan. 1989. The Old and the New in Heterodox Stabilization Programs: Lessons from the Sixties and the Eighties. Unpublished manuscript. The World Bank, October.

Sargent, T. J., and N. Wallace. 1973. Rational Expectations and the Dynamics of Hyperinflation. *International Economic Review* 14:328–50.

————. 1981. Some Unpleasant Monetarist Arithmetic. *Federal Reserve Bank of Minneapolis Quarterly Review:* 1–17.

2

Stabilization in High-Inflation Countries: Analytical Foundations and Recent Experience[1]

I. Introduction

Consider an economy, such as Argentina or Israel in the early 1980s, which has the following characteristics:

(1) There is a high rate of inflation at a three-digit annual level that has prevailed for several years.

(2) There is widespread use of formal and informal indexation.

(3) There is a relatively large stock of public debt and a large budget deficit (over 10 percent of GDP).

(4) There is a statistically weak link between the budget deficit and the inflation rate.

(5) There is an accommodative monetary policy.

(6) The government has an important role in setting key nominal variables, such as prices of public-sector utilities and subsidized food products.

(7) It is commonly understood that adopting policies that markedly increase the rate of unemployment is politically infeasible.

(8) There is a relatively large stock of foreign debt and a balance-of-payments deficit.

(9) There have been several past attempts to disinflate, none of which succeeded. In fact, these attempts often ended with an acceleration of inflation in subsequent periods.

Now suppose that the authorities choose the goals of immediately reducing the inflation rate to below 20 percent per year on a permanent basis and of

Reprinted with permission from *Carnegie-Rochester Conference Series on Public Policy* 28 (1988):9–84.

1. This research was partially supported by the Foerder Institute for Economic Research and the Archie Sherman Fund for research of International Economic Relations. For comments we would like to thank Eitan Berglas, Allan Drazen, Stanley Fischer, Allan Meltzer, Assaf Razin, and Zvi Sussman, as well as participants at the April 1987 Carnegie-Rochester Conference and seminars at the University of Chicago, the Stockholm School of Economics, and Tel Aviv University.

improving the economy's external position. Conventional macroeconomic theory suggests that in order to achieve these goals, a set of contractionary fiscal and monetary policies must be adopted, and that for these policies to affect expectations, it is important that they be perceived by the public as credible and sustainable. There are at least two potential difficulties with adopting such policies that were envisioned by policymakers and their economic advisors in some of the countries under consideration. First, the policies are likely to result in an increase in the rate of unemployment due to downward wage rigidity (see [7] above). Second, in order to effect a fiscal contraction, it is typically necessary to sharply increase prices of the public-utilities sector, with the objective of reducing the losses of public-sector enterprises and to reduce the extent of product subsidization. At the same time, balance-of-payments developments require a devaluation of the domestic currency (which is overvalued). If indeed implemented, the nominal adjustments and alignment of relative prices would lead to an immediate price increase, which would then be transmitted, through indexation, into wage increases and increases in other nominal variables. These, in turn, will increase inflationary expectations and result in higher inflation.

Given these perceived difficulties, as well as political resistance to cutting budget deficits, it is perhaps not surprising that policies of this type have not been commonly observed. Instead, most previous anti-inflation policies have consisted of managing the exchange rate and other nominal variables (such as public-sector tariffs and wages) to achieve a given target for the inflation rate. Although in some cases these policies were planned to be accompanied by fiscal and monetary restraint, this did not materialize, and so the end result was a failure to reduce inflation (e.g., Israel in 1982–83 and Argentina in the late 1970s). Moreover, since these policies resulted in distortions in the structure of relative prices (e.g., overvaluation of the domestic currency and low prices of food products), they typically ended with the introduction of sharp corrective adjustments in the previously managed nominal variables.

Against this background, a new set of disinflation policies was adopted from 1985 on by several high-inflation countries. These new disinflation strategies (referred to as "heterodox") are based on the following main ingredients:

(1) The public sector takes a series of measures to reduce the size of its budget deficit to a level below 5 percent of GDP.[2] This is achieved primarily by imposing higher and new taxes and by experiencing an increase in real tax revenue (in the presence of time lags in the process of tax collections) as a result of the decrease in the inflation rate (the so-called Tanzi-effect). In the longer run, the government intends

2. Sargent (1982) emphasizes the role of budget-deficit reductions in ending hyperinflations of the 1920s.

also to reduce its spending as well as the size of the public sector. Monetary policy is planned to be restrictive, though some monetization of the economy is expected following the reduction in the inflation rate.

(2) At the time of implementing the program, there is a discrete adjustment of the exchange rate, wages, prices of subsidized commodities, and public-sector tariffs. These are effected to align previously distorted relative prices to levels that seem sustainable for a period of at least several months. Following these one-shot adjustments, nominal variables are frozen (through administrative controls) at their new levels.[3] These controls are imposed for a limited period of time, and it is announced that they will be gradually lifted thereafter (though the exact date for their lifting is not known ahead).

(3) Upon adoption of the program, many existing indexation arrangements are abolished, at least temporarily. Thus, there is no automatic compensation for the initial jumps in the exchange rate and prices. Instead, it is stipulated that wages will be allowed to increase only after agreements to that effect are reached between government, private-sector employers, and labor trade unions. These agreements, together with the government's future adjustment of prices and exchange rates, are to shape the path of key nominal variables in a synchronized way that will avoid large fluctuations in relative prices.

The main objectives of this paper are to review the recent plans and their actual implementation,[4] and to explore analytical foundations of four sets of issues which are at the heart of the new programs:

(a) the connection between budget deficits and the rate of inflation;
(b) the role of exchange-rate management in an anti-inflation plan and its connection with budgetary policies;
(c) the available policy options for disinflating economies that feature wage and price inertia and monetary accommodation;
(d) the role of wage and price controls in the disinflation process.

While we are not able to provide a complete analysis of these issues, our discussion imposes some analytical discipline on recent controversies. This helps to clarify important issues and to identify directions for further research.

Section II provides a review of the disinflation plans adopted in four countries: Argentina, Israel, Brazil, and Bolivia. Given the great similarity of the comprehensive plans implemented in Argentina and Israel, we focus most of

3. Dornbusch (1982) provides arguments in support of combining wage-price controls and exchange-rate targeting with the more conventional measures of monetary and fiscal restraint as integral components of stabilization policies in developing countries. Interestingly, the use of price and wage controls as an ingredient of stabilization plans in high-inflation economies is new; controls were not used in stopping previous hyperinflations (see Dornbusch, Simonsen, and Fischer [1986]).

4. For previous discussions of the recent plans, see Dornbusch, Simonsen, and Fischer (1986); Knight, McCarthy, and van Wijnbergen (1986); Blejer and Liviatan (1987); and Dornbusch and Simonsen (1987).

our discussion on these two countries. Section III deals with the connection between budget deficits and inflation. Section IV considers open-economy issues, and in particular the role of exchange-rate management in the disinflation process. In section V we discuss the phenomenon of inflationary inertia, which is widely believed to exist in these economies, and examine the implications of wage indexation and nonsynchronized wage- and price-setting rules. We characterize macroeconomic policies that can disinflate such economies. The role of wage-price controls is also discussed in this context. Section VI concludes the paper.

II. Recent Anti-Inflation Plans

In this section we review policy measures that were included in recent disinflation plans and discuss the resulting macroeconomic performance. The plans are presented, together with the views about the functioning of the economies that stood behind their formation. Our assessments are provided in the analytical sections that follow. We deal with Argentina, Bolivia, Brazil, and Israel but focus our discussion on the plans adopted by Argentina and Israel in 1985.

A. The Austral Plan

Argentina's inflation history for 1960–1986 is depicted in figure 2.1. It can be seen that three-digit annual inflation rates persisted continuously from the

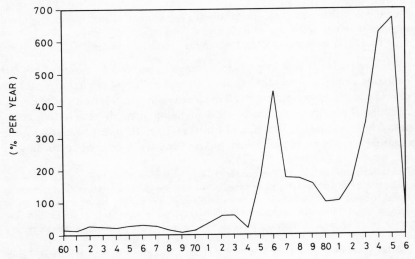

Figure 2.1   Inflation in Argentina, 1960–86.

mid-1970s. The Austral Plan, named after the new currency, was adopted on June 14, 1985. The main goal was to drastically reduce the inflation rate, which reached a level close to 2,500% annually in May 1985. Table 2.1 presents quarterly data on the development of key macroeconomic variables before and after the adoption of the plan.

Policy Measures. The most salient policy goals and measures that were included in the Austral Plan are as follows:[5]

1. Fiscal Policy: the fiscal goal was set to reduce the combined deficit of the nonfinancial public sector and the central bank from a level of about 12% of GDP to a level of no more than 2–3% of GDP. It was estimated that a deficit of this magnitude would be fully financed by foreign capital inflow and thus would eliminate altogether the need for credit expansion by the central bank to finance the public-sector deficit. To achieve the fiscal goal, several specific measures were adopted which were supposed to result in an increase in tax collections of 6% of GDP, a decrease in government spending of about 0.5% of GDP, and a decrease of 3.5% of GDP in the operating losses of the central bank. The planned increase in tax receipts reflected an increase in specific taxes as well as an increase in the real value of tax collections that arises when there are nonnegligible collection lags and the inflation rate is drastically reduced. Among the taxes that were imposed or raised under the plan are those affecting: exports, gasoline, imports, and bank transactions. The plan, then, substituted explicit taxes for the inflation tax.

2. Monetary Policy: initially, monetary policy was based on the assumption of zero inflation, and thus included a commitment of no money printing to finance public-sector deficits. First, a monetary reform was introduced with one unit of the new currency (austral) being equal to 1,000 existing pesos. In order to avoid large profits or losses to debtors and creditors who engaged in previously set contracts, a system of deindexation of contracts denominated in pesos was established. The system consisted of a table of "disagio" that provided daily conversion rates from pesos to units of the new currency. This table was applied to rental contracts, to saving deposits, and to borrowing and lending agreements. Second, there was a restructuring of interest rates by the central bank. In particular, it was planned that nominal interest rates would be set at levels that ensured positive expected real interest rates for both deposits and loans. Third, the central bank imposed ceilings on the levels of credit to the private sector. It also planned to use more intensively open-market operations as its policy instrument, and to reduce its high degree of intervention (as well as the government's) in the process of financial intermediation.

3. Wage, Price, and Exchange-Rate Freeze: the plan included a series of controls

5. Some of the sources for our discussion are: *Novedades Economicas* (a monthly publication by the Fundacion Mediterranea, Cordoba, Argentina), Central Bank and IMF publications and reports, and reports appearing periodically in *International Currency Review*. See also the papers mentioned in note 3 above.

Table 2.1
Macroeconomic Indicators for Argentina
(1983:I–1986:IV)

Period	Inflation (% monthly)	GDP (Index)	Industrial Employment (index)	Industrial Real Wage (index)	Budget Deficit (% of GDP)	M_1 Growth (% monthly)	M_5 Growth (% monthly)	Real Interest Rate (% monthly)	Real Exchange Rate (Basket index)	Real Exchange Rate ($ index)	Trade Deficit ($ mil.)
1983:											
I	13.40	100.00	101.80	86.80	7.00	3.70	7.40	0.80	120.00	124.40	957.0
II	11.70	104.20	100.40	96.10	8.25	14.70	12.30	0.07	108.90	118.90	922.0
III	17.00	109.10	97.70	104.90	9.00	9.40	11.90	3.83	93.70	111.10	793.0
IV	18.00	112.26	100.20	112.30	15.80	28.90	22.30	1.93	99.20	120.00	660.0
1984:											
I	16.60	114.73	104.40	120.60	12.50	14.10	17.00	1.38	94.50	110.20	1294.0
II	17.80	119.21	102.80	127.60	12.30	17.90	15.40	3.67	88.20	106.10	1350.0
III	22.90	120.28	101.30	128.50	9.75	11.00	14.40	8.90	81.60	102.80	754.0
IV	18.00	123.89	103.10	131.60	10.75	23.20	18.10	1.20	93.90	93.70	124.0
1985:											
I	24.10	122.40	108.00	122.00	11.50	12.90	19.80	1.33	91.20	121.00	830.0
II	28.40	116.77	100.30	116.20	12.30	33.00	35.30	4.17	99.67	128.70	1642.0
III	3.80	107.31	93.80	105.10	3.30	12.20	11.00	4.63	109.00	135.70	1331.0
IV	2.50	103.56	94.40	103.20	5.60	11.50	7.10	3.70	107.70	128.00	782.0
1986:											
I	3.10	103.97	98.90	105.30	4.50	0.80	4.60	3.77	105.30	117.70	550.0
II	4.40	109.90	94.40	105.60	2.80	7.90	6.40		102.00	109.30	722.0
III	7.50		92.50		2.60				102.30	102.00	582.5
IV	5.36								100.00	99.00	582.5

Notes: Inflation is measured by the percentage change in the CPI. Industrial employment is an index of the number of workers, and the industrial real wage is an index of average hourly real wages. The budget deficit (measured by cash flows) includes the nonfinancial public sector and the central bank and is expressed as a percentage of GDP. Real interest rates are regulated 30 days borrowing rates minus monthly inflation. Real exchange rates are adjusted for differentials in consumer prices. The sources are: International Financial Statistics, published by the IMF; Novedades Economicas and Newsletter, published by Fundacion Mediterranea, Cordoba, Argentina; and Indicadores de Cojunctura, published by FIEL, Buenos Aires, Argentina.

on prices and wages, as well as fixing the austral/dollar exchange rate. Prior to setting wages, prices, and the exchange rate at the levels to be subsequently frozen, it was necessary to adjust them to levels that seemed to be sustainable over a considerable period of time. Specifically, the following alignments were made. Just before the adoption of the plan in June 1985, the government announced a wage increase of 22.6% and an increase of 25.1% in retirement pensions. Public-sector prices (e.g., public transportation and electricity) were considerably increased in May and June 1985, in order to catch up with previous inflationary developments. The domestic currency was devalued by 18% against the dollar on June 11, 1985. All prices, wages, salaries, and other forms of compensation were frozen at their levels as of the date of the plan's implementation, and maximum prices were decreed on about eighty popular consumption items. The new exchange rate was set at 1 dollar = 0.8 austral and was announced to remain at this level for a considerable time period. The authorities also announced that these controls were to be gradually eliminated through a series of sectorial agreements and negotiations at some point in the future—yet provided no specific date for such a change.

Developments. In terms of the policies implemented and the results obtained, the period following the adoption of the Austral Plan can be divided into three subperiods: (i) June 1985 to February 1986; (ii) March 1986 to August 1986; and (iii) September 1986 to the present (April 1987). Our discussion relies on the quantitative evidence provided in table 2.1.

The first subperiod shows a marked reduction in the monthly inflation rate, from 32 percent in June 1985 to 6 percent in July and to a monthly average of 2.5 percent over the period August 1985–February 1986. During most of this period, the controls on prices, wages, and the dollar exchange rate were maintained at the original levels set in the plan. However, the sharp decrease in real wages that occurred after its adoption led to a series of wage demands that brought about nominal wage increases over this period. Moreover, as the economy's production began to recover in late 1985 and early 1986, labor employment increased, and associated with it were wage increases in the private sector. These increases also contributed to higher wage demands by public-sector employees. Most prices of public utilities were maintained constant over this period and so was the austral/dollar exchange rate. This resulted in a real appreciation of the domestic currency, which would have been larger were it not for the depreciation of the dollar in international currency markets that took place at that time. Price controls were not followed by the emergence of important shortages. Among the controls, those on wages were the least effective.

While the first stage of the Austral Plan exhibited some success in disinflating the economy, the monetary-fiscal policies that were actually adopted were not entirely supportive. On the fiscal side there was no reduction in the size of the public sector, and the deficit was reduced only to about double the level that could be financed from abroad. The failure to achieve the plan's fiscal goals was due mainly to lack of control over spending by the public sector. For example, social security payments and salaries to military personnel increased over this period over and above what was originally planned. Monetary policy was quite expansionary, resulting in average increases in real-money balances of about 10 percent per month. While part of this monetization reflected increased money demand and foreign capital inflow, as originally conceived, a substantial portion (about 60 percent of money creation) can be attributed to deviations from the plan's goals, and this part materialized mostly in the form of rediscounts by the central bank to public-sector entities. Despite increased monetization in the economy, the ex-post real interest rate showed a marked increase to about 5 percent per month in the early stages of disinflation.

The second stage of the Austral Plan represents an attempt to realign some of the key nominal and relative prices that were "distorted" during the first stage. A leading example is the austral/dollar exchange rate which was maintained fixed until April 1986. Given the observed real appreciation of the austral relative to the dollar, the authorities began devaluating the domestic currency in order to regain competitiveness, and this was achieved through a series of mini-devaluations in the following months. At the same time there was an upward adjustment of public-sector tariffs (to avoid increasing losses of public enterprises) and wage pressures were continuously growing. For example, in July 1986, the government agreed to have wage increases of up to 25 percent for the rest of 1986. Although initially these were presented as "corrective" measures, the general perception was that the government had decided to stop fixing the exchange rate and public tariffs as anti-inflation measures and moved instead to a policy of mini-devaluations and gradual increases in wages and other prices. Monetary and fiscal policies were more contractionary in this period than in the previous one, but they were still too expansionary compared to the authorities' goals.

The result of the above developments was a noticeable increase in the inflation rate, which tripled relative to its previous level, to an average of about 7 percent per month over this period. Aggregate economic activity showed an upward trend.

The resurgence of relatively high inflation prompted the third stage of the plan, which started in late 1986. This stage consisted of an attempt at combating inflation again, though this time with a much more contractionary fiscal and monetary policy. As far as fiscal policy was concerned, the goal was similar to that included in the original plan, and the available evidence indicates that this goal is being achieved since September 1986 (mostly through higher taxes). Moreover, the authorities seemed committed to reducing the number of public-sector employees by at least 10 percent during 1987. Regarding monetary policy, the central bank has reduced its rediscounting and has imposed effective ceilings on credit to the private sector. The authorities' goal was to have monthly increases in the money supply of about 4–5 percent, which is about 40 percent lower than the average monthly increases over June 1985–September 1986. These monetary policies have resulted in an increase in real interest rates and a credit squeeze on the private sector.

Together with these monetary and fiscal policies, the authorities started gradually devaluating the domestic currency and also allowing increases in wages and public-sector prices within governmentally decreed authorized "bands." Thus, the policy of fixing the exchange rate at a certain level, and then waiting for a few months until this level is adjusted again, was substituted by a policy of mini-devaluations. While the official goal was to have an inflation rate not higher than 3 percent per month, most Argentine analysts agreed that a monthly rate around 4 or 5 percent was a more realistic forecast for 1987.

Summing up, although the original goal was the eradication of inflation, the updated goal as of early 1987 seemed to be to maintain inflation at the two-digit level, preferable below 50 percent per year. While the plan had initial success in disinflating the economy, the accompanying fiscal and monetary policies were too expansionary to be consistent with the nominal prices imposed by official controls. Thus, there was a lack of coordination between the price-controls policy and fiscal and monetary policies. Some of the price and wage controls were not effective, and key relative prices began to move in what were commonly thought to be unsustainable directions. This created the need for corrective measures that were implemented in the second stage of the program. As of the first quarter of 1987, the current stage of the Argentine stabilization effort featured a combination of more contractionary fiscal and monetary policies, together than an attempt to control and synchronize from month to month the rates of increase of wages, the exchange rate, and prices.

B. The Israeli Stabilization Plan

As shown in figure 2.2, three-digit annual inflation is a relatively recent phenomenon in Israel, dating from the end of the 1970s. Israel's plan was announced on July 1, 1985. Its main target was to reduce inflation from the previous level of 10–15 percent per month to a level of less than 2 percent per month. The plan was also intended to bring about an improvement in Israel's balance of payments. Macroeconomic developments for periods be-

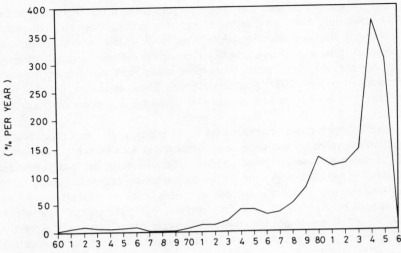

Figure 2.2   Inflation in Israel, 1960–86.

fore and after the adoption of the plan are summarized in table 2.2, which is used as the basis of our following discussion.

Policy Measures. The specific policy measure and goals were as follows:[6]

1. Fiscal and Monetary Policies: at the time of adoption of the plan, Israel featured one of the world's highest ratios of public-sector debt to GNP: about two. Accordingly, the main fiscal goal was to reduce the budget deficit of the public sector to a level that would ensure no further growth in real domestic and external debt. This implied that the domestic budget deficit had to be reduced from its prevailing level of close to 15 percent of GDP to no more than 5 percent of GDP. A number of fiscal measures were taken in order to achieve this target, most of which concentrated on raising net tax revenue. Specifically, new taxes were imposed (e.g., on cars, property, and travel abroad), and there was a substantial cut in subsidies to basic goods such as food and transportation (e.g., there was a 75 percent increase in the price of bread, and a 27 percent rise in fuel prices). At the same time, Israel received emergency aid from the United States government amounting to a total of $1.5 billion to be spread evenly over 1985 and 1986 (this figure represented about 6 percent of Israel's yearly GNP), which further contributed to the reduction in the budget deficit.

Concerning monetary policy, measures were taken to limit credit expansion to the private sector and to reduce the effective degree of liquidity of bank deposits that were linked to foreign exchange. In addition, the authorities planned to take measures to

6. The following discussion is based on various reports and publications of the Treasury and the Bank of Israel, as well as on Bruno (1986, 1987). See also the papers mentioned in note 3 above.

ensure a more intensive use of open-market operations in the implementation of monetary policy.

2. Fixing the Exchange Rate: the plan envisioned the nominal exchange rate of the dollar as being a key anchor for other nominal variables. After an initial devaluation of 19.1 percent, the exchange rate was fixed at 1.5 shekels per dollar.

3. Wage and Price Freeze: the view was that given the substantial price shocks induced by the devaluation and the cuts in subsidies, the maintaining of existing wage indexation agreements would have resulted in a new round of inflationary-spiral effects. In order to avoid this development, and in order to help disinflate the economy, the plan included a temporary (three-month) suspension of existing indexation arrangements. Since in the absence of other measures this suspension would have resulted in a sharp cut in real wages, the trade union demanded compensation which materialized in the following planned wage increases: 14 percent of gross wages, to be paid on August 1, a one-time 12 percent payment on September 1, and 4 percent to be paid at the beginning of each one of the first three months of 1986. In addition, formal indexation in the form of 80 percent compensation for previous month's inflation rate was reestablished beginning December 1, 1985, only if inflation exceeded 4 percent per month (contrasted with 12 percent before the adoption of the program). April 1986 was determined as the date at which wage negotiations would resume. Indexation of financial assets remained unaltered.

After the initial devaluation and the upward adjustment of prices, the government legislated a full price freeze for a period of three months. For the period thereafter, the authorities announced their intention to gradually eliminate price controls, though their exact timing and magnitude remained uncertain.

Developments. Analysis of the economy's performance under the plan can be subdivided into two main periods: before and after January 1987. Before the adoption of the new policy measures, monthly inflation was typically in the 10–15 percent range. Upon implementation of the plan, the inflation rate increased in July 1985 to 27.5 percent, reflecting the stepwise alignment of the exchange rate and other prices and a marked gradual deceleration thereafter. The rate of inflation was 2 percent per month during the last quarter of 1985, and 1 percent per month during the first quarter of 1986. By the end of 1986 the inflation rate was about 2–2.5 percent per month.

Perhaps equally impressive is the performance of the public-sector domestic deficit. From substantial domestic deficits before July 1985, the public-sector budget went into a surplus on a cash-flow basis; see table 2.2. Three key factors were responsible for this development: an increase in government tax collections, a decrease in government payments in the form of subsidies, and the arrival of United States emergency aid. Even though the figures show a sharp fiscal adjustment, some of its components (as, e.g. United States emergency aid) are of a temporary nature (see below).

Table 2.2
Macroeconomic Indicators for Israel
(1983:I–1986:IV)

Period	Inflation (% monthly)	GDP (index)	Employment (thousands)	Real Wage, Private Sector (index)	Real Wage, Public Sector (index)	Budget Deficit (% of GNP)	M_1 Growth (% monthly)	M_5 Growth (% monthly)	Real Interest Rate (% monthly)
1983:									
I	6.70	28.10	1323.00	108.00	113.00	4.00	13.00	6.80	0.80
II	7.40	27.00	1343.00	99.80	107.50	1.10	0.70	8.40	0.50
III	7.50	26.90	1347.00	102.60	108.70	6.80	5.10	8.90	1.40
IV	15.90	26.70	1344.00	88.30	88.40	3.80	10.80	16.30	4.10
1984:									
I	12.50	27.10	1325.00	92.20	90.30	8.70	11.70	13.60	2.80
II	16.00	26.70	1331.00	98.20	107.40	4.90	10.10	14.10	3.00
III	16.70	27.70	1361.00	98.80	110.30	12.30	12.90	16.40	5.90
IV	15.50	27.70	1342.00	96.00	106.00	10.10	19.20	17.10	6.80
1985:									
I	10.30	28.60	1364.00	101.00	99.90	8.50	14.90	12.00	5.80
II	13.70	29.20	1352.00	94.00	97.80	4.40	6.60	13.40	5.40
III	11.50	28.30	1333.00	86.50	85.80	0.50	16.90	8.60	5.90
IV	2.20	27.00	1350.00	88.20	84.10	-0.90	6.70	3.80	6.80
1986:									
I	0.60	28.20	1354.00	101.50	90.10	-0.70	15.70	4.50	4.30
II	2.20	28.30	1359.00	102.30	107.00	-4.40	0.90	1.10	1.30
III	1.00	28.56	1379.00	102.80	105.80	-2.40	7.00	3.20	2.60
IV	3.00	27.70	1377.00	106.70	105.70	-4.10	4.20	3.20	1.80

Period	Real Exchange Rate (basket-index)	Real Exchange Rate (dollar-index)	Controlled Prices (ratio to CPI)	Trade Deficit ($ millions monthly)	Private Consumption (index)	Unemployment ($ of labor force)
1983:						
I	91.00	95.80	99.00	242.30	20.60	4.50
II	87.50	93.00	98.00	318.10	20.30	4.50
III	89.00	97.00	96.50	331.70	19.99	4.10
IV	94.20	104.00	103.00	266.70	19.40	4.90
1984:						
I	94.60	103.90	110.80	197.10	18.50	5.60
II	94.40	103.80	105.90	253.70	18.80	5.80
III	92.50	104.00	99.00	280.60	19.80	5.60
IV	94.70	107.00	97.80	108.80	18.30	6.40
1985:						
I	101.00	115.80	102.80	124.70	19.00	5.90
II	108.00	121.90	111.00	216.20	18.80	6.50
III	114.00	125.00	128.00	163.60	17.70	7.50
IV	108.00	115.00	118.00	142.40	19.50	6.70
1986:						
I	106.00	109.60	117.40	152.40	20.00	7.20
II	100.00	101.30	120.60	216.20	20.50	7.90
III	99.00	100.60	120.80	210.70	21.30	6.80
IV	97.00	98.40	118.40	207.70	21.33	6.60

Note: Inflation is measured by the percentage change in the CPI. Employment is the number of employed persons (in thousands). The budget deficit (measured by average cash flows) is expressed as a percentage of GNP. The real interest rate is the effective monthly rate on credit lines for businesses minus the inflation rate. Controlled prices represent the ratio of the price level of controlled goods and services to the CPI. Private consumption is an index in constant shekels. The trade account is the excess of imports over exports in $ millions, monthly averages.

Sources: Various issues of *Annual Report and Recent Economic Developments,* published by the Bank of Israel; and *Israeli Monthly Statistics,* published by Israel's Bureau of Statistics.

Turning to the behavior of key relative prices, consider first the real exchange rate of the shekel against the U.S. dollar and against a basket of foreign currencies (including the dollar). Following the devaluation of the shekel at the initial stage of the plan, both real exchange rates increased (i.e., the domestic currency depreciated) during the third quarter of 1985. However, from that time on there was a marked real appreciation of the domestic currency—primarily against the U.S. dollar. This appreciation was just a result of combining the fixed-exchange-rate policy, that was maintained up to January 1987 (see below), with positive domestic inflation. At the same time that the shekel/dollar exchange rate was maintained fixed, the dollar depreciated in world currency markets, so that effectively the shekel *depreciated* against foreign currencies other than the dollar. Moreover, the observed declines in international prices of oil and commodities were additional external developments that helped maintain the fixed-exchange-rate policy. The real appreciation with respect to the basket was milder than with respect to the dollar. In any case, the inverted-U shapes of real-exchange-rate levels indicate that while the competitiveness of Israeli products was relatively high at the start of the period, it continuously deteriorated. In August 1986 the authorities decided to peg the exchange rate to a basket of foreign currencies rather than to the dollar. Towards the end of 1986 pressure was mounting to have a devaluation that would offset existing trends.

Second, we turn to real wage behavior. It can be seen in figure 2.3 that the plan initially strengthened a downward trend in real wages in the private sector that prevailed in early 1985. The same holds for real wages in the public sector. Real wages in public and private sectors reached their lowest levels in the six months following the adoption of the plan. However, both these variables have shown marked increases from the end of 1985, with public-sector wage increases typically lagging behind those of the private sector. Both real wages show a U shape, and after a temporary erosion have come back to their average (or even higher) levels before the plan. Regarding the indexation arrangements, in April 1986 a two-year agreement was signed, stipulating a cumulative threshold inflation rate of 7 percent (below which indexation payments are not yet made) and an indexation coefficient ranging from 70 to 90 percent, depending on the actual inflation rate. Under this agreement a monthly average inflation rate of 1.5 percent would result in an indexation adjustment of 70 percent of cumulative inflation once every four or five months (see Bruno [1986]).

Third, we turn to controlled prices and their relation to the overall CPI. Upon looking at past periods, it can be seen that the policy of slowing down the monthly rate of increase of governmentally determined prices adopted in 1982–83 resulted in a very low ratio of these prices to the CPI. The 1985 plan began with a marked upward adjustment of these prices, which was

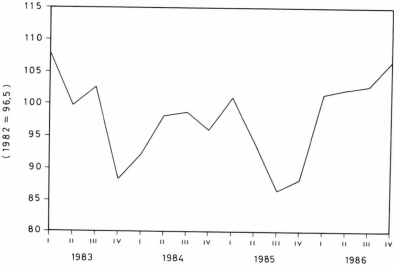

Figure 2.3   Israel—private sector real wage rate.

subsequently partially offset, yet leaving the ratio of controlled prices to CPI at a higher level in 1986 than before the plan. The controls did not lead to shortages in the economy, and by the end of 1986 many controls were removed.

Monetary policy was only initially conducted in a way consistent with disinflation. Towards the second half of 1986 credit and money aggregates expanded fast, in considerable excess of their targets. The sharp disinflation was associated with high ex-post real interest rates on the free segment of bank borrowing, about 6–7 percent per month, until the last part of 1985. However, these credit lines constituted a small fraction of total credit, with much lower interest rates applying to the larger government-directed credit component. Real interest rates have decreased since then, and by the end of 1986 they were at the 1.7 percent monthly level.

The Israeli disinflation did not lead to a marked decrease in employment or real output. As shown in figure 2.4, initially employment continued the downward trend that existed at the beginning of 1985. However, since the end of 1985 there has been a marked increase in employment and in economic activity, which have either returned to or passed the average level of pre-July 1985. The rate of unemployment increased in third quarter of 1985 and in the first quarter of 1986, but from then on it has been continuously decreasing.

The plan resulted in an initial improvement in the trade account, but this proved to be a temporary phenomenon. Rising real wages and consumption together with the real appreciation of the shekel, have led to increases in

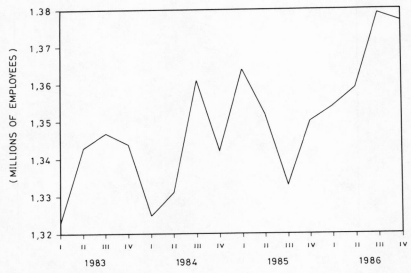

Figure 2.4   Israel—employment.

imports and a smaller growth in exports that have brought the trade deficit back to its pre-plan level. Since United States emergency aid was received over the 1985–86 period, the unfavorable developments in the trade account did not manifest themselves in the form of reserve losses or increased foreign borrowing—so that the overall balance of payments brought about a decline in foreign indebtedness.

Last, figure 2.5 describes a U-shaped behavior of private consumption, which decreased in the quarter following the implementation of the plan (and thus continued a trend from the previous quarter), but then increased continuously, starting with the last quarter of 1985. In fact, private consumption reached a peak level during 1986.

Towards the end of 1986, the marked real appreciation of the shekel and increases in real wages resulted in a loss of competitiveness and raised serious doubts about the desirability of maintaining the prevailing exchange-rate level. Accordingly, on January 13, 1987 a new package of policy measures was adopted, one that represented an updating and correction of previous measures. Specifically, the new package contained the following main ingredients: (i) a devaluation of 10 percent of the shekel, resulting in a new exchange rate of 1.65 shekels per dollar. The authorities emphasized once again their intention of maintaining a fixed exchange rate with respect to the basket of currencies; (ii) an upward adjustment of prices of subsidized products. For example, the price of bread was increased by 20 percent and that of milk by 14 percent; and public transportation fares are scheduled to increase by

30 percent in April. The government returned to statutory price controls for a period of one year, up to April 1988; (iii) a new tripartite agreement between government, the trade union, and the employers stipulated a postponement of 2.7 percentage points out of the next indexation payments, and the Treasury decreed a decrease of 2.7 percent in national insurance payments made by employers. The latter agreed to abstain from passing over cost increases that will result from the devaluation, and from other price adjustments, into prices of manufactured products.

While the official forecasts were that due to these adjustments inflation would have accelerated during the first quarter of 1987, the overall outlook for economic policy during 1987 remained uncertain. The reason was that there were signs that the public-sector budget deficit would be higher than the level that seemed consistent with inflation rates in the order of 2–3 percent per month. Government spending was forecasted to increase, United States emergency aid was not forthcoming in 1987, and the government had intro- duced a tax reform package that effectively reduced marginal income tax rates which would result in lower tax revenue. The new outcome was likely to be a public-sector budget deficit of about 4 percent of GDP of 1987.

Comparing the economy of Israel at the present time with that before the adoption of the plan suggests that most real economic variables have not changed noticeably (recall the U shapes that characterize the behavior of sev- eral of these variables, such as the real wage rate, employment and private

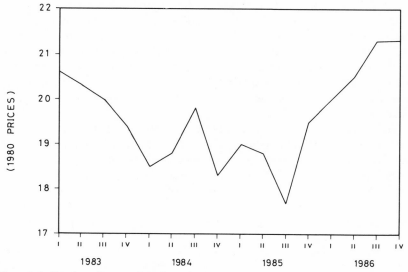

Figure 2.5   Israel—private consumption.

consumption). In fact, disinflation during 1986 has been accompanied by booming real wages and private consumption. The most striking change is the decrease in the size of the government budget deficit.

C. Other Stabilization Plans

We now discuss the policies adopted by Brazil and Bolivia.

C.1. The Cruzado Plan. During most of the 1980s, Brazil featured annual inflation rates at three-digit levels. (See figure 2.6, which gives quarterly inflation rates expressed in percentages per month). In 1984 and 1985 the annual inflation rate settled at 220 percent, and in early 1986 there was an acceleration of inflation to an annual level of about 400 percent. Under these circumstances, the authorities decided to attack inflation, and on February 28, 1986, they adopted a set of policy measures that form the Cruzado Plan. The plan implemented a currency reform, replacing old currency units by cruzados. Brazil's initial conditions seemed more favorable than those of Argentina and Israel in that they featured a continuous trade surplus, high growth of GDP, and a budget deficit no larger than 4 percent of GDP.

The basic idea underlying the plan was that Brazil's inflation was mostly inertial, and that as such it can be eradicated by using statutory wage and price controls without necessarily requiring fiscal and monetary contraction. The main policy measures included the following:[7] (i) prices were frozen at their prevailing levels for an indeterminate time horizon; (ii) the exchange rate was fixed at the level of 13.80 cruzados per dollar; (iii) wages were frozen at a new level in cruzados. This level was determined according to the average purchasing power of wages during the previous six months plus a wage increase of 8 percent. These steps brought about an effectively large increase in real wages at the start of the program. Wage indexation was suspended as long as inflation did not go beyond 20 percent; (iv) indexation of government bonds was suspended for one year, and a table was announced for converting old currency units into new ones.

The Cruzado Plan has not succeeded in reducing inflation. Even though inflation was reduced to about 1–1.5 percent per month within the first six months, inflationary pressure has been gradually accumulating, and it erupted by the end of 1986 and the beginning of 1987—inflation running at an annual rate of 500 percent for the first quarter of 1987. There are at least two weak points in the plan and its implementation. First, instead of aligning relative prices and reducing real wages before establishing price controls (as was the

---

7. Some of the sources for our discussion are: *Indicadores de Cojunctura* (various issues); reports appearing in *International Currency Review* (various issues); and IMF publications and reports. See also the papers mentioned in note 3 above.

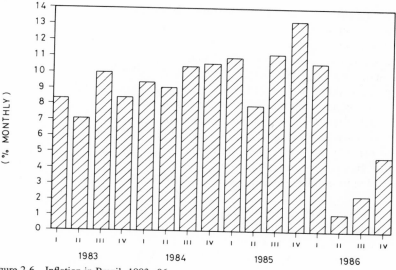

Figure 2.6   Inflation in Brazil, 1983–86.

case in Argentina and Israel), the plan began with a sharp increase in real wages, and the authorities froze prices at their existing levels as of February 1986. For some products, like beef, milk, and some consumer durables, this implied very low relative prices. The latter were maintained, in many cases, only through increased subsidies from the government to producers. Acute shortages and black markets developed for these products, with sellers typically asking buyers to pay agios (surcharges) well above official prices, and an environment of *suppressed* inflation developed. Faced with extremely distorted relative prices, many producers shut down their lines of production, thus further contributing to the shortages. Second, while the Plan contained a forecast of the budget deficit for the public sector in the order of 0.5 percent of GDP, the actual figure for 1986 turned out to be 10 times larger, namely, 5 percent of GDP. Lower tax revenues, higher government spending, increased losses of public enterprises, and increased subsidies all contributed to this development. In addition, monetary policy turned out to be much more expansionary than initially forecasted by the authorities. Output growth continued at a relatively fast pace and the trade account showed continued surpluses though at remarkably lower levels than before the plan, reflecting increased imports and decreased exports. These developments enhanced Brazil's difficulties in effecting interest payments on foreign debt, and in the first quarter of 1987 the government announced a temporary suspension of these payments.

The combination of generalized shortages and expansionary fiscal and monetary policies were viewed towards the end of 1986 as signaling an imminent collapse of the policy. Accordingly, on November 21, 1986 (following elections to Congress) the authorities adopted a second set of packages (the Cruzado II Plan) which mostly included stepwise upward price adjustments for numerous products; for example, electricity prices were increased by 40 percent, water tariffs by 45 percent, and mail service by 80 percent. These adjustments have continued during the first months of 1987 and have generated higher recorded inflation for that period—though, to the regret of wage earners, some of these adjustments were defined as "surcharges" and as such were not included in the inflation rate used for wage indexation payments. Rather than have a zero inflation target as in the original plan, the authorities attempted to stabilize the inflation rate for 1987 at the level of 50–60 percent.

C.2. Bolivia's New Economic Policy. Perhaps the most remarkable attempt to combat inflation in the 1980s is that of Bolivia.[8] During the first half of 1985 this country had an inflation rate of 20,000 percent per year, and in the summer of the same year the monthly inflation rate was around 60 percent (see figure 2.7). Money creation, and thus inflation, was the method used by the government in financing its budget deficit of about 30 percent of GDP—at a time when explicit tax revenue amounted to less than 5 percent of GDP. Other initial conditions included trade account deficits, generalized use of price controls and rationing, large operating losses of public enterprises, and a continued trend of decreasing output per capita (the latter decreased by 30 percent from 1980 to 1985).

The New Economic Policy was introduced on August 29, 1985. Its main objectives were to reduce inflation to a single-digit level, to restore external balance, and to lay the basis for a growth recovery. The policy consisted of the following main measures: (i) a dismantling of controls on prices, interest rates, and exchange rates. The exchange rate was initially floated, following a devaluation of about 90 percent, and later on replaced by a managed exchange rate. A general market liberalization was adopted; (ii) the imposition of strict controls over public finances aimed at sharply reducing the budget deficit. To this end, the program stipulated cuts in government spending in the form of support to public enterprises and subsidies to production and a tax reform establishing well-defined value-added, income and property taxes that would substitute for the inflation tax. In addition, to further enhance the fiscal contraction, wages in the public sector were frozen for periods of several months, and the government eliminated more than 15,000 jobs in the public

---

8. For an extensive discussion of the Bolivian case, see Sachs (1986). See also *IMF Survey,* January 26, 1987.

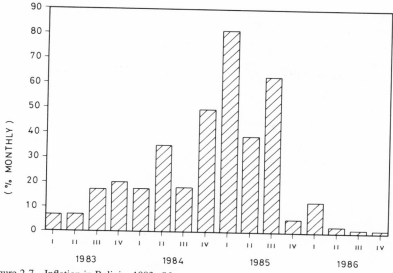

Figure 2.7   Inflation in Bolivia, 1983–86.

sector; (iii) the adoption of several structural and institutional measures, such as a process of rationalization of state enterprises and of reduction of the size of the public sector.

The results are so far impressive. The inflation rate for 1986 was less than 2 percent per month and a similar forecast held for 1987. Most of the measures included in the Plan materialized. Specifically, the authorities freed goods, financial, and labor markets; raised prices of public utilities (e.g., the price of gasoline was raised from $0.04 per liter to $0.30); and started a restructuring of state enterprises (especially the state mining company). In May of 1986 the government introduced a comprehensive tax reform that included taxes on net worth of enterprises, on landholdings and other assets, a 10 percent value-added tax, and a 10 percent complementary income tax. As a result of the tax reform and cuts in government spending, the budget deficit of the public sector has settled at 6 percent of GDP out of which 5 percent is externally financed. The main unresolved issue was the continued decrease in output (which declined in 1986 by 3 percent), made worse in 1986 by a deterioration in the country's terms of trade associated with the marked decline in prices of tin and hydrocarbons in international markets. In addition, there has been a widening in the current-account deficit in 1986 due to increased imports and reduced exports. Despite this, there has been a significant repatriation of capital which has more than offset the current-account developments, thus resulting in an increase in the country's international reserves.

The evidence so far indicates that Bolivia has succeeded in stopping an acute and chronic hyperinflation by using a combination of contractionary fiscal-monetary policies and a package of institutional and structural reforms. In contrast to the other countries discussed above, Bolivia's anti-inflation policy did not include price controls. On the contrary, the stabilization plan dismantled previous existing controls and proceeded to liberalize markets.

III. Budget Deficits and Inflation

During the public discussion that preceded the design of recent stabilization programs, a major argument in favor of unorthodox measures was that the inflationary process in Argentina, Brazil, and Israel is not of the "textbook" type, and it should not therefore, be combated by means of traditional measures. This argument was, of course, not new—it was at the heart of thinking that led to disinflation attempts by means of exchange-rate management in Argentina (1978–81), Chile (1978–82), and Israel (1982–83) (see chapter 8), and the thinking that led to the "package deal" policies in Israel (1984–85) that relied on price-wage agreements and controls. An important justification of the search for new explanations of the inflationary process and their policy implications was the observation that budget deficits were not strongly and positively correlated with the rate of inflation. Therefore, it was argued, the major source of inflationary pressure was not the budget deficit. For example, Liviatan and Piterman (1986) stressed that while the domestic-deficit-to-GNP ratio followed over time an inverted U shape (increasing from 4.1 percent in 1963–72 to 22.1 percent in 1973–77 and then down to 13.2 percent in 1978–83), the inflation rate continuously rose (from 7.4 percent per year in 1963–72 to 32.8 percent in 1973–77 and to 107.5 percent in 1978–83).[9] This argument was of major importance in the Israeli debate, and it was used to justify earlier attempts to disinflate without a fiscal adjustment.

Whatever merits explanations of the inflationary process that do not rely on budget deficits might have (we will discuss them at a later stage), it is important to understand that even in those cases in which the budget deficit is the sole source of inflationary pressure, one may observe periods in which this correlation is weak. Hence, the lack of a strong correlation of this type cannot be used on its own to reject the conventional approach. The importance of fiscal discipline is also apparent from the fact that programs that were implemented without restraining the budget deficit did not succeed.

The usual view that budget deficits and inflation are positively correlated rests on a steady-state analysis of the type presented in figure 2.8. Curve I

9. Furthermore, the correlation coefficients between quarterly movements in inflation and in the budget-deficit-to-GNP ratio are 0.47 and 0.41 for Israel and Argentina, respectively, over the three years that preceded the disinflation plans.

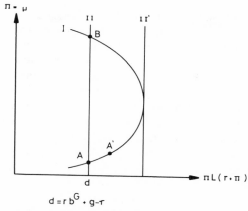

Figure 2.8   Determination of the steady state inflation rate.

describes the functional relation between the inflation rate π (with the inflation rate being equal to the rate of money growth μ) and the inflation-tax revenue $\pi L(r + \pi)$, where $L(\cdot)$ is the demand for real balances and r is the real interest rate. Curve II describes the budget deficit which is equal to $rb^G + g - \tau$ (b^G is the real value of government debt, g is real spending, and τ is real net taxes) and m denotes real balances; $m = L(r + \pi)$ in equilibrium.[10] Standard demand-functions for money, such as the Cagan type, imply that the two curves have two intersection points, such as A and B in the figure, which correspond to low and high inflation equilibria. Assuming that by controlling the money growth rate the government drives the economy to the low-inflation equilibrium, point A is actually observed.[11]

Now suppose that the budget deficit increases. Then curve II shifts to the right and the equilibrium shifts from A to A' (the largest budget deficit that can be financed by the inflation tax is given by curve II', which represents Friedman's maximum inflation tax). Hence, a higher budget deficit is associated with a higher inflation rate and lower real balances. The higher budget deficit may result from lower taxes, higher spending, or higher debt. Higher debt may result from an attempt to temporarily reduce the rate of money growth to combat inflation, which will eventually lead to a larger budget deficit as a result of larger outlays for debt servicing, and thereby to higher infla-

10. Curve II in figure 2.1 is drawn under the assumption that real taxes τ do not depend on the inflation rate. If tax revenue declines with increases in inflation, the curve is upward-sloping, which does not change the arguments in the text.

11. The answer to the question which of the two possible long-run equilibria will actually be observed depends on the nature of government policy out of steady state and on the formation of expectations. This issue has been treated in Sargent and Wallace (1987); Bruno (1987); and Bental and Eckstein (1990).

tion. Hence, without a fiscal adjustment it may be possible to trade off lower inflation in the near future for higher inflation in the distant future. This is the essence of Sargent and Wallace's (1981) monetarist arithmetic.

The difficulty with the direct application of this analysis to the countries under discussion is that a steady-state analysis is quite inappropriate for these episodes (there also exists the problem that the analysis is for a closed economy while these countries are rather open, but this is inconsequential for the problem at hand as long as the exchange rate is more-or-less floating). That this is the case is illustrated by the data for Israel and Argentina in tables 2.3 and 2.4, which describe the evolution of budget deficits and their financing. It is seen from these data that most of the financing of budget deficits was done by means of debt issues which have been raising the debt/income ratio. In Israel the debt/income ratio was about two just before the implementation of the program. It is also clear from these data that despite the acceleration of inflation in the eighties, revenue from base money creation did not change much, contrary to the prediction of the steady-state model. Some may argue (see, e.g., Bruno [1987]) that the latter represents a move from a low- to a high-inflation equilibrium, such as from point A to B in the figure. However, the evidence on the evolution of public debt seems to be inconsistent with this interpretation.

A possible interpretation of what has happened relies on the observation that these countries have been pursuing macroeconomic policies which were unsustainable in the long run, a feature that was manifested in large budget deficits and growing public debt. Consequently, it was expected that a major policy change will take place. Under these circumstances expectations of a

Table 2.3
The Financing of the Public Sector's Domestic Deficit, Israel 1981–1986 (in % of GDP)

	1981	1982	1983	1984	1985	1985:II	1986
1. Deficit (excl. interest	9.4	6.3	3.3	8.3	3.0	−0.2	−2.6
2. Interest	2.2	3.6	2.8	3.8	5.9	5.9	5.3
3. Domestic deficit (1 + 2)	11.6	10.0	6.0	12.1	9.0	5.7	2.6
Financing:							
4. Base money creation	2.0	1.8	2.3	2.9	6.5	10.6	1.9
5. Domestic net debt	8.1	8.3	−1.0	0.8	−1.2	−6.1	−0.4
6. Foreign exchange sales	1.9	2.6	6.3	8.6	4.8	2.2	2.5

Source: Bank of Israel, *Annual Report (1986).*

Table 2.4
The Financing of the Public Sector's Deficit, Argentina, 1980–1986 (in % GDP)

	Total Deficit (1)	Base Money Creation (2)	Domestic Net Debt (3)	External Financing (4)
1980	11.3	3.2	2.8	5.3
1981	16.4	2.9	6.5	7.0
1982	17.2	4.1	7.2	5.9
1983	12.7	1.0	10.2	0.9
1984	11.3	3.9	8.9	−1.5
1985:				
I	9.3	3.2	7.7	−1.5
II	23.4	11.4	9.3	2.6
III	5.5	3.5	1.5	0.5
IV	8.3	3.2	0.5	4.6
1986:				
I	6.8	1.7	2.2	3.0
II	6.0	3.4	−0.2	2.8
III	6.9	4.5	0.9	1.5

Sources: Cavallo and Pena (1983); Novedades Economicas (December 1986); and International Financial Statistics.

future policy change have major implications for current macroeconomic behavior, in particular when there is uncertainty about the timing of the policy change. This raises the question of whether such expectations alter the positive relation between budget deficits and inflation that emerges from steady-state analysis. It turns out that the answer to this question is in the affirmative, at least for some forms of expected policy changes. We know of no empirical study that has explored this issue in detail, and will, therefore, present the theoretical arguments.

Consider an economy in which a representative individual maximizes the discounted flow of utility:

$$\int_0^\infty e^{-\beta t} \left[u(c, \ell) + v\left(\frac{M}{P}\right) \right] dt,$$

where β is the subjective discount rate, c is consumption of the single available good, ℓ is leisure, M is the stock of money holdings, and P is the price of the consumption good (the arguments of $u(\cdot)$ and $v(\cdot)$ are time-dependent). The individual faces a standard intertemporal budget constraint, which reflects the existence of a perfect capital market in which a bond issued by the government is traded. The bond is denominated in terms of the consumption good and it pays a real interest rate r. The individual pays a lump-sum tax τ

in each period and tax on labor income at the rate λ. The evolution of government debt is given by:

$$b^G = rb^G + g - \tau - \lambda(1 - \ell) - \mu m, \qquad (2.1)$$

where $1 - \ell$ is labor supply and the real wage rate is equal to one.

Now consider a situation in which current policy consists of fixed values of (g, τ, λ, μ), such that initially public debt is growing over time. Assuming perfect foresight, it can be shown that in this case the equilibrium real interest rate is equal to the discount rate β, and debt grows faster than the rate of interest, thereby violating the individual's transversality conditions. In this sense the initial macroeconomic policy package is unsustainable in the long run.

Suppose, therefore, that it is expected that the government will change its policy. First, suppose that it is known with certainty that the policy change will take place at time T, and that it will bring the economy at once to a steady state. It is shown in Helpman and Drazen (1986) that if the public believes that lump-sum taxes will be used for stabilization, then real balances will be constant over time and so will the inflation rate, which will be equal to the rate of money growth. If the public believes that the policy switch will consist of raising the rate of money growth, then real balances will decline over time and the rate of inflation will increase over time. The same pattern emerges when the public believes that stabilization will be effected by an expenditure cut, provided the elasticity of demand for money with respect to the interest rate is smaller than one—the usual case. Here the demand function for money is implicitly described by the equilibrium requirement:

$$\frac{v'(m)}{\theta} = r + \pi, \qquad (2.2)$$

where θ is the marginal utility of consumption, which can be shown to remain constant at all points in time before the policy-switch date and the right-hand side is equal to the nominal interest rate. This implies a negative relationship between the inflation rate and the real stock of money on the adjustment path. However, when the public expects stabilization to be effected by an increase in the labor tax rate, real balances are rising over time and the inflation rate is declining over time. In all cases the budget deficit is rising over time, with the basic deficit $g - \tau - \lambda(1 - \ell)$ being constant (the rising overall deficit results from increases in government debt).

These results indicate that indeed when money financing is considered to be the long-run option, the rate of inflation will be rising and so will the budget deficit, thereby generating a positive association between them. However, when a fiscal correction is considered to be the long-run option, then a rising deficit can be associated with a rising, a constant, or a declining rate of inflation, depending on whether a spending cut, a lump-sum tax increase, or an increase in labor taxation is believed to be the corrective instrument.

This analysis rested on the assumption that the timing of stabilization is known with certainty. The more realistic assumption that there is uncertainty about the timing of stabilization further weakens the link between budget deficits and inflation. This issue is studied in detail in Drazen and Helpman (1990). Consider first the case in which stabilization will be effected by money financing. In this case the real interest rate will still be equal to the private discount rate, but the nominal interest rate will include a risk premium which compensates holders of nominal assets for the prospect of a price-level jump in the event stabilization takes place (unexpectedly). This risk premium can be positive or negative, depending on whether an upward or a downward price jump is expected. In any case real balances will be falling over time and the nominal interest rate will be rising over time as in the certainty case. The budget deficit will also be rising over time as in the certainty case. However, now, due to the existence of the risk premium, a rising nominal interest rate does not reflect a rising rate of inflation. The rate of inflation is equal to the nominal interest rate minus the real interest rate $r = \beta$, minus the risk premium. Hence, if the risk premium rises sufficiently fast, the rate of inflation may be declining despite the rising budget deficit. Figure 2.9 shows a simulated time pattern of inflation for a simple nonpathological example reported in Drazen and Helpman (1990). In this example the budget deficit is rising, while inflation is rising initially and declining thereafter.

The foregoing discussion shows clearly that there is nothing odd about finding a weak relation between inflation and budget deficits, as in the Israeli data, even if one maintains that the budget deficit is the major source of inflationary pressure. Naturally, in this framework a constant deficit that is fi-

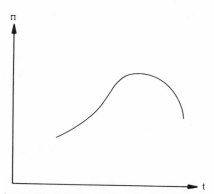

Figure 2.9   Example of a possible inflation path with a rising budget deficit.

nanced by means of an inflation tax implies a constant rate of inflation. It is also shown in Drazen and Helpman (1990) that uncertainty about the timing of a stabilization to be effected by a budget cut can generate cyclical movements in real balances and in inflation rates. This strengthens the case for the lack of a strong link between inflation and budget deficits. Hence, the lack of such a link in the data should not necessarily lead one to conclude that it is possible to disinflate without a fiscal adjustment.

Theory suggests that immediate budget balance is not necessary for an immediate ending of an inflationary process. What is required is an assurance that, if sustainable budget balance is not achieved on impact, it will be achieved in the future, so that there will be no need to rely on printing money. The difficulty is, of course, to generate this assurance, and immediate reductions in the budget deficit help to build up credibility in the new policy. This point has been emphasized by Sargent (1982), and also by Dornbusch (1982) who held a different view on efficient stabilization methods. However, the necessity of budget balancing was not generally accepted in the countries under consideration before 1985, and it was rejected in Brazil even as late as 1986.

Although plausible, the argument that links current budgetary performance to the formation of expectations has not been made precise. On the other hand, it is the case that programs which did not pay due attention to budget deficits have failed. One may therefore conclude that there is a clear case for long-term budget balancing, and that an immediate reduction of the budget deficit is most helpful, both because it has a favorable effect on expectations and because it makes easier the adjustment of fiscal policy to the long-run goal. These arguments are supported by the evidence from Israel, Argentina, and Brazil. Indeed, in Israel, which made the largest budgetary adjustment, inflation remained low for the largest span of time; second in this ranking is Argentina which made a moderate budgetary adjustment and had some reduction in inflation; and last is Brazil which made no budgetary adjustment and its plan has collapsed.

Although in this section we have stressed the role of budget deficits, we do not wish to argue that they were necessarily the sole source of inflationary pressures. We deal below with other possibilities, and with their relation to budget deficits.

IV. Exchange-Rate Management

A major ingredient of recent stabilization programs is a fixed exchange rate during the first phase. The use of exchange-rate management for disinflation purposes is not new. It has been used, for example, in the German program of 1923 and in the French program of 1926, as well as in the Argentine and

Chilean programs of the late 1970s and the Israeli program of 1982–83. What is different in recent programs is the composition of policies; in Argentina, Brazil, and Israel the exchange-rate freeze was accompanied by price and wage controls. The effects of price and wage controls will be analyzed in the next section, where we will also discuss the use of an exchange-rate freeze in that context.

One rationale that was suggested for exchange-rate management, such as a fixed exchange rate, as a component of a stabilization package has to do with its relative efficiency in disinflating with smaller output losses as compared to monetary policy. It is well known that in an economy with complete information and no distortions or rigidities, exchange-rate targets or monetary targets are equivalent policies. However, this equivalence need not hold in the presence of incomplete information, distortions, or rigidities. For example, Fischer (1988) has demonstrated that in an economy with multiperiod wage contracts, in which policy fundamentals have been adjusted for disinflation purposes, exchange-rate targets dominate monetary targets under some configurations of the underlying parameters, but are dominated under other configurations. His overall conclusion was, however, that the former possibility is more likely. The question raised in this analysis is an extremely important one. However, given the particular model used to answer it, the robustness of the result remains an open issue.

Notice that the foregoing discussion relied on the assumption that fundamentals, such as budgetary policy, have already been brought in line with the inflation target. Yet this was not always the case, and it is certainly not always apparent from government actual performance at the beginning of a stabilization program. This raises the issue of sustainability of exchange-rate management. Accordingly, we analyze in this section the relationship between exchange rate and budgetary policies.

It is indeed the case that an exchange-rate freeze together with a fiscal package that makes it sustainable in the long run brings inflation at once to foreign levels, provided the economy settles on a steady state. This is easily seen for an economy with traded goods only, in which the domestic price level P is equal to the foreign price level P^* times the exchange rate ε. In this case the rate of inflation π is equal to the foreign inflation rate π^* plus the rate of currency devaluation $\dot{\varepsilon}/\varepsilon$. Hence, if the exchange rate is constant, $\pi = \pi^*$. In the somewhat more complicated case in which there also exist nontraded goods, this point can be seen as follows. In a steady state the relative price of traded goods, often defined as the real exchange rate, i.e., $p = \varepsilon P^*/P_N$, where P_N is the price of nontradables, is constant. Assume also for the rest of this section that the foreign price of traded goods P^* is constant (the modifications required in order to allow for changing P^* are trivial). Hence, if the exchange rate is constant, then the price of nontradables is also constant.

Therefore, the price of tradables εP^* and the price of nontradables P_N are constant, and so is every price index that is built on them.

The assumption that the economy is in a steady state is essential for this conclusion as long as there are nontradable goods. For instance, suppose the economy is not in a steady state. In particular, suppose that aggregate spending is rising over time, bringing about a declining real exchange rate p (as happened in Israel in 1986). This real exchange-rate appreciation holds in terms of both p and another commonly used index of the real exchange rate $q = \varepsilon P^*/Q$, where Q is a price index which is a linear homogeneous function of the price of traded and the price of nontradable goods (here q is an increasing function of p). In this case

$$\frac{\dot{Q}}{Q} = \frac{\dot{\varepsilon}}{\varepsilon} + \frac{\dot{P}^*}{P^*} - \frac{\dot{q}}{q} = \frac{\dot{q}}{q},$$

so that the rate of inflation in terms of the price index Q is positive, despite the exchange-rate freeze. It is apparent from this discussion that an exchange-rate freeze can bring inflation to a halt only if the accompanying policies make the freeze sustainable and bring about stability of the real exchange rate. It is also clear from the data presented in section II that the second condition was not satisfied, because inflation was not brought to a halt, nor was it reduced to relevant foreign levels (by pegging the exchange rate to the dollar, the inflation rate declines to dollar price inflation of traded goods if the second condition is satisfied). Whether the first condition was satisfied is to some degree a matter of judgment. It was clearly violated in Argentina and Brazil, and in our judgment it was also violated in Israel, if one projects budgetary policy from past experience. This raises two questions. First, what other policies are required in order to support a given exchange-rate policy in general and an exchange-rate freeze in particular? And second, what are the real effects of exchange-rate management?

In order to answer the first question, it is necessary to consider the budgetary implications of exchange-rate management. For this purpose the relevant budget is the consolidated budget of the government and the central bank. While typically the central bank manages foreign-exchange reserves and the treasury manages government debt, quite often the ability to rebuild depleted reserves depends on the size of government debt. It is most convenient to think in terms of the simplest case in which foreign-exchange reserves and government debt bear the same real interest rate. In this case exchange-rate management affects the evolution of net debt through the induced movements in reserve holdings. Naturally, reserve movements do not depend only on the exchange rate. For example, they depend also on other factors that determine the demand for money, such as income and interest rates. Some of these variables, on the other hand, depend on the degree of control on international capital movements. Hence, reserve and net debt movements depend on a variety of policies, the exchange-rate policy being only one of them. However, the question on the sustainability of the policy package can be reduced to the following: does the implied evolution of net debt ensure solvency? If, for example, equation 2.1 is interpreted as the consolidated budget with b^G representing net government debt, then the solvency requirement reduces to the question of whether $e^{-rt}b^G$ is strictly positive as time goes to infinity. If it is not, the policy package is sustainable. In this case simple integration of (2.1) implies solvency in the sense that the present value of taxes, including the inflation tax, is equal to the present value of expenditures plus initial net debt.

It is clear from this discussion that if there exists a sustainable policy, then there also exist many others. For if a given trajectory of taxes, monetary injections, and spending is consistent with a trajectory of a managed exchange rate, then an increase in current spending on, say, tradables, together with a sufficiently large reduction in spending on tradables in the future, is also a sustainable policy (think especially about a small country). A current tax reduction with a sufficiently large increase of taxes in the future should also do the job. What matters is the matching of government outlays and receipts in present value terms. This makes clear the point that sustainability depends crucially on fiscal management, that there exist degrees of freedom in the choice of instruments that will be adjusted to the exchange-rate policy, and that there exist degrees of freedom as to the timing of use of these instruments.

This brings us to the second question; namely, what are the real effects of exchange-rate management? It has been demonstrated by Helpman (1981) and Lucas (1982) that in the absence of distortions and in the presence of Ricardian equivalence, intertemporal balancing of the government budget ensures that exchange-rate management will have no real effects. Namely, changes in the time pattern of the exchange rate will induce changes in the time pattern of reserve holdings and net debt which will not feed back into private decision making. Here the absence of distortions is crucial, as has been demonstrated, for example, by Aschauer and Greenwood (1983). In fact, the presence of distortions often destroys Ricardian equivalence, which is also essential for neutrality of exchange-rate policies. However, Ricardian neutrality may not exist even in the absence of distortions, as happens, for example, when there are finite lifetimes of economic agents who live in different periods. In the latter case, which is of practical relevance, future tax liabilities are not fully incorporated into the budget constraints of the currently alive population, making the government's outstanding debt part of private wealth (see Leiderman and Blejer [1988] for a survey).

The latter case has been studied by Helpman and Razin (1987) in the context of an exchange-rate freeze, using a Yaari-Blanchard-type consumption function (see Blanchard [1985]). As an unexpected exchange-rate freeze generates a capital gain for the currently alive population (because the unexpectedly low exchange-rate level increases the real value of nominal asset holdings, such as money balances) and this capital gain is not fully offset by future tax liabilities due to the absence of Ricardian equivalence, it brings about an increase in private consumption and a worsening of the trade account. Future tax liabilities increase because the exchange-rate freeze brings about reserve losses which increase net government debt, and the servicing of the larger debt together with the solvency requirement imply the need for future reductions in the budget deficit. These are achieved in this exercise by means of higher taxes (expenditure cuts will be discussed at a later stage). As time goes by and the share of the population that enjoys the capital gain declines while the share of the population that faces only tax liabilities increases, consumption tends to decline until it becomes lower than in the absence of an exchange-rate freeze. This demonstrates a channel through which exchange-rate management leads to temporarily high private consumption, a worsening of the trade account, reserve losses, and larger government net debt.[12] These features were observed during the exchange-rate-managed disinflation attempts in Argentina and Chile in the late seventies, and Israel in 1982–83, which did not include budgetary restraint with the slowdown of devaluations (see Edwards [1985]; Corbo, de Melo, and Tybout [1986]; chapter 8). In fact, these outcomes do not depend on the details of the particular model that has been described above; the logic of the argument applies to many circumstances in which future tax liabilities are not fully incorporated into the budget constraints of those who experience capital gains with the inception of exchange-rate management. Moreover, the tendency towards an increase in aggregate spending is strengthened if one takes account of the existence of durables. The temporarily low real exchange rate, if indeed it is perceived to be temporary, induces earlier purchases of durable consumer goods, stockpiling of industrial inventories, and earlier investment in machines and equipment, thereby increasing spending and causing reserve losses (see Dornbusch [1985]).

It is shown in Helpman and Razin (1987) that under these circumstances exchange-rate management has real effects unless very specific tax policies are implemented with the choice of an exchange-rate path. These tax policies are intended to undo the redistributional effects of the exchange-rate policy, and they are typically difficult to calculate. One major feature of these policies is that they require immediate adjustments—any postponement generates real effects.

12. For an empirical test of this channel using time-series data for Israel, see chapter 19.

In order to concentrate on other issues, assume for the rest of this section that there is no breakdown of Ricardian equivalence as a result of finite lives. This leaves room for real effects that result from distortions or from different forms of budgetary adjustments. An example of the former is the recent analysis by Calvo (1986), who uses two models in which the nominal interest rate affects private real consumption. In the first case, which relies on an effective consumption cash-in-advance constraint, consumption is a decreasing function of the nominal interest rate. A temporary reduction in the rate of devaluation with an eventual recourse to money financing generates via the interest parity condition temporarily low interest rates. This is so because the eventual recourse to money financing leads to rates of devaluation that are equal to the rate of money growth, which is higher than the initially low rate of currency devaluation (see also van Wijnbergen [1986]). This is just another example of monetarist arithmetics (see Sargent and Wallace [1981]). Hence, consumption is high during the time span of low rates of currency devaluation, and low afterwards when money financing is pursued. In this case the initial rise in consumption in response to low interest rates worsens the trade account of the balance of payments and brings about added reserve losses, thereby generating effects which are similar to those described above. Observe, however, that while in the previous case the consumption and balance-of-payments effects stemmed from a tilt in the consumption profile as a result of finite lifetimes, with no need to abandon exchange-rate management, here it stems from the eventual abandonment of exchange-rate management which leads to a distortion via a changing nominal interest rate. Which effect is more important is an empirical matter, although both produce similar results which seem to be consistent with the above-mentioned episodes.

In fact, after several months following the Argentine and Israeli plans of 1985, the consumption and trade data showed a noticeably similar pattern to what has happened during the above-mentioned exchange-rate-based stabilization efforts, despite the presence of price and wage controls. One may, therefore, argue that the considerations that we have described have also a bearing on these episodes, because indeed following the initial major adjustments described in section II, what remained was essentially a fixed-exchange-rate policy. We will discuss the Israeli case in more detail at a later stage. Here, we would like to express our view that a reliance on a consumption function which depends on the nominal interest is not very satisfactory in the explanation of these events, and that we find the alternatives more appealing.

Expectations of an eventual abandonment of exchange-rate management have played a major role in these and other episodes. The importance of this possibility for current macroeconomic performance has been formally studied in recent years, beginning with the work of Krugman (1979) and continuing with that of Lizondo (1983), Obstfeld (1984), Flood and Garber (1984), Blanco and Garber (1986), van Wijnbergen (1986), and Drazen and Helpman (1987a; 1987b). The typical view was that a failure to support the exchange rate with current policies leads to the abandonment of exchange-rate management and to money financing of the budget deficit (see, however, Drazen and Helpman [1987a; 1987b] for the role of fiscal policy). Three major conclusions have emerged from this analysis. First, if the timing of the policy collapse is known with certainty, there will be no premium on foreign exchange, and there will be no exchange-rate jump at the collapse point. Second, if there is uncertainty, then there will be a risk premium on foreign exchange which will drive the nominal interest rate, and there will be typically an upward exchange-rate jump at the collapse point. Third, balance-of-payments developments prior to the collapse depend on whether the collapse is followed by a fiscal adjustment and the nature of this adjustment, with the limiting case being a fiscal adjustment that prevents a collapse of the exchange-rate policy.

These findings shed substantial light on the recent as well as earlier stabilization efforts, because in all of them exchange-rate management was pursued without immediately balancing the budget. For this reason one can view these stabilization efforts as two-stage programs: the first stage begins with exchange-rate management and other adjustments, while in the second stage either a further fiscal adjustment takes place or the first-stage exchange-rate policy is abandoned. More complicated variants are also possible, but the simple two-stage variant suffices in order to clarify the issues at hand.

Take as an example a modified version of the model that was discussed in the previous section. Now suppose that it deals with an open economy in which there are two goods; a traded and a nontraded good. The nontraded good replaces leisure. The utility function is:

$$u(c, c_N) + v\left(\frac{M}{Q}\right),$$

where c is consumption of traded goods, c_N is consumption of nontradable goods, and Q is a price index (a linearly homogeneous function of the price of tradables and nontradables). Assume that there is free capital mobility and that the foreign-currency price of tradable goods is constant. The following discussion is based on Drazen and Helpman (1987a) (with a slight change of notation). If there is no uncertainty, the consumer's optimal program implies:

$$v'(mq)\frac{q}{\theta} = r + \frac{\dot{\varepsilon}}{\varepsilon}, \tag{2.2'}$$

where $m = M/\varepsilon$ are real balances in terms of tradable goods; $q = \varepsilon P^*/Q$ is the real exchange rate, measured as the ratio of the price of tradable goods to the price index Q; θ is the marginal utility of tradables; and r is the foreign interest rate on foreign-currency denominated assets.

Assuming for simplicity that the subjective discount rate β is equal to the interest rate r implies that the marginal utility of consumption of tradables, θ, does not vary with time. Hence, if government spending on tradables and nontradables and its lump-sum taxes are constant during the first stage of the program; i.e., the stage at which it maintains an exchange-rate freeze, then the constancy of the marginal utility of consumption of tradables and market clearing imply constant private consumption of traded and nontraded goods (there is no growth). Therefore, the real exchange rate is also constant during this phase. These considerations together with (2.2′) imply that during the period in which the exchange rate is constant, there is price stability (recall the discussion at the beginning of this section) and real money balances m are constant. However, real balance holdings depend on the marginal utility of consumption and on the real exchange rate.

Now suppose that the public expects the current exchange-rate policy to be maintained forever, but as current macroeconomic policies imply a growing public debt that is inconsistent with solvency, the public expects a policy adjustment at a known date T. For simplicity, let the adjustment bring the economy to a steady state. Naturally, under these circumstances it cannot expect recourse to money financing, because money financing requires a positive rate of inflation, which is inconsistent with a fixed exchange rate in a steady state. It can be shown that if lump-sum taxes are expected to be used, there is balance in the current account of the balance of payments prior to T; if a budget cut on traded goods is expected there is a deficit on current account; and if a budget cut on nontraded goods is expected there is a surplus on current account (provided the marginal utility of tradables is increasing with the consumption of nontradables). In the first two cases there is no run on reserves, while in the last case there is a run on reserves at T if the elasticity of the demand for money with respect to the interest rate is smaller than one—the usual case. If, on the other hand, the public expects the exchange-rate policy to be abandoned at T and to be replaced by money financing of the budget deficit (the case originally analyzed by Krugman), there will be current-account balance and a run on reserves at the policy switch point, but no exchange-rate jump. In fact, every second-stage policy package that includes a budget cut on nontraded goods or recourse to money financing induces a run on reserves. The run on reserves is induced by a downward shift in the demand for money at the policy switch point. In the case of a budget cut on nontradables, the decline in the demand for money is caused by a depreciation of the real exchange rate, while in the case of money financing it is caused by a rise of the nominal interest rate.

These considerations show clearly that a change in the public's expectations about the second-stage policy adjustment can induce shifts in consumption and the current account. Thus, for example, if the implementation of a program generates expectations of a second-stage budgetary adjustment in the form of a budget cut on nontraded goods, and in the course of time these expectations change towards higher taxes or money financing, then the change of expectations will bring about an immediate worsening of the trade and current accounts. This seems to be relevant, for example, to the case of Israel in 1985, where the original plan included projections of budget cuts on non-tradable services, such as education and social services, but which were not forthcoming. If the public considered it to be a signal that they will not be forthcoming in the future as well, it might have induced a rise in consumption and a worsening of the trade account, which have indeed taken place.

The cases considered so far imply that abandoning of exchange-rate management produces no discontinuity in the exchange-rate path. In practice, however, it seems that a typical collapse of an exchange-rate policy involves a large discrete devaluation. The latter possibility (together with other relevant features) can be explained by the presence of uncertainty, especially about the policy switch time. This type of uncertainty introduces a risk premium in the nominal interest rate, which is equal to the product of the conditional density of a policy switch (that is, conditional on no switch taking place so far) and the capital loss on money holdings in the event a switch takes place now. If the above conditional density is rising with net government debt, then the nominal interest rate is rising over time and the demand for real balances is falling. The latter generates reserve losses (see Drazen and Helpman 1987b). Hence, instead of a one-time run on reserves in the certainty case, in the case of uncertainty the adjustment starts early, and it is characterized by continuous reserve depletion. Moreover, in the uncertainty case the abandoning of exchange-rate management induces a discrete devaluation, such as those observed in Argentina in 1981, in Chile in 1982, and in Israel in 1983. In fact, the existence of mass points in the probability distribution function or discontinuities in the density function of the timing of a policy switch generate runs on reserves that are not necessarily associated with an actual abandonment of exchange-rate management. The economic interpretation of these characteristics is that the public believes that the particular point in time is a point at which a policy switch is most likely to take place, and that can be related to political or economic events.

Finally, the presence of uncertainty can contribute to the explanation of the very high real interest rates that have been observed immediately after the implementation of the programs that relied on an exchange-rate freeze. Recall that the real interest rate is calculated as the difference between the nominal interest rate and the actual rate of inflation. If there is initially low confidence in the program, and in particular in the success of the exchange-rate policy, the risk premium resulting from a possible policy switch may be substantial.

This leads to high nominal interest rates. In this case a successful program that reduces at once the rate of inflation generates data which imply high real interest rates on the basis of this calculation. The less confidence there is in the policy, the higher will be the real interest rate. By the same token, the more confidence the public develops towards the success of the program, the lower becomes the real interest rate.

V. Price Wage Dynamics

The notion that the inflation rate includes an important inertial component was shared by those who shaped the stabilization plans of Argentina, Brazil, and Israel. The basic idea was that due to formal and informal indexation arrangements, to staggered price-setting, to slowly adjusting expectations, and to the existence of monetary accommodation, the inflation rate was largely predetermined. In Dornbusch and Simonsen's (1987:4) words,

> Inertial inflation means that inflation today is approximately equal to what it was yesterday. . . . The reason for this persistence or inertia is primarily formal or informal indexation interacting with staggered wage setting. This may take the form of a legally imposed wage rule according to which wage adjustments today are based on the inflation over the past year or the past six months. It may also be that much more informal wage bargaining may lead to the same result. Other than through wage indexation the same mechanism also works via expectations. In setting their prices firms will have to estimate their own cost increases and the price increases of competing firms. The best guess is that, cyclical and supply shock factors aside, inflation today will be approximately what it was yesterday.

Consequently it was argued that anti-inflation policies are not likely to succeed unless they directly break the existing inflationary inertia.

The fact that movements in inflation have own-persistence is apparent from table 2.5. The table gives sample autocorrelations of monthly inflation for Argentina, Brazil, and Israel. It can be seen that these autocorrelations start at relatively high levels and decay slowly with increased lags. Whether this own-persistence proves the existence and importance of inflationary inertia is a controversial issue that we take up later on in this section.

There are several ways in which inflationary inertia arising from wage-price dynamics can be modeled. One central view, which is evident from the above quotation, stresses the role of multiperiod nominal contracts and wage indexation (see, for example, Taylor [1980]).[13] As far as the latter is concerned,

---

13. Apart from wage indexation, indexation of financial assets proves to be also important; it prevents the erosion of private wealth as a result of inflation. Consequently, the inflation tax can

Table 2.5
Sample Autocorrelations of Monthly Inflation

Lags	Argentina (80:5–84:12) (56 obs.)	Brazil (71:2–85:12) (179 obs.)	Israel (71:2–85:6) (1973 obs.)
1	0.82	0.85	0.72
2	0.70	0.80	0.61
3	0.63	0.80	0.58
4	0.53	0.76	0.54
5	0.52	0.74	0.61
6	0.54	0.77	0.65
7	0.46	0.73	0.57
8	0.41	0.73	0.50
9	0.39	0.73	0.51
10	0.34	0.69	0.49
11	0.32	0.68	0.48
12	0.37	0.67	0.55

there can be formal agreements that stipulate wage increases in response to past price increases or current wage adjustments in anticipation of future price increases ("ex-post" and "ex-ante" indexation, respectively, in the terminology of Fischer [1984]).

Given a path of nominal wages and a path of expected price movements, there is an implied expected path of real wages and employment, provided employment depends on real wages. If under these circumstances the rate of inflation is unexpectedly reduced, say by a stabilization program, and the path of nominal wages remains unchanged, then real wages rise above and employment declines below the expected levels. Hence, there is an output cost associated with the disinflation, and this cost is due to nominal wage stickiness. Moreover, a given unexpected contraction of aggregate spending for disinflation purposes has a smaller disinflationary effect in the presence of backward-looking wage indexation than in its absence. In order to attenuate the loss of output that is generated by disinflation under these circumstances, it is suggested that wage controls be used at the start of a disinflation program. Such controls also help to achieve a given disinflation with a smaller demand contraction.

This mechanism, that implies an inverse relationship between unexpected inflation and real wages and a positive relationship between inflation and em-

---

be collected only from money or near monies. Thus, the base of the inflation tax is relatively small, and it shrinks as inflation increases. These features justify the modeling of such economies as economies in which private holdings of nonmonetary assets, such as bonds, are denominated in real terms, as we have done in the previous sections, and as we will do in what follows.

ployment, may contribute to the explanation of certain short-run fluctuations in Argentina, Brazil, and Israel. However, it cannot explain some major price, wage, and employment developments. If indeed this mechanism was the sole source of wage changes, then during inflationary periods, and especially during periods of rapid inflation, one would observe declining real wages and rising employment. In contrast to this prediction, there are major episodes in which high and accelerating inflation was associated with rising real wages. Thus, for example, the acceleration of inflation in Argentina from levels of around 100–150 percent per year in 1981–82 to 300 and 600 percent levels in 1983–84 was accompanied by a large increase in real wages (more than 30 percent). Similarly, in Israel the rise of inflation from about 10–20 percent per year in the early 1970s to around 100 percent in the early 1980s was accompanied by a real wage increase of more than 20 percent, and the further acceleration of inflation to around 350 percent in 1984 was accompanied by a further rise in real wages of about 16 percent. In Israel in particular there was a secular upward trend in inflation, real wages, and employment during the seventies and early eighties, contrary to the predictions of the backward-looking wage indexation model. These increases in real wages cannot be attributed to rising labor productivity and have to be attributed to other factors (see Helpman and Leiderman [1987] for a further discussion of this point).

In order to deal with episodes in which inflation was associated with rising real wages, it is necessary to specify a wage process that does not rely entirely on backward-looking indexation. We will describe such a process and use it to explain rising inflation with rising real wages. Apart from dealing with these secular trends, we will use the model to discuss empirical measurement of inflationary inertia, to derive policies that are helpful for disinflation, and to shed light on the observed policy packages. For this purpose we assume that wages are governed by forward-looking considerations and, for simplicity, abstract from backward-looking elements altogether. The following discussion is based on Helpman and Leiderman (1987b).

Our setup consists of a modified version of Blanchard's (1986) wage-price spiral model. In this framework firms set in advance nominal prices for a limited period of time, forming expectations about wage and demand developments in the future, and workers set in advance nominal wages for a limited period of time on the basis of expected future price developments. Prices and wages are set at different points in time, thereby representing nonsynchronization between these variables, a feature that is considered to be central to the understanding of these episodes (see Bruno [1986; 1987] and Dornbusch and Simonsen [1987]). Monetary policy is assumed to be accommodative in a way that will be explained later. Monetary accommodation is believed to be relevant for Argentina, Brazil, and Israel (see, for example, Bruno and Fischer [1986] for a discussion of Israel).

Assume that firms choose prices for a two-period time interval in every even period t, and that workers choose the nominal wage rate for a two-period time interval in every odd period t. Taking a Spence-Dixit-Stiglitz type specification of preferences for differentiated products with a constant elasticity of substitution (see Spence [1976] and Dixit and Stiglitz [1977]) and with a fixed number of firms, the decision problem of a typical firm in period t even is:

$$\max_{p_t,\ t\ \text{even}} p_t d_t(p_t) - w_{t-1}\phi[d_t(p_t)] + \beta_t[p_t d_{t+1}(p_t) - w_{t+1}\phi[d_{t+1}(p_t)]],$$
(2.3)

where p_t is the price set for two periods at time t (t even), w_t is the nominal wage set by workers at time t (where t is odd) for a two-period time interval, β_t is the one-period nominal discount factor (equal to one over one plus the nominal interest rate), $d_t(p_t)$ is the demand function, and $\phi(d)$ is labor requirement per unit output (labor is the only variable input). The demand function is given by

$$d_t(p_t) = \left(\frac{p_t}{P_t}\right)^{-\sigma} a_t, \quad \text{for all } t,$$

where P_t is the price level, a_t is the level of real spending per firm, and σ is the elasticity of substitution in consumption and the elasticity of demand. The price level is defined by

$$P_t = \left[\frac{1}{n}\sum_{i=1}^{n} p_{ti}^{1-\sigma}\right]^{1/(1-\sigma)},$$

where p_{ti} is the price charged by firm i (the index i was dropped in the preceding discussion of the representative firm).

Workers choose the nominal wage rate for a two-period time interval to ensure that the present value of two-period wages equals a predetermined present value of real purchasing power ω_t. Namely:

$$w_{t-1} + \beta_{t-1}w_{t-1} = \omega_{t-1}(P_{t-2} + \beta_{t-1}P_t) \quad \text{for } t \text{ even.}$$
(2.4)

Here ω represents the average real wage rate requested by workers, with the averaging taking into account the timing of payments.[14]

Equations 2.3 and 2.4 constitute the basic system describing wage-price dynamics. Following the standard approach to economies with differentiated

14. The wage-determination rule that is described in (2.4) corresponds to 'ex-ante' indexation in the terminology of Fischer (1986). In his model, this type of indexation leads to a shorter recession with a smaller sacrifice ratio in terms of lost output than backward-looking indexation.

products of the above-described type, we deal with symmetric equilibria in which all variables are equally priced. In this case the price level is equal to the price of a single variety; i.e., $P_t = p_t$. Assuming a constant real interest rate with ρ denoting the real discount factor, and perfect foresight (we will discuss expectational errors at a later stage), these equations can be combined to yield (recalling that in this case $\beta_{t-1} = \rho p_{t-1}/p_t = \rho p_{t-2}/p_t$ and $\beta_t = \rho$ for t even):

$$1 = R\frac{1+\rho}{1+\dfrac{\rho a_{t+1}}{a_t}}\left[\frac{\omega_{t-1}\phi(a_t)}{x_t+\rho} + \frac{\omega_{t+1}\phi(a_{t+1})x_{t+2}}{x_{t+2}+\rho}\left(\frac{\rho a_{t+1}}{a_t}\right)\right] \qquad (2.5)$$

for t even, where $R = (1 - 1/\sigma)^{-1}$ is the markup coefficient, $x_t = p_t/p_{t-2}$ (i.e., one plus the two-period inflation rate) and $\phi(\cdot)$ is the marginal labor requirement (the derivative of $\phi(\cdot)$).

Equation 2.5 describes the evolution of inflation as an implicit function of the markup, the real interest rate, the evolution of real wages, and the evolution of demand. This is a forward-looking equation in which current inflation x_t depends on expected future inflation x_{t+2}.

First, consider the case in which real spending, the required real wage rate, and the inflation rate are constant. In this case (2.5) reduces to:

$$R\omega\phi(a) = \frac{x+\rho}{\rho x+1}. \qquad (2.6)$$

It is easy to see that for positive real interest rates ($\rho < 1$), the rate of inflation is higher the higher the markup, the required real wage rate, the marginal labor requirement, and the lower the real interest rate. If marginal labor requirement is rising with output (i.e., marginal costs are increasing), then inflation will be higher the larger real spending.

In order to discuss inflationary dynamics, we assume a positive real interest rate, and for simplicity we also assume that real spending and the required real wage rate are constant. Then the inflationary dynamics can be described by means of figure 2.10. The curve that relates x_{x+2} to x_t is rising, going to infinity as x approaches $\bar{x}$ from below, and going to minus infinity as x approaches $\bar{x}$ from above. It intersects the 45° line at the steady-state point A, with a slope larger than one. It is clear from the figure that perfect foresight and expected positive prices require expected and actual rates of inflation to be in the interval $(x, \bar{x})$ in all time periods. This, however, is satisfied if and only if the expected rate of inflation is equal to the steady-state level. Hence, in this case perfect foresight leads to a constant rate of inflation, equal to the steady-state level.

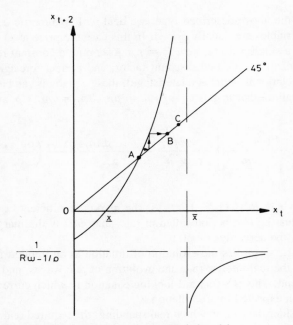

Figure 2.10   Dynamics of inflation in the price wage spiral model.

Consider an economy in a steady-state equilibrium at point A in figure 2.10, with $R\omega\phi > 1$, which implies a positive rate of inflation. In order to reduce the long-run inflation rate it is required to reduce the real wage rate ω, or the markup R, or the marginal labor requirement ϕ, or to increase the real interest rate. If this is done, the curve in figure 2.10 shifts to the northwest, so that the new steady-state point is to the left of A on the 45° line. With perfect foresight, expectations adjust immediately to the new long-run level, and so does the actual rate of inflation. No other expectations are consistent with perfect foresight and positive prices in all time periods. Hence, in this case there can be no gradual transition to the new long-run equilibrium—there is no inflationary inertia. In fact, long-run feasibility, perfect foresight, and a positive real interest rate imply that every permanent shock leads to an immediate adjustment of the rate of inflation to its new steady-state level. Naturally, transitory disturbances do generate gradual adjustment (see below).

This model predicts that a once-and-for-all increase in the real wage rate, in the profit rate (the markup), or in real spending (when the marginal labor requirement is rising with output) lead to a once-and-for-all increase in the inflation rate. Thus, it can account for a time series of inflation rates in the form of "steps" as has been argued by some observers to have existed in

Israel (see e.g., Bruno [1986]). On the other hand, it is inconsistent with the view that a one-time expansionary nominal shock leads to inflationary inertia and to an eventually ever-higher inflation rate (see Liviatan and Piterman [1986]), despite the fact that we assume a fully accommodating monetary policy; here real permanent shocks are required for the inflation rate to change in steps.

This model suggests that the rate of inflation can be reduced by means of an incomes policy (provided the nature of the price and wage determination processes does not change, such as the length of time during which nominal prices are fixed). The policy should consist of a reduction in the real wage rate or the profit rate. Naturally, monetary and fiscal adjustments are required to support the reduction in the rate of inflation; we will discuss these necessary adjustments in subsection B. While it has been argued that price and wage controls are needed in order to break inflationary inertia (see, for example, Dornbusch [1982]), this forward-looking model of a wage-price spiral does not support this claim (backward-looking wage indexation can justify such claims, as we have described above). On the other hand, an incomes policy by means of price and wage controls can be helpful under some circumstances in bringing about a decline in the real wage or markup that is needed for disinflation purposes. The argument that controls were needed in order to bring about a reduction in real wages was central in the design of the Israeli program. This, however, is not the only incomes policy that can achieve this result, and the model is silent on the issue of which incomes policies are relatively more efficient.

The model highlights the importance of inflationary expectations. In particular, it supports the view that in a stabilization program that is based on a permanent change in the relevant parameters, it is necessary also to change inflationary expectations. Suppose the public does not believe that the change is permanent. Then it does not reduce its inflationary expectations to the new long-run steady-state level. Suppose that the permanent policy change shifts the long-run equilibrium from point B in figure 2.10 to A. If inflationary expectations remain temporarily at the old level, then inflation will start rising, and if they do not adjust in the course of time, they will lead to nonfeasibility. Naturally, rational economic agents are expected to adjust their expectations, and the exact path of transition depends on the nature of this adjustment. Hence, in order to avoid temporarily high inflation rates, it is important to influence expectations by convincing the public that the change is permanent. Some argue that this can be achieved by price controls (see Dornbusch and Simonsen [1987]). However, the considerations that lead to this claim, as well as the broader issues of a policy's credibility and the public's adjustment of expectations, are outside the scope of the present model.

We have already discussed permanent changes in the markup, the real wage rate, the real interest rate, and real spending. However, since in the observed stabilization programs there were also temporary changes in these variables, we now discuss the effects of such changes. Consider an economy in a high-inflation equilibrium, say at point C in figure 2.10. Now suppose that the authorities bring about a permanent reduction in the markup or the real wage rate, so that the new long-run equilibrium is at point B, at which the inflation rate is lower. However, suppose that the program brings about a temporarily larger drop in the real wage rate and markup, to a temporarily higher real interest rate, and to a temporary real spending decline. These are features of the Argentine and Israeli data. Under these circumstances the real wage rate, the markup, and real spending and output are expected to increase over time, while the real interest rate is expected to decline. In this case the curve that is relevant for a description of the dynamic trajectory is located to the left of point B, such as the curve that goes through point A. This curve will typically shift over time. However, for expositional purposes, suppose it does not. Then the arrowed path describes the resulting dynamics, where the length of time during which the temporary parameters are in effect determines the initial point; the system has to hit B at the point in time at which all the underlying parameters reach their new steady-state values. It is clear from the figure that under these circumstances the inflation rate drops on impact and rises thereafter, until it settles at the new steady-state level. This pattern does not change when there are upward shifts in the curve as a result of a gradual adjustment of the real wage, the markup, the real interest rate, and real spending. The initial undershooting of the inflation rate in response to a temporary over-shooting of the real interest rate, real wage decline, and real spending decline, followed by a gradual upward adjustment of the inflation rate, seems to fit the facts reported in section II.

In this model employment is demand-determined. Hence, in the last example employment decreases on impact, along with the decrease in demand, and rises later on as demand picks up over time, as has happened in Argentina and Israel. Different inflation rates can be associated with a given level of employment, provided real spending is constant. Consequently, disinflation does not require lower employment even temporarily.

This discussion was based on the assumption that monetary policy is fully accommodative. If during an inflationary period money growth is not accommodated to the inflation rate, then the real value of nominal assets is reduced. If this brings about a decline in real spending, the result is lower output and employment. Moreover, if real spending is expected to decline, these expectations lead to upward pressure on the inflation rate. Naturally, this presumes that the mechanism of price and wage determination does not change in face of rising unemployment, which is not plausible. One may expect ω to change in face of prolonged unemployment and one may also expect under these circumstances changes in the process of wage-price determination.

A. *Implications for Measured Real Wages*

We now consider implications for measured real wages $w_t/P_t = w_t/p_t$. This discussion is confined to steady states. It can be shown that in the present model, starting with a positive rate of inflation, an increase in the rate of inflation increases the periodic fluctuations in the measured real wage rate irrespective of the factor that causes the rate of inflation to rise (be it the markup, the real wage ω, real spending, or the real interest rate). Clearly, the measured wage rate is larger in odd periods (in which the nominal wage is adjusted) and smaller in even periods (in which prices are adjusted). Figure 2.11 describes the time pattern of measured real wages. The difference between the solid graph and the broken-line graph is that in the latter ω is larger than in the former (and so is the resulting inflation rate). An increase in the rate of inflation via an increase in ω increases the measured real wage rate in odd periods and reduces it in even periods. And if ω increases and R declines so that $R\omega$ does not change, and therefore the rate of inflation does not change too, this induces an increase in fluctuations of the measured real wage rate. The peak real wage goes up and the trough real wage declines. Fluctuations in the real wage rate also reflect fluctuations in the share of labor in output. Although the fluctuations in real wages depicted in figure 2.11 are similar to fluctuations that result from backward-looking wage indexation (see, for example, Dornbusch and Simonsen [1987]), they are caused by entirely different factors.

B. *Closing the Model*

We have discussed price-wage dynamics under the assumption that the monetary authority pursues an accommodating monetary policy, assuming a given

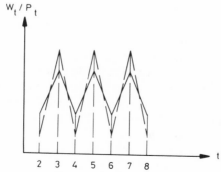

Figure 2.11   Fluctuations in measured real wages.

time pattern of real spending a_t. It is shown in Helpman and Leiderman (1987) that there exists a wide range of spending patterns that are consistent with general equilibrium considerations, given that individuals maximize the discrete-time analogue of the objective function employed in previous sections; i.e.,

$$\sum_{t=0}^{\infty} \rho^t \left[u(c_t) + v\left(\frac{M_t}{p_t}\right) \right],$$

subject to the usual intertemporal budget constraint. However, this requires the government to pursue an appropriate budgetary policy in order to accommodate the demand for money and ensure solvency. Thus for example, if disinflation leads to a loss of inflation tax revenue, it is necessary to increase other taxes or to reduce spending. The timing of these adjustments is not unique, although credibility considerations suggest making them as soon as possible, and in particular with the inception of a stabilization program.

It can be shown that in this setup employment is determined by real spending and that there exists a continuum of equilibria which differ in employment levels. This point is important, because it shows that in an environment in which workers make wage demands irrespective of employment, and oligopolistic firms price goods according to $MR = MC$, real-demand management plays a role in the determination of employment.

C. Price-Wage Controls

We have seen that price-wage controls have been part of several of the stabilization plans described above, and we have already discussed some of the rationales for their use. Here we expand the discussion of the role of controls. Three of the arguments for controls are based on the need to break inflationary inertia: inertia that is claimed to arise from backward-looking wage indexation, from the staggering of price-setting, and from a slow adjustment of inflationary expectations. We have already dealt with the first type of inertia. Indeed, in that case wage controls can break the inertia and enable disinflation at lower transitional output and employment costs. Observe, however, that in this case there is no need for price controls; the control of nominal wages cuts off current inflation from past wage contracts. Nevertheless, it is sometimes argued that labor unions refuse to agree to a wage freeze without price controls and the fixing of the exchange rate. This was indeed the Israeli case.

The second argument is based on the notion that prices are not adjusted continuously and that different firms adjust prices at different points in time (see, for example, Sheshinski and Weiss [1977] and Blanchard [1983]). In this case a reduction in money growth and in aggregate demand brings about disinflation at a slower pace than in an economy with synchronized price-setting. Therefore, by bringing about faster synchronization of price adjustments, price controls are thought to be a mechanism that speeds up the disinflation process. To the extent that price-staggering coexists with backward-looking wage indexation, these arguments call for wage and price controls, with part of the price controls being achieved by means of fixing the exchange rate.

The third argument concerns expectations. It is argued that in an economy with a history of inflation and failed disinflation efforts, inflationary expectations do not decline on impact with the inception of a stabilization program. Rather, expectations adjust slowly, as there is a gradual process of learning the new policy and its degree of success. Under these circumstances effective price controls may speed up the downward adjustment of inflationary expectations.

Having explained some of the main arguments advanced by proponents of wage and price controls in recent stabilization programs, we now discuss several of the difficulties that arise from their use. The foremost difficulty is to choose the controlled levels of wages, prices, and the exchange rate to make them compatible with each other and with the underlying monetary and fiscal policies. This is especially the case if controls are to affect expectations to make the disinflation policy credible. Incompatibility of these choices may lead to shortages, to unemployment, and to speculative attacks on the exchange rate, thereby endangering the entire stabilization program. This is more so once it is recognized that the economy is subjected to regular random shocks, and in particular in view of the uncertainties that are generated by a major stabilization program per se. In the Israeli case, for example, the external shocks, e.g., the decline of the dollar to which the domestic currency was pegged and the decline in raw-material prices, were rather favorable in the sense that they helped sustain the fixed-exchange-rate policy. It is not clear, however, how successful the policy would have been in the presence of adverse external shocks.

Since there are economic costs associated with controls, with part of the costs stemming from the risks associated with the ability to sustain them for a prolonged period of time, it is necessary to carefully weigh these costs against potential benefits they may contribute to the disinflation process. This cost-benefit calculation has also to take into account the eventual need to remove the controls, the effects of uncertainty about how and when they will be removed, and the consequences of their removal. Brazil is a case in point which shows apparent high costs associated with the controls policy. These costs showed up in the form of shortages, black markets, and the disruption of economic efficiency. Israel is a case in point which shows that controls may not be very costly. In this case there were no apparent shortages, black markets, or disruption of economic efficiency. The major difference between these countries appears to be that the initial alignment of controlled prices, wages, the exchange rate, and monetary and fiscal policies was approximately compatible in Israel (with external shocks enhancing this compatibility), but it was not in Brazil.

We now turn to an examination of the implications of price-wage controls in the context of our specific model. While the model is not capable of shedding light on the role of controls in breaking inflationary inertia that stems from backward-looking wage indexation, it does provide insights on the other two arguments. Moreover, it helps to explain why controls need not lead to shortages and the role of controls in the incomes policy that is required in order to disinflate in the presence of price-wage staggering.

The first thing to be noticed is that in the presence of such controls the previous wage- and price-setting equations are no longer relevant, because price controls prevent firms from choosing prices and wage controls prevent workers from choosing wage rates. In particular, if the government imposes a price-wage combination in all time periods, firms can only choose how much to produce up to the demanded quantity of goods, while workers can only choose how much to work up to the demanded quantity of labor. Hence, employment is determined by the demand for labor.

In order to analyze the effect of controls on output and in order to see whether they will result in shortages, it is useful to contrast competitive with oligopolistic market structure (the following discussion is based on Helpman [1988]). Panel (a) in figure 2.12 describes a competitive market in which D is the demand curve and MC is the marginal cost curve, assuming that a unit of labor produces a unit of output (this assumption sharpens the analysis). In a competitive equilibrium, price equals marginal cost and the supplied quantity is determined at the intersection point A. Now, if the government imposes price-wage controls in the form of upper ceilings, then the wage controls shift down MC and the price controls are effective only if the controlled price is below the new wage rate (otherwise the equilibrium price is lower than the price ceiling). Hence, with effective price controls at the level p^c, shortages (excess demand) arise.

Now consider an oligopolistic market structure. The marginal cost, demand, and marginal revenue curves of a typical firm are described in panel (b). Without price controls the intersection of the marginal cost with the marginal revenue curve at point A determines the profit-maximizing quantity and price p. In the presence of price-wage controls there are two relevant possibilities. The first arises when the price ceiling p^c is above the wage rate but below the

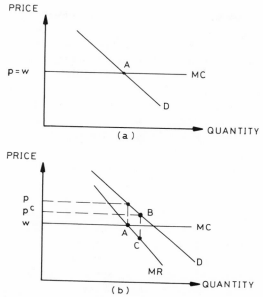

Figure 2.12   Price controls under competition and oligopoly.

profit-maximizing price, as drawn in the figure (taking now MC to represent marginal costs at the controlled wage rate). In this case the controls make marginal revenue horizontal at the level p^c up to point B, then dropping to C, and coinciding with the MR curve for larger quantities. The firm's optimal policy is to supply the demanded quantity at the controlled price; there are not shortages. The firm is making positive profits, with $p^c - w$ being the profit margin.

The second case arises when the controlled price drops below the wage rate. In this case supply drops to zero, just like in the competitive case, and shortages emerge.

In the wage-price spiral model, the market structure is oligopolistic. Hence, price-wage controls with the property $w^c \leq p^c$ need not bring about the cessation of production. Assume that this is indeed the case. Then inflation stops immediately, firms supply the resulting demand, and employment is determined by the demanded output level. The government is requested to accommodate the demand for money and to be intertemporally balanced.

Two additional points should be noted. First, output and employment can still be at a continuum of levels; expectations of many employment levels are self-sustaining. Second, the model implies that in order to stop inflation it is sufficient to control either prices or wages. Naturally, the choice of instrument affects the distribution of income between labor and profits, but both lead to price-wage stability. Price-wage controls enable a choice of a specific income distribution. In Israel, for example, the plan has caused a major income re-distribution from profits to wages (the share of wages in domestic income has risen by about seven percentage points between 1984 and 1986).

In relating this model-specific analysis to the observed disinflation pro-grams, we draw the following main conclusions. First, the existence of an oligopolistic market structure may account for the casual observation that price controls did not lead to shortages in Argentina and Israel (although this has to be qualified by noting that some of the controls were not effective). Second, as explained in detail in Helpman (1988), this type of market structure can also account for the observed comovement of real wages, em-ployment, and the trade account in Israel during the period of price con-trols—namely, the rise in real wages and employment and a deterioration of the trade account, starting with the last quarter of 1985; comovements that are not readily explainable by a model with a competitive market structure. Third, although wage and price controls may contribute to disinflation in an economy characterized by a price-wage spiral of the above-described type, they are not the only instruments that can achieve it. Hence, even in those cases in which an incomes policy is required, our analysis does not identify apparent advantages to these types of controls.

D. Testing for Inertia

The existence and relevance of inertia in the above-discussed inflationary epi-sodes is an open empirical question. It has been quite common (at least in the Israeli debate on this issue) to use autoregressive representations for inflation in order to empirically assess inertia. Consider, for example, the analysis by Bruno and Fischer (1986). They show that in quarterly inflation autoregres-sions for Israel, the size and sum of coefficients on the first and second lags have increased over time along with the inflation rate. For 1965:I–1971:I this sum is 0.56; for 1975:III–1978:IV it is 0.87; and for 1979:I–1982:IV it is 1.04. Their conclusion is that the evidence supports the notion that there is considerable inertia in the inflationary process in Israel and that this inertia has been growing.

In what follows we use the foregoing analytical framework of wage-price dynamics in order to point out limitations of this approach and to suggest an alternative route for empirical research. An important limitation of using in-flation autoregressions to assess inertia is that in the countries under study the inflation rate is nonstationary. Consequently, some of the inflation autocorre-lations are likely to be spurious and may not necessarily capture the inertia phenomenon. In order to illustrate this point, we have estimated inflation

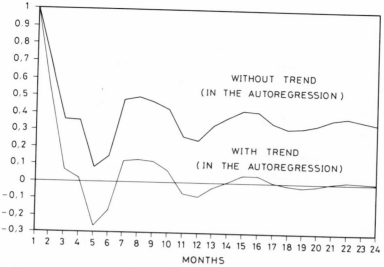

Figure 2.13   Inflation responses to a unit standard deviation inflationary shock—Argentina.

autoregressions without and with the inclusion of a deterministic time-trend variable.[15] Instead of using them directly, we have calculated the implied moving-average representations (or impulse-response functions) given in figures 2.13, 2.14 and 2.15. We have used monthly data for Argentina (80:5–84:12); Brazil (73:1–85:12); and Israel (70:12–83:9), where in each case the time period is chosen so that there is no apparent break in the inflation process.

The evidence in the charts is quite clear. When time trends are not included, there seems to be some long-term persistence of shocks to the rate of inflation. However, the results are sensitive to inclusion of a time trend in the autoregressions. When this is done, the impulse-response functions show that a one-time inflation shock has only short-lived effects on subsequent inflation rates, thereby raising doubts about the existence of inertia. These findings hold for all three countries.

Having established that findings from inflation autoregressions are not robust with respect to the inclusion of time-trend variable, the next question is why, if at all, such a variable should be included in the equations? More generally, what seems to be a proper test of inertia? To answer these ques-

15. Obviously, other detrending methods could be used; see Nelson and Plosser (1981) and Watson (1986). As will become clear later on, our view is that this issue should be resolved on the basis of what is implied by the theoretical model being investigated. The AR equations that we estimated regress the inflation rate on a constant and six lagged values of inflation. As explained in the text, we also ran these equations with the addition of a time-trend term.

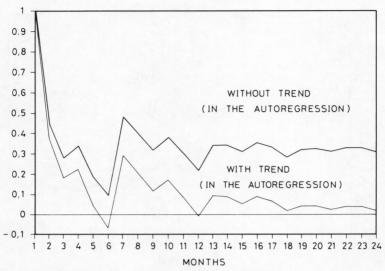

Figure 2.14   Inflation responses to a unit standard deviation inflationary shock—Brazil.

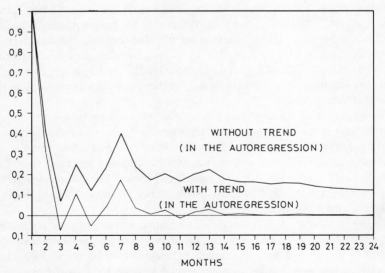

Figure 2.15   Inflation responses to a unit standard deviation inflationary shock—Israel.

tions, let us go back to the price-wage spiral model developed in this section. Equation 2.5 gives the model's implicit solution for the inflation rate as a nonlinear function of the markup, the evolution of required real wages, the real interest rate, the evolution of demand, and expected future inflation. Clearly, for some configurations of changes in these factors over time (e.g., rising real wage rates and constant real spending), the model is capable of generating a highly persistent series of inflation rates of the type that have been used to claim the existence of inertia, despite the fact that the model does not produce inertia per se. Hence, univariate inflation autoregressions do not provide direct evidence on inflationary inertia. In order to test the hypothesis of inflationary inertia, it is necessary to formulate a model that embodies it and face it with data.

VI. Concluding Remarks

Recent stabilization programs have been generating evidence which enables close examinations of competing views about the desirability of various policies. Although it is premature to reach final judgment on existing controversies, we draw tentative conclusions at the present time.

First, an immediate reduction of the budget deficit is important for successful disinflation. Postponement of this adjustment need not fail a program, but only if the government succeeds in building up confidence in its fiscal discipline by other means. An immediate reduction of the deficit seems to be an effective means of generating credibility, even if further adjustments may be required in the future. Argentina, Bolivia, and Israel are cases in point. All these countries used immediate fiscal adjustments, despite the face that it was clear at the time that further adjustments would also be needed (including Israel which did not have a budget deficit in 1986, but in which some revenue was only temporary, such as certain taxes and emergency foreign aid). Brazil, on the other hand, did not rely on a contractionary fiscal policy in the Cruzado Plan and was indeed the least successful in combating inflation.

Second, a credible exchange-rate freeze does not necessarily eliminate inflation, and it does not seem to be a prerequisite for a quick reduction of the inflation rate. The latter point is illustrated by Bolivia's program, which did not include such a freeze. The former is illustrated by the other prorams. In fact, the entire issue of the role of an exchange-rate freeze is difficult to resolve on the basis of recent experience. The difficulty is most apparent in the case of Israel, which has maintained a fixed exchange rate longer than the other countries. On the one hand, the accompanying policies, and in particular fiscal policy, were most supportive, and the decline in the dollar, oil prices, and other commodity prices (which were to a large extent unexpected) helped greatly to sustain the fixed exchange rate. Hence, unexpectedly favorable external circumstances were instrumental in supporting the exchange-rate policy. On the other hand, there was indeed hardly any pressure on the exchange rate, and its time path helped to reduce inflation through a decline in the rate of increase of the price of traded goods. But inflation was not eliminated. Rising spending that began in the fourth quarter of 1985, which was fed by private consumption, drove up prices of nontraded goods.

In assessing the usefulness of exchange-rate targets in a stabilization package, it is necessary to take into account the degree to which the central bank can control intermediate monetary targets, such as credit. In some cases, such as Argentina and Israel, the institutional structure makes monetary control difficult to attain. When this is coupled with the fact that a major stabilization program brings about large shifts in the demand for financial assets, it may be concluded that it is sometimes preferable to supplement intermediate targets with exchange-rate targets, despite the well-known dangers of exchange-rate management. In retrospect it seems that, under the prevailing circumstances, the exchange-rate freeze contributed successfully to disinflation in Israel.

Third, the experience of Argentina and Israel shows that price and wage controls did not generate shortages and severe disruptions, although this statement has to be qualified in view of the fact that it is not clear how effective these controls have been in practice (especially in Argentina). The experience of Brazil, however, shows that controls may lead to substantial shortages and disruptions. Differences in the programs of these countries show that in order to avoid these phenomena, a careful alignment of relative prices and aggregate spending is required before the imposition of controls. This may be possible for economies in which oligopolistic market structures are prevalent. Under these circumstances controls need not cause severe losses of employment and output. On the other hand, prolonged controls may be quite damaging, even if the resulting harmful effects are not as visible as shortages, because relative prices can hardly be expected to be at their efficient levels. It is also clear from our analysis and from Bolivia's experience that successful disinflation can take place without controls. Even in the case of Israel, which has implemented a successful "heterodox" program so far, price controls have played a minor role in the disinflation process relative to budgetary, monetary, wage, and exchange-rate policies.

References

Aschauer, D., and J. Greenwood. 1983. A Further Exploration in the Theory of Exchange Rate Regimes. *Journal of Political Economy* 91:868–75.

Bental, B., and Z. Eckstein. 1990. The Dynamics of Inflation with Constant Deficit under Expected Regime Change. *Economic Journal* 100:1245–60.

Blanchard, O. J. 1983. Price Asynchronization and Price Level Inertia. In *Inflation, Debt, and Indexation,* ed. Rudiger Dornbusch and Mario Henrique Simonsen. Cambridge: MIT Press.

————. 1985. Debt, Deficits and Finite Horizons. *Journal of Political Economy* 93:223–47.

————. 1986. The Wage Price Spiral. *Quarterly Journal of Economics* 101:543–66.

Blanco, H., and P. Garber. 1986. Recurrent Devaluation and Speculative Attacks on the Mexican Peso. *Journal of Political Economy* 94:148–66.

Blejer, M. I., and N. Liviatan. 1987. Fighting Hyperinflation: Stabilization Strategies in Argentina and Israel, 1985–86. *IMF Staff Papers* 34:409–38.

Bruno, M. 1986. Sharp Disinflation Strategy: Israel 1985. *Economic Policy* 2:379–402.

————. 1987. Israel's Stabilization: The End of the Lost Decade? *Economic Quarterly* 37:914–925 (Hebrew).

————, and S. Fischer. 1986. The Inflationary Process: Shocks and Accommodation. In *The Israeli Economy: Maturing through Crises,* ed. Yoram Ben-Porath. Cambridge: Harvard University Press.

Calvo, G. A. 1986. Temporary Stabilization: Predetermined Exchange Rates. *Journal of Political Economy* 94:1319–29.

Cavallo, D. F., and A. Pena. 1983. Deficit Fiscal, Endeudamiento de Gobierno y Tasa de Inflacion: Argentina, 1940–1982. *Estudios Economicos,* April–June.

Corbo, V., J. de Melo, and J. Tybout. 1986. What Went Wrong with the Recent Reforms in the Southern Cone. *Economic Development and Cultural Change* 34:607–40.

Dixit, A., and J. E. Stiglitz. 1977. Monopolistic Competition and Optimum Product Diversity. *American Economic Review* 67:297–308.

Dornbusch, R. 1982. Stabilization Policies in Developing Countries: What Have We Learned? *World Development* 10:701–8.

————. 1985. External Debt, Budget Deficits, and Disequilibrium Exchange Rates. In *International Debt and the Developing Countries,* ed. Gordon W. Smith and John T. Cuddington. Washington, D.C.: World Bank.

————, and M. H. Simonsen. 1987. Inflation Stabilization With Incomes Policy Support: A Review of Recent Experience in Argentina, Brazil and Israel. Occasional paper, Group of Thirty, New York.

Dornbusch, R., M. H. Simonsen, and S. Fischer. 1986. Stopping Hyperinflation: Past and Present. *Weltwirtschaftliches Archiv* 122:1–46.

Drazen, A., and E. Helpman. 1990. Inflationary Consequences of Anticipated Macroeconomic Policies. *Review of Economic Studies* 57:147–64.

————. 1987a. Stabilization with Exchange Rate Management. *Quarterly Journal of Economics* 102:835–55.

————. 1987b. Stabilization with Exchange Rate Management under Uncertainty. In *Economic Effects of the Government Budget,* ed. E. Helpman, E. Sadka, and A. Razin. Cambridge: MIT Press.

Edwards, S. 1985. Stabilization with Liberalization: An Evaluation of Ten Years of Chile's Experiment with Free Market Policies, 1973–1983. *Economic Development and Cultural Change* 33:223–54.

Fischer, S. 1988. Real Balances, the Exchange Rate and Indexation: Real Variables in Disinflation. *Quarterly Journal of Economics* 103:27–50.

————. 1986. Exchange Rate Versus Money Targets in Disinflation. In *Indexing, Inflation, and Economic Policy,* by S. Fischer. Cambridge: MIT Press.

Flood, R. P., and P. Garber. 1984. Collapsing Exchange-Rate Regimes: Some Linear Examples. *Journal of International Economics* 17:1–14.

Helpman, E. 1981. An Exploration in the Theory of Exchange-Rate Regimes. *Journal of Political Economy* 89:865–90.

————. 1988. Macroeconomic Effects of Price Controls: The Role of Market Structure. *Economic Journal* 98:340–54.

Helpman, E., and A. Drazen. 1986. Future Stabilization Policies and Inflation. In *Finance Constraints, Expectations and Macroeconomics*, ed. M. Kohn and S. C. Tsiang. Oxford: Oxford University Press.

Helpman, E., and L. Leiderman. 1987. Wages, Prices, and Inflationary Inertia. Manuscript. Tel Aviv University.

Helpman, E., and A. Razin. 1987. Exchange Rate Management: Intertemporal Trade-offs. *American Economic Review* 77:107–123.

Knight, P. T., F. D. McCarthy, and S. van Wijnbergen. 1986. Escaping Hyperinflation. *Finance and Development* 23:14–17.

Krugman, P. R. 1979. A Model of Balance-of-Payments Crises. *Journal of Money, Credit and Banking* 11:311–25.

Leiderman, L., and M. I. Blejer. 1988. Modelling and Testing Ricardian Equivalence: A survey. International Monetary Fund, *IMF Staff Papers*, 35:1–35.

Liviatan, N., and S. Piterman. 1986. Accelerating Inflation and Balance of Payments Crises, 1973–1984. In *The Israeli Economy: Maturing Though Crises*, ed. Yoram Ben-Porath. Cambridge: Harvard University Press.

Lizondo, J. S. 1983. Foreign Exchange Futures Prices under Fixed Exchange Rates. *Journal of International Economics* 14:69–84.

Lucas, R. E., Jr. 1982. Interest Rates and Currency Prices in a Two-Country World. *Journal of Monetary Economics* 10:335–60.

Nelson, C. R., and C. I. Plosser. 1981. Trends and Random Walks in Macroeconomic Time Series: Some Evidence and Implications. *Journal of Monetary Economics* 10:139–62.

Obstfeld, M. 1984. Balance-of-Payments Crises and Devaluation. *Journal of Money, Credit, and Banking* 16:208–17.

Sachs, J. 1986. The Bolivian Hyperinflation and Stabilization. Working Paper no. 2073. NBER.

Sargent, T. J. 1982. The Ends of Four Big Inflations. *Inflation: Causes and Effects*, ed. Robert E. Hall. Chicago: University of Chicago Press, for NBER.

Sargent, T. J., and N. Wallace. 1981. Some Unpleasant Monetarist Arithmetic. *Federal Reserve Bank of Minneapolis Quarterly Review* 5:1–17.

————. 1987. Inflation and the Government Budget Constraint. In *Economic Policy in Theory and Practice*, ed. Assaf Razin and Efraim Sadka. New York: Macmillan.

Sheshinki, E., and Y. Weiss. 1977. Inflation and Costs of Price Adjustment. *Review of Economic Studies* 50:287–303.

Spence, M. 1976. Product Selection, Fixed Costs, and Monopolistic Competition. *Review of Economic Studies* 43:217–36.

Taylor, John B. 1980. Aggregate Dynamics and Staggered Contracts. *Journal of Political Economy* 88:1–23.

van Wijnbergen, S. 1986. Fiscal Deficits, Exchange Rate Crises and Inflation. In *Budget Effects of the Government Budget,* ed. E. Helpman, A. Razin, and E. Sadka. Cambridge: MIT Press.

Watson, M. W. 1986. Univariate Detrending Methods with Stochastic Trends. *Journal of Monetary Economics* 18:49–75.

3

Real Wages, Monetary Accommodation, and Inflation

1. Introduction

The notion that inflation includes an important predetermined component, referred to as inflationary inertia, has influenced the design of recent disinflation policies in Argentina, Brazil, and Israel. It was argued that conventional policies are not likely to succeed unless this inertia, which is mainly attributed to the coexistence of a wage-price spiral and monetary accommodation, is eliminated (see, for example, Bruno [1986] and Dornbusch and Simonsen [1987]).

While the role of monetary accommodation in enhancing persistence of inflation does not seem to be controversial, the role of inertia is controversial. There are at least two ways of dealing with the wage-price spiral. The first stresses the interaction between backward-looking wage indexation and staggered wage and price-setting. Since typically such indexation does not provide full compensation for past inflation, this mechanism implies an inverse relation between movements in real wages and inflation; i.e., declining real wages in periods of high and accelerating inflation and rising real wages in periods of disinflation. There exists evidence for high-inflation countries that does not conform to these implications. In particular, there were substantial increases in real wages preceding and during major episodes of high and accelerating inflation in Israel and Argentina (see chapter 2). Specifically, it is seen in figure 3.1 that the rise of inflation in Israel from about 10–20 percent a year in the early 1970s to around 100 percent in the early 1980s was accompanied by a real wage increase of more than 20 percent, and the further acceleration of inflation to close to 400 percent in 1984 was accompanied by a further rise in real wages of about 16 percent.[1] In the case of Argentina, real

Reprinted with permission from *European Economic Review* 34 (July 1990):897–912.
1. In the chart the real wage corresponds to the yearly average per employee post, and inflation is measured by the percentage change in the CPI. The source for these series are various issues of the *Annual Report* by the Bank of Israel.

wage increases of more than 40 percent between 1972 and 1974 preceded the acceleration of inflation from less than 50 percent in 1974 to more than 400 percent in 1976, marked real wage decreases between 1974 and 1977 preceded the more than halving of the inflation rate that occurred between 1976 and 1977/78, and further real wage increases have accompanied the upsurge of inflation in the early 1980s.

The foregoing evidence implies that longer-term wage developments have been governed to a large extent by factors other than backward-looking wage indexation. This observation provides the motivation for focusing our analysis on forward-looking wage and price determinations. We develop a model that embodies a wage-price spiral and monetary accommodation, and use it to investigate inflationary dynamics. We show that inflationary inertia need not be a characteristic of this type of an economy, despite the fact that the data it produces may be mistakenly interpreted as exhibiting inflationary inertia. We explain how the model accounts for the positive association between real wages and inflation, and how it is possible to disinflate an economy with these characteristics.

For the purpose of this study we develop a modified version of Blanchard's (1986) model, in which there is monopolistic competition and nonsynchronized decision making by firms and workers about price and wage changes.[2] In particular, we allow for autonomous changes in real wages, positive discounting, and use exact functional forms. In order to concentrate on the mechanism that generates the positive comovement of real wages and inflation, we abstract from backward-looking wage indexation.

In our model there is a staggering in the setting of wages and prices and monetary accommodation. The emerging time pattern of inflation depends on a set of fundamentals that includes the level of real wages, the markup, the real interest rate, and real spending. When these parameters are constant, perfect foresight leads to a constant rate of inflation, implying that there is no inflationary inertia. That is, despite the existence of a wage-price spiral and monetary accommodation, current inflation is not affected by past inflation. To the extent that fundamentals change over time, the model implies that steady-state inflation is higher the higher are real wages, the markup, and real spending, or the lower is the real interest rate. Moreover, rising real wages over a given time interval imply a rising rate of inflation.

Models of price-wage spirals (Blanchard's model notwithstanding) build on competing claims by workers and firms for the economy's output. These claims are usually reconciled by means of employment adjustments with inflation playing at most a temporary role. We underline the possibility that

---

2. Zeira (1989) has used a differently modified version of Blanchard's model in order to describe inflationary inertia. He also dealt with different issues.

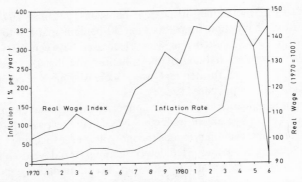

Figure 3.1   Inflation and real wages in Israel (1970–86).

inflation can be a permanently reconciling factor. Namely, even with complete real wage rigidity the competing claims of workers and firms can be reconciled with a finite level of inflation. This, however, requires positive discounting of the future. In fact, we show that the range of real wages within which inflation is bounded depends on the real discount rate. This point is of independent interest.

The paper is organized as follows. Section 2 describes the basic model. Section 3 derives its implications for disinflation, for the comovement of inflation and real wages, and for inflationary inertia. This analysis is restricted to partial equilibrium. A general equilibrium underpinning is provided in section 4. Section 5 concludes by pointing out some limitations of recent empirical tests of inflationary inertia in view of our analysis and by discussing possible extensions.

2. Wages and Prices

In this section we develop our model of staggered wages and prices. Prices are set in even periods for a two-period time interval and nominal wages are set at odd periods for a two-period time interval. Labor is the only variable input in production. Let $d_t(p)$ be the demand curve faced by a representative firm in period t, where p is the price it charges for its product, and let $\phi(a)$ be its labor requirement for producing output a (i.e., the inverse of the production function). Then if w_t stands for the nominal wage rate set by workers in period t odd, and β_t stands for the one-period nominal discount factor in period t, the representative firm's decision problem can be written as:

$$\max_{p_t} p_t d_t(p_t) - w_{t-1}\phi[d_t(p_t)] \tag{3.1}$$

$$+ \beta_t[p_t d_{t+1}(p_t) - w_{t+1}\phi[d_{t+1}(p_t)]], \ t \text{ even}$$

We assume oligopolistic competition amongst firms producing differenti-ated products. Preferences are of the Spence-Dixit-Stiglitz type with a con-stant elasticity of substitution σ. Hence, the demand function is

$$d_t(p) = \left[\frac{p}{P_t}\right]^{-\sigma} a_t, \quad \text{all } t, \tag{3.1a}$$

where P_t is a price index of the available varieties and a_t is real aggregate spending per firm (see Appendix). Every firm has an identical demand and cost structure. Therefore, in a symmetrical equilibrium $P_t - p_t$, and the above-described pricing decision implies:[3]

$$P_t = \frac{R}{1 + \beta_t a_{t+1}/a_t} \left[w_{t-1}\phi(a_t) + \beta_t\left(\frac{a_{t+1}}{a_t}\right)w_{t+1} \right.$$
$$\left. \times \phi(a_{t+1}) \right], \quad \text{for } t \text{ even}, \tag{3.2}$$

where $R = 1/(1 - 1/\sigma)$ is the markup factor and $\phi(\cdot)$ is the derivative of $\phi(\cdot)$, thereby representing marginal labor requirement. Marginal labor re-quirement is rising with output if and only if marginal costs are rising with output.

We assume that the nominal wage rate is set for a two-period time interval such that the present value of two-period wages equals a predetermined pres-ent value of real purchasing power ω_t. Since the latter is taken as exogenous to the model, the analysis embodies a form of real wage rigidity. Specifically, the wage rule is:[4]

$$w_t + \beta_t w_t = \omega_t(p_{t-1} + \beta_t p_{t+1}), \quad \text{for } t \text{ odd}. \tag{3.3}$$

Equations 3.2 and 3.3 describe the basic wage-price spiral model. It can be seen that past and future wages are taken into account by firms when setting prices, and similarly past and future prices are taken into account by workers when setting wages. Although the processes of wage-price determination are

3. We employ a standard Nash equilibrium concept. If the problem was formulated as a repeated game other equilibria would be possible.

4. In this formulation workers require nominal wages that are equivalent over the two-period horizon of the contract to receiving ω_t in real terms in each one of the two periods. Alternatively, it could have been assumed (as suggested by a referee) that the fixed parameter is not ω_t but rather the discounted present value of real wages over the two periods. Both formulations yield similar results, except for the effect of the real interest rate on inflation.

not derived here from first principles,[5] they capture what is believed to be an observed nonsynchronization of these variables and enable us to analyze in a tractable framework the effects of changes in key parameters, such as autonomous shifts in real wages, on the inflationary process. The consistency of the present formulation with general equilibrium considerations is discussed in section 4.

3. Inflation Dynamics

Now assume that the real interest rate is positive and constant, and let ρ, $0 < \rho < 1$, be the real discount factor (equal to one over one plus the real interest rate). Then $\beta_t = \rho P_t/P_{t+1}$. Since $p_t = p_{t+1}$ for t even, we obtain:

$$\beta_t = \begin{cases} \rho & \text{for } t \text{ even,} \\ \dfrac{\rho p_{t-1}}{p_{t+1}} & \text{for } t \text{ odd.} \end{cases}$$

Combining this with (3.2)–(3.3) yields:

$$1 = R \frac{1 + \rho}{1 + \alpha_t \rho} \left[\frac{\omega_{t-1} \phi(a_t)}{x_t + \rho} + \alpha_t \rho \frac{\omega_{t+1} \phi(a_{t+1}) x_{t+2}}{x_{t+2} + \rho} \right], \qquad (3.4)$$

where $\alpha_t = a_{t+1}/a_t$ is the growth factor of demand per firm and $x_t = p_t/p_{t-2}$ is one plus the two-period inflation rate. This equation describes the determination of current (period t) inflation as an implicit function of the markup, the real interest rate, the evolution of real wages, the evolution of demand, and expected future inflation.[6]

In order to study inflation dynamics, we specialize the model at this point by assuming that real wages ω_t and real demand per firm a_t are constant over time (the case of rising real wages is discussed in the sequel). In this case (3.4) reduces to:

$$1 = R\omega\phi(a) \left[\frac{1}{x_t + \rho} + \frac{\rho x_{t+2}}{x_{t+2} + \rho} \right] \quad \text{for } t \text{ even.} \qquad (3.5)$$

5. It is possible to generalize the wage rule so as to incorporate also backward-looking elements, such as in Taylor (1980). However, it is convenient to concentrate on the simplified version for current purposes.

6. Equation 3.4 implicitly describes the rate of inflation that reconciles the competing claims by workers in (3.3) and firms in (3.2). Inflation can assume this role because wages and prices are set in different time periods. Alternative timing conventions for setting prices and wages will assign inflation different reconciling roles.

It is useful to begin the discussion with the case of a constant rate of inflation; i.e., $x_t - x$ for all t even. This is applicable to steady states, but it may also apply to situations in which the economy is not in a steady state, as we explain in section 4. In this case (3.5) implies:

$$R\omega\phi(a) = \frac{x + \rho}{\rho x + 1}. \tag{3.6}$$

It is easy to see that in (3.6) x is an increasing function of $R\omega\phi$ if and only if $\rho < 1$. Hence, if the real interest rate is positive, higher values of the real wage rate, the markup, or the marginal labor requirement are associated with higher constant inflation rates. It is also straightforward to see from (3.6) that for a given value of $R\omega\phi$ the rate of inflation is a decreasing function of the real interest rate (an increasing function of ρ) if the real interest rate and the inflation rate are positive.[7]

Equation 3.6 is highly nonlinear. It implies that small changes in the real wage rate, the markup, or marginal labor requirement may bring about large changes in the rate of inflation. To see this point, consider the case in which prices are adjusted every six months, so that the elementary time unit is one quarter. Let the quarterly real interest rate be 1.5 percent. Then, if $R\omega\phi = 1$ there is price stability, and if, say, the real wage rate increases by 0.1 percent the rate of inflation increases to 14.4 percent per half year. A further increase in the real wage rate or marginal labor requirement by 0.1 percent increases the rate of inflation to 31 percent per half year. This shows clearly the high elasticity of the inflation rate with respect to costs.

In what follows we consider the case in which

$$\rho < R\omega\phi < \frac{1}{\rho}.$$

which ensures the existence of an equilibrium with a constant rate of inflation. In this case equation 3.5 implies the functional relationship between x_t and x_{t+2} as described in figure 3.2. The curve is rising, going to infinity as x approaches $\bar{x}$ from below, and going to minus infinity as x approaches $\bar{x}$ from above. It intersects the 45° line at the steady state point A, with a slope larger than one. It is clear from figure 3.2 that perfect foresight and expected positive prices require expected and actual values of x to be in the interval $(x, \bar{x})$ in all time periods. This, however, is satisfied if and only if the expected rate of inflation is equal to the constant level represented by point A. Hence, in

---

7. The partial derivative of x with respect to ρ that is implied by (6) is $(x^2 - 1)/(1 - \rho^2)$.

this case perfect foresight leads to a constant rate of inflation as long as the underlying parameters are constant; i.e., inflation does not depend on predetermined factors.

In this model unexpected permanent shocks to fundamentals bring about permanent changes in the rate of inflation, and there is no inflationary inertia. The model suggests that in order to permanently disinflate an economy with these characteristics it is necessary to generate some combination of decreases in the real wage rate, the markup, and marginal labor requirement, and an increase in the real interest rate. As discussed in chapter 2, models of this class are useful for analyzing recent anti-inflation plans such as those implemented in Israel and Argentina in mid-1985, where the initial impact of the policy measures featured decreases in the real wage and markup and an increase in the real interest rate.

While the foregoing discussion was confined to unexpected permanent shocks, it turns out that anticipated changes in key parameters may generate a gradual rise in inflation which can mistakenly be interpreted as inflationary inertia. Consider a gradual increase in the real wage rate ω_t, with a_t being constant. It is easy to see from (3.4) that this brings about a rightward shift of the curve that passes through A in figure 3.1. If $\omega_1 = \omega'$ and it rises over time until it reaches a constant level ω from time $t = T$ on, then on a perfect foresight path the rate of inflation at time T has to be the constant rate of inflation that corresponds to the wage rate ω (i.e., the solution to [3.6]).

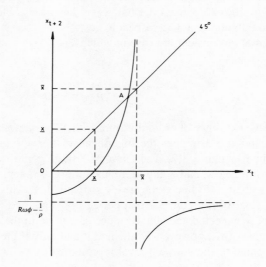

Figure 3.2

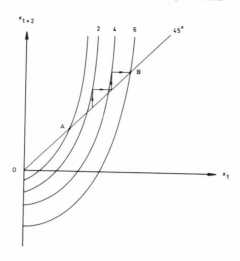

Figure 3.3

Solving (3.4) backwards produces the unique perfect foresight path. In terms of our diagram, figure 3.3 describes the adjustment path for a two-period increase in real wages. If the real wage was constant at the level ω_1 the rate of inflation would have been constant at point A. However, since $\omega_3 > \omega_1$, the relevant curve is more to the right, such as curve 2. Hence, in period 2 the system has to be on curve 2. Similarly, in period 4 it has to be on curve 4 and in period 6 on curve 6. Moreover, in period 6 it has to be at point B. Therefore, moving backwards we identify the arrow path as the equilibrium trajectory. It is clear that on this trajectory the rate of inflation is rising, and so is positively autocorrelated, thus possibly giving the impression that there is inflationary inertia. Yet the latter interpretation is not valid in the current context.

4. General Equilibrium Considerations

So far we have discussed price-wage dynamics under the assumption that monetary policy accommodates the resulting price developments. We have also assumed a given time pattern of real spending per firm, a_t. We now develop an explicit model of intertemporal choice that provides general equilibrium underpinnings for this analysis. It is assumed for this purpose that the number of firms is n in every time period. Hence, n is also the number of available varieties. In addition, there exist indexed bonds that are freely traded in the capital market. These bonds can be issued by the government or the private sector.

Consider a representative individual that maximizes the discounted flow of utility:

$$\sum_{t=0}^{\infty} \rho^t \left[u(c_t) + v\left(\frac{M_t}{p_t}\right) \right]$$

subject to the budget constraint:

$$\sum_{t=0}^{\infty} \delta_t \left[c_t + \frac{M_{t+1} - M_t}{p_t} \right] \leq \sum_{t=0}^{\infty} \delta_t (y_t - \tau_t) + (1 + r_{-1})b_{-1}. \quad (3.7)$$

Here the utility level depends on real consumption and real balance holdings, where the dependence on real consumption is derived from a Spence-Dixit-Stiglitz utility function with a fixed number n of equally priced varieties.[8] The period t real discount factor is denoted by δ_t (discounted from time t to time 0), M_t stands for nominal money balances, y_t for real income, τ_t for lump-sum taxes, r_{-1} for the real interest rate in the period prior to zero, and b_{-1} for bonds acquired in the period prior to zero. If $b_{-1} > 0$, these bonds have been issued by the government, and if $b_{-1} < 0$, the bonds have been issued by the private sector. The evolution of private bond holdings is described by:

$$b_{t+1} = (1 + r_t)b_t + y_t - \tau_t - c_t - \frac{M_{t+1} - M_t}{p_t}.$$

Let θ be the multiplier of constraint 3.7. Then the first-order conditions for the consumer's maximization problem are:

$$\rho^t u'(c_t) = \delta_t \theta, \qquad t = 0, 1, 2 \ldots \quad (3.8)$$

$$\rho^{t+1} v' \frac{(m_{t+1})}{p_{t+1}} = \theta\left(\frac{\delta_t}{p_t} - \frac{\delta_{t+1}}{p_{t+1}}\right), \qquad t = 0, 1, 2 \ldots \quad (3.9)$$

where m_t is real balance holdings.

In what follows we deal with the case in which real income y_t is constant;

---

8. Let $u^\circ(U)$ be the original utility function from which $u(\cdot)$ has been derived, with $U = [\int_{i\in I} c_i^\gamma]^{i/\gamma}$ where c_i is consumption of variety i and $0 < \gamma < 1$ (see Appendix). Then if p is the price of every variety, it is optimal to choose equal quantities $c_1 = a$. Given real consumption spending c this yields $a = c/n$, where n is the number of available varieties. Hence, we can define $u(c) = u^\circ(n^{1/\gamma - 1}c)$, which is used in the text.

i.e., $y_t = y$. It will be shown that this is indeed an equilibrium (albeit not the only one). Assume also that government spending is the same in all time periods at the level g, and that its allocation across varieties is the same as in the private sector. In this case

$$c_t = c = y - g,$$

which implies with the aid of (3.8) that $\delta_t = \rho^t u'(c)/\theta$. However, since by definition $\delta_0 = 1$, this yields $\theta = u'(y - g)$ and $\delta_t = \rho^t$ for all t. Applying these results to (3.9) yields

$$\frac{v'(m_{t+1})}{u'(y - g)} = \frac{p_{t+1}}{\rho p_t} - 1 \qquad \text{for all } t. \tag{3.10}$$

This equation provides a link between inflation and real money holdings, given real income y, real government spending g, and the real interest factor ρ. In order for this equation to be satisfied at each point in time while price movements are determined by the process described in the previous section, the government has to accommodate the demand for money. It is, therefore, necessary to see whether and how this can be done.[9]

Taking b^G_{-1} to be the government's outstanding debt, and using $\delta_t - \rho^t$, the government's consolidated intertemporal budget constraint is:

$$\sum_{t-0}^{\infty} \rho^t \left[\tau_t + \frac{M_{t+1} - M_t}{p_t - g} \right] = (1 + r_{-1})b^G_{-1}. \tag{3.11}$$

The left-hand side represents the present value of its income minus spending, where income is derived from lump-sum taxes and monetary injections. The right-hand side represents its liabilities at time zero. This implies the evolution of government debt according to

$$b^G_{t+1} = \rho^{-1}b^G_t + g - \tau_t - \frac{M_{t+1} - M_t}{p_t}.$$

Naturally, in equilibrium $b_t = b^G_t$.

---

9. Observe that the analysis in the previous section implied that $p_{t+1} - p_t$ for t even. Therefore, in this case (3.10) implies that real balance holdings are higher in even periods than in odd periods. The amplitude of these fluctuations in real balance holdings is smaller the lower the rate of inflation.

The government is solvent as long as (3.11) is satisfied. This intertemporal budget constraint can also be written as:

$$\sum_{t=0}^{\infty} \rho^t \tau_t = (1 + r_{-1})b_{-1}^G + \sum_{t=0}^{\infty} \rho^t \left(\frac{g + m_t - m_{t+1}p_{t+1}}{p_t} \right), \quad (3.11')$$

which implies that given a) the inflation path that is determined by means of the mechanism described in the previous section; b) the implied real balance holdings that are described in (3.10); c) the real spending level g; and d) accommodation of the demand for money; the right hand side of (3.11') is given. Therefore, this determines the present value of lump-sum taxes. Naturally, there is more than one time pattern of taxes that ensures solvency, and with each feasible pattern there is an associated pattern of government debt. However, the substitution of debt for taxes has no real effects (there is Ricardian neutrality). Hence, as long as taxes can be chosen so as to ensure intertemporal balancing of the government budget, the government can indeed pursue an accommodating monetary policy. Given some natural restrictions on the level of taxes at each point in time (such as the requirement that taxes cannot exceed income), this leaves a wide range of cases in which this policy is feasible.

It remains to discuss the consistency of a constant real income level y with the predetermined price-wage dynamics. Recall that we assumed that government spending g is allocated across varieties in the same way as in the private sector. Hence, aggregate spending per firm is

$$a = \frac{(c + g)}{n} = \frac{y}{n}.$$

On the other hand, employment is given by

$$\ell = n\phi^{-1}(a) = n\phi^{-1}\left(\frac{y}{n} \right),$$

where $\phi^{-1}(\cdot)$ may include fixed costs. Hence, as long as y is low enough so that ℓ is below the full employment level (assuming an inelastic labor supply), we have an equilibrium configuration. Namely, if individuals expect such y to be their real income in every period (from wages and profits), and firms expect y to be the level of aggregate spending in every time period, then indeed these will be equilibrium values. The pattern of inflation, on the other hand, is determined according to the mechanism described in the previous section. Since every level of real income y that leads to less than full employment of labor is an equilibrium value, there is a continuum of equilibria with constant income and consumption. In fact, there also exist many others in which private consumption, and therefore also aggregate spending, change over time (while government spending is constant). In the latter case the real interest rate is not the same in all time periods.

Observe that given constant values of (a, ω), and the constant real interest rate, the rate of inflation is constant. In this case government debt may be growing over time if higher taxes are expected in the future. Hence, there may be constant inflation despite the fact that the economy is not in a steady state. In addition, rising marginal costs imply higher inflation for a higher real spending level per firm, while higher real spending implies higher employment. Therefore, in this type of an economy one may observe a long-run Phillips curve, although it may be argued that this model is not suitable for long-run analysis because in the long run the rules for determining prices and wages may change.

Can the government affect employment? The answer is yes if private sector expectations are such that an increase in public spending makes people believe that income will be higher. If expectations satisfy this condition, then an increase in public spending brings about expectations of higher income, which induces in turn higher aggregate spending and higher employment. Given rising marginal costs the result will be higher inflation. Consequently, the correspondingly lower demand for real balances has to be accommodated, implying the need to adjust the present value of tax revenue in order to satisfy (3.11').

5. Concluding Remarks

We have analyzed the dynamics of inflation in an economy characterized by a forward-looking, staggered, price and wage determination process, and by monetary accommodation. In our model, inflation reconciles the conflicting claims of workers and firms. The model is capable of generating a positive association between real wages and inflation, of the type that has been observed in some high-inflation countries. It generates a price-wage spiral but does not result in inflationary inertia. We have identified changes in key underlying parameters that are required in order to disinflate an economy with these characteristics.

Our results can be used to question the meaning of recent research that has used autoregressive representations in order to empirically assess inflationary inertia. Consider for example the analysis by Bruno and Fischer (1986). They show that in quarterly inflation autoregressions for Israel the size and sum of coefficients on the first and second lags have increased over time along with the inflation rate. For 1965:I–1971:I this sum is 0.56, for 1975:III–1978:IV it is 0.87, and for 1979:I–1982:IV it is 1.04. Their conclusion is that the evidence supports the notion that there is considerable inertia in the inflationary process in Israel and that this inertia has been growing over time.

In the light of our model, an important limitation of using univariate inflation autoregressions to assess inertia is that the latter do not explicitly allow for changes in fundamentals. Equation 3.4 describes the inflation rate as an implicit function of the markup, the evolution of the target real wage, the real interest rate, the evolution of aggregate demand, and expected future inflation. Thus, from this model's standpoint inflation autoregressions that do not allow for changes in these factors are misspecified. Another problem with the above-mentioned autoregressions, discussed in chapter 2, arises from the fact that no detrending was applied despite the fact that inflation appears to be nonstationary. The upshot is that there seems to be no meaningful model-free test of inflationary inertia. In order to test this hypothesis, it is necessary to formulate an explicit model that embodies it, allowing for changes in the forcing variables, and then test it directly.

In order to sharply focus on the new features of our wage-price spiral we have intentionally disregarded backward-looking wage indexation that prevails in many high-inflation economies. In principle, our forward-looking mechanism is complementary to conventional backward-looking wage indexation and stabilization programs have to address both. Indeed, reductions in the degree of indexation have been used in early stages of disinflation programs in an attempt to deal with the latter. Our model underlines the need for additional steps that have been used in recent programs, such as the lowering of target real wages.

Our analysis can be extended in several directions in an attempt to relax some of the restrictive assumptions that were used. First, the rules of wage and price determination can be modified so as to include the effects of backward-looking wage indexation. Second, the assumption of perfect foresight could be relaxed. When discussing the effects of government policies on inflation, credibility characteristics of these policies can also be considered. Third, wage-setting rules could be derived from first principles by explicitly taking into account workers' and trade unions' objectives. Fourth, the extent of staggering could be expanded, by allowing some firms or sectors and some workers to change their prices and wages every period. Naturally, the ways in which these extensions and modifications alter our results remains to be determined in future work.

Appendix

Let the utility function of the representative individual be of the Spence-Dixit-Stiglitz type with a constant elasticity of substitution and a continuum of varieties. Then it can be represented as:

$$U = \left[\int_{i \in I} c_i^\gamma di^{1/\gamma}, \right. \tag{3A.1}$$

where i is an index of varieties, I is the set of available varieties, c_i is consumption of variety i, and $0 < \gamma < 1$ is a parameter. The elasticity of substitution is given by $\sigma = 1/(1 - \gamma)$. This utility function implies the demand function for variety i:

$$c_i = \left[\frac{p_i}{P} \right]^{-\sigma} a, \tag{3A.2}$$

where P is a price index and $a = A/(Pn)$ is real spending per variety (or per firm). Here, A stands for nominal spending and n for the number of firms. The number of firms is defined as:

$$n = \int_{i \in I} di$$

and the price index P is defined as:

$$P = \left[\frac{1}{n} \int_{i \in I} p_i^{1-\sigma} \right]^{1/(1-\sigma)}$$

References

Blanchard, O. 1986. The Wage Price Spiral. *Quarterly Journal of Economics* 101: 543–66.

Bruno, M. 1986. Sharp Disinflation Strategy: Israel 1985. *Economic Policy* 2:379–402.

Bruno, M., and S. Fischer. 1986. The Inflationary Process: Shocks and Accommodation. In *The Israeli Economy: Maturing Through Crises,* ed. Y. Ben-Porath. Cambridge: Harvard University Press.

Dixit, A., and J. E. Stiglitz. 1977. Monopolistic Competition and Optimum Product Diversity. *American Economic Review* 67:297–308.

Dornbusch, R., and M. H. Simonsen. 1987. Inflation Stabilization with Incomes

80   *Chapter Three*

Policy Support: A Review of Recent Experience in Argentina, Brazil and Israel. Group of Thirty, New York.

Spence, M. 1976. Product Selection, Fixed Costs, and Monopolistic Competition. *Review of Economic Studies* 43:217–36.

Taylor, J. 1980. Aggregate Dynamics and Staggered Contracts. *Journal of Political Economy* 88:1–23.

Zeira, J. 1989. Inflationary Inertia in a Wage-Price Spiral Model. *European Economic Review* 33:1665–83.

4

Comparing Macroeconomic Performance before and after Disinflation in Israel

I. Introduction

The Israeli stabilization program of 1985 is generally considered one of the most successful programs of recent years, in that it rapidly disinflated the economy from inflation rates of about 400 percent per year to rates between 15–20 percent per year. While much attention has been devoted to the heterodox components of the program and their analytical foundations,[1] relatively little work has been done quantitatively comparing the structure and performance of the macroeconomy before and after the program. Yet such a comparison can be regarded as a key ingredient in an overall evaluation of the pros and cons of programs such as that of Israel.

Accordingly, the main objective of this paper is to examine how macroeconomic performance has changed after the implementation of the stabilization program and to determine whether these changes conform with the predictions of standard macroeconomic models. We investigate, using simple time-series techniques applied to monthly data for 1980–88, the changes that have taken place in the time-series properties of key macroeconomic variables after the stabilization program of 1985. Special attention is given to changes in the tradeoff between inflation and unemployment which are apparent after the program.

The notion that a change in the policy regime should cause changes in the relationships among macroeconomic variables is quite familiar since Lucas's (1976) critique. We focus here on some of the empirical implications of this critique. Comparing policy regimes before and after 1985 suggests that the post-program regime is characterized by a tight fiscal policy, and by a sharp decrease in the degree of exchange-rate accommodation as

---

1. See, e.g., chapter 2, Blejer and Liviatan (1987); Bruno (1986); Bruno and Piterman (1988); Fischer (1987); Kiguel and Liviatan (1988); and Liviatan (1989).

reflected in the fixing of the exchange rate, which was viewed as the main anchor for the nominal system. For other nominal variables it is less clear whether and how their rules of behavior have changed after the program. Prices of controlled goods and services were periodically adjusted to changes in the rate of inflation. Monetary policy was mainly conducted so as to provide indirect support for the exchange-rate anchor and it did not target directly monetary aggregates such as M_1 or M_2. Wage policy resulted in slow transition of COLA and of other institutional features of the wage-setting process toward a low-inflation position. The upshot of this discussion for the analysis that follows is that it seems plausible to hypothesize that the program brought a decrease in the degree of accommodation of nominal policy variables, effected mainly through a decrease in exchange-rate accommodation.

Policy-regime changes such as the above can be expected to have affected relations between key macro variables. First, less accommodative exchange-rate and nominal policies can cause changes in the form of the tradeoff between inflation and unemployment. Second, these less accommodative policies are likely to result in changes in the persistence (or inertia) of inflation and other nominal variables. Third, to the extent that after the program there is a more dominant role of real shocks relative to nominal shocks, as it is likely to be the case given the less active role of nominal policy variables after the program, it is likely that there would be changes in the relations between variabilities of relative prices, relative wages, and relative outputs across sectors in the economy. Moreover, this enhanced importance of real vs. nominal shocks can, by itself, result in changes in the form of the inflation/unemployment tradeoff. Fourth, lack of credibility of the new policies can result in high real wages, high real interest rates, and a consumption boom at the start of the stabilization program and thus importantly affect the transition of the economy to its new equilibrium. Identifying these types of changes in macroeconomic performance is the focal point of this research.

The paper is organized as follows. Section II briefly describes the main changes in the behavior of nominal policy variables brought about by the stabilization program. It also discusses the predictions of standard macro models for the likely impact of these changes on the economy. Section III provides evidence on macroeconomic performance in the Israeli economy before and after the disinflation program. We investigate and interpret the time-series behavior by key macro variables and characterize their changes in terms of means, standard deviations, correlations, responses to shocks, and degree of persistence. We also examine changes in the comovements of cross-sectional variabilities of relative prices, wages, and outputs. Changes in the tradeoff between inflation and unemployment (Phillips curve) are discussed and analyzed in section IV. Section V concludes the paper.

II. The Change in Regime: Facts and Models

We begin this section by describing briefly the main nominal policy rule changes brought about by the 1985 program. Later on, we turn to a discussion of standard macroeconomic models in order to get analytical guidance as to what to expect when comparing the Israeli economy before and after the program.

A. Some Facts

Since the Israeli program has been described in detail elsewhere (see note), we focus here briefly on its main aspects, which are relevant to analysis of the effects of changes in the rules governing the evolution of nominal policy variables. Comparing the policy regimes before and after the program suggests that there were at least five main changes brought about by the disinflation program. First, there was a fiscal contraction as the public sector sharply reduced its fiscal deficit by about 9 percent of GNP. About half of this reduction was effected by a decrease in public-sector consumption and the remaining half by increasing taxes.

Second, the government adopted a fixed-exchange-rate regime.[2] Fixing the exchange rate was conceived as a key element in anchoring the nominal system at a low-inflation equilibrium. The Israeli shekel was initially pegged to the U.S. dollar, but later on (August 1986) the pegging was done relative to a basket of foreign currencies.[3] Thus, the authorities abandoned the previous policy of using devaluations in a one-sided manner to affect real wages and external balance, and adopted the view that further changes in exchange-rate policy would have to reflect cooperative agreements between government, labor, and employers. It is in this spirit that the devaluations of January 1987 and of December/January 1988/89 have to be interpreted. Since the fixed-exchange-rate policy, coupled with other internal and external developments, resulted in marked real appreciation trends of real exchange rates, it was changed early in 1989 toward more flexibility. That is, the exchange rate is being targeted now within a relatively fixed band rather than at a specific fixed rate.

Third, there have been changes in wage policy toward disinflation. It ap-

2. The shekel was devalued by 10 percent in January 1987 and by 13 percent in January 1989. Since the latter date the exchange rate is targeted within a band of ±3 percent.
3. This was facilitated by a $1.5 billion grant from the U.S. government.

pears that after the program there was an increase in the importance and length of nominal contracts and an increase in the fraction of wage changes that are due to agreements at the company or plant level as opposed to centralized collective agreements.[4] Of special interest in this context is the evolution of the cost-of-living agreement (COLA). COLA's structure has been gradually changed so that the trigger level of inflation (for actual payment of indexation) has been raised and the frequency of COLA payments has been reduced. The agreement reached in February 1989 stipulates wage indexation payments once every six months (and not every three months as before), at a rate of 85 percent of the excess of the inflation rate beyond 3 percent during these six months. Though these changes represent important adjustments in the transition to a low-inflation economy, one can certainly question why progress in this direction has been relatively slow in the face of the fast disinflation that took place and whether the present agreement is indeed appropriate under the current rates of inflation of less than 20 percent per year. The slow adjustment of COLA's structure may well reflect partial lack of credibility of the stabilization program.

Fourth, there was a shift to a tight monetary policy. Immediately after the program the monetary authority targeted commercial bank credit to the private sector, which was considered as an additional nominal anchor. Later on, there was a shift toward targeting real M_3 with a view toward the economy's international reserves position. In addition, real interest rates were kept high to affect the current account and the state of aggregate demand. Obviously, some of the observed increases in M_1 and other shekel-denominated assets capture the effects of disinflation on the composition of private portfolios. Fifth, in Israel government directly determines prices of goods and services whose weight in the consumer price index is of about 20–30 percent; for example, prices of public transportation, gasoline, and basic foodstuffs. Given the sizable weight of these controlled prices, and their importance in government (subsidies) budget, the stabilization program stipulated a government policy of changing them at a rate compatible with the attempted low inflation.

Overall, the policy regime after the program features a decrease in the degree of exchange-rate accommodation. This decrease was supported by a tight fiscal policy. Whether and how the degree of accommodation of other nominal policy variables changed after the program remains an open question.

B. Models

What are the possible implications of these facts for macroeconomic performance? Here we attempt to answer this question in the light of two classes

4. For a detailed discussion, see Artstein and Sussman (1988).

of standard macro models: contracting models and imperfect information models.[5]

i. Contracting Models. Models of the Fischer (1977)-Taylor (1979) variety emphasize the role of contractual rigidities in generating real costs of disinflation. In particular, the models posit a nonstate contingent structure of overlapping multiperiod wage contracts. As a result, ending inflation is generally costly (in terms of unemployment) because firms and workers are locked into long-term nominal contracts that were negotiated on the basis of price and wage expectations formed in the past.[6] A tradeoff between the variance of inflation and the variance of output arises from these frameworks. In these models, the degree of accommodation of nominal policy variables plays a key role in determining the shape of this tradeoff between output and inflation variabilities. For example, high monetary accommodation to nominal wage shocks generally results in higher output stability but at the cost of generating higher price instability.

To sharpen the discussion, consider the impacts of a decrease in the degree of nominal exchange-rate accommodation in the context of Dornbusch's (1982) open-economy analysis of contracting models. The exchange rate is postulated to affect both demand and supply sides of the macroeconomy, and some of the results are ambiguous depending on the relative strength of these two effects. The analysis indicates that a decrease in exchange-rate accommodation lowers the variability of prices and has ambiguous effects on the variability of output. The latter is decreased when the cost channel of exchange rates dominates, but it is increased if the aggregate demand role of the real exchange rate dominates. To the extent that the move toward lower exchange-rate accommodation is accompanied by decreased monetary accommodation, there is a further decrease in price variability and a dampening or even offsetting of the effects on output variability that arise from the supply-side effects of the exchange rate. Numerical examples provided by Dornbusch (1982) indicate that starting with high degrees of exchange-rate and monetary accommodation, a decrease in the former accompanied by no major change in the latter leads to a marked reduction in price variability with only a minor change in output variability. The model has also implications for persistence[7] and for the impact of unanticipated disturbances on output. Specifically, when

5. We do not examine here the more recent real business cycle approach because its implications for short-run impacts of stabilization policies remain yet to be analyzed.
6. This class of models implies that there can be a costless disinflation only if there is a gradual tightening of fiscal and monetary policies with a timing that pays attention to the persistence in nominal wages that was built in by old wage contracts.
7. In this model persistence is defined as the first-order autoregressive coefficient of a given dynamic variable.

the aggregate demand effect dominates, a decrease in monetary or exchange-rate accommodation lowers the persistence of wages and prices through time and raises the impact of unanticipated disturbances on output. This discussion of persistence has to be qualified, however, in that it assumes no change in the frequency of wage and exchange-rate adjustments. To the extent that a disinflation program results in less frequent exchange-rate and wage adjustments, it can contribute toward higher and not lower persistence of nominal disturbances. Thus, a more complete analysis would indicate ambiguous effects of exchange-rate accommodation on persistence. Taking into account changes in the frequency of exchange-rate and wage adjustments following disinflation would strengthen the above-described rise in the impact of unanticipated disturbances on output in response to a decrease in exchange-rate accommodation.

ii. Imperfect Information Models. These models posit that agent's imperfect information about current and future real and nominal shocks is the main factor explaining observed Phillips curves. Movements in output and other real variables can result from changes in nominal variables only to the extent that the latter are not fully known with certainty. In Lucas's (1973) setup, producers cannot fully determine the extent of relative price change from current information about their own nominal price. Under these conditions, the slope of the aggregate supply schedule (inverse Phillips curve) depends on the relative importance of real (relative) vs. nominal (aggregate) shocks. The higher the importance of real (relative) shocks, the flatter becomes the aggregate supply schedule in the [price, output] plane, and probably the stronger is the tradeoff between inflation and unemployment.

To the extent that following a disinflation program there is a diminished role of nominal shocks and, other things equal, the program can result in a more pronounced observed tradeoff between inflation and unemployment. While there are some methods for measuring the relative importance of real vs. nominal shocks, additional information on this issue can be obtained by examining the comovements between the variabilities of prices and outputs across sectors in the economy. As shown by Cukierman (1983), imperfect information models imply (under some restrictive assumptions regarding parameter values) that when nominal aggregate shocks dominate, these variabilities can be expected to move in opposite directions. That is, an increase in the variance of nominal aggregative shocks reduces demand-and-supply-relative price elasticities in each market and thus results in higher relative price dispersion but lower output variability across sectors. However, cross-sectional output and price variabilities would move in the same direction in the presence of dominant real shocks. Thus, under the maintained hypothesis of these models it may be expected that while before a major disinflation program these output and price variabilities moved in opposite directions, they moved in unison after disinflation.

III. Time-Series Evidence and Comparisons

In this section, we present time-series evidence on changes in the relations between key macro variables that occurred after the program. We assemble and interpret the evidence in the light of the models discussed in the previous section. We start by looking at summary statistics such as means and standard deviations—the latter taken here as a measure of the degree of variability of different variables—as well as by examining changes in contemporaneous cross-correlations. Then, we investigate how the dynamics of selected variables changed after the program by studying their responses to shocks. We first consider responses to own shocks and later on responses to shocks in other variables. Then we turn to evidence on the cross-sectional variabilities of output growth, a real wage growth, and relative prices which provide indication as to whether there has been a change in the type of shocks that are dominant. Last, we investigate whether the persistence of economic fluctuations changed after the program. We conclude the section by summarizing the key findings and by discussing the extent to which they conform with the models.

A. Summary Statistics

Our discussion in this subsection is mainly based on table 4.1 and figures 4.1–4.4.

i. Means. The first two columns of panel *a* in table 4.1 report monthly means for a set of macroeconomic variables before (i.e., 1980:2–1985:6) and after (i.e., 1986:1–1988:12) the disinflation program of 1985. It can be seen that before the program prices, money, wages, and nominal exchange rates were increasing at a rate of about 9 percent per month. The stabilization program resulted in a remarkable reduction in the rate of inflation to a rate of about 1.3 percent per month. Growth rates for other nominal variables changed in different patterns. Some variables feature a lower rate of growth than the rate of inflation in the post-stabilization period, but others increased at much higher rates than inflation. Specifically, while exchange rates for the dollar and the basket of foreign currencies depreciated at a lower rate than inflation, there were relatively high rates of growth of nominal wages, M_1, and credit in the later period. Overall there have been two patterns (see figures 4.1 and

Table 4.1

Summary Statistics—Israel: 1980–1988 (monthly data)

a. Means, Standard Deviations, and Coefficients of Variation[a]

Variable (% rate of change)	Mean[b]		Standard Deviation[b]		Coefficient of Variation[b]	
	(B)	(A)	(B)	(A)	(B)	(A)
CPI	9.36	1.34	5.03	0.89	2.70	0.59
Price of controlled goods	9.48	1.39	6.44	1.04	4.38	0.78
Price of free goods	9.32	1.33	4.95	0.98	2.63	0.71
Nominal wage	9.83	2.46	7.85	6.50	6.27	17.18
Exchange rate (basket)	8.71	0.70	5.29	1.55	3.21	3.43
Exchange rate (dollar)	9.37	0.21	5.05	1.35	2.72	8.67
M1 money	8.23	3.81	7.90	8.30	7.58	18.08
M3 money	10.03	1.67	6.27	2.74	3.92	4.50
Credit	9.20	3.22	5.26	1.64	3.01	0.84
Interest rate[c]	11.44	3.75	5.12	0.62	2.29	0.10
Industrial production	0.73	0.51	8.78	9.62	105.60	181.46
Employment	0.20	0.16	1.52	1.31	11.55	10.73
Rate of unemployment[c]	5.13	6.58	0.78	0.97	0.12	0.14
Consumption	0.69	0.91	7.16	5.05	74.30	28.03
Real wage	0.47	1.11	7.80	6.48	129.45	37.83
Real exchange rate (basket)	−0.64	−0.64	3.25	1.78	−16.50	−4.95

	DM₁	DM₃	DC	DPC	DER	INT
Real exchange rate (dollar)	1.43	−1.13	3.35	1.73	7.86	−2.64
Real relative price of controlled goods	0.13	0.05	3.24	0.85	80.75	14.45
Real interest rate[c]	2.09	2.41	3.79	1.22	6.87	0.62
Trade deficit[d]	244.91	237.46	62.65	66.09	16.03	18.40
Trade deficit/GDP[e]	0.12	0.08	0.031	0.023	0.008	0.006

b. Correlations Matrix for Inflation and Selected Nominal Variables[f]

	DP	DW	DM₁	DM₃	DC	DPC	DER	INT
DP	1.00							
DW	.33 (.08)	1.00						
DM₁	.17 (−.27)	.46 (.33)	1.00					
DM₃	.66 (−.33)	.28 (.12)	.48 (.60)	1.00				
DC	.66 (−.10)	.40 (.34)	.41 (.32)	.64 (.32)	1.00			
DPC	.87 (.62)	.19 (.04)	.19 (−.19)	.61 (−.39)	.55 (.04)	1.00		
DER	.80 (−.00)	.34 (−.19)	.32 (−.09)	.73 (.15)	.80 (.33)	.67 (.10)	1.00	
INT	.72 (−.27)	.40 (.04)	.37 (.31)	.58 (.46)	.78 (.24)	.59 (−.17)	.75 (.23)	1.00

(continued)

Table 4.1 (*continued*)

c. Correlations Matrix for Inflation and Selected Real Variables[g]

	DP	UNE	DIP	DEMP	DCON	DRER	RIR	DRW
DP	1.00							
UNE	.38	1.00						
	(−.21)							
DIP	−.17	.23	1.00					
	(−.10)	(.19)						
DEMP	−.26	.14	.49	1.00				
	(−.25)	(−.00)	(.54)					
DCON	−.27	.06	.34	.12	1.00			
	(.02)	(.09)	(.19)	(.04)				
DRER	−.24	.17	.50	.29	.25	1.00		
	(−.50)	(.07)	(−.03)	(.14)	(.05)			
RIR	−.35	.35	.21	.23	.27	.45	1.00	
	(−.87)	(.07)	(.00)	(.16)	(−.00)	(.54)		
DRW	−.31	−.05	.17	.40	.30	.19	.33	1.00
	(−.05)	(−.01)	(.39)	(.35)	(.06)	(−.14)	(.08)	

[a] Data sources: Bank of Israel and Central Bureau of Statistics.

[b] Columns (B) refer to the period 1980:2−1985:6; i.e., before the implementation of the 1985 stabilization program. Columns (A) apply to the 1986:1−1988:12 post-stabilization period.

[c] Level (and not rate of change).

[d] Level, in millions of dollars.

[e] Trade deficit in domestic currency units divided by a monthly measure of GDP.

[f] The variables DP, DW, DM$_1$, DM$_3$, DC, DPC, and DER denote the rates of change of the CPI, nominal wage, M_1, M_3, credit, controlled prices, and nominal (basket) exchange rate. INT denotes the nominal interest rate. Each entry gives a correlation coefficient for the period 1980:2−1985:6. Figures in parentheses are correlation coefficients for the period 1986:1−1988:12.

[g] The variables DP, DIP, DEMP, DCON, DRER, and DRW denote the rates of change of the CPI, industrial production, employment, consumption, real exchange rate, and real wage. UNE and RIR denote, respectively, the rate of unemployment and real interest rate. Each entry gives a correlation coefficient for the period 1980:2−1985:6. Figures in parentheses are correlation coefficients for the period 1986:1−1988:12.

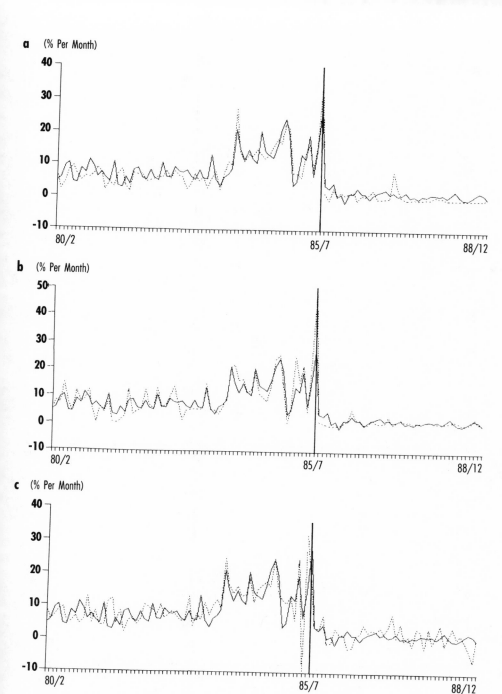

Figure 4.1 (a) The rate of inflation and the rate of devaluation (basket) (——— = inflation; . . . = devaluation (basket). (b) The rate of inflation and the rate of change of controlled prices (——— = inflation; . . . = rate of change of controlled prices). (c) The rate of inflation and money (M_3) growth (——— = inflation; . . . = M_3 growth).

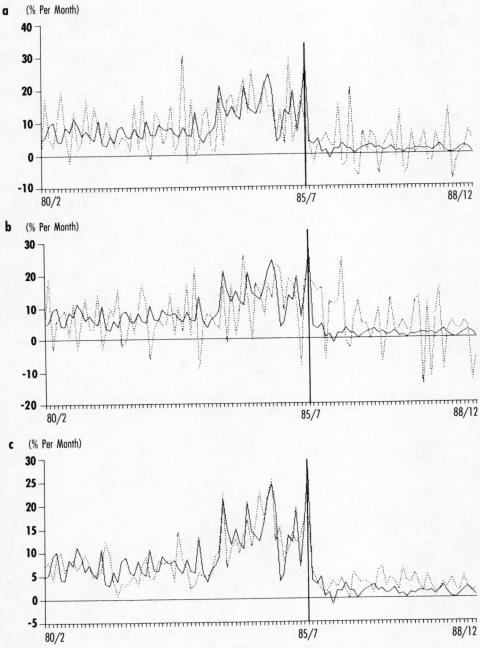

Figure 4.2 (*a*) The rate of inflation and nominal wage growth (——— = inflation; . . . = nominal wage growth). (*b*) The rate of inflation and money (M_1) growth (——— = inflation; . . . = M_1 growth). (*c*) The rate of inflation and the rate of change of credit.

4.2). Some nominal variables have shown movements that have been aligned well in the later period with those in the rate of inflation; see figure 4.1 for evidence on the growth rates of the nominal exchange rate, controlled prices, and M_3 money. However, there has been some *nonsynchronization* after the program between the growth rates in wages, M_1 money, and credit and the rate of inflation; see figure 4.2.

Turning to real variables, there has been a slowdown in the rate of growth of industrial production[8] and of employment after the disinflation, from monthly growth rates of 0.73 and 0.20 percent respectively before the program to rates of 0.51 and 0.16 after the program. These, however, have not been major changes; see figure 4.3. Quantitatively more important changes show up for the rate of unemployment, which increased from 5.13 percent to 6.58 percent, and in private consumption purchases, which have increased at a more rapid rate in the later period; see figure 4.4. Though the rate of unemployment increased immediately after the implementation of the program, this increase partly represents a continuation of existing trends from before the program. In addition, from the first quarter of 1986 on there was a downward trend in unemployment—a trend that was reversed in 1988 and early 1989 and has resulted in a rate of unemployment of about 8 percent.

It is straightforward to translate the evidence in the first panel of table 4.1 into evidence regarding relative-price type variables. Some of these calculations are reported in the third panel of the table. Two key features of the data are the almost tripling in the rate of growth of the real wage in the later period and the real appreciation of the Israeli shekel, as inflation exceeded the rate of devaluation during that period. Despite the sharp increase in the real interest rate at the start of the program, the real interest rate for the 1986–88 period is only slightly higher (on average) than in the previous period. However, since it is likely that there has been a fall in the risk-premium component of the interest rate, associated with a decrease in inflation uncertainty, the "net" real interest rate may well be much higher after the program than before it.

The evidence on the monthly trade deficit indicates that, despite some reduction immediately after the program, in dollar terms the deficit has remained quite unchanged after the program at a level of about $240 million; see figure 4.3. However, the deficit was somewhat reduced in real terms and relative to GDP.

ii. Standard Deviations. The middle two columns of table 4.1, panel *a,* can be used to analyze changes in the variability of these variables, measured by their standard deviations. For most nominal variables, there has been a de-

---

8. Domestic gross investment increased significantly in 1986 but its rate of growth fell.

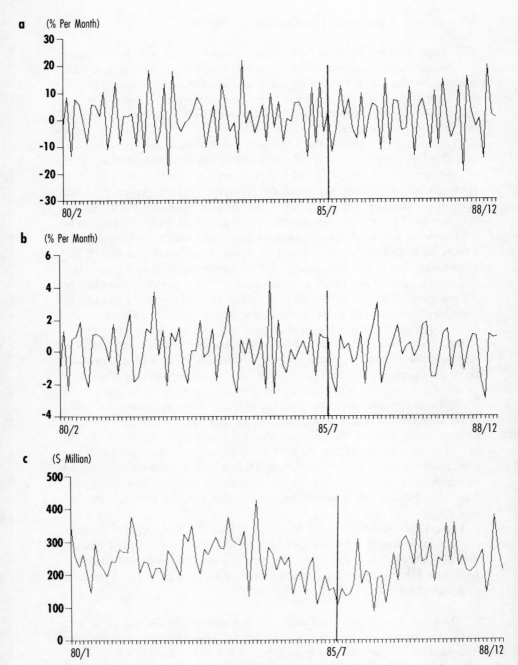

Figure 4.3 (a) The rate of growth of industrial production. (b) The rate of growth of employment. (c) The trade deficit.

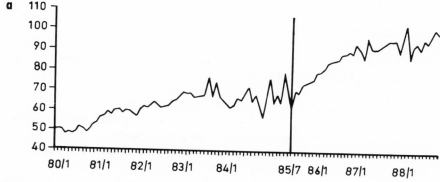

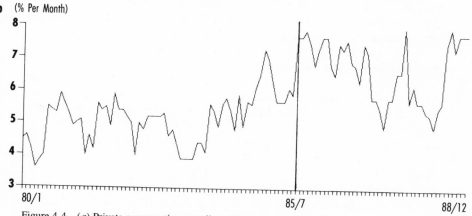

Figure 4.4   (a) Private consumption spending. (b) The rate of unemployment.

crease in their standard deviations, along with the above-discussed decrease in mean rates of growth. In particular, the standard deviations of inflation and most other nominal variables after the program are at levels of about 20–30 percent of their previous levels; a similar pattern holds generally for coefficients of variation also reported in table 4.1.[9]

In contrast to this general pattern, there has been a relatively minor change in the variability of the rates of growth of nominal wages and of M_1 after the program. Thus, for these variables the observed decreases in their mean rates of growth were not accompanied by a decline in their standard deviations—a somewhat puzzling finding. We have checked changes in the standard deviations of these two variables for each one of the three years from 1986 to 1988. It appears that the standard deviations of the rate of growth of nominal wages

9. Notice that coefficients of variation would not be well-defined measures of variability for variables whose means are close to zero.

and of M_1 have remained high for each one of these years. Specifically, the standard deviation of movements in wage growth were 8.05, 5.99, and 5.63 in 1986, 1987, and 1988 respectively, and those for M_1 growth were 7.52, 8.15, and 8.56 respectively. This evidence indicates that the relatively high variabilities of these variables during 1986–88 are not the result of particularly high variability in a given year; not only that changes in the mean growth rates of wages and M_1 have not been synchronized with the rate of inflation, but nonsynchronization has also been present when comparing changes in the standard deviations of inflation and of these two variables; again see figure 4.2 for general evidence on such nonsynchronization. Among the possible reasons for these phenomena we can mention the following: (i) the adjustment of M_1 may well be the net result of gradual and time-varying shifts in agents' portfolios toward shekel-denominated assets; (ii) the adjustment of wages may reflect increased staggering and sectorial variability as well as interference of economy-wide wage norms with sectorial adjustments toward equilibrium; see Artstein and Sussman (1988).

The volatilities of real variables have changed less markedly, if at all, after the program than those of the nominal variables. The standard deviations of the rate of growth of industrial production and of the rate of unemployment increased in the later period. On the other hand, the standard deviations of the rates of growth of employment and of consumption decreased in the later period. The variability of the trade deficit has not changed much after the program. For relative-price type variables there is generally some decrease in their variability after the program.

These findings suggest that generally there has been a decrease in the relative variability of nominal vs. real quantity variables in the post-stabilization period. This conclusion would not be incompatible with characterizing the later period as one in which there has been an increase in the quantitative importance of real shocks as compared to that of nominal shocks. In addition, the notion that when inflation is sharply reduced this induces less variability, both over time and across sectors, in relative-price variables is supported by the data.

iii. Cross-Correlations. Cross-correlations between monthly movements in inflation and in other key nominal variables are reported in panel *b* of table 4.1 for the periods before and after the disinflation program. Before the 1985 stabilization program, there were relatively large correlations between inflation, rates of growth of monetary aggregates (M_1, M_3, and credit), the nominal interest rate and the rate of change of the exchange rate. These monthly cross-correlations generally reached values in the .65–.80 range. The period after 1985 features a marked reduction in these correlations. In fact, some of them became negative, such as the correlations between inflation and monetary aggregates. This may well capture a shift toward a less indexed nominal side of the economy and toward smaller accommodation after the program.

The evidence supports the notion that before the plan there was a strong and close association between monthly movements in key nominal variables. This has changed after the implementation of the plan, in that there are now much weaker links within the nominal side of the system.

Cross-correlations between monthly movements in inflation and selected real variables are reported in panel c of table 4.1. Not surprisingly, the correlations between monthly movements in inflation and in real variables are much smaller than those reported in part b of the table. Upon comparing correlations before and after the program, notice that while before mid-1985 there was a positive link between inflation and the rate of unemployment, the relation between these variables becomes negative in the later period. Thus, the statistical (monthly) Phillips curve appears to have changed as a result of the program.

Considering jointly the evidence in panels b and c of table 4.1 reveals that the signs and sizes of cross-correlations between monthly movements in inflation and in other macroeconomic variables have generally changed after the disinflation plan. These changes are more pronounced for the nominal variables than for the real variables—a pattern that held also generally for comparisons involving means and standard deviations.

B. Responses to Shocks

Having discussed the evidence on some summary statistics, we turn now to an examination of whether and how the dynamics of key macroeconomic time series have changed after the implementation of the disinflation program. To achieve this goal, bivariate autoregressions are estimated and transformed into moving average form (or impulse-response functions) in which the impact of shocks can be measured. The estimated equations are of the form

$$x_t = \sum_{i=1}^{4} A_i x_{t-i} + e_t, \tag{4.1}$$

where $x_t = (\pi_t, y_t)'$, with π denoting the rate of inflation and y denoting any other variable entering the autoregression (e.g., y may denote the rate of growth of money). The moving average for this system is given by

$$x_t = \sum_{i=0}^{\infty} B_i e_{t-i}, \tag{4.2}$$

where the B_i matrices can be obtained from the A_i matrices; see Sims (1980). For our purposes, it is convenient to orthogonalize the covariance matrix of the e's thus yielding the representation

$$x_t = \sum_{i=0}^{\infty} C_i e^*_{t-i}, \qquad (4.3)$$

where e^* denotes the orthogonalized disturbances.

Bivariate autoregressions such as in equation 4.1 were estimated for the rate of inflation and another variable selected those appearing in table 4.1. Each such run was implemented on monthly data twice: for the 80:6–85:6 period (before the disinflation program) and for the 85:12–88:12 period. Before we discuss changes in the impacts of shocks, it is well to turn to table 4.2 which reports evidence on the *size of the shocks* in both time periods. The shocks in the system are measured by the estimated disturbances in the econometric equations; thus, wage shocks are the disturbances to the bivariate regression of the rate of change of wages on four own lagged values, four lagged values of the rate of inflation, and a constant. For inflation shocks, we used the disturbances from the autoregression including lagged inflation

Table 4.2
The Size of the Shocks: Standard Deviations of Estimated Disturbances

	1980:6–1985:6	1985:12–1988:12
Inflation	3.85	0.68
Wage Growth	7.18	5.55
M_1 Growth	6.48	7.91
M_3 Growth	5.08	2.45
Credit Growth	4.15	1.57
Devaluation (Basket)	4.08	1.53
Devaluation (Dollar)	3.57	1.26
Inflation of Controlled Prices	5.79	0.96
Nominal Interest Rate	1.22	0.20
Unemployment	0.49	0.77
Industrial Production Growth	6.46	6.29
Employment Growth	1.38	1.00
Consumption Growth	6.25	3.96
Trade Deficit/GDP	0.026	0.024

Note: Each entry is the standard deviation of the estimated disturbance from bivariate autoregressions that used four lagged values of inflation and of the other relevant variable and a constant. The figures for inflation are based on autoregressions that had lagged inflation and wage growth as explanatory variables.

and wage growth as explanatory variables. The size of the shocks is measured by the standard error of the estimated disturbances.

The evidence reported in table 4.2 is quite consistent with that reported in table 4.1. That is, the size of most nominal shocks has generally decreased by a large extent. Standard deviations of nominal shocks in the post-1985 period are at about 25–35 percent of their levels before the program. The exceptions are shocks to nominal wage growth and to M_1 growth, which had in the later period standard deviations of the same order of magnitude as in the first period. For real variables, the picture is somewhat different in that for most shock-type quantity variables there have been only relatively minor changes in standard deviations. Thus, *this evidence tends to support the notion that real shocks have become more important relative to nominal shocks in the period after the 1985 stabilization program.*

To examine the nature of the changes in the dynamic responses to shocks we use figures 4.5 to 4.8 and begin by looking at the responses of each variable of interest to its own shocks. The first chart in figure 4.5 depicts the response of inflation through time to a unit shock (i.e., one standard deviation) in the rate of inflation in period 1 as calculated for the periods before and after the disinflation program. The figure also reports responses of wage growth and of M_1 growth to respective own unit shocks. Two main features are salient in figure 4.5. First, there is generally less own-persistence in the impact of the shocks in the first two or three periods. For example, against the same unit shock to the inflation rate there is a smaller rate of inflation by period 4 after the program than before. Second, there has been an increase in the variability of the responses through time after the program. There is now more pronounced cyclicality in the process of convergence following the shocks.

Figure 4.6 presents evidence on responses to own shocks for variables that have been subject to greater control by policymakers than those in the previous figure. These are the rate of change of the exchange rate (basket), the rate of change of controlled prices, and the rate of change of credit. It is seen that for each one of these variables responses to own shocks show less persistence after the program, especially in the first few periods immediately after the shocks and there is a somewhat faster convergence back to the steady state or control values of zero. This seems to be consistent with stronger attempts by policymakers to bring these nominal variables back to their preshock levels more rapidly than in the period before the program.

Responses of real variables to unit shocks in their values are presented in figure 4.7. Shocks to the rate of growth of employment and to the rate of unemployment seem to have slightly larger persistence in the first periods after the shocks. Altogether, however, there are no major changes in the responses of real variables to their own shocks after the 1985 program.

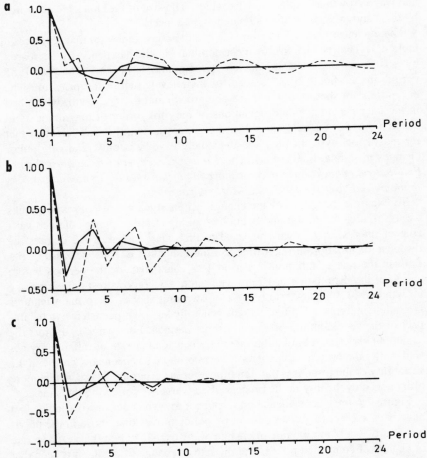

Figure 4.5   Responses to own shocks: Inflation, wage growth, and M_1 growth (———— = before the program; . . . . . = after the program), (*a*) The rate of inflation. (*b*) The rate of change of the nominal wage. (*c*) The rate of change of M_1.

Some evidence regarding changes in cross effects before and after the program is provided in figure 4.8. In all cases we consider the effects of inflation shocks on other variables. The first two charts depict the responses of wage growth and M_1 money growth to unit shocks in inflation. It can be seen that these shocks generate a *less accommodating* short-term response of nominal wages and M_1 in the post-program period. These responses show a great degree of volatility, or cyclicality, in the later period. Considering the effects of

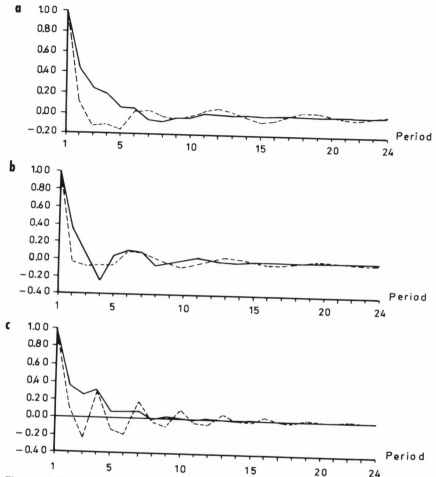

Figure 4.6   Responses to own shocks: Exchange rate, controlled prices, and credit (———— = before the program; . . . = after the program). (*a*) The rate of change of the basket exchange rate. (*b*) The rate of change of controlled prices. (c) The rate of change of credit.

inflation shocks on the rate of change of the exchange rate, in the third chart of the figure, indicates that the shocks have a much smaller impact and result in somewhat less variability of the rate of change of the exchange rate than before the program. This probably reflects the *decrease in exchange-rate accommodation* implied in the use of the exchange rate as a policy variable in the process of disinflation. The last chart in the figure gives the responses of employment growth to inflation shocks. After the program, there is a stronger

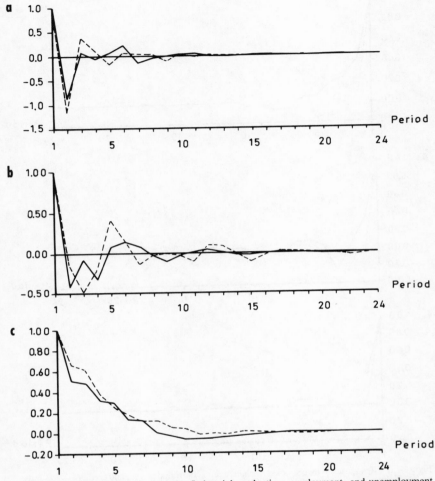

Figure 4.7 Responses to own shocks: Industrial production, employment, and unemployment (———— = before the program; . . . . . = after the program). (*a*) The rate of change of industrial production. (*b*) The rate of change of employment. (*c*) The rate of unemployment.

short-run impact of inflation shocks on the rate of change of employment and the latter's responses show higher volatility than before—this last finding is similar to that reported above for wage and M_1 growth.

Another type of cross effect arises from considering the response of inflation to shocks in the other variables. The evidence, not reported here in charts for brevity, is straightfoward: *shocks in other variables have a much smaller impact on the rate of inflation after the program.* Thus, the disinflation pro-

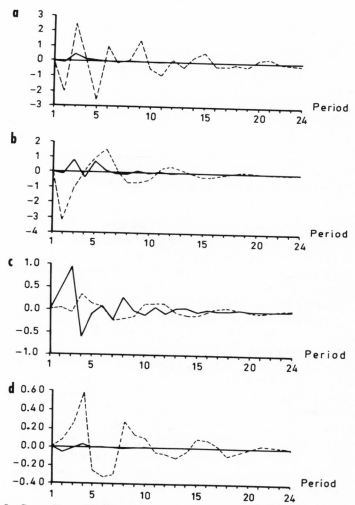

Figure 4.8   Cross effects of inflation shocks (———— = before the program; . . . = after the program). (a) On the rate of change of wages. (b) On the rate of change of M_1. (c) On the rate of change of the basket exchange rate. (d) On the rate of change of employment.

gram appears to have weakened the link going from shocks to key macro variables to the process of inflation.

C. Cross-Sectional Variabilities

The conclusion, based on tables 4.1 and 4.2, that there is a less important role of nominal vs. real shocks after the program, is now further verified by

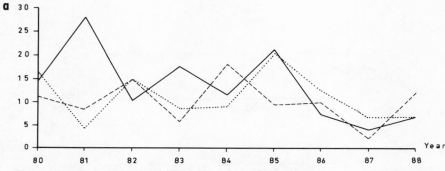

Figure 4.8a   Cross-sectional variabilities (———— = relative prices; - - - - - = relative outputs;
. . . . . = relative wages).

turning to cross-sectional variabilities. We discussed in the previous section
the predictions of imperfect information models regarding the direction of comovement between price and output cross-sectional variabilities. Figure 4.8a
plots three measures of variability: of relative prices (across ten broad categories in the CPI), relative growth rates of output (across six main sectors
such as industry, agriculture, construction, etc.), and relative rates of growth of
real wages (across nine main sectors). We consider the latter two measures as
applying to real variables. In each case, variability is measured by weighted
cross-sectional variances.[10]

There are two salient features of figure 4.8a. First, there has been a decrease in cross-sectional variabilities after the 1985 program. In particular,
the index of dispersion of relative prices after the disinflation has become
about one-third of its value before the program. This finding is in line with
the observed positive correlation between inflation and relative price dispersion that has been documented for several countries. Similarly, there has been
a decrease of about 20 percent in the variability of real wage growth rates
after 1985. There has been a somewhat slower downward adjustment of relative real wage growth variability than that of relative prices.[11] Second, notice
the form of comovement between these three measures of dispersion before
and after the program. Up to 1984 there was generally a common movement
of the variabilities of output growth and real wage growth, in *opposite* direction to that of the variability of relative prices. Thus, *periods with high price
variability were typically also periods of low variability of output growth and
wage growth across different sectors.* This pattern *changed after 1985,* in that

10. The data source for our calculations is the Bank of Israel's *Annual Report* (various issues).
11. This may partly reflect the interference of economy-wide range wage norms imposed by
the program with different stages of adjustment to long-term equilibrium of different sectors. See
Artstein and Sussman (1988).

the three variabilities appear to be *positively correlated* since then. Using these patterns to classify time periods according to the relative importance of real vs. nominal shocks, as suggested in the previous section, provides further support to the hypothesis that real shocks have become more dominant after the program. Notice also that while 1987 was a year with remarkably low values of our three measures of dispersion, they all show increases in 1988 and especially so the variability of output growth rates.

D. Persistence of Fluctuations

Has there been a change in the degree of persistence of macroeconomic fluctuations after the disinflation program? We interpret persistence in a time-series sense and measure it by the variance ratio, used recently by Cochrane (1988). Consider time series for a given variable, say the rate of inflation π_t. The variance ratio consists of dividing $(1/k)$ times the variance of k-differences in π by the variance of its first differences:

$$V(k) = \left(\frac{1}{k}\right)\left[\frac{\text{var}(\pi_t - \pi_{t-k})}{\text{var}(\pi_t - \pi_{t-1})}\right]. \qquad (4.4)$$

One extreme case of persistence is when π_t follows a random walk. In this case, the variance of k-differences in π grows linearly with k and the variance ratio is equal to one. Under these conditions fluctuations in π are permanent and the underlying process is nonstationary. At the other extreme is the case in which π_t follows a stationary (mean-reverting) process. The variance of k-differences in π_t approaches then a constant equal to twice the variance of the series and the variance ratio approaches zero for large k; in this case, fluctuations in π are transitory. Between these two extremes there are cases in which fluctuations in π are partly permanent and partly temporary, as when the series are a combination of a random walk and a stationary component. In these more general cases the variance ratio provides a measure of the relative importance of the permanent component, in that for large k it settles down to the ratio of the innovation variance of the random walk component to the variance of first differences.

Variance ratios adjusted for small sample bias are reported in table 4.3 and figure 4.9 provides plots of the ratios for four variables: the rate of inflation, the rate of unemployment, the rate of change of the real exchange rate, and the real interest rate. For each variable the ratios are reported for periods before and after the disinflation program. In each case we used monthly data and $k = 13$. Caution is suggested in regarding the findings as definitive because small samples are being used and standard errors are not provided.

Comparing persistence before and after the program yields two main pat-

Table 4.3

Variance Ratios [V(k); Equation 4.4 in Text]

						k							
	1	2	3	4	5	6	7	8	9	10	11	12	13
Inflation:													
B	1.00000	0.73707	0.50000	0.42241	0.26293	0.16379	0.22845	0.23276	0.16810	0.15948	0.13793	0.09483	0.16379
A	1.00000	0.58876	0.69231	0.40828	0.31361	0.13609	0.14793	0.17751	0.20710	0.19527	0.16568	0.11834	0.11834
Wage growth:													
B	1.00000	0.38268	0.20042	0.21089	0.16061	0.11453	0.12709	0.13757	0.07542	0.10824	0.09776	0.05168	0.10265
A	1.00000	0.53662	0.17209	0.28132	0.19863	0.10500	0.15639	0.13618	0.09611	0.13060	0.10804	0.03904	0.10214
Devaluation:													
B	1.00000	0.71366	0.52785	0.46580	0.30140	0.28583	0.28687	0.22598	0.20930	0.18554	0.17763	0.15859	0.16933
A	1.00000	0.67048	0.50835	0.40333	0.24658	0.24872	0.23060	0.22258	0.23357	0.17257	0.18878	0.18758	0.19087
Controlled prices:													
B	1.00000	0.69781	0.54636	0.33400	0.20838	0.19766	0.20184	0.21346	0.17373	0.13295	0.12852	0.13032	0.16921
A	1.00000	0.71828	0.54833	0.42852	0.33582	0.32976	0.24679	0.23018	0.10757	0.14290	0.12978	0.10757	0.12669
M1 growth:													
B	1.00000	0.38670	0.24433	0.18247	0.18539	0.11433	0.12373	0.10939	0.07666	0.12047	0.08487	0.05750	0.07757
A	1.00000	0.51536	0.27167	0.26406	0.14228	0.13555	0.14792	0.15681	0.10752	0.10619	0.11527	0.05837	0.11292
Real interest Rate:													
B	1.00000	0.68221	0.42582	0.35292	0.19905	0.13669	0.19244	0.20529	0.15381	0.15823	0.13612	0.09459	0.15113
A	1.00000	0.85366	0.81460	0.70741	0.65854	0.71494	0.74586	0.76572	0.67311	0.63091	0.59823	0.64258	0.68555

Real exchange Rate:													
B	1.00000	0.59958	0.36146	0.29204	0.12783	0.13341	0.18042	0.15791	0.11462	0.10623	0.11007	0.06904	0.10982
A	1.00000	0.90368	0.79649	0.54128	0.31707	0.19207	0.21744	0.26867	0.32048	0.27551	0.25110	0.18555	0.20703
M3 growth:													
B	1.00000	0.19266	0.21137	0.15831	0.14188	0.10033	0.13165	0.08900	0.08475	0.08116	0.07961	0.06362	0.08779
A	1.00000	0.51014	0.32540	0.30281	0.20196	0.20079	0.18361	0.21716	0.15512	0.14415	0.15733	0.10906	0.13237
Trade deficit:													
B	1.00000	0.67213	0.29946	0.27400	0.28237	0.18835	0.18890	0.20058	0.17194	0.16209	0.15144	0.15678	0.13547
A	1.00000	0.53362	0.29464	0.29246	0.27303	0.18391	0.18956	0.21099	0.11565	0.14587	0.13975	0.11685	0.10997
Employment growth:													
B	1.00000	0.38710	0.34441	0.20406	0.13763	0.14860	0.10332	0.11677	0.13610	0.09435	0.10406	0.03600	0.09064
A	1.00000	0.77404	0.47957	0.23888	0.18269	0.22716	0.15018	0.15535	0.20282	0.23128	0.14135	0.06653	0.13552
Unemployment rate:													
B	1.00000	0.70774	0.68333	0.62857	0.64286	0.51786	0.50833	0.40923	0.33542	0.28155	0.25000	0.20923	0.24881
A	1.00000	0.82031	0.79279	0.70579	0.71591	0.67614	0.66104	0.57582	0.45543	0.34357	0.32067	0.30575	0.32031
Industrial production growth:													
B	1.00000	0.30294	0.23441	0.17457	0.13388	0.08461	0.11530	0.09399	0.07784	0.08954	0.08396	0.03030	0.00840
A	1.00000	0.34508	0.20635	0.18977	0.15483	0.07901	0.15599	0.07479	0.08338	0.10747	0.07277	0.04631	0.10196
Credit growth:													
B	1.00000	0.60812	0.42183	0.33465	0.26656	0.32297	0.26259	0.18055	0.20625	0.16418	0.16625	0.19000	
A	1.00000	0.67387	0.27260	0.31657	0.21801	0.20960	0.09434	0.21405	0.12913	0.15762	0.14307	0.07059	0.17060

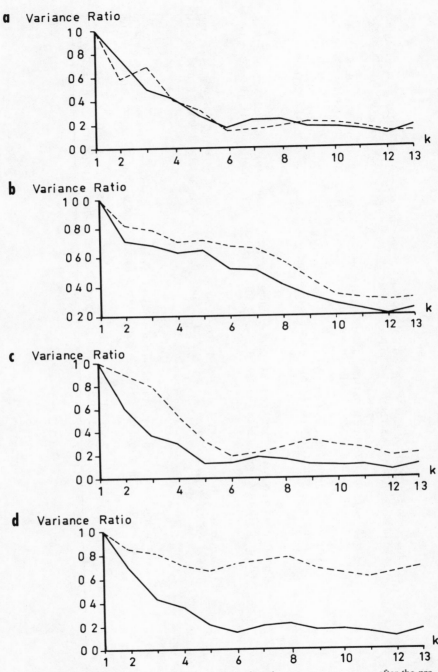

Figure 4.9 Selected variance ratios (———— = before the program; . . . . . = after the program). (*a*) The rate of inflation. (*b*) The rate of unemployment. (*c*) The rate of change of real exchange rate. (*d*) Real interest rate.

terns. On the one hand, no major change in variance ratios shows up for the nominal variables such as the rate of inflation, and the rates of growth of M_1, wages, controlled prices, the nominal exchange rate, etc. See in this context the first chart in figure 4.9 which gives the variance ratio for the rate of inflation. It is seen that before and after the program fluctuations in inflation were primarily transitory, as indicated by the variance ratios of 0.16 and 0.12 respectively (for $k = 13$).[12]

Variance ratios for real variables, on the other hand, yield a somewhat different pattern. The ratios reported in table 4.3 indicate that there has been an increase in the degree of persistence of fluctuations in some real variables after the program, especially so for the rate of unemployment, the rate of change of the real exchange rate, and the real interest rate (see their variance ratios plotted in figure 4.9). This increased persistence of unemployment after the program may well reflect a process of structural adjustment and reallocation of resources across sectors; see section IV below.

E. Relating the Findings to the Models

In summarizing and interpreting the evidence presented above we would like to highlight six main results. First, it seems safe to characterize the post-1985 regime as one with a lower degree of exchange rate, and perhaps overall nominal accommodation. That is, there is weaker transmission of changes in the rate of inflation into changes in other nominal variables after the program. This finding is especially relevant for contracting models, where changes in the degree of accommodation of nominal policy variables play an important role in changing macroeconomic performance. We discussed earlier (in section II) the predictions of these models regarding the effects of lowering the degree of nominal accommodation and will explain shortly how these predictions fit the data.

Second, changes in the size of the shocks and in the direction of comovements of cross-sectional variabilities generally indicate a larger role of real vs. nominal shocks after disinflation. To the extent that this enhanced importance of real shocks can be associated with a greater role of relative disturbances, then imperfect information models would predict that this will induce an increase in economic agents' responsiveness to perceived relative prices— an effect that may result in a flatter Phillips curve.

Third, there appears to be a more pronounced tradeoff between inflation and unemployment in the later period. This is consistent with the analysis of contracting models, which predict that lowering the degree of nominal policy

12. Notice, however, that there are subperiods before the program in which inflation persistence may have well increased, as in the inflation outburst that occurred from late 1983 to mid-1985; see again figure 4.1.

accommodation should result in a larger impact of unanticipated disturbances on output and on other real variables. This finding is also in line with imperfect information models, as discussed above. In the next section we will discuss the statistical links between inflation and unemployment in the transition from high to low inflation.

Fourth, the tradeoff between output variability and inflation variability, if it exists, has shifted downward such that inflation variability has diminished and output variability shows very little change. Interestingly, this pattern conforms quite well with the outcomes from numerical examples applied to open-economy contracting models by Dornbusch (1982); see our discussion in section II above.

Fifth, the evidence on changes in persistence is not clearcut. Perhaps this is not surprising given the theoretical ambiguities that arise when analyzing the impact of lower nominal accommodation on persistence in contracting models.

Sixth, after the program there has been a decrease in the dispersion of relative prices across different sectors. Thus, the idea that reducing inflation leads to a decrease in the high-inflation-induced "noise" component of relative prices seems to be supported by the evidence. Also, real relative-price type variables such as real exchange rates and real interest rates exhibit lower variability through time after the program.

While we obviously recognize that our findings are not based on definitive tests of a model or set of models, we regard the evidence presented thus far as harmonious with the predictions of standard macroeconomic models.

IV. The Changing Nature of the Inflation/Unemployment Tradeoff

This section provides further evidence on the inflation/unemployment tradeoff before and after the program. We begin by examining statistical and econometric Phillips curves before and after the program and move on to investigate the relations between the rate of unemployment and three important variables: the real exchange rate, the real interest rate, and the real wage. We focus on the timing of changes in unemployment and on the difficulties in attempting to account for the observed timing with standard macro models.

Four years after the implementation of the stabilization program it has become clear that the remarkable disinflation that took place, from inflation rates of about 9.3 percent per month to rates of about 1.3 percent per month, has been accompanied by an increase in the rate of unemployment from about 5 percent per month before the program to about 8 percent in early 1989; see figure 4.10 for half-yearly data.

The observed empirical relation between inflation and unemployment exhibits a positive association between these variables in the high-inflation pe-

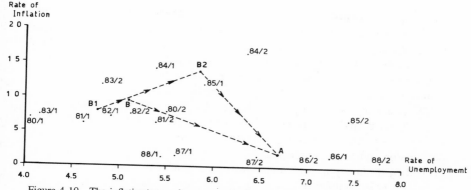

Figure 4.10   The inflation/unemployment tradeoff (correlation coefficient = 0.32). Note: The data plotted are half-yearly averages. *B* indicates the averages before the program and *A* after the program. *B*1 indicates the averages for the 1980–83 period and *B*2 those for the 1984–85:1 period.

riod and practically no systematic relation about stabilization. By contrast, *inflation and unemployment appear to be strongly negatively related when comparing the means of these variables before and after stabilization*. Thus, with the benefit of hindsight, the empirical Phillips curve for the high-inflation period had no predictive value with regard to what was to be anticipated after the program.

These facts raise the question of why the empirical relation between these two variables is so different within regimes as compared with the transition between regimes, and especially what are the causes for the negative relation in the latter case. The case of the transition is of course the more important aspect of this discussion since it is only in this case that a tradeoff is indeed observed. In what follows, we suggest some answers to these questions.

A. The High-Inflation Period

In this period the behavior of inflation and unemployment seems to reflect the economy's reaction to policymakers' actions intended to influence another policy target: the economy's external balance. When the balance of payments gets into a crisis and international reserves are being depleted—as in 1979–80 and 1983–84—this consideration probably takes precedence over the targets of having low inflation and unemployment. In fact, both inflation and unemployment may become instruments in dealing with such a crisis. Under these circumstances, and assuming an indexed economy, a positive association may emerge between inflation and unemployment. Yet this association has nothing to do with the tradeoff between these variables that is relevant in the context of a disinflation program. When the stress on the balance of payments is relieved, there is probably room for policymakers to shift attention toward stabilizing inflation. However, this shift did not materialize in the period before 1985. Although an attempt was made to combat inflation back in 1982–83, it was not supported by an adjustment in fiscal and monetary fundamentals. Therefore, it seems plausible that such attempt did not confront a tradeoff between inflation and unemployment.

The reasoning behind a positive association between inflation and unemployment in periods of balance of payments crises is as follows. Handling these crises normally requires improving competitiveness by effecting a real devaluation and a drop in real wages. In principle, the latter could be accomplished by a reduction in nominal wage growth which possibly will also induce a decrease in inflation. However, in a highly indexed economy in which workers are not willing to make wage concessions the adjustment is somewhat different. Put a bit more formally, we can express the average real wage over a given period (say a year), w^R, in such an economy as

$$w^R = g(w^P, \pi, n) \tag{4.5}$$
$${\scriptstyle(+)}\ {\scriptstyle(-)}\ {\scriptstyle(+)}$$

where w^P denotes the peak real wage (i.e., at the time of the COLA payment) and n denotes the frequency of COLA's per year. When improving competitiveness requires at least some drop in real wages (unless workers are willing to change the wage agreement as reflected in w^P and in n) the only viable alternative is to raise π. This can be accomplished by raising the rate of devaluation (as in the 1984 crisis) and by raising public-sector prices (as in 1980). In fact, the evidence provided in figure 4.11 indicates that there were severe cuts in real wages in the context of the upward adjustments in the rate of inflation that followed the 1979 and 1984 balance-of-payments crises.

What about unemployment? Since the solution of a balance-of-payments crisis typically involves also contractionary fiscal and monetary policies, in order to reduce spending and imports, there may be a tendency for the rate of unemployment to rise. This is intensified by government's direct attempts to restrict growth of employment in the public sector. These combined policies may contribute toward increased unemployment; see figure 4.11 for evidence in this regard for the 1979 and 1984 episodes. The overall outcome of these policies is compatible with observing a positive link between inflation and unemployment. This link is somewhat confirmed by the regression equations 1 and 2 in table 4.4. These are univariate and multivariate Phillips-curve type equations. In both cases, the coefficient on the rate of unemployment is positive, and in equation 1 it is significantly different from zero.

In between these two balance-of-payments crises, the exchange rate was used, especially for about one year after September 1982, as a means to re-

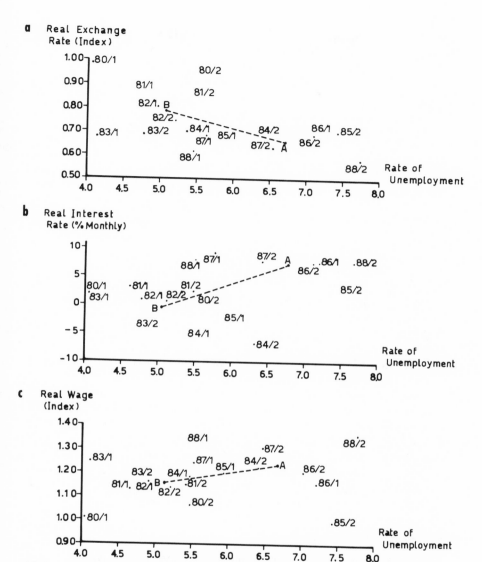

Figure 4.11 See note to fig. 4.10. (a) The real exchange rate and the rate of unemployment (correlation coeff. = 0.54). (b) The real interest rate and the rate of unemployment (correlation coeff. = 0.35). (c) The real wage and the rate of unemployment (correlation coeff. = 0.22).

Table 4.4
Simple Phillips-Curve Regressions

I. Before the Program (1980:4–1985:6)

$INF_t = -2.625 + 0.455INF_{t-1} + 4.813\text{Log}(UNE)_t$ (1)
    (6.171)   (0.126)   (4.080)
    $R^2 = 0.293$ $DW = 2.029$ $SER = 4.327$
$INF_t = 0.389 + 0.056INF_{t-1} + 0.467DPC_t + 0.345DER_t + 0.623\text{Log}(UNE)_t$ (2)
    (2.907)   (0.069)   (0.053)   (0.079)   (1.938)
    $R^2 = 0.851$ $DW = 1.876$ $SER = 2.021$

II. Entire Sample (1980:4–1988:12)

$INF_t = 8.953 + 0.672INF_{t-1} - 3.950\text{Log}(UNE)_t$ (3)
    (3.776)   (0.072)   (2.113)
    $R^2 = 0.488$ $DW = 2.22$ $SER = 4.279$
$INF_t = 4.053 + 0.151INF_{t-1} + 0.424DPC_t + 0.296DER_t - 1.799\text{Log}(UNE)_t$ (4)
    (1.649)   (0.043)   (0.044)   (0.061)   (0.919)
    $R^2 = 0.906$ $DW = 1.894$ $SER = 1.850$

Note: The notation is as follows: *INF:* rate of inflation; *UNE:* rate of unemployment; *DPC:* rate of inflation of controlled prices; *DER:* rate of change of exchange rate. Figures in parentheses are standard errors.

duce inflation by adopting a policy of devaluing at a rate of 5 percent per month which was about 2 percent below the ongoing rate of inflation. The fact that now inflation was used as a target was not sufficient to create a tradeoff in the course of the policy. Thus, the point 83/1 in figure 4.10 is one with relatively low inflation and low unemployment. What appears to be a main explanation for this outcome is the combination of the direct effect of slowing down devaluations on the rate of inflation, and the lack of credibility of the policy which stimulated consumption spending and hence economic activity. These effects of perceived temporariness and of lack of credibility of government policies are further explored in what follows.

B. The Post-Stabilization Period

For the period after the stabilization program, figure 4.10 indicates no clear pattern of relation between inflation and unemployment. There were two peaks for the rate of unemployment; one in the second half of 1985, immediately after the program, and the other one in the second half of 1988. In early 1989, the rate of unemployment reached an overall peak level of about 8 percent. It is evident that disinflation was achieved quite rapidly, yet unemployment increased only gradually through time. In fact, the points for 1986 through 1988 in figure 4.10 suggest movements in the rate of unemployment that were not accompanied by changes in the rate of inflation. Consequently, the statistical Phillips curve for this period is approximated by a horizontal line.

C. The Tradeoff in the Transition

Despite these mixed patterns within subperiods, it is evident that comparing the economy's position before and after the program (see the broad averages plotted in points B and A of figure 4.10) yields a statistical tradeoff between the rates of inflation and unemployment. This is somewhat confirmed by the econometric evidence provided in table 4.4, equations 3 and 4. Both the latter suggest that when one considers the entire 1980–88 period for estimation purposes, the coefficient describing the inflation/unemployment tradeoff becomes negative and marginally significant. Thus, while a positively sloped statistical Phillips curve may have prevailed in the period up to mid-1985, and no clearcut relation emerged for the post-1985 period, *the statistical tradeoff emerges when comparing the pre- and post-program periods*. It is precisely when a strong disinflation is attempted and achieved that we see an inverse relation between inflation and unemployment arising from the data.

Modern macroeconomic theory treats the Phillips curve as a reduced-form relation. Behind it there is a set of fundamental factors that determine its shape. Changes in these factors are the existing macroeconomic policies, their credibility, the private sector's expectations, the type of shocks affecting the economy, and the existing rigidities in the system. To further examine how some of these factors are captured in the inflation/unemployment tradeoff in the transition from high to low inflation, we present in figure 4.12 the relations in the data between the rate of unemployment and three important relative-price type variables: the real exchange rate, the real interest rate, and the real wage. Comparing the half-year averages in figure 4.12 before and after the stabilization program suggests a clearcut pattern: the increase in the rate of unemployment after the program was accompanied by a real exchange-rate appreciation, by an increase in the real interest rate, and by an increase in the real wage. And these links are more pronounced when comparing performance across the pre and post periods than when looking at the relations within each subperiod.

Examining the figures and the data suggests that the behavior of the rate of unemployment after the program followed a cycle consisting of *three phases*. In the initial stage of six to nine months inflation was simply reduced by a combination of orthodox and heterodox policies. This was accompanied by an increase in unemployment for about a year and a drop in industrial production for about two to three quarters. However, the size of these recessionary tendencies was relatively small: a spectacular disinflation was then effected without major losses in output.

The second phase is characterized by a *boom in private consumption spend-*

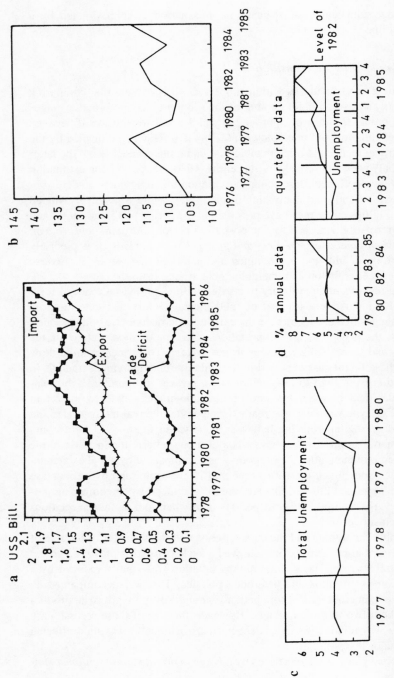

Figure 4.12 Trade balance, real labor cost, and unemployment. (*a*) Trade balance (seasonally adjusted) 1978–86 (billions of U.S. dollars, 1980 prices). Source: Bank of Israel, *Annual Report* (1986), 182. (*b*) Real labor cost per unit of output in business sector 1975–85 (average 1971–75 = 100). Source: Bank of Israel, *Annual Report* (1985), 76. (*c*) Rate of unemployment 1977–80 (quarterly percentage, seasonally adjusted). Source: Bank of Israel, *Annual Report* (1980). (*d*) Employment and unemployment 1974–85. Source: Bank of Israel, *Annual Report* (1985).

ing in 1986–87 which stimulated economic activity. The main features and explanations for this boom have been analyzed in more detail in an earlier paper by Liviatan (1989). The data indicate that while private consumption spending amounted to 53 percent of GDP in 1984–85, this ratio increased to 59 percent during 1986–88. Though partially offset by decreases in private investment and public consumption, these changes in consumption dictated the direction of change in total domestic uses which increased by 9 percent in 1986 and by 6.1 percent in 1987. GDP growth for these years was 3.6 and 5.2 percent respectively. Overall, then, the 1986–87 period was one of booming private consumption and economic activity, high real wages[13] and real interest rates, and a low real exchange rate.[14] Liviatan (1989) discussed several explanations for the consumption boom after stabilization and reached the conclusion that the boom is most probably due to an initial perception that stabilization is only temporary[15]—an argument which is in line with recent theoretical work by Calvo (1986) and by Helpman and Razin (1987).

Phase three started in 1988, when there was a slowdown in private consumption growth and in the growth of GDP, which was about 1.6 percent for that year. Industrial production started to fall and unemployment reached unprecedented levels in 1989. While these recent developments have not yet been fully analyzed, it appears that an important part of the recent increase in unemployment can be explained by a combination of factors that resulted in a profit squeeze for the business sector in recent years. First, the cycle discussed above was such that it resulted in persistently high real interest rates, high and increasing real wages, and continuous real appreciation of the Israeli shekel. Second, there were decreases in subsidies to the corporate sector, and an increase in tax rates on corporate profits. Third, there was a decrease in the public sector's demands for goods and services from the private sector— a decrease that was probably perceived by the business sector as permanent. Fourth, the uprising in the occupied territories contributed to a downturn in economic activity.

In addition to these factors, it appears that the recent increase in unemployment reflects a slow adjustment of the economy's structure to the new economic environment with low inflation. This adjustment entails *major reallocations of resources among sectors*. Thus, factors of production had to be reshuffled between financial and nonfinancial activities to accommodate the

13. The fact that output growth accelerated in spite of the growth of real wages suggest that the economy was driven by demand factors.

14. Helpman (1988) has argued that some of these comovements cannot be accounted for by models of pure competition. Instead, they can be explained by using a framework of oligopolistic competition.

15. Similar booms have been documented for several Latin American countries after the implementation of stabilization programs; see, e.g., Liviatan (1989).

decrease in the intensity of the former. Similarly, in the high-inflation regime many large combines (such as government and labor-union enterprises and transportation cooperatives) relied on government support in periods of financial and liquidity crises. Such support was gradually eliminated after the program and therefore these combines had to contract their activities.

Interestingly, these allocative effects of disinflation have great similarity with those in the aftermath of the German hyperinflation; see Garber (1982). During the hyperinflation in Germany, there was a policy of subsidizing the capital-goods industry through the inflation tax revenue. When this source of revenue was terminated and a "Rationalization Period" was started, a major reallocation of resources was required, with capital and labor moving out of the capital-goods industry. It is this reallocation that, in Garber's view, generated the transitional costs of disinflation which showed up in a decrease of industrial production by about 20 percent in less than one year and an increase in the rate of unemployment to 22 percent of union members. Similarly to the case of Israel, these developments did not occur immediately after disinflation but instead emerged with a lag (that is, one-and-a-half years after the November 1923 reform).

Finally, we relate these developments to standard macroeconomic models such as those discussed in section II. In these models, imperfect information and contractual rigidities determine the transition path of the economy from high to low inflation. Once these imperfections and rigidities are removed, disinflation is not predicted to have an impact on real output, unemployment, and other real variables. The fact that the rate of unemployment has markedly increased to about 8 percent only three years after the program does not appear to be explained by the existence of these imperfections and rigidities. Thus, even if agents correctly perceive and predict the new policy regime and even under a heterodox policy package, there may be real costs associated with disinflation to the extent that the latter entails a process of structural adjustment consisting of major reallocations of resources across sectors.

V. Conclusions

Much of the evidence obtained from comparing macroeconomic performance in Israel before and after the stabilization program of 1985 conforms well with standard macro models. The decreases in exchange-rate and nominal accommodation and the enhanced importance of real, as opposed to nominal, shocks that characterize the post-program regime appear to have strengthened the tradeoff between inflation and unemployment. They have also been associated with a decrease in inflation variability and no major change in the stability of output or other real variables. Cross-sectional variabilities, of relative prices, outputs, and real wages, have changed in a direction compatible with the notion that indeed real shocks have become more dominant in the low-inflation economy.

What are less standard from the standpoint of conventional theories are the immediate and abrupt reduction in the rate of inflation, and the timing and form of the impact of disinflation on real variables. For more than two years after the program there was a private consumption boom that was accompanied by increases in economic activity and by relatively high real wages and real interest rates and a low (appreciated) real exchange rate. It is only in the beginning of the fourth year after the program that the consumption boom stopped, economic activity was stagnant, and there was a rise in the rate of unemployment. *It seems difficult to explain these developments solely on the basis of models stressing the role of imperfect information and contractual rigidities.* The consumption boom appears to be closely related to partial lack of credibility of the program and of the exchange-rate policy. Apparently the public perceived the changes as mainly temporary. In addition, the recent rise in unemployment seems to reflect, to an important extent, the beginning of a process of *structural adjustment* whereby resources are reallocated across the economy to conform with the new low-inflation equilibrium. This process may involve a reduction of growth in the transitional stage, but will enable an increase in long-term growth after the completion of the adjustment.

Considering the Israeli program as a laboratory experiment in heterodox policy, we can address its implications so far for the well-known debate between gradualism vs. shock treatment in the process of stabilization. From the point of view of reducing inflation, the program seems to have had the same advantage as of shock-treatment policies: There was a *sharp and immediate disinflation* after mid-1985. This was probably due to the use of multiple nominal targets (such as a fixed exchange rate and price-wage controls) in conjunction with adjustments in fundamentals right at the start of the program—a mix that makes the program heterodox. From the perspective of the real costs of disinflation, the program resembles more a gradualist policy. The real costs, in the form of increased unemployment, were *postponed* for several years and in the transition there was actually a boom in economic activity. Which of these features of the results of the program are specific to Israel and which ones are common to heterodox policies applicable to other countries is an important question that needs to be addressed in the future.

References

Artstein, Y., and Z. Sussman. 1988. Wage Policy during Disinflation: The Israeli Stabilization Program of 1985. Discussion Paper 88.07, Research Department, Bank of Israel.

Blejer, M., and N. Liviatan. 1987. Fighting Hyperinflation-Stabilization Strategies in Argentina and Israel 1985–86. *IMF Staff Papers* 34, no. 3:403–38.

Bruno, M. 1986. Sharp Disinflation Strategy: Israel 1985. *Economic Policy* 2: 379–402.

Bruno, M., and Sylvia Piterman. 1988. Israel's Stabilization: A Two Year Review. In *Inflation Stabilization: The Experience of Israel, Argentina, Brazil, Bolivia, and Mexico*, ed. M. Bruno, G. D. Tella, R. Dornbusch, and S. Fischer, eds., Cambridge, Mass.: MIT Press.

Calvo, G. A. 1986. Temporary Stabilization: Predetermined Exchange Rates. *Journal of Political Economy* 94:1319–29.

Cochrane, J. 1988. How Big Is the Random Walk in GNP? *Journal of Political Economy* 96:892–919.

Cukierman, A. 1983. *Relative Price Variability and Inflation: A Survey and Further Results*. Carnegie-Rochester Series on Public Policy 19:103–38.

Dornbusch, R. 1982. PPP Exchange Rate Rules and Macroeconomic Stability. *Journal of Political Economy* 90:158–65.

Fischer, S. 1977. Long Term Contracts, Rational Expectations, and the Optimal Money Supply Rule. *Journal of Political Economy* 85:191–206.

———. 1987. The Israeli Stabilization Program 1985–86. *American Economic Review* 77:275–78.

Garber, P. 1982. *Transition from Inflation to Price Stability*. Carnegie-Rochester Series on Public Policy 16:11–42.

Helpman, E. 1988. Macroeconomic Effects of Price Controls: The Role of Market Structure. Economic Journal 98:340–54.

Helpman, E., and A. Razin. 1987. Exchange Rate Management: Intertemporal Trade-offs. *American Economic Review* 77:107–23.

Kiguel, M., and N. Liviatan. 1989. The Old and the New Heterodox Stabilization Programs: A Study of the Sixties with Perspective of the Eighties. Unpublished manuscript. The World Bank.

Liviatan, N. 1989. Israel's Stabilization Cycle with Some Reference to Latin American Experience. Preliminary manuscript. The World Bank.

Lucas, R. E., Jr. 1973. Some International Evidence on Output Inflation Tradeoffs. *American Economic Review* 63:326–35.

———. 1976. *Econometric Policy Evaluation: A Critique*. Carnegie-Rochester Series on Public Policy 1:19–46.

Sims, C. A. 1980. Macroeconomics and Reality. *Econometrica* 48:1–48.

Part II: Devaluation, Money, and
Inflation: Dynamic Interactions

5

Overview

Macroeconomic models for open economies can give rise to a whole variety of dynamic relations between currency depreciation, inflation, and money growth depending on the policy rules, the source of shocks, and the economic structure that are specified. Some models envision an autonomous role for exchange-rate depreciation in the inflationary process, and stress the potential inflationary inertia that may arise from these shocks. Other models view exchange-rate depreciation as a policy variable that is reacting mainly to the cumulative differential between domestic and foreign inflation. Similarly, while some models assume that the monetary authorities effect their policy through money supply or domestic credit targets, others posit the existence of monetary accommodation to exchange-rate and price shocks. For most specifications, the parameters governing the extent of exchange-rate accommodation and of monetary accommodation can have a key role in determining the economy's performance in terms of output and price variability (see, e.g., Dornbusch [1982]).

Since much of the controversy about inflation in Israel and elsewhere originates in different views about these issues and about the structure of the economy, it would be useful for theoretical and policy analysis to let the data inform us what the dynamic patterns of interaction that characterize a given sample are. These considerations motivated the work in the present part. Specifically, vector autoregression and statistical causality methods are applied to time series for Israel in an attempt to quantitatively assess the underlying patterns of intertemporal correlation in the data. Instead of testing here a specific structural model, the focus is on using relatively model-free statistical methods in order to uncover any empirical regularities in the data. These regularities, in turn, can be used to determine which classes of models are not compatible with the information in the sample (see Sims [1980]).

Although each individual chapter concentrates on its own specific theme, there are two key issues that appear in most parts of the analysis: the relation between inflation and domestic currency depreciation, and the existence of monetary accommodation to price and exchange-rate shocks. Both these issues have been at the center of policy discussions on the inflation process in Israel and elsewhere. I use here data for the period before disinflation in Israel. In addition, data for Argentina and Chile are used in parts of the part.

Consider the first issue, dealing with the bivariate relation between the rate of inflation and the rate of depreciation of the domestic currency, a relation often known as the vicious circle. One class of models in the literature, and of policy arguments, has emphasized exchange-rate pass-through effects on prices. That is, changes in the exchange rate tend to have direct and indirect effects on the domestic price level. An example of that are cost-push frameworks, where an exchange-rate depreciation raises the price of imported inputs and thus exerts upward pressure on prices of domestic final goods and services. In some versions of these models, slowing down the rate of depreciation of the domestic currency is a prerequisite for slowing down the rate of inflation.

Yet another class of models views exchange-rate depreciation as determined mainly through a backward-looking policy-reaction function. According to this function, the rate of depreciation chosen by the authorities for period t is a function of lagged values of the differential between domestic and foreign rates of inflation. If followed continuously, this policy rule could help prevent a loss of competitiveness of domestic products even under highly inflationary conditions.

Empirical analysis of the intertemporal relation between inflation and currency depreciation can exploit the fact that these two views imply restrictions on time-series data. Indeed, this relation is examined below using Granger-causality methods and vector autoregressions. When this is done, a key finding that arises is that the pattern of interaction between inflation and currency depreciation depends on the exchange-rate regime: as the regime gets closer to a fixed-exchange-rate system, there is more of a unidirectional significant causality running from inflation to exchange-rate depreciation.

A first body of evidence on this issue appears in chapter 6 which uses quarterly data for Israel from 1969 to 1979. For most of this period Israel had either a fixed exchange rate with periodic adjustments in import duties and export subsidies or a crawling peg (up until October 1977). Only by the end of 1977 was there a shift to a managed float. For this period, I find that there is a statistically significant causality from movements in inflation to domestic currency depreciation. Significant causality in the reverse direction is not evident in the data. However, it is shown in subsequent chapters in this part that a different pattern emerges after 1977, when the exchange rate became more flexible through a managed float policy. There I find strong bivariate relations between innovations in inflation and in currency depreciation. In particular, a sizable fraction of the forecast error variance of inflation is then accounted for by exchange-rate innovations (see chapters 8 and 9).

In my view, this dependence of the pattern of results on the exchange-rate regime is quite plausible. Under a semifixed exchange-rate system the authorities usually intervene to support the prevailing exchange rate. Thus, there is little room for month-to-month, or even quarter-to-quarter, exchange-rate fluctuations and there is not much scope for inflationary impact of these fluctuations. Large devaluations are effected in this regime only as a measure of last resort, typically in response to speculative runs on foreign currencies and after the domestic economy has accumulated a substantial excess of domestic over foreign inflation. It is this direction of statistical causality from inflation to depreciation that characterizes the data for the semifixed-exchange-rate period. On the other hand, as more room for exchange-rate volatility is allowed, the exchange rate becomes more of an asset price which exhibits relatively large fluctuations, and domestic prices become more sensitive to these fluctuations. That is, the evidence indicates that the price-setting mechanism depends on the exchange-rate regime, a finding that conforms with the Lucas (1976) critique.

Furthermore, the results reported in this part explain, to a large extent, the emphasis of heterodox programs on fixing the exchange rate during disinflation and stabilization. The impulse-response functions discussed below indicate that although no medium- or long-run inflation inertia arises from exchange-rate shocks, a temporary slowdown in the rate of depreciation of the domestic currency is accompanied by a temporary slowdown in inflation and in money growth. Moreover, exchange-rate innovations account for a sizable portion of forecast error variance in inflation and in money growth. Accordingly, heterodox stabilization programs can be interpreted as attempts to eliminate for some time period the strong links between exchange-rate depreciations at time t and rates of inflation and money growth in subsequent periods. Yet, as indicated by the evidence for Israel in the early eighties, and for Argentina and Chile in the late seventies, if the fixing of the exchange rate is not accompanied by adjustment of fiscal and monetary fundamentals then disinflation may well turn out to be purely transitory.

As far as monetary accommodation is concerned, the pure monetary textbook case of exogenous money shocks driving up inflation is not transparent in the data. Instead, there are quite complicated relations between money growth, exchange-rate depreciation, and inflation. Much of the evidence below suggests that exchange-rate-depreciation shocks and inflation shocks account for a sizable portion of the forecast error variance of money growth. This would be consistent with the existence of monetary accommodation of price and exchange-rate shocks. At the same time, there is also some evidence for statistical causality in the other direction. As shown in chapter 7, the statistical relation between inflation and money growth may well vary according to the frequency of observations, the time period, and the definition of the money aggregate. Coupled with the evidence on the central role of the exchange rate, these findings can provide a rationale for the use of an exchange-rate anchor instead of a money-aggregate anchor in heterodox disinflation programs.

References

Dornbusch, R. 1982. PPP Exchange Rate Rules and Macroeconomic Stability. *Journal of Political Economy* 90:158–65.

Lucas, R. E., Jr. 1976. *Econometric Policy Evaluation: A Critique.* Carnegie-Rochester Series on Public Policy 1:19–46.

Sims, C. A. 1980. Macroeconomics and Reality. *Econometrica* 48:1–48.

6

Dynamic Interactions between Inflation and Devaluation in Israel

I. Introduction

Do increases in the rate of devaluation cause subsequent increases in the rate of inflation, or do they follow previous accelerations in inflation? This is certainly one of the most controversial economic questions in Israel. The purpose of this chapter is to assess the empirical link between the rate of change of the nominal exchange rate and the rate of inflation in Israel by using a statistical method that can account for dynamic interactions between these variables. I use quarterly data for the period 1969–79 and define the exchange rate as the effective nominal exchange rate for imported goods and services.

Economic theory indicates that both the exchange rate and the rate of inflation are endogenously determined and depend on the behavior of fundamentals.[1] From this perspective it is not entirely meaningful to study the direct link between movements in inflation and in devaluations. However, such a study is of interest from the standpoint of economic behavior in the short run, defined as that length of period for which the system has not fully adjusted to changes in fundamentals. It is common to assume that in such a short run there exist temporary price and exchange-rate rigidities that manifest themselves in the form of different speeds of adjustment of both these variables, thus providing interest on documenting the statistical links between devaluation and inflation.[2]

Translated from Hebrew and reprinted with permission from *Economic Quarterly* 107 (December 1980):375–80.

1. In this context, see Helpman (1980). On the effects of movements in government spending on external balance and the rate of devaluation, see Razin (1980).

2. Examples of these rigidities are: a fixed-exchange-rate regime, with only periodic adjustments in the level of the official exchange rate, and the direct governmental setting of several prices of goods and services in the economy, such as the prices of public transportation, electricity, bread, etc.

There are two main approaches for analyzing the relation between inflation and devaluation, both in general and in Israel. One approach stresses the cost-push inflationary impact of increases in the rate of devaluation; see, e.g., Bruno (1978). An increase in the rate of devaluation raises prices of intermediate and final imported goods. If wage indexation exists, these price increases may well translate into wage increases. Thus, according to this view increases in the rate of devaluation may bring about increases in the rate of inflation. An important policy implication of this view is that the authorities may well aim at slowing down the rate of devaluation in an attempt to disinflate the economy.

Several empirical studies that are directly or indirectly based on this approach have been conducted in Israel; see e.g., Artstein and Sussman (1978) and Halevi and Blejer (1978). These studies derive a reduced-form equation that expresses the rate of inflation as the dependent variable and the rate of devaluation as one of the explanatory variables. Econometric estimates typically indicate that there is a strong, positive, and statistically significant link between movements in devaluation and inflation, and this evidence is regarded as providing support to the above-mentioned approach.

Another approach focuses on the role of devaluations in restoring external competitiveness following periods in which domestic inflation exceeded foreign inflation. For example, expansionary monetary and fiscal policies that persist for some time under a quasi-fixed exchange rate may lead to an increase in domestic inflation, a worsening in the economy's external position, and to a deterioration in the country's external competitiveness as reflected in a cumulative increase in the relative price of domestic vs. foreign goods. Following these developments, the authorities may wish to devalue the domestic currency in an attempt to shift competitiveness back toward its initial level. Under this approach, the rate of devaluation chosen by the authorities at a given time is primarily a function of current and past changes in domestic inflation. Empirical evidence produced by Michaely (1975: ch. 5) and by Halevi (1977) seems consistent with this approach.

While most previous empirical investigations of the interaction between devaluation and inflation in Israel specified equations that are consistent with only one of the two aforementioned approaches, a more general methodology is followed in the present work. That is, I examine this interaction without imposing a priori restrictions on the direction of causality. The analysis is based on implementing causality tests as those advanced by Granger (1969) and Sims (1972).[3] The word causality should be interpreted here only in the statistical sense: a variable x is said to "Granger cause" a variable y to the

---

3. See Ronn and Ben Zion (1978) for use of causality tests to policy variables in Israel.

extent that changes in x help predict changes in y. There is extensive literature on the limitations of attempting to provide structural interpretations to the results of causality tests and of using the results of statistical causality tests to determine overall (nonstatistical) patterns of causality. All these considerations should be taken into account when interpreting the results of the present analysis.

II. Methodology

In what follows I use two sets of causality tests. The first is based on Granger's (1969) specification and relies on estimating the following equations:

$$\Pi_t = \Sigma a_i \, L^i \, \Pi_t + \Sigma b_i \, L^i \varepsilon_t, \quad \text{and} \tag{6.1}$$

$$\varepsilon_t = \Sigma c_i L^i \, \Pi_t + \Sigma d_i \, L^i \varepsilon_t, \tag{6.2}$$

where Π denotes the rate of inflation, ε is the rate of change of the nominal exchange rate (a positive value meaning devaluation of the domestic currency), L is the lag operator, such that for any variable x, $L^i x = x_{t-i}$, and the summation signs apply for lags 1 through n. Equations 6.1 and 6.2 express the rate of inflation and the rate of devaluation at time t as functions of lagged values of these variables. The null hypothesis for Granger-causality tests in this context is that there is no bidirectional causality; that is, $b_i = c_i = 0$ for all i. Statistical rejection of the null hypothesis would indicate the presence of causality from devaluation to inflation (if the hypothesis $b_i = 0$ is rejected) and/or from inflation to devaluation (if the hypothesis $c_i = 0$ is rejected). To implement the Granger tests, univariate versions of 6.1 and 6.2 are estimated and are used to calculate the pertinent F statistics.

The second set of causality tests to be reported corresponds to Sims's (1972) specification and is based on estimating equations of the following form:

$$\Pi_t = \Sigma h_i \, L^i \varepsilon_t, \quad (i = -m, \ldots 0, \ldots m), \quad \text{and} \tag{6.3}$$

$$\varepsilon_t = \Sigma k_i L^i \Pi_t. \tag{6.4}$$

That is, the rate of inflation at time t is projected on past, present, and future values of the rate of devaluation, and conversely for equation 6.4. The null hypothesis for these tests is that the coefficients on future variables in these equations are zero; that is, $h_i = k_i = 0$ for negative values of i. As in the case of Granger's tests, equations 6.3 and 6.4 are estimated both under the restrictions of the null hypothesis and then unrestricted, and an F statistic is calculated to perform the test.

III. Empirical Results

The data base for this study consists of quarterly observations from 1969:II to 1979:II. The variable Π is represented by the rate of inflation of the consumer price index. ε measures the rate of change of the nominal effective exchange rate that applies to imports.[4] It is important to stress that there were changes in the exchange-rate system during the sample period. In particular, there was a shift in mid-1975 toward a crawling peg system, and a financial and foreign-exchange liberalization in October 1977. It would be desirable in future work to shift attention to monthly data in order to separately analyze the different subperiods. Table 6.1 reports the results of Sims's causality tests. Equation 6.5 projects the rate of inflation at time t on past and current values of the rate of devaluation, and it can be seen that there are no strong links from devaluations to inflation. However, equation 6.6 indicates that there is a positive and generally significant relation between inflation at time t and subsequent devaluations; see, e.g., the impact of inflation on the rate of devaluation three quarters into the future. The F statistic based on both these equations is 3.0 with (4, 26) degrees of freedom. It indicates that the null hypothesis is rejected at the 5 percent level.

Equations 6.7 and 6.8 express the rate of devaluation as the left-hand-side variable which is projected on past, current, and future values of the rate of inflation. It can be seen that no statistically significant links from current values of devaluation to future rates of inflation are detected. Specifically, the F statistic in this case is much smaller that its critical value thus indicating nonrejection of the null hypothesis.

Table 6.2 provides evidence on Granger-causality tests. Equation 6.9 is a fourth-order autoregression for the rate of inflation, and equation 6.10 adds four lagged values of the rate of devaluation as explanatory variables. No strong and statistically significant effects of lagged devaluations on current inflation are detected, and the F statistic obtains a value of 0.8 which is smaller than the five percent critical value of 2.7 (with (4, 32) degrees of freedom)). This is evidence in support of nonrejection of the null hypothesis.

Equations 6.11 and 6.12 project the rate of devaluation on own lagged values and on lags of the rate of inflation. The explanatory power of equation 6.11, the autoregression for the rate of devaluation, is markedly increased upon adding four lagged values of inflation rates as explanatory

---

4. The data sources are: Central Bureau of Statistics and Bank of Israel, various publications. The effective nominal exchange rate for imported goods and services is composed of the official (formal) exchange rate and any taxes or tariffs on imported goods and services.

Table 6.1
Estimates for Sims-Causality Tests

$$\Pi_t = 0.05 + (0.11 + 0.05L + 0.15L^2 - 0.09L^3 + 0.01L^4)\varepsilon_t$$
$$(3.27) \quad (1.09) \quad (0.51) \quad (1.42) \quad (0.80) \quad (0.08)$$
$$R^2 = 0.2674 \quad DW = 2.09 \quad SER = 0.04 \quad RHO = 0.37$$
(6.5)

$$\Pi_t = 0.03 + (0.14 + 0.02L + 0.10L^2 - 0.12L^3 - 0.07L^4)\varepsilon_t$$
$$(1.84) \quad (1.59) \quad (0.24) \quad (0.99) \quad (1.12) \quad (0.68)$$
$$+ (0.17L^{-1} + 0.05L^{-2} + 0.24L^{-3} + 0.19L^{-4})\varepsilon_t$$
$$(1.83) \quad (0.57) \quad (2.63) \quad (2.04)$$
$$R^2 = 0.4961 \quad DW = 1.92 \quad SER = 0.04 \quad RHO = 0.20$$
(6.5)

$$\varepsilon_t = 0.002 + (-0.32 - 0.17L - 0.24L^2 + 0.87L^3 + 0.75L^4)\Pi_t$$
$$(0.09) \quad (0.91) \quad (0.52) \quad (0.81) \quad (2.48) \quad (2.07)$$
$$R^2 = 0.3400 \quad DW = 1.92 \quad SER = 0.07 \quad RHO = 0.09$$
(6.7)

$$\varepsilon_t = 0.01 + (0.02 - 0.21L - 0.32L^2 + 0.64L^3 + 0.98L^4)\Pi_t$$
$$(0.40) \quad (0.06) \quad (0.51) \quad (0.88) \quad (1.66) \quad (2.39)$$
$$+ (0.19L^{-1} + 0.37L^{-2} - 0.39L^{-3} - 0.46L^{-4})\Pi_t$$
$$(0.52) \quad (1.01) \quad (1.09) \quad (1.31)$$
$$R^2 = 0.4225 \quad DW = 1.94 \quad SER = 0.07 \quad RHO = 0.08$$
(6.8)

Note: For notation and explanation of the equations, see text. Figures in parentheses are estimated standard errors. L is the lag operator. *SER* is the standard error of estimate, and *RHO* denotes the *MA1* coefficient of each equation's error term.

Table 6.2
Estimates for Granger-Causality Tests

$$\Pi_t = 0.02 + (0.11 + 0.07L + 0.36L^2 + 0.36L^3)\Pi_{t-1}$$
$$(1.38) \quad (0.68) \quad (0.43) \quad (2.39) \quad (2.13)$$
$$R^2 = 0.4848 \quad DW = 1.99 \quad SER = 0.04$$
(6.9)

$$\Pi_t = 0.02 + (0.10 + 0.10L + 0.38L^2 + 0.43L^3)\Pi_{t-1} +$$
$$(1.37) \quad (0.55) \quad (0.64) \quad (2.39) \quad (2.13)$$
$$+ (-0.06 + 0.06L - 0.16L^2 - 0.01L^3)\varepsilon_{t-1}$$
$$(0.57) \quad (0.66) \quad (1.77) \quad (0.01)$$
$$R^2 = 0.5325 \quad DW = 1.96 \quad SER = 0.04$$
(6.10)

$$\varepsilon_t = 0.04 + (0.30 - 0.22L - 0.01L^2 + 0.07L^3)\varepsilon_{t-1}$$
$$(2.27) \quad (1.76) \quad (1.27) \quad (0.02) \quad (0.39)$$
$$R^2 = 0.1095 \quad DW = 1.92 \quad SER = 0.08$$
(6.11)

$$\varepsilon_t = -0.002 + (0.08 - 0.31L - 0.16L^2 - 0.16L^3)\varepsilon_{t-1}$$
$$(0.10) \quad (0.44) \quad (1.95) \quad (1.03) \quad (0.98)$$
$$+ (-0.05 + 0.01L + 0.78L^2 + 0.53L^3)\Pi_{t-1}$$
$$(0.17) \quad (0.01) \quad (2.73) \quad (1.46)$$
$$R^2 = 0.4103 \quad DW = 1.93 \quad SER = 0.07$$
(6.12)

Note: See note to table 6.1.

variables. This is reflected in the F statistic that obtains a value of 4.0, which is higher than the critical 5 percent value of 2.7, thus indicating rejection of the null hypothesis.

IV. Conclusions

This chapter has empirically examined the statistical dynamic interactions between quarterly movements in the rate of inflation and in the rate of devaluation in Israel during the period from 1969 to 1979. The results of Granger and Sims causality tests are unambiguous. The evidence indicates that there is statistically significant causality from movements in inflation to devaluations. Significant causality in the reverse direction is not evident in the data. A plausible interpretation of these findings, along the lines of the second approach discussed in the introduction to the chapter, is that following periods of increases in the domestic rate of inflation the authorities intervene to produce larger devaluations of the domestic currency in an attempt to at least partially restore external competitiveness. Similarly, according to this view, the implementation of contractionary monetary and fiscal policies that would put downward pressure on the rate of inflation would also result in a slowdown in the rate of devaluation.[5]

References

Artstein, Y., and Z. Sussman. 1978. The Dynamics of Inflation in a Fully Indexed Economy Subject to Price Shocks. Mimeo. Bank of Israel.

Bruno, M. 1978. Exchange Rates, Import Costs, and Wage-Price Dynamics. *Journal of Political Economy* 86 (June):379–404.

Granger, C. W. J. 1969. Investigating Causal Relations by Econometric Models and Cross-Spectral Methods. *Econometrica* 37 (July):424–38.

Halevi, N. 1977. The Impact of Inflation on Exchange Rates: The Israeli Example. Discussion Paper 7711. Jerusalem: Falk Institute.

Halevi, N., and M. I. Blejer. 1978. Devaluation and Inflation in Israel: Empirical Evidence. In *Explorations in the Economy of Israel 1977*, 30–38. Jerusalem: Israeli Economic Association (Hebrew).

Helpman, E. 1980. Foreign Exchange Market Intervention. *The Economic Quarterly* 105 (June):112–15 (Hebrew).

Michaely, M. 1975. *Foreign Trade Regimes and Economic Development: Israel*. N.Y.: Columbia University Press.

5. A skeptical reader might interpret the present results as suggesting that although statistically changes in inflation appear to cause changes in devaluation, true causality might be in the reverse direction to the extent that movements in inflation primarily reflect expectations of future devaluations.

Razin, A. 1980. The Effects of the Government Budget on Real Devaluation and the Trade Balance. *The Economic Quarterly* 105 (June): 105–12 (Hebrew).

Ronn, E., and U. Ben Zion. 1978. Exogeneity of Macroeconomic Policy Variables. In *Explorations in the Economy of Israel 1977*, 149–60. Jerusalem: The Israeli Economic Association.

Sims, C. A. 1972. Money, Income, and Causality. *American Economic Review* 62: 540–52.

7

The Interaction between Inflation and Monetary Aggregates in Israel

1. Introduction and Main Findings

Most attempts—in this country and abroad—to explain the accelerated inflation of the last decade take account of the effect of monetary factors, and there is in fact a variety of empirical evidence which shows that their role is a dominant one.

The monetary developments experienced by Israel in recent years (some of them resulting from the 1977 liberalization of foreign currency) and its high inflation (up to three digits) provide an excellent quasi-laboratory environment for research into the interactions between monetary variables and the rate of inflation—research that can contribute to our understanding and help the monetary authorities to evaluate their policies. Such a study should be based on a structural model of the monetary sector, a model that contains behavioral equations and the budget constraints of economic agents. To the best of our knowledge, no such analytical model has yet been completed. Indeed, its construction depends on the answer to several empirical questions; for example, should one assume price rigidity in the long, short, or medium run? Do changes in the quantity of money affect prices? And if so, what is the mechanism through which the effect works, and what are the lags involved? Since these are still open questions, we believe that it is better at this stage to examine the facts without forcing them into a specific structural model; in this way we hope to reveal the empirical regularities of the connection between money and inflation, and to use them in the construction of an appropriate model.[1]

The aim of the present study is, therefore, to examine the relationship between monetary variables and inflation in recent years, using econometric time-series tools. The emphasis is on forecasting, that is, on the contribution

Reprinted with permission from *Bank of Israel Economic Review* 55 (1983):48–60.
1. For an extensive discussion of this approach, see Sims (1980).

of the monetary variables to the statistical significance of the explanation of inflationary developments, and vice versa. In order to explore these problems we use tests of causality; in interpreting the results, the correct statistical meaning of causality as defined in what follows should be borne in mind.

In the course of this study we examined a large number of monetary aggregates. The findings relate to the period January 1972–September 1980. We use monthly and quarterly data for 1972–80 and, for the discussion of the money supply, annual data for 1954–79. The monthly data serve to examine short-term interactions; the quarterly data serve for the medium run, and the annual data for the long run.

From the outset, the monthly tests showed that the relationships have not been stable—a natural break can be seen following the 1977 reform of the foreign-currency regime, and the sample is therefore divided at this point. The quarterly and annual data, however, contain too few observations to make it possible to split the period.

The monthly data were run twice—once seasonally adjusted and once unadjusted. It turned out that the results were not very sensitive to the seasonal adjustment.

The monthly variables enter the monthly and quarterly tests:

M_1 = Means of payment
M_2 = M_1 + negotiable certificates of deposit + time deposits
M_3 = M_2 + current resident deposits (foreign currency) + resident time deposits (foreign currency)
M_4 = M_3 + bonds held by the public
C_0 = total bank credit
B_1 = money base narrowly defined
G_0 = government and Jewish Agency injection
G_1 = injection stemming from government demand surplus.

The first six variables are stocks, and we therefore use their rate of change; the remaining two are flows, and their period values were used.

Table 7.1 presents the annual rate of change of the variables. As can be seen, the proportion of those containing linked elements (M_3 and M_4) has risen at the expense of the unlinked aggregates.

The short-run test (monthly data) indicates that the causal relationships are not constant. Before the 1977 reform, M_1 affects prices, as does credit, though somewhat less strongly; there is no converse effect of prices on money. After 1977, on the other hand, the effect of money on prices weakens, while the effect of prices on money is dominant. A possible explanation of this pattern is connected with dollarization and with the increase in the weight of the linked elements in the public's portfolio of liquid assets. It is not yet possible to check whether the quarterly or annual data show a similar reversal of causality, since the series are not yet long enough.

The credit variable, which is to a large extent under the control of the central bank, turns up in several of the equations as the variable whose effect on inflation has the highest significance after the foreign-currency reform. This effect has a lag of several months and disappears in the medium run. A thorough study of how credit fits into the inflationary process and the country's macroeconomic system would therefore seem to be a promising topic for future research.

In the medium run (quarterly data) there is no significant effect of money on inflation, a result that to a large extent contradicts the common opinion that an increase in the quantity of money (however defined) accelerates inflation in the medium run. On the other hand, it was found that while prices do not affect the linked aggregates (M_3 and M_4), they have a significant effect on the others. A possible explanation is that the price increase instantaneously raises the value of linked assets, a relationship which is evident in the monthly data for the post-reform period. The public's portfolio is unbalanced and unlinked assets are adjusted in response. Other explanations are of course possible.

In the long run, money affects prices with a two-year lag, and monetary changes evidently do affect inflation with such a lag. The reverse causality was also significant—price increases entail changes in the quantity of money.

Our results were in several respects similar to those obtained for other countries. Thus the absence of any strong short- or medium-run effect of money on prices and its presence in the annual data is a pattern found also in the United States. The finding on the effect of prices on money is consistent with

Table 7.1
The Monetary Aggregates
(% change over the preceding year)[a]

	M_1	M_2	M_3	M_4	C_0	B_1	CPI
1973	32.30	18.54	18.46	50.06	32.14	25.96	26.40
1974	17.99	10.71	13.42	43.11	70.80	9.30	56.18
1975	21.69	15.30	18.69	16.85	30.20	4.80	23.50
1976	27.07	24.28	33.02	19.09	38.70	46.00	38.00
1977	38.78	36.00	64.18	44.86	85.39	51.60	42.50
1978	45.10	38.50	100.10	70.78	55.26	27.29	40.10
1979	30.51	31.00	84.10	92.82	115.30	12.88	111.40
1980	97.74	113.18	134.10	146.97	133.86	98.43	132.94

[a] Calculated from end-year figures (December–December).

Table 7.2
Summary of Findings

Long Run		Medium Run		Short Run	
$M \rightarrow P$	$P \rightarrow M$	$M \rightarrow P$	$P \rightarrow M$	$M \rightarrow P$	$P \rightarrow M$
$M_1 \rightarrow P$	$P \rightarrow M_1$		$P \rightarrow M_1$	Pre-reform	
			$P \rightarrow M_2$	$M_4 \rightarrow P$	
			$P \rightarrow G_0$	$C_0 \rightarrow P$	
			$P \rightarrow G_1$	Post-reform	
			$P \rightarrow B_1$	$M_4 \rightarrow P$	$P \rightarrow M_3$
			$P \rightarrow C_0$	$C_0 \rightarrow P$	$P \rightarrow M_4$
					$P \rightarrow C_0$

Symbols: M, monetary variable; P, prices; arrows indicate the direction of Granger causality (see below); $\dashrightarrow$ indicates that the causal relation was found for some but not all lags.

those of Kleiman and Ophir (1972) as well as with some studies of hyper-inflation (Sargent and Wallace, 1973, and Frenkel, 1977).

To sum up the principal findings (see table 7.2): (a) The monetary aggregates do not for the most part affect inflation in the short and medium run, the exception being credit (C_0) and M_4. (b) In the long run, M_1 affects inflation with a two-year lag. (c) As regards the effect of inflation on the monetary aggregates, we find that it affects linked assets (M_3, M_4) in the short run; in the medium run, it affects the unlinked but not the linked variables. (d) In the long run, inflation again affects M_1.

Section 2 discusses the methodology of causality tests; section 3 contains a brief survey of earlier work on related topics, in Israel and abroad. The findings are in section 4, and section 5 concludes the paper.

2. Methodology

Macroeconomic studies based on time-series data nowadays rest on two general econometric modelling approaches. The first specifies a structural model (such as the Bank of Israel's model) in which economic theory[2] plays a central role in the a priori formulation of equations and constraints. The idea here is to accommodate the data within a general theoretical framework.

The second approach is the analysis of time series, in which the data play the central role, both in formulating the equations and in testing constraints. Once the empirical work is complete, the findings are incorporated into a theoretical framework.

This is, of course, a simplified presentation of the two approaches, which

2. Our maintained hypothesis derives from the theory (Granger and Newbold, 1977).

interact in empirical work as Granger and Newbold (1977:7) put it, "it is almost a tautology to say that the optimum approach should probably involve the best features of each." The two approaches must therefore be viewed as complements rather than substitutes.

In recent years there have been many monetary innovations in Israel. The new developments have not yet been explained—fully or in part—by a theoretical model, and construction of such a model encounters many difficulties. Much depends on future research. In the present state of the art, we can resort to the second approach, in an attempt to discover the empirical regularities of the interactions between money and prices, so as to indicate the direction of theoretical research. The present study relies mainly on time-series analysis.

The principal criterion by which an econometric time-series study is to be judged is of course the predictive power of its equations. In the last ten years a literature has grown up on this topic under the label of causality, a concept that is interpreted as follows: if a variable X gives a prediction of variable Y which is better than one using information U, from which X has been excluded, X is said to cause Y.[3] Define $\sigma^2(Y|U)$ as the variance of the forecast error of Y, conditional on information U. Then X causes Y if

$$\sigma^2(Y|U) < \sigma^2(Y|U - X), \tag{7.1}$$

where $U - X$ is information U *less* series X. This is Granger's (1969) definition of causality. Clearly, causality may run both ways, and in that case

$$\sigma^2(Y|U) < \sigma^2(Y|U - X) \tag{7.2}$$
$$\sigma^2(X|U) < \sigma^2(X|U - Y).$$

This meaning of causality is identical with neither the philosophical meaning[4] nor the everyday definition.

As an example, take an economy in which, by assumption, inflation is due solely to monetary factors, that is to say, an economy in which changes in the quantity of money cause (in the dictionary sense) changes in inflation. If in a given year economic agents expect a significant increase in the quantity of money in the next year, it is reasonable to assume that this expectation will raise prices in the current year, that is, before any increase has occurred in the money stock; the next year, the money stock does rise, as expected. The

3. Information U contains all current and past data on Y and any other series likely to help in the prediction of Y, including series X.

4. In the philosophical sense, there is a causal relationship between two factors if a change in one is a necessary condition of a change in the other.

econometrician carrying out a causality test for this economy will get an un-
equivocal result—the increase in the quantity of money is Granger-caused by
the price increase, whereas, on our assumption, the opposite is true. Thus
when expectations play a dominant part in the system of variables analyzed
(e.g., stock-exchange variables), causality tests may give a misleading picture
of the causal relationship (in the ordinary sense). If, however, the tests indicate the direction of (statistical) causality, any model constructed must be
consistent with the test result.

The most important practical problem in defining causality is the choice of
U and the choice of predictive model. Granger recommends concentrating on
two series, X and Y, to include the lags of both in U, and to make do with
linear predictions. Under these constraints, Granger's test is a simple F test
of the significance of a group of variables that includes the 'causal' series,
with several lags:

$$Y_t = \alpha_1 Y_{t-1} + \alpha_2 Y_{t-2} + \cdots + \alpha_n Y_{t-n} + \varepsilon_t \tag{7.3}$$

$$Y_t = \beta_1 Y_{t-1} + \beta_2 Y_{t-2} + \cdots + \beta_n Y_{t-n} + \gamma_1 X_{t-1}$$
$$+ \cdots + \gamma_n X_{t-n} + \delta_t. \tag{7.4}$$

The test is

$$H_0 : (\gamma_1, \gamma_2, \ldots, \gamma_n) = 0$$
$$H_1 : \text{otherwise}, \tag{7.5}$$

This test has statistical validity if the random errors ε_1 and δ_1 in (7.3)–(7.4)
are normally distributed without serial correlation.[5] The main difficulty arises
because of the possibility that

$$\sigma^2(Y \mid Y, X) < \sigma^2(Y \mid Y)$$
$$\sigma^2(Y \mid X, Y, Z) \nless \sigma^2(Y \mid Y, Z) < \sigma^2(Y \mid Y); \tag{7.6}$$

in other words, if there is a third variable which is the cause of Y, its omission
can lead to erroneous conclusions.

In his seminal 1972 paper Sims developed a causality test based on a

---

5. The F test, which tests for serial correlation of order n, failed to reject the null hypothesis
(no serial correlation) in all equations.

significance test for leads. By the Sims test, Y formally causes X if $(\beta_1, \beta_2, \ldots, \beta_m) = 0$ in

$$Y_t = \sum_{i=0}^{n} \alpha_i X_{t-i} + \sum_{j=1}^{m} \beta_j X_{t+j} + \varepsilon_t. \quad (7.7)$$

We chose to use Granger's rather than Sims's test, for two reasons: (a) The Sims test has statistical validity only if the X and Y series have been transformed into a stationary series by filtering (Sims 1972:545). The test is sensitive to the choice of filter, a choice that is controversial.[6] The Granger test is preferable from this point of view since it uses the crude series (a feature that also improves one's intuitive understanding of the results), and increases the validity of the test. (b) Sims himself has proved that if the assumptions underlying his test hold, the two tests are identical. For reasons of convenience, we decided to work with the Granger test. We should add that Sims shows that tests of causality are in general tests of statistical exogeneity, and it is chiefly this that makes the Sims test important. To illustrate: if

$$Y_t = \sum_{i=-k}^{n} \beta_i X_{t-i} + \varepsilon_t \quad (7.8)$$

(where k is the expected length of lag) and the Sims test rejects the hypothesis $H_0: \beta_k = \cdots = \beta_0 = 0$, the estimates obtained from regression 7.9 will be biased and inconsistent as a result of the omission of variables correlated with the explanatory variables of this regression:[7]

$$Y_t = \sum_{i=1}^{n} \beta_i X_{t-i} + \delta_t, \quad (7.9)$$

The conclusion is that the Sims model, as formulated in 7.9, produces consistent estimates if and only if there is neither Granger nor Sims causality from Y to X.

Some time-series exhibit seasonality. If it is assumed that both X and Y do so, the question arises whether they should be deseasonalized. If the seasonality of Y is Granger-caused by the seasonality of X, a test on deseasonalized data biases the conclusions. However, this is not very likely, since the relationship will hold regardless of seasonal factors if X causes Y. In that case the

6. See Schwert (1977); Auerbach and Rutner (1978); and Zellner (1979).
7. This correlation is due to the strong serial correlation found in all macroeconomic series, as can be seen in (7.9), $\delta_i = \sum_{i=-k}^{n} \beta_i X_{i-1} + \varepsilon_t$.

test will probably not be sensitive to deseasonalization. If, on the other hand, it is assumed that series X is seasonal while the series Y is not, failure to deseasonalize X (when it is the dependent variable) is liable to give spurious significance to Y. When Y is the dependent variable, this problem does not arise.

We carried out all tests with and without deseasonalizing. The price data are strongly seasonal (rising at the time of the festivals—October, November, April, May), while the monetary data are not. The data were deseasonalized by introducing a dummy variable for each month as an additional explanatory variable; most of the findings were not sensitive to this procedure. When the findings are reversed, the matter must be investigated further.

The literature on the choice of lag is scanty, and it is usual to try out different lags in order to discover regularities in the data. It is customary to use the same lags for X and Y, a convention that has no theoretical justification; however, there are far too many possible lag combinations for it to be feasible to estimate them all. We too follow the conventional course: if it is assumed that an increase in the money stock affects prices with a lag of years, we can reject the hypothesis that money causes inflation in the short run, and it can be argued that money does not affect prices beyond the effect of lagged prices on prices. At the same time, the price increase can be explained by an increase in the quantity of money in the less recent past.

In practice this can be tested by

$$Y_t = \sum_{i=1}^{n} \alpha_i Y_{t-i} + \sum_{j=1}^{m} \beta_j X_{t-k+j} + \varepsilon_i. \tag{7.10}$$

The test here is the one used earlier for

$$H_0: \beta_1 = \cdots = \beta_k = 0$$

$$H_1: \text{otherwise.}$$

We tried a few experiments on these lines. The results were not satisfactory, but we believe that this line of investigation is worth pursuing.

3. A Brief Survey of Related Research

An econometric study connected with our topic was carried out by Kleiman and Ophir (1972 and 1975) for the economy of Israel for 1955–65. This study showed that in Israel, inflation affects the quantity of money; this could, for example, be due to the government's efforts to maintain a constant real deficit. In order to do this, the government creates means of payment against each increase in the rate of inflation. Similarly, if the central bank's policy is in accordance with the real-bills doctrine, it will inject liquid assets into the system with each increase in the rate of inflation.

Another related study is Blejer and Leiderman (1980), which examines some monetary aspects of Israel's inflation in 1977–79. The authors apply causality tests to the connection between inflation and three definitions of money and find that M_3 is the only monetary variable to give a significant explanation of monthly changes in the rate of inflation (M_3 is the definition of money that includes deposits denominated in foreign currency).

Several studies on similar topics and using similar tools have been carried out in the U.S. economy. Feige and Pearce (1979) examine the contribution to the explanation of inflation of lags in the quantity of money, and they also take inflation lags into account. They found that in order to forecast inflation from quarterly data it is sufficient to look at past inflation rates—monetary (and fiscal) variables do not make a significant contribution to the explanation. Sims (1972) and Williams, Goodhart, and Gowland (1976) obtained similar results for the United Kingdom. Brillembourg and Khan (1979), who used annual data covering about one hundred years, reached entirely different conclusions in their investigation of similar questions in the United States; they found that the quantity of money affects the rate of inflation with a two-year lag, the effect being significant. Thus studies in the United States have found a long-run but not a short- or medium-run effect of money on inflation. These results accord with the view that in the short run prices are fairly inelastic with respect to monetary changes, and that this rigidity tends to disappear in the longer run.

Other studies have investigated the European hyperinflations, particularly those of the 1920s (see for example Sargent and Wallace, 1973, and Frenkel, 1977). Here, a clear effect of inflation on money is found, the reverse effect being absent. This result is similar to that of Kleiman and Ophir (1972) for Israel, and it appears to be due to the efforts of governments to maintain a constant real deficit.

The studies so far cited use causality tests. Among those using more structural models of the economy of Israel, Artstein and Sussman (1978) found that the growth rate of the quantity of money in the conventional definition has a significant but quite small effect on the rate of inflation.

4. The Findings

As mentioned, we examine the interactions between inflation and money, using monthly, quarterly, and annual data for the short (three to six months lag), medium (two to four quarters), and long run (one to two years) interactions, respectively. The monthly data are divided into two subperiods with the break at the 1977 foreign currency reform. Results referred to as significant are significant at 5 percent unless otherwise stated.

The Effect of Monetary Variables on Inflation

The Short Run. Before the reform: The results are presented in panel I of table 7.3. As can be seen, the only monetary variable to show significant Granger causality from money to inflation is M_4, whose coefficient has an F exceeding the critical value in all regressions in which it is lagged from three to six months. All other coefficients of the monetary variables are nonsignificant, with that of credit, C_0, the only one for which F approaches the critical value.

After the reform: The results are shown in the lower part of panel I of table 7.3. Again, most of the explanatory variables have nonsignificant coefficients. The exceptions are C_0, whose coefficient is significant in the three-month and four-month lag equations; and M_4, with a significant coefficient only with the four-month lag (elsewhere it is on the borderline of significance).

The Medium Run. The results are shown in panel II of table 7.4. As can be seen, no causality from M to P is found.[8]

The Long Run. The F test was applied to M_1 for 1954–79 (table 7.5). The F value is significant at 10 percent only with the two-year lag.

The Effect of Inflation on the Monetary Variables

The Short Run. Before the reform: Table 7.3, panel II, shows the F statistic for the null hypothesis that inflation does not affect money. The results are unambiguous: inflation does not affect money, however defined, all F statistics being well below the critical value. These results hold also when the data are deseasonalized by dummy variables.

After the reform: The results are shown in the lower part of table 7.3, panel II: (a) M_3 and M_4, which contain inflation-linked elements, are strongly affected by inflation, in all equations and for all lags tested; (b) the credit variable, C_0, is significantly affected only with the three-month lag; the effect weakens with longer lags and becomes nonsignificant; and (c) none of the other monetary variables are affected by inflation.

---

8. The F statistic for G_1 (injection due to the government's demand surplus) verges on significance with a 2-quarter lag, but is definitely nonsignificant with the 4-quarter lag.

Table 7.3

Granger Causality Test of the Short-Run Interaction of Money on Prices (monthly data)[a]

(F values)

Lag Months	M_1	M_2	M_3	M_4	G_0	G_1	B_1	C_0	Critical F Value
1. The Effect of Money on Prices									
Pre-reform (1/1972–10/1977)									
Seasonally adjusted									
1–3	0.80	0.76	0.52	3.13*	1.88	0.82	3.14*	2.72	2.80
1–4	0.66	0.99	1.05	3.10*	1.50	1.48	2.03	2.38	2.57
1–5	0.58	0.87	0.81	2.98*	1.11	1.09	1.84	1.81	2.44
1–6	0.53	0.80	0.70	2.42*	0.86	0.88	1.52	1.79	2.35
Unadjusted:									
1–3	0.08	0.18	0.36	3.94*	1.00	1.43	1.93	2.08	2.76
1–4	0.14	0.45	0.52	3.50*	0.72	1.22	1.44	1.61	2.52
1–5	0.13	0.40	0.32	4.52*	0.46	1.05	1.00	1.25	2.39
1–6	0.20	0.48	0.36	3.63*	0.86	1.11	0.95	1.10	2.29
Post-reform (11/1977–9/1980)									
Unadjusted:									
1–3	1.30	0.75	2.02	2.57	1.34	1.41	0.47	6.57*	2.96
1–4	1.18	1.09	2.02	3.37*	0.69	0.66	0.95	3.48*	2.76
1–5	0.43	0.35	2.26	2.23	1.33	0.68	1.50	2.12	2.64
1–6	0.38	0.30	2.03	1.76	1.63	1.35	1.54	1.79	2.57
II. The Effect of Prices on Money									
Pre-reform (1/1972–10/1977)									
Seasonally adjusted:									
1–3	0.63	0.46	0.60	1.11	0.56	0.56	0.65	0.58	2.80
1–4	1.12	1.08	0.40	0.66	0.73	0.47	1.13	0.87	2.57
1–5	0.84	0.79	0.36	0.56	0.60	0.36	0.80	0.51	2.44
1–6	0.80	0.75	0.46	1.18	0.74	0.36	1.16	0.40	2.35
Unadjusted:									
1–3	0.60	0.61	0.35	0.85	0.97	1.12	1.77	0.73	2.76
1–4	0.54	0.66	0.35	0.63	0.85	0.84	1.59	0.66	2.52
1–5	0.41	0.47	0.31	0.60	0.86	0.85	1.28	0.51	2.39
1–6	0.34	0.40	0.24	1.37	1.40	0.70	1.60	0.66	2.29
Post-reform (11/1977–9/1980)									
Unadjusted:									
1–3	1.07	1.38	4.52*	3.55*	2.37	0.99	0.76	3.01*	2.96
1–4	1.49	1.33	3.74*	4.31*	2.74	1.42	0.94	2.43	2.76
1–5	1.11	1.23	3.85*	3.74*	2.03	1.03	0.76	1.79	2.64
1–6	1.45	1.89	4.05*	2.93*	1.81	0.98	0.57	2.38	2.57

[a] Asterisk denotes significant at 5 percent.

Table 7.4
Granger Causality Test of the Medium-Run Interaction of Money and Prices (quarterly data):
1/1972–III/1980
(F values)

Lag Quarters	M_1	M_2	M_3	M_4	G_0	G_1	B_1	C_0	Critical F Value
I. The Effect of Money on Prices									
1–2	0.20	0.19	0.25	0.98	0.40	3.00	0.17	0.54	3.35
1–4	0.17	0.32	0.50	0.40	0.55	0.48	0.35	0.20	2.76
II. The Effect of Prices on Money									
1–2	4.68*	7.50*	2.25	1.45	8.03*	3.25*	3.48*	3.17	3.35
1–4	3.19*	3.06*	0.78	0.77	3.35*	3.90*	1.32	0.53	2.76

*Significant at 5 percent.

Table 7.5
Granger Causality Test of the Long-Run Interaction of M_1 and Prices (annual data): 1954–79
(F values)

Lag Years	I. The Effect of M_1 on Prices		II. The Effect of Prices on M_1	
	M_1	Critical F value	M_1	Critical F value
1	1.63	2.96	9.26**	4.32
1–2	3.04*	2.62	5.37**	3.55

*Significant at 10 percent.
**Significant at 5 percent.

The Medium Run. The results are shown in table 7.4, panel II: (a) the effect of inflation on M_1, M_2, G_0, and G_1 is highly significant; (b) the F statistics for M_3 and M_4 are nonsignificant at all lags; (c) credit and the narrowly defined money base (C_0, B_1) are significantly affected by inflation with the two-quarter lag; with four quarters, the effect is not significant.

The Long Run. Again only M_1 was tested (table 7.5). The F statistic is well above the critical value and the null hypothesis is thus rejected. That is, inflation affects M_1 in the long run.

5. Concluding Remarks

Thus study has presented a method of using econometric tests to investigate the causal relations between monetary variables and inflation, in the short, medium, and long runs. We found that in Israel the relationship runs both ways—there is no dominant unidirectional causality.

The interactions are unstable over time; the economic reasons for this should be investigated and an attempt made to incorporate them explicitly in a structural model.[9] One factor which might cause the interactions to vary between runs is the public's adjustment to its portfolio to inflation. The case of varying the portfolio may also affect inflation itself.

We also found that the dynamics of the interaction change over time—for example, results that apply to the short run are not always applicable to the medium or long run. The choice of horizon is therefore a central issue for any study in this field.

These results strongly suggest that there is a need to study the structure of the mechanisms of the effect of money on inflation and vice versa. Consider, for example, the significant effect of inflation on money. Two alternative mechanisms are possible: (a) some of the important monetary aggregates contain linked assets, which are automatically revalued by any price change; or (b) changes in the rate of inflation are often accompanied by monetary changes arising from other causes, such as the government's attempt to finance a given real deficit by printing money; monetary accommodation of the central bank; or the external sector's reaction to changes in the rate of inflation and its effects on the money base; and so forth. An important question here is now much of the causality stems from (a) and how much from (b).

Finally, an important conclusion emerges from this study on the construction of a structural model: since the interactions found operate in both directions and there is no dominant direction of causality, it follows that in the Israeli economy money and inflation are endogenous to the macroeconomic system.

References

Artstein, Yael, and Zvi Sussman. 1978. The Dynamics of Inflation in a Fully Indexed Economy Subject to Price Shocks. Mimeograph. Jerusalem: Bank of Israel.

Auerbach, Robert D., and Jack L. Rutner. 1978. A Causality Test of Canadian Money and Income: A Comment on Barth and Bennett. *Canadian Journal of Economics* 11, no. 3 (August):583–93.

Blejer, Mario I., and Leonardo Leiderman. 1980. Monetary Aspects of the 1977–79 Inflation in Israel. Sapir Development Center Discussion Paper no. 80–10. Tel Aviv: Tel Aviv University.

Brillembourg, Arturo, and Mohsin S. Khan. 1979. The Relationship between Money,

---

9. In order to investigate the instability found, long time series should be used.

Income, and Prices: Has Money Mattered Historically? *Journal of Money, Credit, and Banking* 11, no. 3 (August):358–65.

Feige, Edward L., and Douglas K. Pearce. 1976. Economically Rational Expectations: Are Innovations in the Rate of Inflation Independent of Innovations in Measures of Monetary and Fiscal Policy? *Journal of Political Economy* 84, no. 3 (June): 499–522.

———. 1979. The Casual Causal Relationship between Money and Income: Some Caveats for Time Series Analysis. *Review of Economics and Statistics* 61 (November):521–33.

Frenkel, Jacob A. 1977. The Forward Exchange Rate, Expectations, and the Demand for Money: The German Hyperinflation. *American Economic Review* 67, no. 4 (September):653–70.

Granger, C. W. J. 1969. Investigating Causal Relations by Econometric Models and Cross-Spectral Methods. *Econometrica* 37, no. 3 (July):424–38.

Granger, C. W. J., and Paul Newbold. 1977. The Time Series Approach to Econometric Model Building. In *New Methods in Business Cycle Research*, ed. Christopher A. Sims, 7–22. Minneapolis: Federal Reserve Bank of Minneapolis.

Kleiman, E., and T. Ophir. 1972. The Adjustment of the Quantity of Money to Changes in the Price Level in Israel, 1955–65. *Bank of Israel Economic Review* 39 (August):3–27.

———. 1975. The Effects of Changes in the Quantity of Money on Prices in Israel, 1955–65. *Bank of Israel Economic Review* 42 (January):15–45.

Michaely, Michael. 1981. Inflation and Money in Israel since the 1977 Tax Reform. *Economic Quarterly* 28, no. 109 (July):3–24 (Hebrew).

Sargent, Thomas J., and Neil Wallace. 1973. Rational Expectations and the Dynamics of Hyperinflation. *International Economic Review* 14, no. 2 (June):328–50.

Schwert, G. 1977. Tests of Causality: The Message in the Innovations. Graduate School of Management Working Paper 77-4. Rochester, N.Y.: University of Rochester.

Sims, Christopher A. 1972. Money, Income, and Causality. *American Economic Review* 62, no. 4 (September):540–52.

———. 1980. Macroeconomics and Reality. *Econometrica* 48, no. 1 (January): 1–48.

Williams, David, C. A. E. Goodhart, and D. H. Gowland. 1976. Money, Income, and Causality: The U.K. Experience. *American Economic Review* 66, no. 3 (June):417–23.

Zellner, Arnold. 1979. Causality and Econometrics. In *Three Aspects of Policy and Policymaking: Knowledge, Data and Institutions,* ed. K. Brunner and A. H. Meltzer. Carnegie-Rochester Conference Series on Public Policy, vol. 10. Amsterdam, New York, Oxford: North-Holland.

8

Slowing Down Devaluation, Monetary Accommodation, and Inflation: A Comparison of Argentina, Chile, and Israel

I. Introduction

Problems of inflation and external deficits are not unique to Israel. Many other countries have attempted to deal with both these problems through measures similar to those adopted in Israel. The list of such measures is quite extensive and includes: crawling pegs, exchange-rate indexation to a basket of currencies, budget cuts, wage and price controls, package deals, and slowing down devaluations to the point of even fixing the exchange rate.

The experience of some Latin American economies is quite similar to that of Israel and it seems that much can be learned by way of comparison of the different policies and performances. It is for this reason that we focus the present investigation on two countries in addition to Israel: Argentina and Chile. It turns out that there are common patterns across these countries in terms of the policies adopted as well as in the responses to these policies. The period under analysis corresponds to the late seventies and early eighties, up until 1983. Thus, we discuss here the period before the inflation-stabilization plans adopted in Argentina and Israel in mid-1985.

The chapter is organized as follows. Section II provides the background conditions that gave rise in each country to the policies of the late seventies, and section III analyzes macroeconomic developments under these policies. Section IV provides econometric evidence on the relation between devaluation, inflation and monetary accommodation for each one of the three countries. Such evidence is generated by analysis of trivariate vector autoregressions. Although some of the results turn out to differ from country to country, some common patterns are observed. In particular, there is a great similarity in the findings for Chile and Israel. In all these countries there is evidence of monetary accommodation in that the money stock changes in

Translated from Hebrew and reprinted with permission from the *Economic Quarterly* 132 (July 1987): 19–33.

response to changes in prices or the exchange rate. In addition, there is a relatively strong impact of changes in the exchange rate on the rate of inflation, though such impact is much weaker in Israel than it is in the other two countries. These and other findings are discussed at length in section IV. Section V deals with the constraints on policy that are implied by exchange-rate management and with the conditions under which anti-inflationary programs based on exchange-rate management are likely to succeed.

II. Background for the Policies Adopted in the Late Seventies

The period from mid- to late seventies features highly volatile macroeconomic conditions in Argentina, Chile, and Israel. Under these conditions inflation accelerated, there were increases in external debt and in government budget deficits, and there was a marked slowdown in the rate of growth. The policies that were adopted were supposed to deal with these developments and to bring about a greater degree of macroeconomic stability. Some of these policies were aimed at improving economic efficiency especially through liberalization and structural reform measures. Other policies were directed toward stabilizing these economies by reducing inflation and improving the external balance position. These latter stabilization policies constitute the focal point of our analysis.[1]

Stabilization policies were adopted in Argentina and Chile when inflation rates rose to 2,300 percent per year in Argentina (March 1976) and to 1,000 percent per year in Chile (September 1973). In both these countries the policies were adopted in a two-stage sequence. First, conventional measures of monetary and fiscal contraction were adopted, and large devaluations were effected in order to improve external competitiveness. As a result of these measures there was an improvement in the countries' external position and a decrease in the rate of inflation. Despite the latter, inflation rates remained at relatively high levels, namely 166 percent per year in Argentina (end of 1978) and 50 percent per year in Chile (end of 1977).

Accordingly, the main purpose of the second stage in the programs was to achieve further disinflation. It was decided in both these countries to manage the exchange rate for anti-inflationary purposes. In particular, it was argued that managing the exchange rate can provide an anchor to the public's inflation expectations, which were partly blamed for not adjusting downward enough. Thus, in the course of 1978 both Argentina and Chile adopted a "tablita" exchange-rate policy which consisted of announcing a list of nominal exchange rates that the authorities planned at each point in time into the

---

1. For further analysis of stabilization policies in Latin America, see Ardito Barletta, Blejer, and Landau (1984); and Corbo, de Melo, and Tybout (1986).

future. An extreme version of this policy held in the case of Chile, where the authorities actually fixed the exchange rate from June 1979 to June 1982.

In the case of Israel, inflation gradually accelerated throughout the seventies, while a variety of exchange-rate policies were in effect. In 1975, a crawling-peg regime based on devaluations at the rate of 2 percent per month was adopted. Then in 1976–77 the crawling peg became more flexible and the exchange rate was indexed to a basket of foreign currencies. By October 1977, upon the change in government, an economic reform and foreign-exchange liberalization was implemented and the exchange rate was allowed to float. Existent controls on international movements of capital were eliminated in January 1978, but then brought back early in 1979. By 1979 inflation got closer to three-digit figures (in annual terms) and the Bank of Israel adjusted the nominal exchange rate according to a PPP (purchasing power parity) rule. Despite an attempt in late 1979 of fiscal and monetary contraction, inflation rates continued to accelerate. This prompted the decision by finance minister Mr. Aridor to manage the exchange rate in order to achieve disinflation. Specifically, it was announced that the domestic currency will be devalued from October 1982 on at a rate of 5 percent per month. As in Argentina and Chile, it was hoped that this policy would anchor inflationary expectations. The policy was abandoned in October 1983 in favor of, again, a PPP rule for the exchange rate. After a few experiments in 1984 and early 1985 with "package deals," that is agreements between government, trade unions, and employees about wages and price increases, a new stabilization plan was adopted in mid–1985.

In summary, each one of the countries considered adopted, at some point in the late seventies or early eighties, a policy of managing the exchange rate in an attempt to reduce the rate of inflation. It was argued that such a policy can play a key role in affecting inflation expectations, and in particular in breaking the inertia of these expectations. Interestingly, the use of exchange-rate management for disinflation objectives is relatively new in Israel where previous exchange-rate policies (such as in the sixties and early seventies) were mainly aimed at improving external competitiveness. Obviously, there were differences in the accompanying monetary and fiscal policies adopted by the three countries. These policies can play an important role in determining the success of exchange-rate management, an issue to be further discussed below.

III. Main Macroeconomic Developments

A. *Annual Averages*

Table 8.1 provides evidence on macroeconomic performance in the three countries based on broad averages of annual data. In Argentina and Chile, the

Table 8.1
Main Developments (averages of yearly data)

Variable	Chile					
	65–70	71–73	74–76	77–78	79–81	82–83
Inflation[a]	12	23	150	358	79	30
Devaluation[a]	36	110	389	56	7	42
Budget deficit[b]	2	16	5	1	−2	3
Real wage[c]	98	98	69	82	100	82
Unemployment[d]	6	5	14	14	12	22

Variable	Argentina				
	65–73	73–75	76–78	78–80	81–83
Inflation[a]	24	78	246	128	189
Devaluation[a]	13	66	178	65	285
Budget deficit[b]	3	12	8	8	18
Real wage[c]	125	154	100	118	111
Unemployment[d]	6	2	3	2	5

Variable	Israel				
	65–67	68–73	74–77	78–80	81–83
Inflation[a]	6	11	36	84	127
Devaluation[a]	4	6	26	69	122
Budget deficit[b]	2	7	14	15	14
Real wage[c]	74	80	91	100	116

Source: International Financial Statistics, and Corbo, de Melo, and Tybout (1986).
[a] expressed as percentage per year.
[b] expressed as percentage of GDP.
[c] index (the base level varies from country to country).
[d] percentage of labor force.

early seventies mark the transition from the inward-oriented policies of the mid-sixties (with heavy protection of domestic production) to the crises that prompted the design and implementation of stabilization programs. It is notable that in this translation there was a sharp increase in government budget deficits from about 2–3 percent of GNP to about 12–16 percent of GNP. In addition, both inflation and the rate of devaluation accelerated in both countries in the early to mid-seventies.

Examining the columns for 1976–78 for Argentina and for 1974–76 for Chile indicates that during the first step of these countries' programs there was a decrease in the ratio of government budget deficit to GNP. Despite this, and other orthodox anti-inflation measures, the rate of inflation actually increased as did the rate of devaluation. In both countries, however, the former dominated the latter thus giving rise to a trend of real appreciation of the domestic currency.

Turning now to the second stage of the policy, which involved exchange-rate management, it can be seen that there was a noticeable slowdown in the rate of devaluation and in the rate of inflation. The government budget deficit remained unchanged in Argentina (with a deficit of about 8 percent of GNP) yet in Chile further budget cuts were effected (in fact, Chile's government budget was in surplus in 1979–81). During the 1979–81 period there was a marked increase in the real wage in Chile, and the rate of unemployment remained at its previously high levels.

Despite its partial success at slowing down inflation, the policy of exchange-rate management was abandoned in the early eighties. The 1981–83 and 1982–83 columns in table 8.1 for Argentina and Chile correspond to the first few years after such a policy change. The main reason for abandoning these policies is that other macroeconomic policies were not adjusted enough to support exchange-rate management as a sustainable policy. In both countries the observed real appreciations were accompanied by a deterioration in the countries' external positions and by erosion of international reserves and capital flight. Thus, expectations of a change in policy and of large devaluations quickly emerged and strengthened these trends. The nonsustainability of the exchange-rate-management policy was clear in Argentina, where the budget deficit was not reduced enough to support this policy (see Dornbusch [1985] for further discussion), but also in Chile where the observed increase in the real wage was generally regarded as unsustainable. Both countries stopped managing their exchange rates in the early eighties.

In the case of Israel, the rate of inflation gradually escalated from 36 percent per year in 1974–77 to 84 percent per year during 1978–80 and then to 127 percent per year during 1981–83. As far as the government budget deficit is concerned there were two main jumps in its size, one from 1965–67 to 1968–73 and another one in the transition to 1974–77. Since 1977 the budget deficit remained relatively stable at 15 percent of GDP. The rate of devaluation generally increased with inflation, yet at a lower rate thus giving rise to a trend of real appreciation of the domestic currency. Real wages were rising since the sixties up to the end of 1983, the time at which exchange-rate management was abandoned for similar reasons as in Argentina and Chile.

This broad discussion and the evidence in table 8.1 suggest three main conclusions at this point. First, while the rates of devaluation and inflation generally moved together in each one of the three countries, a clear pattern of real exchange-rate appreciation was observed under the policy of exchange-rate management. Second, high inflation rates were observed in the three countries only in the seventies. In the transition from the sixties to the seventies there was a sharp increase in the government budget deficit, a fact that conforms with the view that these deficits can play a key role in the acceleration of inflation. However, once these budget deficits reached relatively high levels it is difficult to find a close association between further fluctuations in them and movements in the rate of inflation. In fact, there were periods in which, e.g., inflation accelerated despite the appearance of some reduction in the deficit. Third, while in both Argentina and Chile there were some periods of budget deficit cuts and cuts in real wages in the process of attempting to disinflate, no such experience holds for Israel where the government budget deficit gradually increased up to 15 percent of GNP with accompanying increases in real wages. It is only under the stabilization program of mid-1985 that cuts in the budget and in real wages are observed, for some time, in Israel.

B. Quarterly Data

In this subsection we use quarterly data to discuss in more detail some of the developments under the exchange-rate-management policies.[2] For brevity, we focus our analysis on the rate of inflation, the rate of devaluation, and the real exchange rate in each country.

Figure 8.1 depicts the quarterly rate of inflation in Chile for the period 1977:II to 1983:IV. There is a broad trend of decrease in inflation up until the abandonment of exchange-rate management in early 1982. Interestingly, despite the fact that a fixed exchange rate was established in 1979:IV, it took considerable time for the rate of inflation to start slowing down. Also seen in the figure is the behavior of the rate of devaluation, which began slowing down in early 1978 and was then maintained at zero from 1979:IV to 1982:II. This fixed-exchange-rate episode ended with a large devaluation in 1982:III. Last, figure 8.1 gives the log real exchange rate, which shows the sharp and continuous real appreciation that prevailed from early 1978 to the end of the fixed-exchange-rate regime.

The quarterly data for Argentina are provided in figure 8.2. Although the "tablita" policy that slowed down the rate of devaluation was adopted toward the end of 1978, the rate inflation showed some deceleration only toward the end of 1979. This trend in inflation persisted until early 1981, the time of change in policy. The graph for the rate of devaluation shows the slowdown associated with the "tablita" policy and the large devaluations that were effected in the second and third quarters of 1982 reflecting the abandonment of the policy. As in the case of Chile, the graph for the log real exchange rate

2. The source for the quarterly data used in this section is *International Financial Statistics* published by the International Monetary Fund.

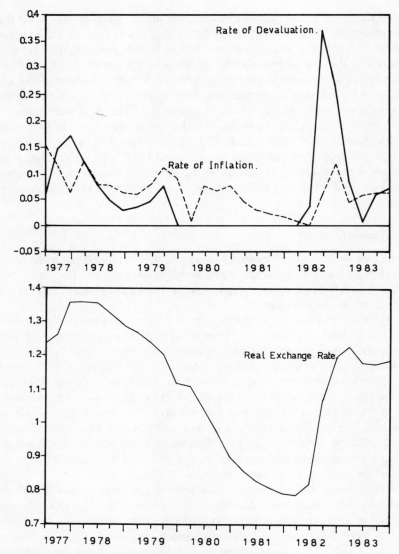

Figure 8.1   Devaluation, inflation, and the real exchange rate in Chile.

shows the marked real appreciation under the policy and the role of the large
devaluations in the early eighties in reversing this trend.

Figure 8.3 gives the evidence for Israel. The rate of devaluation exhibits
some slowdown from the end of 1977 to the end of 1978 and for some quarters between 1982 and 1983. The rate of inflation accelerated up until the first
quarter of 1980 and remained quite high and stable until late 1983. Interest-

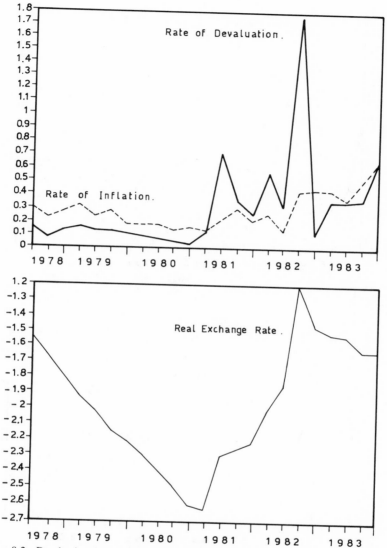

Figure 8.2   Devaluation, inflation, and the real exchange rate in Argentina.

ingly, no noticeable decrease in the rate of inflation showed up during the 1982–83 episode of exchange-rate management. The log real exchange rate, plotted in figure 8.3, shows a general trend of real appreciation, especially in the periods from mid-1978 to mid-1980 and from mid-1982 to mid-1983 (the period of exchange-rate management).

A comparison of developments across these three countries suggests that

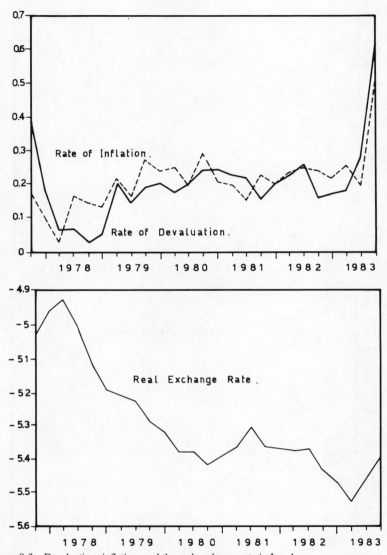

Figure 8.3   Devaluation, inflation, and the real exchange rate in Israel.

the adoption of an exchange-rate-management policy did not have an immediate effect on the rate of inflation. There were considerable lags in generating
some reduction in inflation, lags that could reflect the existence of contractual
rigidities as well as the lack of adjustment of other macroeconomic policy
instruments toward a low-inflation position. In addition, while Argentina and

Chile made extensive use of exchange-rate management for anti-inflation purposes, such a policy was used in Israel only for a short time. Despite these
different experiences, considerable real exchange appreciation was observed
in all three countries.

IV. Dynamic Relations between Devaluation, Inflation, and Money Growth

In this section, we attempt to uncover the main empirical regularities in the
data regarding the dynamic relations between movements in the rate of devaluation, the rate of inflation, and money growth. In particular, we examine
the impact of devaluation shocks on the rate of inflation, the extent to which
changes in money are autonomous or accommodating, and whether devaluation shocks and money shocks can statistically account for a nonnegligible
fraction of observed fluctuations in inflation. We deal with these issues by
estimating and analyzing trivariate vector autoregressions for each country.
We view this as a statistical first pass at the data rather than as a substitute for
constructing and estimating structural models for these countries.

A. Methodology

We follow Sims's (1980) vector autoregression methodology. Specifically, define by X_t the 3×1 vector giving the stochastic processes for the rate of
devaluation (DE), the rate of inflation (DP), and the rate of growth of money
(DM). That is, $X_t = [DE_t, DP_t, DM_t]'$. A second order vector autoregression
for these processes is given by

$$X_t = A_0 + A_1 X_{t-1} + A_2 X_{t-2} + u_t, \qquad (8.1)$$

where A_0 is a (3×1) vector of constants, A_1 and A_2 are (3×3) matrices of
least squares coefficients, and u_t is a (3×1) vector of random disturbances.
The latter are the shocks or innovations in the system, in that they represent
that part of X_t that cannot be linearly predicted by using a constant and two
lagged values of X. Since equation 8.1 is like a reduced form of the system
and there are many possible structures that may give rise to a given set of
A coefficients, caution is suggested if and when attaching structural interpretations to these coefficients.

After the A coefficients are estimated, it is convenient to use them to calculate the moving average representation of X_t which is given by

$$X_t = C_0 + u_t + C_1 u_{t-1} + C_2 u_{t-2} + \ldots + C_i u_{t-i}. \qquad (8.2)$$

Since there may be disturbances that are contemporaneously correlated in the
u-process, it is useful to orthogonalize them following some ordering of the

variables. Upon doing so, one obtains the orthogonalized moving average representation:

$$X_t = K_0 + e_t + K_1 e_{t-1} + K_2 e_{t-2} + \ldots + K_i e_{t-i}, \qquad (8.3)$$

where e is the vector of orthogonalized disturbances. Equation 8.3 is the impulse-response function of the system and the K-parameters are the dynamic multipliers that give the system's response at present and future periods to shocks to components of the e-process. The order of orthogonalization used here is as follows:

$$e_{1t} = u_{1t}; \; e_{2t} = u_{2t} - a_1 u_{1t}; \quad \text{and} \quad e_{3t} = u_{3t} - a_2 u_{1t} - a_3 u_{2t}.$$

That is, shocks to the rate of devaluation enter first, then enter shocks to the rate of inflation, and finally enter shocks to money growth.

B. Empirical Results

We estimated system 8.1 for each country using quarterly data on the rate of devaluation, the rate of inflation and the rate of growth of narrow money. The sample periods are 1977:IV to 1983:IV for Chile and Israel, and 1979:I to 1983:IV for Argentina.[3]

Table 8.2 provides the contemporaneous correlations between the estimated disturbances. It is seen that there are many sizable correlations in the table. For example, the correlation between contemporaneous disturbances to inflation and to devaluation is 0.66 in Israel, and a similar size of correlation applies to the disturbances to money growth and inflation.

Figures 8.4 to 8.6 depict the responses of each one of the three variables considered, in each country, to their shocks. These responses are given starting with the time period (quarter) at which the shock occurs up until two years after the shock. These responses were calculated using the impulse-response functions given in system 8.3.

Figure 8.4 gives the responses to a one-standard-deviation positive shock to the rate of devaluation in each country. There are four main features of the results that are worth emphasizing at this point. First, in all three countries the devaluation shock has relatively short persistence in terms of subsequent rates of devaluation. Thus, the latter converge quite quickly to the rate of devaluation before the shock. Second, in all countries the positive shock to the rate of devaluation is accompanied by increases in money growth. This finding accords with the view that the monetary authorities accommodate such

---

3. For data source, see note 2.

Table 8.2
Contemporaneous Correlations of Residuals

	DE	DP	DM
Argentina:			
DE	1.00		
DP	0.73	1.00	
DM	0.67	0.58	1.00
Chile:			
DE	1.00		
DP	0.15	1.00	
DM	0.11	0.52	1.00
Israel:			
DE	1.00		
DP	0.66	1.00	
DM	0.60	0.65	1.00

Note: This table is based on the disturbances estimated from the vector auto-regression eq. 8.1.

shocks. During the year after the shock, there is an increase in real-money balances in each one of the three countries. Third, while in all cases the devaluation shock is accompanied by an acceleration in the rate of inflation (see especially the case of Israel where such a relation is particularly strong), the former is more sizable thus yielding an increase in real-exchange-rate depreciation. This pattern holds mainly in the short run; in the medium and long runs the trend is reversed in Argentina and Chile and a real appreciation arises. Fourth, while in Chile and Israel all variables tend to return to their preshock levels in about two years, the rate of inflation and the rate of growth of money in Argentina are still at higher values than initially even two years after the shock.

Looked in terms of the policy experiment of interest in this paper, the results indicate how a sudden (and temporary) slowdown in the rate of devaluation will be accompanied by some decreases in the rates of inflation and money growth and by a real appreciation of the domestic currency.

Figure 8.5 plots the responses to a one-standard-deviation increase in the rate of inflation. The main results are as follows. First, there are cross-country differences in the speed of convergence of the rate of inflation back to its preshock level. Chile exhibits the fastest speed of convergence, followed by Israel, where there is a marked volatility of inflation rates in the transition, and Argentina is a case of strongest persistence of the shock. Second, the increase in inflation is accompanied in the short run by a nominal appreciation of each one of the domestic currencies. One possible interpretation of this finding is that the authorities attempt to partially offset the impact of the infla-

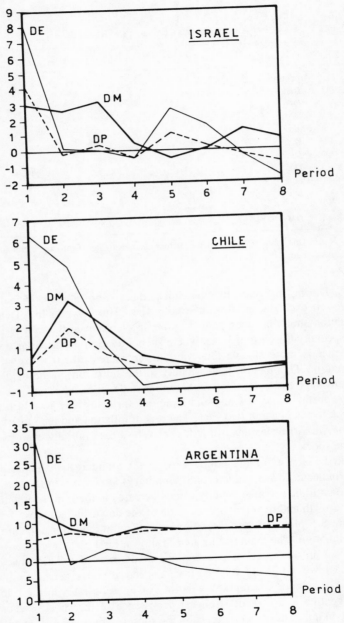

Figure 8.4   Responses to shocks to the rate of devaluation.

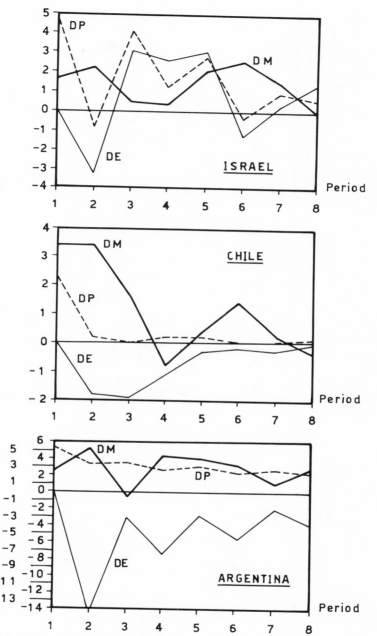

Figure 8.5   Responses to inflation shocks.

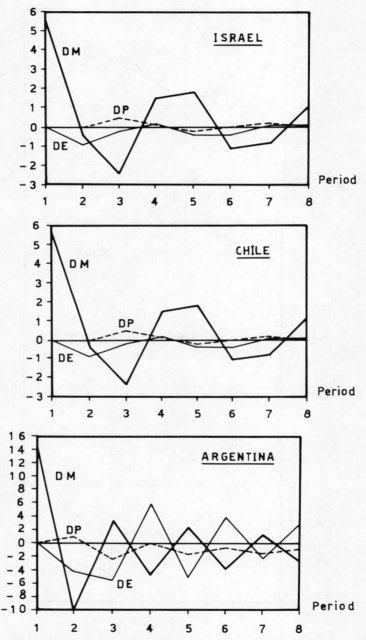

Figure 8.6 Responses to money growth shocks.

tion shock by appreciating the nominal exchange rate. In all cases, real-exchange-rate appreciation arises in response to this shock. Notice also the marked volatility of the rates of devaluation and inflation in Israel. Third, in all cases there is an increase in the rate of growth of money following the shock. Again, one may interpret this as indicating the existence of monetary accommodation. Money growth converges quite quickly to its preshock levels in the cases of Chile and Israel.

Figure 8.6 provides the responses to a money-growth shock. It can be seen that a positive innovation in money growth has little impact on the rate of inflation and thus results in an increase in real money balances. The shock is accompanied in all countries by a nominal-exchange-rate depreciation in the short run. For Argentina and Israel, this is offset in the medium and longer run by nominal devaluations. Thus, the positive money shock is accompanied in the very short run by real-exchange-rate appreciation.

Next, we turn to examining the relative importance of the shocks by means of variance decompositions. That is, we calculate what percentage of each variable's forecast error is accounted for by the different shocks. Forecast errors are defined by

$$X_t - E_{t-i}X_t = e_t + K_1 e_{t-1} + \ldots + K_{i-1} e_{t-i+1}, \qquad (8.4)$$

where E_{t-i} denotes the linear forecast of X_t (based on the estimates of system 8.1) conditional on X_{t-i}, X_{t-i-1}, X_{t-i-2}, etc.

Table 8.3 presents these variance decompositions for each country for a forecast-error horizon of eight quarters (that is, two years) into the future.

Table 8.3
Variance Decompositions of Forecast Errors

| Explained by | Percentage forecast error in: | | |
	DE	DP	DM
Chile:			
DE	87	42	17
DP	11	54	32
DM	2	4	51
Argentina:			
DE	70	82	57
DP	22	16	7
DM	8	2	36
Israel:			
DE	55	27	41
DP	28	69	31
DM	17	4	28

First, consider accounting for forecast-error variance of the rate of devaluation. It can be seen that in Chile 90 percent of forecast error variance is accounted for by own lagged values of the rate of devaluation. In Argentina and Israel, however, shocks to the rate of inflation account for a nonnegligible portion of devaluation's forecast error variance. Money growth shocks appear to have no explanatory power for devaluations.

Shocks to the rate of devaluation have a sizable role in accounting for forecast error variance in inflation in the cases of Argentina and Chile where 82 percent and 42 percent, respectively, of this variance is accounted for by devaluation shocks. Inflation shocks are more autonomous in Israel than in the other countries, though devaluation shocks still have a nonnegligible explanatory power.

Last, consider accounting for money growth's forecast error variance. In Israel, 41 percent of this variance is accounted for by devaluation shocks and 31 percent is accounted for by shocks to inflation. To some extent, these results can be regarded as being consistent with the existence of monetary accommodation. Accommodation appears to be also present in Argentina and Chile, where shocks to devaluation and inflation account for about 50 to 60 percent of forecast-error variance in money growth.

These results highlight the important role of the rate of devaluation for other nominal variables. This may explain the focus on slowing down devaluations in attempting to disinflate these economies. In addition, our findings are compatible with the existence of monetary accommodation in all three countries, though the exact form of accommodation may differ across countries. It appears that in Argentina money growth is mainly related to the rate of devaluation, yet in Chile it is primarily the rate of inflation that affects money growth. Money growth in Israel responds quite sizably to both changes in the rate of inflation and the rate of devaluation. In the next section, we analyze the connection between exchange-rate management and other policies, a connection that is imposed by the economy's long-run constraints on the behavior of international reserves, domestic and external debt, and the financing of the government budget, and we outline the conditions under which exchange-rate management may succeed in reducing inflation (see also Liviatan and Piterman [1984] for a discussion about the specific case of Israel).

V. Constraints on Policy

The common features that we found in many of the results for the three countries under consideration—especially in the relations between nominal variables such as money growth, inflation, and devaluation—provide a motivation for searching for an analytical framework that could possibly account for them. The results in the previous section are compatible with the existence of monetary accommodation to price and exchange-rate changes. The findings are also consistent with exchange-rate policies that were partly autonomous and partly aimed at preserving external competitiveness. In addition, exchange-rate policies were directed to slowing down the economies' rates of inflation. Accordingly, the main objective of this section is to determine under what circumstances and conditions a disinflation policy based on exchange-rate management is likely to succeed, and to indicate whether these conditions prevailed in the three countries under study. The discussion will be at the conceptual and analytical level; no attempt is being made here to provide a model that is focused on a specific country.

Exchange-rate policy can be viewed as one component of an overall package of macroeconomic policies, one whose other main components are monetary and fiscal policy. Thus, there are constraints on exchange-rate policy that arise from the choices made by the authorities for the other components. These constraints do not necessarily apply to the short run, in which there are relatively large degrees of freedom in choosing the level of the exchange rate or the money supply, but rather to the long-term intertemporal relations among the different variables. While, for example, it is possible to maintain an overvalued exchange rate and a large government budget deficit for some time, this policy leads to losses of international reserves and to an increase in the level of public domestic and foreign debt. Therefore, a government that does not aim at defaulting its debt will have to change these policies; otherwise, it may find no resource to serve its debt in the future. The mere existence of expectations by the public about the possibility of default will raise the price of rolling over debt for government and will lead to an increase in the real interest rate.

At each point in time, there is a whole range of expected future feasible policies. Thus, from the public's perspective there is uncertainty about the future course of policy and there may be only partial credibility to policy makers' announcements about their intentions in the future. This uncertainty and lack of full credibility typically lead to the emergence of risk premiums which affect interest rates as well as the expected returns on different assets. In general, the public's expectations about the future course of policy affects behavior and economic performance already in the present period and these expectations sometimes indeed bring about a policy change. A typical example of that is a speculative attack on foreign currencies that ends with an official devaluation of the domestic currency.

These issues can be conveniently analyzed using Helpman and Razin's (1987) framework. For this purpose it will be assumed that government spending is constant, and for simplicity we set it to zero. A disinflation policy based on slowing down the rate of devaluation is shown to bring about a loss of international reserves and an increase in foreign debt. In order for government to be able to repay its debt, the latter has to be prevented from increasing at a rate higher than the real interest rate (we assume for simplicity that there is no growth in the economy). Furthermore, government will have to raise taxes in future periods. If there is no uncertainty about the path of taxes and the exchange rate, it can be shown that the intertemporal relation between exchange rates and taxes has to obey

$$\Sigma R^{-t}(\phi'_t/e_t) = \Sigma R^{-t}[e_{t-1}y(p_{t-1})$$
$$- e_t y(p_t)]/e_t, \; t = 0, \ldots, \infty, \quad (8.5)$$

where R is one plus the real interest rate in terms of traded goods, ϕ'_t is the nominal tax at time t, $y(p_t)$ is real output of traded goods as a function of the relative price of traded and nontraded goods. Thus, $1/p_t$ is the real exchange rate. This way of writing constraint 8.5 assumes that there is no initial debt by government.

The right-hand-side of equation 8.5 gives the present value of the international reserves' losses that would occur in the absence of adjustment of tax policy—where international reserves earn an interest rate of $R - 1$. These losses are due to changes in the demand for money, which equals here nominal output. Thus, in (8.5) the consolidated accounts of government and the central bank are balanced in present-value terms.

The model assumes a finite horizon for each cohort, and each period there is a new cohort of individuals that enter the system. This assumption results in different discount rates for the private agent and the economy as a whole. Thus, the current generation would, other things equal, favor a policy of real appreciation in the short run which is balanced by tax increases to be effected in the longer run. Assuming that the authorities implement a freeze on the exchange rate up to time T, and adjust taxes thereafter to remain intertemporally solvent, the behavior of consumption per capita, private sector's debt, government debt and taxes is given by the following dynamic equations:

$$c_t = (1 - \beta)\{\Sigma(\gamma/R)^\tau[y(P_{t+\tau}) - \phi_{t+\tau}] - Rb_{t-1}\}, \quad t > 0, \quad (8.6)$$

$$b_t = \begin{bmatrix} Rb_{t-1} + c_t - y(p_t) + \phi_t, & t > 0 & (8.7) \\ R^t g, & 0 < t \le T - 1 & (8.8a) \\ R^{T-1}g, & t \ge t & (8.8b) \end{bmatrix}$$

$$\phi_t = \begin{bmatrix} -g, & t = 0 & (8.9a) \\ 0, & 1 \le t \le T - 1 & (8.9b) \\ (R - 1)R^{T-1}g, & t \ge T. & (8.9c) \end{bmatrix}$$

The notation is as follows: c is consumption per capita, β is the saving rate out of wealth, γ is the probability of survival into the next period, b is private sector debt per capita, and b^G is government debt per capita.

From these equations and from the equilibrium conditions in the market for nontraded goods it can be shown that a policy of freezing the exchange rate at its current level leads to an increase in private consumption, to a decrease in private-sector debt, to an increase in government debt (a loss of international reserves), to an increase in the economy's net external debt (that is, an increase in $b_0 + b_0$), and to a real-exchange-rate appreciation. Private consumption will remain higher for some time, and then it will adjust downwards to a level below that which would have prevailed in the absence of this policy. At the same time, the real exchange rate remains appreciated for some time and in the long run increases to the level that would prevail in the absence of the policy. Finally, external indebtedness gradually increases through time.

These responses to a policy of exchange-rate management conform well with the facts in Argentina, Chile, and Israel that were discussed in the previous sections. They can be interpreted as the result of wealth redistribution across generations. That is, slowing down devaluation to combat inflation gives rise to a capital gain to the generations currently alive. The future consequences of the policy, in the form of increased tax burdens, are rolled over to the future generations which will consequently have lower levels of consumption than the current ones. The net result is an increase in the economy's external debt and a real appreciation.

In addition to this interpretation which is based on the specific model discussed above, one may add other factors not included in the analysis. In particular, a temporarily appreciated real exchange rate provides an incentive for increasing, if not advancing, purchases of consumer durables as well as import-intensive investments. These phenomena also prevailed in the three countries, where the policies were followed by large expansions in the levels of aggregate demand.

The fact that sooner or later the policy of exchange-rate management was abandoned in each one of the three countries, with no success on the disinflation front, and the foregoing analysis suggest that this policy can be effective only if it is accompanied by a package of fiscal and monetary measures that make the policy compatible with the long-run constraints of the economy. Otherwise, there are mounting pressures on the balance of payments, on international reserves, and on foreign debt. It is typically under these circumstances that expectations of devaluation arise, expectations which put further pressure on reserves. The latter, in turn, may persist over time thus actually leading to a large devaluation aimed at stopping this process. In fact, the three episodes of exchange-rate management discussed in this paper (Argentina between 1977 and 1982, Chile for 1978–82, and Israel during 1982–83) shared the feature that the slowing down in the rate of devaluation was not accompanied by contractionary monetary and fiscal policies. Thus, the policy had to be abandoned primarily because of the external or balance-of-payments constraints, and in each case a large devaluation marked the transition to a new set of policies. The main lesson from these episodes is that in order for exchange-rate management to succeed it has to be supported by a consistent set of accompanying monetary and fiscal measures.

References

Ardito Barletta, N., M. I. Blejer, and L. Landau, (eds.) 1984. *Economic Liberalization and Stabilization Policies in Argentina, Chile, and Uruguay.* Washington, D.C.: World Bank.

Corbo, V., J. de Melo, and J. Tybout. 1986. What Went Wrong with Recent Reforms in the Southern Cone. *Economic Development and Cultural Change*: 607–40.

Dornbusch, R. 1984. Argentina since Martinez de Hoz. Working Paper no. 1466. NBER, September.

———. 1985. External Debt, Budget Deficits, and Disequilibrium Exchange Rates. In *International Debt and Developing Countries* (ed. G. W. Smith and J. T. Cuddington). Washington, D.C.: World Bank.

Edwards, S. 1985. Stabilization with Liberalization: An Evaluation of Ten Years of Chile's Experiment with Free Market Policies, 1973–83. *Economic Development and Cultural Change*: 223–54.

Helpman, E., and A. Razin. 1987. Exchange Rate Management: Intertemporal Trade-offs. *American Economic Review*: 107–23.

Liviatan, N., and S. Piterman. 1986. Accelerating Inflation and Balance of Payments Crises: Israel 1973–84. In *The Israeli Economy: Maturing through Crises* (ed. Y. Ben-Porath). Cambridge, Mass.: Harvard University Press.

Sims, C. A. 1980. Macroeconomics and Reality. *Econometrica*: 1–48.

9

Foreign Trade Shocks and the Dynamics of High Inflation: Israel, 1978–85

The notion that the process of inflation reaches a self-sustaining momentum or inertia in high-inflation economies, and that it can hardly be stopped by conventional measures of monetary and fiscal policy restraint, has strongly influenced the design of stabilization policies recently adopted in Israel and in Latin American countries such as Argentina and Brazil. The basic idea underlying this "inertia approach" is that due to institutional adjustments, to slowly moving inflationary expectations, and to accommodating monetary and fiscal policies, the stabilizing forces in high-inflation economies are generally weak, thus leaving the inflation rate in a "meta-stable" equilibrium. As a result, it is claimed, even one-time shocks to the price *level* can lead to a long-term rise in the *rate* of inflation. The imposition of price and wage controls and the adoption of a fixed exchange rate as integral components of recent disinflation plans in Israel, Argentina, and Brazil were rationalized as being necessary measures in order to directly stop this inherent momentum or inertia in the inflation process.[1]

In the case of Israel, special attention was given to a hypothesis that focuses on the role of open-economy factors in the propagation mechanism of inflation. This hypothesis specifies a link between balance-of-payments crises, the policy reactions that they generate, and their implications for the process of inflation. According to this hypothesis, balance of payments crises have played a key role in the acceleration of inflation through time. In response to these crises, it is argued, the authorities devalue the domestic currency and lift some of the existing price controls on government-regulated goods and

Reprinted with permission from *Journal of International Money and Finance* 7 (December 1988):411–23.

1. See Dornbusch and Fischer (1986); Dornbusch and Simonsen (1987); and chapter 2 on different possible meanings of inflationary inertia and their role in the design of recent anti-inflation plans. On the concept of "meta-stable" high-inflation equilibrium see Bruno and Fischer (1986).

services such as public transportation, electricity, gasoline, and basic food items. The initial cost-push effects that result from these measures are then quickly translated into an increase in the general price level through widespread indexation in labor and financial markets and through monetary accommodation by the central bank. Since the inflation rate is in a "meta stable" equilibrium, this increase in the price level is transformed into a persistent acceleration in the rate of inflation.[2]

The foregoing view of the inflation process is not uncontroversial. An alternative approach, usually referred to as the 'equilibrium-rational expectations' approach, maintains that any self-persistence in the process of inflation has its roots in the behavior of deeper causal factors such as monetary and fiscal policies. What seems to be a momentum of inflation is interpreted by this approach as a rational response of behavior, expectations, and institutions to an underlying set of current and expected future monetary and fiscal policies. According to this view, it is possible to stop this momentum and to disinflate the economy by generating a credible and permanent change in the policy regime such that the equilibrium rate of inflation under the new set of policies is much lower than the previous one.[3]

Interestingly, similar controversies between theories that link inflation to fundamentals and theories that stress the independent role of balance of payments fluctuations emerged in the context of the German hyperinflation in the early 1920s:[4]

> The main division of opinion regarding inflation and dislocated exchange lies between inflation and balance of payments theories. The former traces causation from quantity of money to domestic prices to rate of exchange; the latter, from real balance factors to rate of exchange, to certain domestic prices, and sometimes further to the quantity of money. (Ellis, 1934:289)

---

2. See Fischer (1984); and Liviatan and Piterman (1986). The notion that monetary policy, and thus inflation, responds to fluctuations in the balance of payments is familiar from the literature on policy reaction functions for open economies; see, e.g., Black (1983). Similar points were made in the discussions following the German hyperinflation:

> There are certain instances in which a rise of prices follows *necessarily* and *inevitably* from the phenomenon of foreign trade and the position of the rate of exchange. . . .
> However great the pressure may be upon the central bank, however much further credit extensions and note issues may seem imperative, further inflation is an act of its own authority for which it is answerable. (Ellis 1934:268–69)

3. See Sargent (1986), especially chapters 3 and 4. Helpman and Leiderman in chapter 2 of this book have shown how expectations of future changes in the policy regime may have affected the dynamics of inflation observed in Israel and in other high-inflation countries.

4. See also Dornbusch (1985); and Sargent (1986).

Given the influential role of the 'inertia approach' for policies actually implemented in high-inflation countries, our purpose in this paper is to empirically examine the extent to which some of its implications conform with Israeli data. In particular, we provide empirical answers to the following questions:

1. Do one-time shocks to key macroeconomic variables give rise to long-term persistence or inertia of inflation?

2. Do foreign trade shocks generate the dynamic response implied by the hypothesis? That is, do increases in the trade deficit lead to a devaluation of the domestic currency, to an increase in prices of controlled goods and services, to monetary accommodation, and to an increase in the general price level?

3. Do devaluations, adjustments in prices of controlled goods and services, and monetary accommodation play a key role in the propagation of inflation?

4. How important, statistically, are these different factors in accounting for fluctuations in the rate of inflation?

In order to accomplish this task, we apply Sims's vector-autoregression analysis to our data set.[5] While we are aware of the potential limitations of this method and especially of attempting to provide structural interpretations to a given set of results, we use it because it is a model-free method that seems appropriate for testing whether the information contained in unrestricted reduced forms linking between a set of key macroeconomic variables conforms with the predictions of the 'inertia approach'.

The paper is organized as follows. Section I provides a brief description of background on the Israeli economy and of the data used in our analysis. Section II reports the results of autoregressive analysis of a five-variable system, using monthly data for Israel for the period 1978:1–1985:5. Section III presents our main conclusions.

I. Background and Data

We base our empirical analysis on monthly data for Israel covering the period from 1978:1 to 1985:5. The main reason for starting our analysis on 1978:1 is that data for periods before the end of 1977 belong to what seems to have been another regime, one of foreign-exchange controls and a fixed or crawling peg for the exchange rate. Policies of liberalizing the foreign exchange market from previously existing controls and of establishing a managed float were adopted by the end of 1977. Our sample ends in 1985:5 because of the fact that in the following month the authorities adopted a comprehensive disinflation program, which included a complete freeze of the exchange rate and the

---

5. For a recent application of this technique to U.S. data, see Litterman and Weiss (1985).

imposition of administrative controls on prices and wages. Thus, observations after that date appear to belong to a different regime than previously.

The most salient feature of the Israeli economy over our sample period is the escalation of inflation,[6] from levels between 50–80 percent in 1978–79, to levels between 120–150 percent in 1980–83, and then to levels between 350–450 percent in 1984–85. Indexation of asset returns and wages was quite extensive during this period. Israeli residents may hold assets with returns indexed to either the exchange rate or the consumer price level. They have also been allowed since the liberalization in 1977 to hold foreign currency and bank accounts denominated in foreign currencies. Wage indexation is part of the centralized agreements negotiated between the trade union, government, and the manufacturers' organization. Although the details of these agreements have varied over the years, most typically they contain a quarterly indexation compensation of approximately 70 percent of the inflation rate in the preceding quarter. In addition, base wages are adjusted once every year or two years. The exchange rate has been determined since the end of 1977 via a managed float, whereby the central bank intervenes in an attempt to avoid having wide fluctuations from purchasing-power parity. International capital movements to and from the economy are not free, and are subject to controls and taxes. The central bank has not conducted an independent or autonomous monetary policy and has not pursued money growth targets over the sample period. Instead, monetary policy has been accommodative and has been constrained by (i) the need to finance part of the government budget deficit, (ii) the requirement of maintaining fixed real interests rates on government indexed bonds, and (iii) the provision of subsidized credit to certain sectors such as exports and industries located in development areas. There is a high degree of government intervention in the economy. The consumption component of government spending is ⅓ of GNP, and there has been a high government budget deficit, amounting to approximately 10–14 percent of GNP over the sample period. Government also has a direct role in setting prices of a set of regulated goods and services (as, for example, public utilities) whose weight in the consumption basket used for calculation of the CPI is between 30 percent and 40 percent. Last, there have been persistent deficits in the current account of the balance of payments. The yearly value of these deficits typically amounted to 20 percent of yearly GNP in our sample. It appears that this situation of continuous external deficits has been the major preoccupation of policymakers in Israel in recent years, and it is precisely the role of shocks to these deficits in the process of inflation that serves as the focal issue of our investigation.

6. For a thorough description and analysis of this and other features of the Israeli economy, see Fischer (1984).

In line with analysis based on the 'inertia approach,' we have included the following five variables in our empirical work: DEF_t is the real value of the monthly trade deficit, calculated by multiplying the dollar value of the deficit by the ratio of the nominal dollar exchange rate to the CPI; DS_t is the monthly percentage change in the exchange rate of the Israeli shekel relative to a basket of five foreign currencies (US dollar, pound sterling, deutschemark, Dutch guilder, and French franc); DPC_t is the monthly percentage change in the price index of goods and services that are subject to government price controls; DM_t is the ratio of public sector monthly monetary infusion to beginning of month's M_1 money supply; DP_t is the monthly percentage change in the consumer price index. The data sources are various reports of the Bank of Israel and the Israeli Central Bureau of Statistics. Throughout, we have used seasonally unadjusted series.[7]

II. Analysis

Let X_t be a (5×1) vector giving the stochastic processes followed by the real trade deficit (DEF_t), exchange rate depreciation (DS_t), controlled prices' inflation (DPC_t), money creation induced by the government budget deficit (DM_t), and inflation (DP_t):

$$X_t = \begin{bmatrix} DEF_t \\ DS_t \\ DPC_t \\ DM_t \\ DP_t \end{bmatrix}$$

The nth order vector autoregression for this process is:

$$X_t = A_0 + \sum_{i=1}^{n} A_i X_{t-i} + \mu_t, \tag{9.1}$$

where A_0 is a (5×1) vector of constants, A_1 through A_n are (5×5) matrices of least squares coefficients, and μ_t is a (5×1) vector of least squares disturbances. The latter are also termed innovations, in that they represent the part of X_t that cannot be predicted linearly from n lagged values of X. Equation 9.1 is the form actually estimated in this section, using monthly data for Israel from 1978:1 to 1985:5. To ensure stationarity and take seasonality into account, we have regressed at a first stage each one of the five dependent variables on a constant, time trend, and eleven seasonal dummies. The vari-

---

7. The complete data set is available upon request from the authors.

ables appearing in (9.1) are the residuals from these first-stage regressions. Due to data transformations, and our setting of $n = 6$, the sample period for the dependent variables is 1978:8–1985:5.[8] The estimated coefficients are difficult to interpret in the present framework, and thus are not reported here. (They are available from the authors upon request.)

Given the estimated parameters of the A matrices, it is possible to solve equation 9.1 for X_t in terms of the u process,

$$X_t = C_0 + \mu_t + C_1 \mu_{t-1} + C_1 u_{t-2} + \cdots + C_j \mu_{t-j}. \qquad (9.2)$$

This is the system's vector moving average representation. Since the μ process is composed of disturbances that may be contemporaneously correlated, it is useful to transform this process into one with contemporaneously orthogonal disturbances. This can be done by imposing a specific ordering of the variables, thus yielding the orthogonalized moving average representation— or impulse-response function

$$X_t = Q_0 + e_t + Q_1 e_{t-1} + Q_2 e_{t-2} + \cdots + Q_j e_{t-j}, \qquad (9.3)$$

where, by construction, the e process contains mutually orthogonal disturbances that are functions of the us. The coefficients of the impulse-response function in (9.3) represent dynamic multipliers, in that they display the current and subsequent responses of the system to shocks in the components of e. The specific variables' ordering used in this section, suggested by the hypothesis to be tested, is as in the list of components of X_t, that is, DEF_t enters first, DS_t second, and DP_t enters last.

Table 9.1 reports the correlation matrix of contemporaneous disturbances. Eight out of the ten reported cross-correlations are of a small order of magnitude. The remaining two cross-correlations are those between controlled prices' inflation and overall inflation, and between exchange-rate depreciation and inflation.

In order to analyze the dynamic effects of shocks we plot in figures 9.1 through 9.5, the responses, derived from the impulse function up to 24 months, to a one-standard-deviation shock in each one of the five variables considered. Each figure corresponds to a different shock occurring in month 1.

Consider first the effects of trade-deficit shocks depicted in figure 9.1. A worsening in the trade deficit is followed by an acceleration in exchange rate

---

8. We have tested systems with four and two lags on each variable against the present specification with six lags, and could not reject the latter at the 5 percent level.

Table 9.1
Correlation Matrix of Contemporaneous Disturbances

	DEF_t	DS_t	DPC_t	DM_t	DP_t
DEF_t	1.00				
DS_t	0.09	1.00			
DPC_t	0.11	0.47	1.00		
DM_t	0.15	0.33	0.03	1.00	
DP_t	0.10	0.60	0.84	0.11	1.00

Note: This table is based on the disturbances of the estimated vector autoregressions, for the period 1978:8–1985:5.

depreciation, in controlled prices' inflation, and in overall inflation. This shock is also followed by an increase in money creation which can be interpreted as reflecting monetary accommodation. The responses of both inflation and money creation reach their peaks by three months after the occurrence of the shock, and the response of exchange-rate depreciation reaches a peak by six months after the shock. Interestingly, the observed propagation mechanism of trade-deficit shocks conforms closely to the open-economy 'inertia approach' described above. However, in contrast to this approach all the responses to a trade-deficit shock are of a temporary nature and no long-term persistence or inertia is detected.

Figure 9.2 gives the dynamic responses to exchange rate depreciation shocks. An increase in exchange rate depreciation is followed by temporary increases in controlled-prices inflation, overall inflation, and money creation. These increases are strongest in the month in which the shock occurs. In terms of the implied effect on the real exchange rate, it can be seen that the increased nominal depreciation is partially offset by the increased inflation. Thus, a nominal depreciation shock induces a depreciation in the real exchange rate, but only temporarily and to a limited extent. This shock has negligible effects on the foreign trade deficit, which tends to decrease in most months after the shock.

Variables' responses to a shock in the inflation rate of controlled goods and services are depicted in figure 9.3. A shock increase in this inflation rate is shown to be followed by short-lived accelerations in exchange-rate depreciation and in overall inflation which are subsequently reversed. The shock is also followed by monetary contraction. These findings are consistent with the view that although increases in controlled prices are inflationary in the short run, they need not be so in medium or long runs—especially in view of the reduction in subsidies that they induce. Thus, typically these increases in controlled prices may lead to a fall in the budget deficit and in money creation

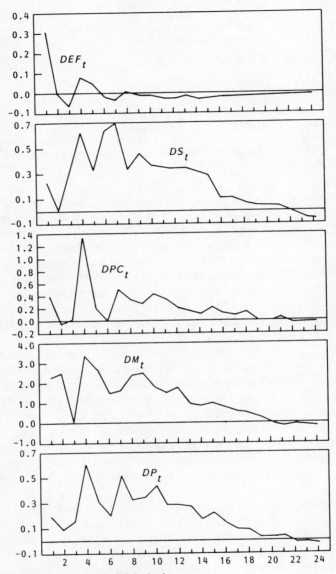

Figure 9.1   Responses to a trade-deficit shock.

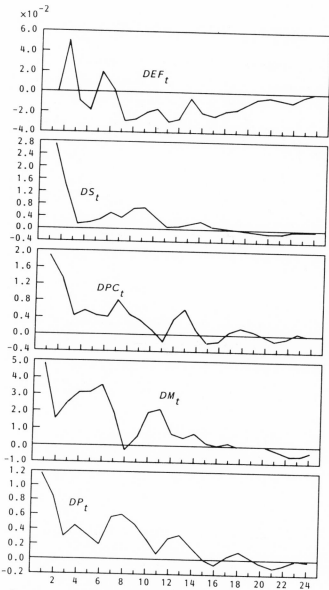

Figure 9.2   Responses to an exchange-rate depreciation shock.

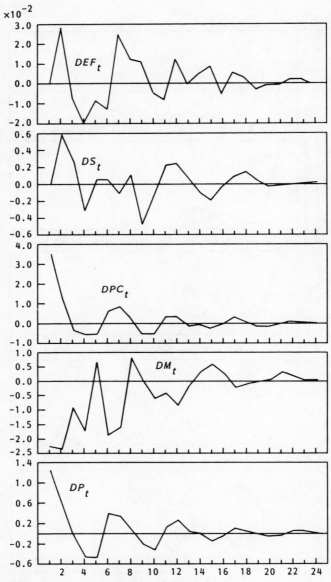

Figure 9.3   Responses to a controlled-prices' inflation shock.

that they induce. Shocks to inflation of controlled prices do not appear to generate long-term inflation inertia. Last, these shocks have only mixed and small effects on the foreign trade deficit.

Figure 9.4 gives the effects of monetary shocks. A shock increase in the monetary infusion induced by the government budget deficit is typically followed by accelerations in exchange-rate depreciation, controlled prices' inflation and overall inflation. Peak responses in these variables occur by three months after the shock. As above, these responses are only temporary. The monetary shock has a somewhat surprising effect on the trade deficit, which mostly moves in an opposite direction than that of the shock.

The dynamics of the system in response to an inflation-rate shock are depicted in figure 9.5. A shock increase in the inflation rate is accompanied by subsequent increases in foreign exchange depreciation. The response of DPC_t shows wide fluctuations. It first decreases and then increases; one possible explanation would be that in the short run the government is attempting to offset the inflationary shock by decreasing DPC_t. As expected, the shock is followed by an appreciation of the real exchange rate. However, its effects on the foreign trade deficit are mixed. Finally, monetary accommodation of this shock is observed in most months within the first year after the shock.

Having traced out the system's responses to innovations, there is still a question as to the relative importance of each type of the shocks in statistically accounting for its own behavior over time as well as that of the other variables. To assess this issue, we turn to the system's variance decompositions, which give the proportion in the forecast error variance of each variable that is accounted for by each one of shock's variances. The j-months ahead error in forecasting X_t linearly from its own past is given by

$$X_t - E_{t-j}X_t = e_t + Q_1 e_{t-1} + Q_2 e_{t-2} + \cdots + Q_{t-j} e_{t-j+1}, \quad (9.4)$$

where $E_{t-j}X_t$ is the linear least-squares forecast of X_t given X_{t-j}, X_{t-j-1}, etc.

Table 9.2 reports variance decompositions for $j = 24$ months. The figures reported in the table indicate that, under the present ordering of variables, trade deficit shocks are mostly autonomous, in that lagged own shocks account for more than 80 percent of own forecast error variance. A similar, yet somewhat weaker, finding holds for exchange-rate shocks and for monetary shocks, despite the accommodation uncovered in the above analysis of dynamic responses. On the other hand, most of the forecast error variance in inflation is accounted for by the variance of foreign exchange depreciation. Interestingly, monetary shocks account for a nonnegligible proportion of forecast error variance of exchange rate depreciation and of inflation. In all cases, the variance of foreign trade deficit shocks has no major role in accounting

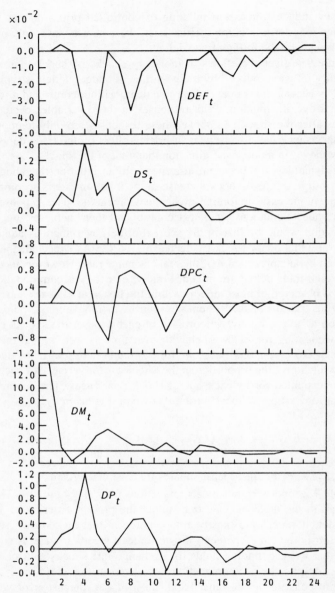

Figure 9.4   Responses to a monetary shock.

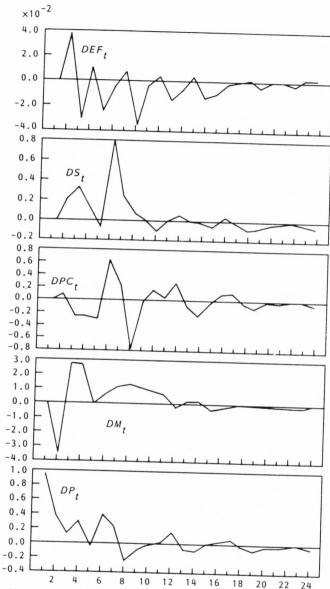

Figure 9.5   Responses to an inflation shock.

Table 9.2
Variance Decompositions of Forecast Errors

By Innovation in	Variables Explained				
	DEF_t	DS_t	DPC_t	DM_t	DP_t
DEF_t	82.54	13.08	8.90	14.21	13.34
DS_t	6.45	55.80	23.48	19.16	31.83
DPC_t	1.86	4.59	48.96	5.47	23.79
DM_t	5.60	21.83	14.27	53.37	18.48
DP_t	3.55	4.70	4.41	7.80	12.55

Note: Each entry gives the proportion of the 24 months ahead forecast error variance for each variable that is accounted for by shocks in itself and in the other variables.

for variances in the other variables considered, and in particular only 13 percent of forecast error variance in inflation is accounted for by these shocks.

III. Conclusions

Our main findings on the role of foreign trade shocks, as well as of other shocks, in the dynamics of inflation in Israel from 1978 to 1985 are as follows:

1. There is no evidence in support of the notion that some shocks give rise to long-term inflation persistence. This finding obviously questions the notion that the inflation rate is in a 'meta-stable' equilibrium.

2. Although some of the results tend to confirm the hypothesis that trade deficit shocks trigger inflationary responses, these shocks turn out to be statistically unimportant in accounting for the behavior of key nominal variables. For example, only 13 percent of the forecast error variance of inflation is accounted for by these shocks, despite the fact that the present orthogonalization procedure allows these shocks to enter first.

3. The results highlight the important role of innovations in exchange-rate depreciation in accounting for the behavior of inflation and of controlled-prices' inflation.

4. Monetary shocks have only a partial role in the propagation mechanism of inflation and some of the evidence is consistent with the existence of monetary accommodation.

Although these findings are informative, there are at least four reasons for suggesting caution in interpreting and applying them. First, the analysis assumes that during the sample period the coefficients characterizing the vector autoregression remained invariant. Unfortunately, the small number of observations available for the period under study prevented us from testing this assumption. Second, we analyze the responses of the variables only with respect to *random* disturbances. There obviously could be important real events affecting the dynamics of inflation in Israel that are not captured by the innovations in the vector autoregression. Third, as previous work (using U.S. data) indicates, the results could be sensitive to changes in the list of variables included in the analysis as well as to the measurement and definition of these variables. Fourth, as suggested by the Lucas critique, the findings of the present vector autoregression analysis may have limited use in determining the effects of changes in policy rules on the propagation mechanism of the inflation process.

Despite these caveats, we find it safe to conclude that key predictions and hypotheses of the "inertia approach" do not conform well with the information in time series for Israel between 1978 and 1985.

References

Black, Stanley W. 1983. The Use of Monetary Policy for Internal and External Balance in Ten Industrial Countries. In *Exchange Rates and International Macroeconomics,* ed. Jacob A. Frenkel. Chicago: University of Chicago Press, for NBER.

Bruno, Michael, and Stanley Fischer. 1986. Israel's Inflationary Process: Shocks and Accommodation. In *The Israeli Economy: Maturing through Crises,* ed. Yoram Ben-Porath. Cambridge: Harvard University Press.

Dornbusch, Rudiger. 1985. Stopping Hyperinflation: Lessons from the German Experience in the 1920's. Working Paper, M.I.T.

Dornbusch, Rudiger, and Stanley Fischer. 1986. Stopping Hyperinflations Past and Present. *Weltwirtschaftliches Archiv* 1, no. 122:1–46.

Dornbusch, Rudiger, and Mario H. Simonsen. 1987. Inflation Stabilization with Incomes Policy Support: A Review of Recent Experience in Argentina, Brazil, and Israel. New York: Group of Thirty.

Ellis, Howard S. 1934. *German Monetary Theory.* Cambridge: Harvard University Press.

Fischer, Stanley. 1984. The Economy of Israel. In *Monetary and Fiscal Policies and Their Application,* ed. Karl Brunner and Allan H. Meltzer. Carnegie-Rochester Conference Series on Public Policy, vol. 20. Amsterdam: North-Holland.

Litterman, Robert M., and Laurence M. Weiss. 1985. Money, Real Interest Rates, and Output: A Reinterpretation of Postwar U.S. Data. *Econometrica* 53 (January):129–55.

Liviatan, Nissan, and Sylvia Piterman. 1986. Accelerating Inflation and Balance-of-Payments Crises: Israel 1973–1984. In *The Israeli Economy: Maturing through Crises,* ed. Yoram Ben-Porath. Cambridge: Harvard University Press.

Sargent, Thomas J. 1986. *Rational Expectations and Inflation.* New York: Harper and Row.

Sims, Christopher A. 1980. Macroeconomics and Reality. *Econometrica* 48 (January):1–48.

Part III: Seigniorage, Money Demand, and Inflation

10

Overview

The chapters in this part deal with the relation between the rate of inflation, the demand for money, and government seigniorage. To a large extent, the research here was motivated by the observation that there was no strong link between government's revenue from money creation and the rate of inflation (see part I). In spite of the marked increase in the rate of inflation from the 1970s to the mid-1980s, the ratio of seigniorage to GNP was quite stable at about 2–3 percent per year. Are these observations compatible with the existence of a stable relation between the stock of real-money balances held by the public and the rate of inflation? Can these facts be explained within a framework of optimal intertemporal determination of the inflation tax by the authorities? These are the key questions addressed in this part.

The main motivation for the empirical research on the demand for money that appears in chapter 11 was the hypothesis that to a large extent the acceleration of inflation in the late 1970s was due to a one-time downward shift in the demand for real-money balances. Such a shift, it was claimed at that time, occurred in reaction to the financial and foreign-exchange liberalization implemented in November of 1977. This liberalization enlarged the menu of financial assets that the public could hold, such as bank accounts that were indexed to the level of the exchange rate between the domestic currency and key foreign currencies. Individual investors were attracted to these accounts mainly because the latter provided financial protection against surprise devaluations. The empirical work revealed quite plausible elasticities of money demand with respect to expected inflation, ranging from -0.41 to -0.12. Estimated income elasticities of money demand were above unity. Stability tests indicated that no significant structural change in money demand occurred at the time of the reform. However, a significant break in this function occurred about a year after the reform (i.e., October 1978). The main feature of this break was an increase in the absolute value of money demand's expected-inflation elasticity to about four times its previous value. The observed delay in money demand's change could possibly reflect the existence of a gradual process of learning by the public about the post-liberalization regime. Overall, the evidence indicated that part of the acceleration of inflation could be related to a one-time downward shift in money demand.

Next in chapter 12, I turned to an examination of the extent to which the observed stability of seigniorage over time could be accounted for in an optimizing intertemporal model of a representative consumer—a model that is commonly used in modern monetary theory. The econometric work consisted of estimating the main parameters based on the restrictions implied by the model on the relations between private consumption, real money holdings, inflation, and assets' returns. Several versions of the money in the utility function model turned out to capture well the comovements between these variables during the sample period (1970–1988, quarterly). The estimated parameters were then used in simulations concerning the time path of seigniorage and the welfare cost of inflation. The main findings indicated that while seigniorage rises with the rate of inflation, seigniorage revenue shows only negligible gains when the rate of inflation exceeds 10 percent per quarter. Moreover, seigniorage revenues in the 1980s were calculated to be quite close to the maximal revenues (about 3 percent of GNP) that could be obtained via sustained money creation. We also found that the simulated relation between the rate of inflation and seigniorage conforms more closely to the present optimizing model than to the Laffer-curve relation than arises from models based on a Cagan-type semilogarithmic demand for money. That is, the evidence is at variance with the notion that the rates of inflation in the first half of the 1980s had exceeded the revenue-maximizing rate, and that therefore the authorities could have actually increased revenue by generating a drop in the rate of inflation. Finally, being based on explicit utility maximization, the model allowed us to assess the welfare losses associated with different steady-state rates of inflation. The welfare cost of 10 percent inflation per year is calculated at 0.85 percent of GNP. This is more than double the corresponding figures estimated for the U.S. Moreover, the welfare cost of the high inflation that prevailed in 1980–84 reached the sizable figure of 4 percent of GNP. Thus, the existence of various inflation-indexation mechanisms and of various institutional adaptations to the inflationary process did not eliminate the room for sizable welfare costs of inflation in Israel.

While the foregoing analysis treated government's choice of inflation and of seigniorage as autonomous, the next issue in the research agenda was to develop and estimate a framework that endogenizes the policymaker's choice of these variables. This is done in chapter 13, which contains an empirical investigation based on an application of optimal intertemporal tax-smoothing principles to the inflation tax. An important feature of the model is that the demand for money is derived from first principles (as in the previous chapter) and thus there is an explicit link between its functional form and the social costs of inflation. The policymaker was assumed to attempt to maximize the welfare of the representative individual under full precommitment. The analytical results indicated that optimal intertemporal tax smoothing by the authorities does not necessarily imply that the rate of inflation follows a random walk, as suggested in most previous work. Instead, the model implied more complicated processes for the rate of inflation, which only under specific restrictive assumptions would become a random walk. When the model was implemented on quarterly data for Argentina, Brazil, and Israel, the results provided some supporting evidence in that the model's overidentifying restrictions were not rejected by the data for most of the specifications used. However, we found several data points at which inflation rates were systematically higher than what was predicted by the model. This finding motivated work on extensions of the basic model in order to take into account financial liberalization, state-contingent inflation commitments by the policymaker, and time inconsistency. Indeed, these three factors were shown to be potentially important for explaining the high-inflation observations. In sum, the data for the high- and volatile-inflation episodes in Argentina, Brazil, and Israel indicate that an extended version of an intertemporal optimal tax-smoothing model is a useful starting point for endogenizing policymakers' choices of the inflation tax and seigniorage.

11

New Estimates of the Demand for Money in Israel

In the last few years students of the Israeli economy have shown great interest in the monetary mechanism, an interest aroused by the acceleration of inflation; thus most attempts to explain the latter refer to the behavior of the money market, in particular to the substantial increase in liquidity since the 1977 foreign-currency reform and the substitution revealed by the decline in the demand for local currency and to the growth in the demand for resident deposits (which are denominated in foreign currency) and other money substitutes (see for example Fischer, 1981; and Michaely, 1981).

In order to analyze how these two trends affect the inflationary process, we need to know the empirical properties of the demand for money, since according to macroeconomic theory the response of the system is a function of, among other things, the parameters of money demand. In this context, the stability of the demand for money, the substitutability of money and other assets, and how fast the money market adjusts to shocks are issues of major interest.

In this study we present some new empirical findings. The period covered is 1973–81. Money is throughout narrowly defined as currency in circulation and demand deposits (M_1). We depart from previous work in using monthly data and we do so mainly for two reasons. First, it may reasonably be assumed that economic agents adjust quite rapidly, particularly in an inflationary economy, so that monthly data have a good chance of revealing systematic statistical relationships; second, the additional degrees of freedom allow us to run statistical tests of the stability of money demand, particularly in a comparison of the period before the 1977 reform and the surrounding events with the period that followed. Since the emphasis of our study is empirical, a large selection of alternative equations is provided. In this respect our approach is similar to Goldfeld's (1973; 1976) in his work on the United States.

Section 1 presents the basic estimating model, which includes a money-

Reprinted with permission from *Bank of Israel Economic Review* 60 (1988): 19–35.

demand equation and expectations-formation equations based on rational expectations.[1] Section 2 presents our principal econometric analysis, preceded by a brief preview of the annual data in more general terms. Section 3 compares our findings with those of previous studies, and section 4 concludes the paper.

1. The Model

As in most previous work, real balances are assumed to be an increasing function of income and a decreasing function of expected inflation.[2]

$$m_t^d = h_{0t} + h_1 y_t^e - h_2 \pi_t^e, \tag{11.1}$$

where m^d = log (quantity of real balances demanded)
$\quad\quad y^e$ = log (expected income)
$\quad\quad \pi^e$ = expected rate of inflation
$\quad\quad h_0$ = a deterministic element reflecting the effect of the constant and the time trend on the demand for money. It also captures, at least in part, any significant changes in financial technology; such changes did occur during the sample period and they presumably affected the demand for money.
$\quad\quad$ The h_i are coefficients and t indexes time.

A second assumption of the model is that real balances adjust gradually to the desired level through a partial adjustment mechanism of the form.

$$m_t - m_{t-1} = a(m_t^d - m_{t-1}) + \varepsilon_t, \tag{11.2}$$

where $0 \le a \le 1$ is the adjustment coefficient. Substituting (11.1) into (11.2), we get

$$m_t = ah_{0t} + ah_1 y_t^e - ah_2 \pi_t^e + (1 - a)m_{t-1} + \varepsilon_t. \tag{11.3}$$

This is the main equation estimated here. We also estimated equations containing additional explanatory variables, such as expected depreciation of the currency and the variance of unexpected inflation.

In order to estimate equation 11.3, we need an expectations-formation model. We have chosen a rational-expectations model in which the expecta-

1. Gottlieb and Piterman (1985) deal with expectation models for Israel of this and other types.
2. The hypothesis that there is a linear relationship between speed of adjustment and the rate of inflation failed to get empirical confirmation.

tion variables are identical with conditional optimum forecasts that take account of systematic relationships between the value of the variable in some period and its value in preceding periods.[3]

Specifically, it is here assumed that income and inflation are 12th-order autoregressive processes:

$$y_t = k_{0t} + \sum_{i=1}^{12} k_i y_{t-i} + u_{1t}, \qquad (11.1a)$$

$$\pi_t = b_{0t} + \sum_{i=1}^{12} b_i \pi_{t-i} + u_{2t}, \qquad (11.2a)$$

where the k_i, b_i are empirically determined.[4] Assuming that the residuals u_{1t}, u_{2t} are free of serial correlation, expected income and inflation can be estimated from values predicted by 11.1a − 11.2a as $y_t^e = y_t - u_{1t}$ and $\pi_t^e = \pi_t - u_{2t}$.

The basic model of this study consists of equations 11.1a–11.2a and 11.3. The estimation proceeds in two stages. Equations 11.1a–11.2a are first estimated as auxiliary equations in order to produce the expectations variables of the model; and equation 11.3 is then run. These equations contain deterministic terms of the form

$$h_{0t} = h_0 + h_{01}t + h_{02}t^2$$
$$k_{0t} = k_0 + k_{01}t + k_{02}t^2$$
$$b_{0t} = b_0 + b_{01}t + b_{02}t^2,$$

that is, they are quadratic functions of the time trend.

2. Empirical Results

Before going on to the econometric analysis of the model just described, we use the annual data for a general description of the behavior of real balances and inflation during the sample period. This analysis is not necessarily con-

3. This autoregressive expectations model is not pure rational expectations since it does not include all relevant information. But neither is it pure adaptive expectations since the coefficients are not predetermined. In effect we have here a combination of rational and adaptive expectations.

4. At an early stage of this study we ran a large number of regressions of greater generality than (11.1a)–(11.2a), and the empirical evidence supports the latter. For the effect of incorporating monetary variables in an inflation equation, see Brezis, Leiderman, and Melnick (1983). In the previous version of the present paper, the money-demand equation was also tested on the assumption of adaptive inflationary expectations. The results did not differ much from those of the rational-expectations assumption on which the study rests.

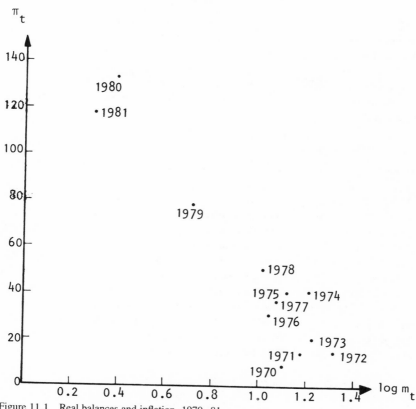

Figure 11.1   Real balances and inflation, 1970–81.

strained by specific assumptions, but despite its limitations it can add to our understanding of the relationship between real balances and inflation.

In figure 11.1 the log of real balances (M_1) is plotted against the average rise in prices for each of the years 1970–81. The expected negative relationship is not in evidence before 1977 because, among other things, the other factors involved (e.g. income) are not constant. From 1977 on, however, there is a clear negative association, reflecting the marked decline in real balances as the rate of inflation stepped up. We have quantified the relationship by calculating the elasticity of real balances w.r.t. inflation, the results being -0.20, -0.46, and -0.42 for 1977–78, 1978–79, and 1979–80, respectively.[5] As we shall see later, similar elasticities are obtained from monthly data, as well as in previous empirical work.

5. This is an oversimplified procedure which fails in going from 1980 to 1981, since it ignores the lag in the adjustment of expectations to actual inflation. In any case, our *ceteris paribus* assumption is not necessarily valid.

The diagram cannot suggest any structural change in money demand in the period following the 1977 reform. Such a change does however emerge from the monthly data of the model, to whose results we now turn.

The data are for 3/1972–12/1981.[6] Real balances are measured as M_1 (average monthly balance) deflated by the CPI. Inflation is represented by the rate of change of the CPI. The income variable, y, is proxied by the monthly index of industrial production.[7]

The Auxiliary Equations

Table 11.1 presents the results for the autoregressive equations used to construct the predicted values of the variables. The table shows equations (11.1a)–(11.2a) and an equation estimating expected depreciation of the currency. These equations should capture any systematic relationship between the current and lagged values of a variable and between the current values and the trend. For lack of space, we cannot go into detail here and comment only that the residuals of the y and π equations are free of serial correlation.[8] The residuals of the π equation are plotted in figure 11.2, which shows that the equation seriously biases expected inflation, chiefly at two points, November 1974 (when there was a sharp devaluation) and November 1977 (the reform), with unexpected inflation coming to 8.7 and 7.5 percentage points respectively. Apart from this and a few other instances, the inflation equation predicts actual inflation sufficiently well for our purposes.[9]

The Basic Money-Demand Equation

The principal money-demand equations estimated are presented in table 11.2. In equation (a), for the entire period, the coefficients of the main economic variables differ significantly from zero and have the expected sign. The predicted and actual values are compared in figure 11.3; the goodness of fit appears to be satisfactory. The parameter estimates, however, are suspect—the

6. Bank of Israel and Central Bureau of Statistics.
7. In the previous version of this paper we also tried to determine the effect of the interest rate on the demand for money. Unfortunately there is no monthly series of effective interest rates covering our entire period and we therefore used quoted rates. As Gottlieb and Piterman (1985) show for quarterly data, there is a fairly high correlation between interest and inflation, and we thus found no significant effect. It can therefore be assumed that the effect of expected inflation as estimated in our money-demand equation (1983) captures the effect of changes in the nominal interest rate.
8. We also found no evidence that the parameters of the equation were unstable over time.
9. We experimented with a dummy variable for two steep devaluations; we also tried subdividing the sample period; neither device improved the estimates. See also Gottlieb and Piterman (1985), who compare autoregressive inflationary-expectation functions with other expectation functions.

Table 11.1
The Auxiliary Equations
Inflation, Output, and Exchange-Rate Expectations *

	Dependent Variable		
Coefficient of	Rate of Inflation	Industrial Production	Rate of Change of Exchange Rate
Sample period	4/1973–12/1981	4/1973–12/1981	10/1978–12/1981
Constant	0.962	5.37	7.26
	0.7	3.8	2.0
Time, t	0.002	0.005	−0.564
	0.1	3.1	2.0
(time)^2, t^2	0.0001	−0.00001	0.006
	0.4	1.3	2.0
Lagged dependent variable			
1	0.33	0.21	0.72
	3.2	2.0	3.5
2	−0.16	−0.02	−0.67
	1.5	0.2	2.6
3	0.15	0.18	0.32
	1.4	1.7	1.1
4	−0.16	−0.08	−0.60
	1.4	0.8	2.1
5	2.00	−0.10	0.42
	1.8	0.9	1.3
6	−0.04	−0.05	−0.35
	0.3	0.4	1.1
7	−0.01	−0.07	0.08
	0.1	0.7	0.3
8	−0.11	−0.05	−0.19
	0.9	0.5	0.7
9	0.09	0.15	0.07
	0.7	1.4	0.2
10	−0.07	−0.20	0.07
	0.6	1.8	0.3
11	0.18	−0.03	−0.00
	1.5	0.3	0.0
12	0.19	−0.01	0.03
	1.7	0.4	0.5
R^2	0.479	0.761	0.698
DW	1.980	1.998	1.910
SE	2.296	0.064	1.740

*Small numerals are t values; R^2 is the coefficient of determination, DW is the Durbin-Watson statistic, and SE is the standard error of the equation.

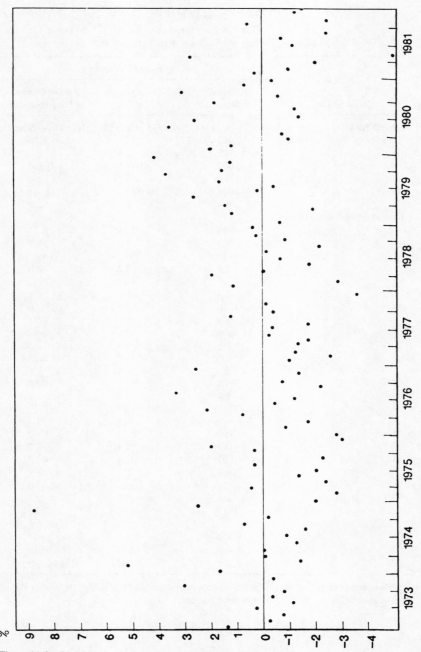

Figure 11.2   Residuals (u_{2t}) of regression (2A) with rate of inflation as dependent variable.

Table 11.2

Selected Estimates of the Basic Money Demand Equation[a]

(Equation 11.3)

Coefficient of	Entire Period 4/73–12/81 (a)	Subdivided at Oct. 1977 4/73–10/77 (b)	Subdivided at Oct. 1977 11/77–12/83 (c)	Subdivided at Sept. 1978 4/73–9/78 (d)	Subdivided at Sept. 1978 10/78–12/81 (e)	Dummy Variables[b] (f)
Constant	−0.86	0.42	−0.47	0.29	2.40	2.11
	1.2	0.3	0.4	0.3	1.0	0.8
Time, t	−0.002	−0.005	−0.008	−0.004	−0.031	−0.03
	2.5	2.4	1.5	2.8	1.7	1.5
$(\text{time})^2$, t^2	$0.2 \cdot 10^{-5}$	$0.4 \cdot 10^{-4}$	$0.3 \cdot 10^{-4}$	$0.3 \cdot 10^{-4}$	$0.1 \cdot 10^{-3}$	$0.1 \cdot 10^{-3}$
	0.3	1.9	1.1	2.0	1.6	1.3
m_{t-1}	0.905	0.839	0.852	0.834	0.708	−0.126
	26.5	10.5	14.6	11.5	6.8	1.0
y^e	0.357	0.234	0.434	0.266	0.366	0.100
	3.1	1.8	1.9	2.0	1.7	0.4
π^e	−1.286	−0.690	−1.652	−0.696	−1.947	−1.251
	4.7	2.0	3.7	2.2	4.1	2.2
R^2	0.9930	0.9498	0.9886	0.9498	0.9878	0.9942
h	0.736	1.975	−0.054	1.338	0.649	
DW	1.866	1.570	2.014	1.734	1.847	1.778
SE	0.0309	0.0269	0.0338	0.0288	0.0290	0.0289

[a]Durbin's h statistic tests for serial correlation when lags of the dependent variable appear as explanatory variables. The null hypothesis (no serial correlation) is rejected at the 5 percent and 1 percent levels by, respectively, $h > 1.96$ and $h > 2.58$. See also note a to table 11.1.

[b]This column gives the γ_i of the equation

$$m = \Sigma_{i=1}^{6}\, \beta_i X_i + \Sigma_{i=1}^{6}\, \gamma_i \delta_i X_i,$$

where $\delta_i = 0$ for $t \le 9/1978$, $\delta_i = 1$ otherwise. The β_i and their t values are as in (d).

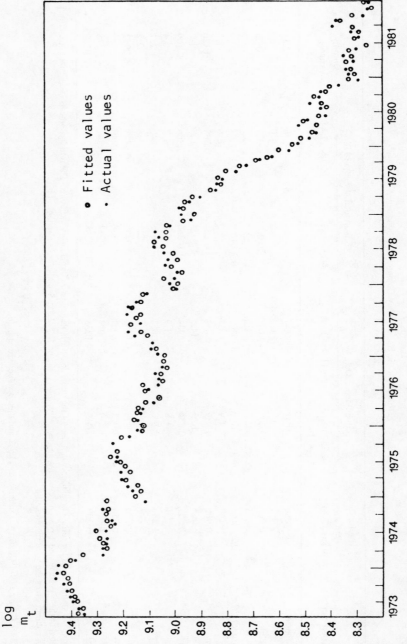

Figure 11.3   Money demand, entire period [(a) in table 11.2] (○ = fitted values; • = actual values).

Table 11.3
Long-Run Demand Elasticity of Money

	Elasticity with Respect to		Average Monthly Rate of Inflation,[b]
	y^e	π^e	%
4/1973–12/1981	3.76	−0.56	4.13
4/1973–9/1978	1.60	−0.12	2.91
10/1978–12/1981	1.25	−0.41	6.18

[a]Calculated from equations (a), (d)–(e) in table 11.2.
[b]Used for the calculation of the inflation elasticity.

adjustment coefficient for real balances is 0.095, or less than 10 percent per month, which implies an average adjustment lag of 9½ months and is equivalent to 26 percent per quarter. This is not particularly slow compared with rates found abroad, but we should have expected it to be much faster in an inflationary economy such as Israel's. The low value of the adjustment coefficient naturally affects the long-run demand elasticity of money (table 11.3). The elasticity w.r.t. y^e is 3.76, which is much higher than found in previous studies. Note also that the coefficient of time is negative, indicating a persistent decline in real balances well beyond the decline ascribable to the acceleration of inflation.

Let us now consider the stability of equation 11.3—specifically, to find out whether any structural change in the demand for money occurred in the period of high inflation. We first tested for a structural change at the time of the 1977 reform by running the equation for each of two subperiods, before and after the reform (respectively [b] and [c] in table 11.2). There is a marked increase in the absolute value of the coefficient of π^e in the later period; and there is no change in the coefficient of time. The Chow test yields $F_{(6,93)} = 1.5$, which is below the critical F value at the 5 percent level, so that stability cannot be rejected.[10] Testing another point of time gave different results. The behavior of real balances (figure 11.3) suggests that if there was a structural change it occurred in mid-1978 rather than at the time of the reform, because that is when inflation moved up to a new plateau. The Chow test shows structural change in money demand at October 1978. We therefore ran equations (d)–(e), with the sample period subdivided at this point. Their explanatory power is high and there is no evidence of serial correlation of the residuals. Several points emerge from a comparison of the two regressions.

10. The possibility that a structural change occurred in mid-1975 (when the crawling peg was introduced) was rejected by a preliminary test which gave $F = 0.8$, even further below the critical F value for 5 percent.

Table 11.4
Adjustment of Real Balances to Quantity Demanded

	Table 2 Equation	Average Lag[a]	Number of Months to Close Gap of[b]	
			50%	75%
4/1973–12/1981	(a)	9.5	6.9	13.8
4/1973–9/1978	(d)	5.0	3.8	7.6
10/1978–12/1981	(e)	2.4	2.0	4.0

[a]Calculated as $(1 - a)/a$, where a is the adjustment coefficient as defined in equation 11.2. See Melnick's (1988).
[b]The value of i satisfying $(1 - a)^i = (1 - x)$, where x is the proportion of the gap closed.

1. The coefficient of π^e is higher in the second period (in absolute value) by a factor of close to 3.

2. Splitting the period raises the adjustment coefficient from 0.095 for the entire period to 0.166 in the first subperiod and 0.292 in the second. This comes to, respectively, 26, 42, and 65 percent per quarter.

3. There is a small change in the coefficient of y^e and a large change in the coefficient of time; although neither is significantly different from zero, these differences seem to be in the right direction. The results show that the speed of adjustment (table 11.4) and the elasticity of money demand w.r.t. inflation are higher in the second period. As can be seen in table 11.3, the long-run inflation elasticity rises from 0.12 to 0.41;[11] the elasticity w.r.t. ye also declines somewhat.

Are these changes statistically significant? Before answering this question for the equation as a whole, let us look at the several coefficients. In equation (f), the regression is run for the entire period with the addition of dummy variables which take the value zero for the first subperiod and the original value for the second, so that the coefficients of (f) are the difference between the corresponding coefficients of (d) and (e). The change in the coefficients is fairly large, but the t values indicate that it is significantly different from zero only in the case of π^e. For the equation as a whole, a Chow test for the subperiods gives $F_{(6,93)} = 3.3$, which is above the critical value at the 1 percent level ($F = 3.0$). That is, the Chow test rejects stability of money demand.

Another way of testing for a possible structural change is to run a simula-

11. In the next section these results are compared with those of previous studies. In our semilogarithmic specification the demand elasticity of money w.r.t. n' rises with inflation. This is another reason for the higher elasticity of the second period (as well as the absolute rise in the coefficient).

tion designed to test how well the estimates for the first subperiod (equation (d)) fit the actual data. The results are shown in figure 11.4. In variant B, the m_{t-1} used to predict m_t is itself predicted by the equation—which puts a strain on the equation; variant A predicts m from actual values of m_{t-1}. The predicted exceeds the actual value in both cases—the pre–October 1978 equation overstates the real balances of the second subperiod. The error of prediction rises over time.

Statistical analysis of the simulations, using Theil's (1961) method, suggests that the main determinant of the variance of the error of prediction (contributing 80 percent of the explanation) is the bias. This is consistent with the occurrence of a structural change in the function.

Expected Devaluation and the Variance of Inflation

We now introduce additional explanatory variables into equation 11.3. One extension is to add expected depreciation of the currency (relative to the dol-

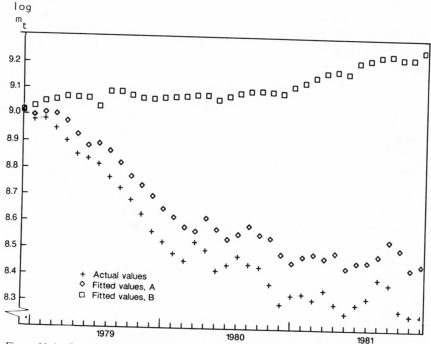

Figure 11.4 Quantity of money in second subperiod predicted by parameters estimated from first subperiod. Note: Fitted values A: m_t predicted from actual values of m_{t-1}; variant B: dynamic prediction with m_t predicted by values of m_{t-1} predicted by the equation (+ = actual values; $\Diamond$ = fitted values, A; $\square$ = fitted values, B).

lar); this represents the marginal alternative cost of holding money. For the period before the foreign-currency reform, we use the NATAD premium;[12] and for the period beginning October 1978, the estimation is by an autoregressive equation of order 12 analogous to equations 11.1a–11.2a (the third equation in table 11.1).

The effect of expected depreciations of the currency on money demand is negative in both subperiods (table 11.5, equations a, c),[13] but significant only in the first. However, when actual rather than expected currency depreciation is used for the second period, the coefficient is negative and significant (equation (b) in table 11.5). These results are in the expected direction, but a fairly strong correlation between expected inflation and expected depreciation of the currency makes it difficult to isolate the effect of the latter.

A second extension is to introduce the variance of unexpected inflation. This can be interpreted as a measure of the risk incurred by holders of real balances, so that under certain assumptions we should expect it to correlate negatively with the demand for real balances.[14] Equations (d)–(f) in table 11.5 are the ones that include this variable, estimated as the moving variance of u_{2t} (see equation 11.2a) over the current month and the five months preceding it. The results confirm that the variance has a negative effect on money demand, but it is significant only for the entire period and the first subperiod.[15]

3. Comparison with Earlier Work

It may be useful to compare our results with those of other empirical studies of Israel's money demand, even though such a comparison can be neither precise nor complete, since the studies differ in sample period, definition, and so forth. We shall focus on two aspects, the elasticities and the question of the stability of money demand after the reform.

Our long-run elasticity estimates were summarized in table 11.3. The elasticity w.r.t. y^e is greater than unity in both subperiods, a result we believe to be consistent with earlier findings (not necessarily based on monthly data): as can be seen in table 11.6, most of the earlier studies give elasticities of close to unity or a little higher. Our elasticity w.r.t. π^c is -0.12 in the first subpe-

---

12. NATAD (foreign securities dividend accounts) were resident foreign-currency deposits originating in receipts from dividends or sales of foreign securities and whose sole permitted use was the purchase of foreign securities. The premium arose from the sale of NATAD dollars at an exchange rate determined in the market. NATAD was superseded by the 1977 reform.

13. Zilberfarb (1983) found a significant negative demand elasticity of money w.r.t. the premium on the black-market dollar (his proxy for expected devaluation).

14. It would, however, appear that models which stress the transactions motive will, under certain assumptions, predict a positive relationship.

15. The entire variance (not just the unexpected component) was also tried, but the results were worse.

Table 11.5

Selected Estimates of the Extended Money Demand Equation[a]

	4/73–10/77 (a)	10/76–12/81 (b)	10/78–12/81 (c)	4/73–12/81 (d)	4/73–9/78 (e)	10/78–12/81 (f)
Constant	−0.35	2.15	2.54	−0.49	1.62	1.21
	0.3	0.9	0.8	0.7	1.6	0.5
Time, t	−0.003	−0.024	−0.032	−0.001	−0.004	−0.020
	1.6	1.3	1.5	1.8	2.8	1.0
$(\text{time})^2$, t^2	$0.2 \cdot 10^{-4}$	$0.1 \cdot 10^{-3}$	$0.1 \cdot 10^{-3}$	$-0.2 \cdot 10^{-5}$	$0.2 \cdot 10^{-4}$	$0.9 \cdot 10^{-4}$
	1.2	1.2	1.4	0.4	2.0	1.0
m_{t-1}	0.886	0.683	0.703	0.897	0.760	0.783
	11.4	6.4	5.6	27.8	11.6	6.2
y^e	0.294	0.397	0.368	0.299	0.143	0.358
	2.3	1.9	1.7	2.7	1.2	1.7
π^e	−0.755	−1.962	−1.938	−0.895	−0.220	−1.657
	2.3	4.2	3.9	3.2	0.7	3.1
Depreciation of sheqel:						
Actual	−0.001	−0.0045				
	2.5	1.8				
Expected			−0.014			
			0.1			
Unexpected variance of inflation:				−0.0134	−0.0172	−0.0098
				3.7	4.4	1.1
R^2	0.9556	0.9868	0.9855	0.9934	0.9584	0.9860
h	0.839	0.271	0.814	3.011	3.644	1.835
DW	1.816	1.935	1.838	1.445	1.241	1.642
SE	0.0256	0.0281	0.0295	0.0291	0.0252	0.0289

[a]See notes a to tables 11.1 and 11.2.

Table 11.6
Demand Elasticities of Narrow Money as Estimated by Previous Studies

				With Respect to			
	Sample Period Interval	Output	Inflation	Expected Inflation	Interest Rate	Lagged Dependent Variable	Premium on Black Market $
Mandell	1966–67 quarter			−0.01 to −0.11 0.008[a]			
Cukierman et al. (1976)[b]	1956–74 year	1.86[c]	−0.066				
Plessner (1976)	1965–74 quarter	0.95	−0.022 0.060[d]		0.001[e]		
Marom (1976)	1960–73 year	1.1[f]		−0.01 to −0.23	−0.16		
Zilberfarb (1979)	1966–75 quarter	1.05 to 1.16	−0.045 to −0.065		−0.51	0.60	
Zilberfarb (1982)	1968–77 quarter	0.84	−0.12		−0.24	0.72	−0.12
Melnick (1982)	1970–80 quarter	0.55	−0.89			0.89	

[a]With respect to expected inflation + interest rate.
[b]Calculated from the coefficients in the source.
[c]With respect to resources at disposal of economy.
[d]With respect to inflation lagged one quarter.
[e]With respect to capital gains on bonds.
[f]With respect to income.

riod and -0.41 in the second; a different, more general method (see note 5) yields almost the same result, which gives us grounds for hoping that it is a good approximation to the actual elasticity of recent years. Similar elasticities w.r.t. the interest rate or inflation or both are reported by Zilberfarb (1983), who uses quarterly data for 1968–77. These are below the 0.89 found by Melnick (1982) from quarterly data for 1970–81.

The stability of money demand since the 1977 reform has been little investigated. A principal conclusion of the present study is that it is very important to determine the date of any break. Previous studies have assumed that it occurred in November 1977 (see Melnick, 1982; and Leiderman and Marom, 1983); the empirical tests employed indicate unequivocally that no significant structural change occurred at that date. However, if one considers that there may have been learning and gradual adaptation, it makes sense to look for a later date, and we have in fact found evidence of a break in October 1978. The change is reflected chiefly in a significant rise in the expected-inflation elasticity of demand for money.

4. Concluding Remarks

Our main findings may be summarized as follows: First, there is no evidence of a change in the behavior of money demand at the time of the 1977 reform. Such a change did occur later, in October 1978, its main manifestation being a significant rise in the elasticity of money demand w.r.t. expected inflation and an increase in the speed of adjustment of real balances to the quantity demanded. Second, the monthly data reveal elasticities w.r.t. y^e and expected inflation which are significantly different from zero. As in previous work, the long-run elasticity w.r.t. y^e is slightly above unity; and in 1979–81, the elasticity w.r.t. expected inflation is -0.4. Third, in 1979–81 real balances adjust at a rate of 29 percent per month, so that the average adjustment lag is only two months.

This study has concentrated on M_1. Obviously, financial adjustments are in reality also made to holdings of other assets—bonds, shares, foreign-currency deposits, and so on. From the point of view of the monetary mechanism and its macroeconomic effects, it is important to determine empirically how a shock is absorbed through the adjustment of supply and demand for a variety of assets. Future work should therefore combine money-demand equations of the type used here with demand equations for other kinds of assets, and the simultaneous financial responses in the system should be analyzed. Such a framework should make it possible to reconsider the definition of money.

Our study has a bearing on the existence and magnitude of inflation tax. The empirical findings indicate that the expected-inflation elasticity of money demand was below unity during the sample period. Acceleration of inflation is therefore still likely to increase the inflation-tax revenue.[16] Our results indicate that the elasticity becomes unitary only at a monthly inflation of 15 percent—a finding that differs from those of several other studies.

References

Brezis, Elise A., Leonardo Leiderman, and Rafi Melnick. 1983. The Interaction between Inflation and Monetary Aggregates in Israel. *Bank of Israel Economic Review* 55 (November):48–60.

Cukierman, A., E. A. Pazner, and A. Razin. 1977. A Macroeconomic Model of the Israeli Economy, 1956–74. *Bank of Israel Economic Review* 44 (November): 29–64.

Fischer, Stanley. 1982. Monetary Policy in Israel. *Bank of Israel Economic Review* 53 (May):5–30.

Goldfeld, Stephen F. 1973. The Demand for Money Revisited. *Brookings Papers on Economic Activity* 3:577–638.

Leiderman, Leonardo, and Arie Marom. 1983. New Estimates of Money Demand in Israel. Research Department Discussion Paper no. 83.09. Jerusalem: Bank of Israel.

———. 1976. The Case of the Missing Money. *Brookings Papers on Economic Activity* 3:683–730.

Marom, Arie. 1977. The Demand for Money in Israel. *Bank of Israel Economic Review* 44 (November):100–133.

Melnick, Rafi. 1982. Two Aspects of Money Demand in Israel, 1970–81. Research Department memorandum (Hebrew).

———. 1988. Two Aspects of the Demand for Money in Israel, 1970–81. *Bank of Israel Economic Review* 60.

Melnick, Rafi, and Meir Sokoler. 1984. The Government's Revenue from Money Creation and the Inflationary Effects of a Decline in the Rate of Growth of G.N.P. *Journal of Monetary Economics* 13, no. 2 (March):225–36.

Michaely, Michael. 1981. Inflation and Money in Israel after the 1977 Reform. *Economic Quarterly* 28, no. 109 (July):115–36 (Hebrew).

Plessner, Yakir. 1976. The Demand for Money. In *Israel Economic Papers 1976,* ed. Nadav Halevi and Yaakov Kop, 214–22. Jerusalem: Israel Economic Association and Falk Institute.

Theil, Henri. 1961. *Economic Forecasts and Policy.* Amsterdam: North-Holland.

Zilberfarb, Ben-Zion. 1979. The Demand for Money in Israel, 1966–1973. *Economic Quarterly* 26, no. 101–2 (September):326–32.

———. 1983. Topics in the Demand for Money in Israel. *Bank of Israel Economic Review* 55 (November):61–76.

---

16. The revenue may, however, fall if inflation steps up, since the government's obligations are for the most part indexed while its assets are not. On this point see Melnick and Sokoler (1984).

12

Seigniorage and the Welfare Cost of Inflation: Evidence from an Intertemporal Model of Money and Consumption

1. Introduction

A common feature of many high-inflation episodes is the lack of a strong positive association between the size of the budget deficit, government seigniorage revenue, and the rate of inflation. Consider for example the case of Israel in the 1980s. In spite of the increase in the rate of inflation from about 130 percent in 1980 to about 400 percent in 1984, the government-deficit-to-GNP ratio showed a small increase, from 17 to 19 percent, and so did the seigniorage-to-GNP ratio, which increased only from 2.1 to 2.9 percent.[1] That this feature applies to the European hyperinflations of the 1920s was indicated by Sargent and Wallace (1973). With the exception of the last (extreme-inflation) observations, the data on seigniorage from these hyperinflations are generally without marked trends despite the rapid increase in inflation.[2]

These "stylized" facts have been used to question models that stress the role of seigniorage and of budget deficits in the inflationary process. Previous research has focused on two main explanations for these facts. First, models based on a Cagan-type semilogarithmic demand for money generally give rise to a Laffer curve and dual inflationary equilibria. These models imply that beyond a specific (revenue-maximizing) rate of inflation, seigniorage revenue decreases in response to increases in the rate of inflation (see e.g. Bruno and Fischer [1990]; and Sargent and Wallace [1987]). Thus, wide fluctuations in the rate of inflation need not be accompanied by noticeable movements in seigniorage revenue, and a given amount of seigniorage can be collected at

Reprinted with permission from *Journal of Monetary Economics* 29 (June 1992): 389–410.
1. See Meridor (1988: table 3).
2. For evidence of rather weak, and time-varying, statistical links between seigniorage, budget deficits, and inflation in low inflation industrial countries see King and Plosser (1985).

either a high or a low rate of inflation. The second main explanation stresses the role of time-varying expectations of shifts in fiscal policy. Although the rate of inflation and the budget deficit increase together over time in application of future monetization of the deficit, the anticipation of future increases in taxes gives rise to a negative correlation between inflation and the deficit.[3] Thus, changes over time in the public's expectations of how high budget deficits will be closed in the future (e.g., through increases in taxes against money creation) give rise to various possible statistical links between deficits, seigniorage, and inflation.

In this chapter we propose another explanation. We show that an empirically based parameterization of an optimizing model with money in the utility function is capable of accounting for the "stylized" facts embodied in time series for Israel, without resorting to an ad hoc semilog demand for money or to expectations of future regime change. The analysis and results below provide a characterization of money demand and of the behavior of seigniorage that differs from those derived from models that directly postulate a semilog demand for real-money balances. Moreover, we discuss the association between primitive parameters, such as the degree of risk aversion, and seigniorage revenue and report calculations of the welfare costs of different rates of inflation.

The first part of the chapter deals with estimation, on quarterly times series for Israel, of the parameters of a model that treats consumption and money-demand behavior as jointly arising from a single optimizing framework of a representative agent, as in modern monetary theory (see, e.g., Sidrauski [1967]).[4] To do so, we focus on the restrictions implied by the nonlinear Euler equations that characterize the first-order conditions of optimization by a representative consumer, as in Hansen and Singleton (1982) and Eichenbaum, Hansen, and Singleton (1988). Thus, our research is related to recent work that has tested some of the implications of intertemporal monetary models using time-series data (see, e.g., Singleton [1985]; Ogaki [1987]; Poterba and Rotemberg [1987]; Marshall [1988]; and Finn, Hoffman, and Schlagenhauf [1990]). While these investigations used data for the U.S., here we are particularly interested in exploring and testing the implications of an optimizing representative-consumer framework using data from an economy featuring wide fluctuations in inflation and in monetary aggregates such as Israel in the period 1970–88. It is challenging for intertemporal models to attempt to account for observed consumption and money-holdings behavior in this volatile

3. See Drazen and Helpman (1990); a very clear exposition of this result is provided by Blanchard and Fischer (1989:512–17). See also Bental and Eckstein (1990).
4. See also Sargent (1987: ch. 4); and Blanchard and Fischer (1989: ch. 4).

environment, one in which there were relatively large costs and benefits associated with agents' decisions about how and when to shift purchasing power from one period to another.

After obtaining estimates for the key parameters, the second and main part of our work consists of comparing steady states of the model assuming different rates of inflation to determine whether the implied relation between seigniorage revenue and the rate of inflation conforms with the "stylized" facts and with the implications of a standard semilog money-demand model. Using estimated and observable parameters, we find that seigniorage rises with the rate of inflation. However, although seigniorage revenue markedly increases when there is a shift from no inflation to an inflation rate of 10 percent per quarter, there are only negligible gains in seigniorage from increases in inflation beyond that rate. Our calculations indicate that seigniorage revenues in the 1980s were quite close to the maximal revenues (about 3 percent of GNP) that could be collected by the government. The simulated relation between seigniorage and the rate of inflation appears to more closely conform with the data than the Laffer curve that arises from a model based on a Cagan-type money demand.

In addition, we quantitatively assess the welfare losses associated with different steady state rates of inflation. We calculate the steady-state welfare cost of a moderate inflation of 10 percent per year at 0.85 percent of GNP, which is more than double most of the available estimates for the U.S.[5] The welfare cost of a rate of inflation of 168 percent per year, the average in Israel for the period 1980–84, reaches the sizable figure of 4 percent of GNP.

The paper is organized as follows. Section 2 deduces the restrictions that are imposed on the data by a model that includes money in the utility function, and discusses some steady-state implications of the model. Section 3 describes the estimation method, data, and results. Section 4 uses parameter estimates from the previous section along with observable parameters and with a set of auxiliary assumptions about a hypothetical steady state to determine the model's quantitative implications for the relation between seigniorage and the rate of inflation and for the welfare costs of inflation. Section 5 contains brief concluding remarks.

---

5. Fischer (1981) and Lucas (1981) calculated these costs for the United States at 0.3 and 0.45 percents of GNP respectively. McCallum (1989) estimates the welfare cost of 10 percent inflation in the United States at 0.28 percent of GNP. Cooley and Hansen's (1989) estimate is 0.39 percent of GNP. However, our estimate for Israel is lower than the estimates by Den Haan (1990) and Gillman (1991) for the United States. See Gillman (1990) for a comparison of alternative measures of this welfare cost.

2. The Model

The economy is populated by infinitely lived families, with population growing at rate n. Each household maximizes expected discounted utility

$$E_0 \sum_{t=0}^{\infty} \beta^t U(m_t, c_t^*), \tag{12.1}$$

where E_0 denotes expectations conditional on information available at time 0, β is a subjective discount factor, m denotes real money balances per capita,[6] c^* denotes consumption services per capital, and $U(\cdot)$ is a concave utility function that is increasing in both its arguments. Consumption services are assumed to be related to purchases according to the simple relation $c_t^* = c_t + \delta c_{t-1}$, where δ is a fixed parameter and c denotes actual purchases of consumer goods. Thus, consumption purchases at time t directly affect consumption services in both t and $t + 1$.[7] In spite of the time separability of utility defined over consumption services and real-money balances, the indirect utility function defined over consumption purchases and real-money balances is temporally nonseparable.

Each household's budget constraint, in per capita real units, is given by

$$b_t = b_{t-1}(1 + r_{t-1})(1 + n_t)^{-1} \tag{12.2}$$
$$+ m_{t-1}[(1 + n_t)(1 + \pi_t)]^{-1} + y_t - m_t - c_t,$$

where b_t, m_t, and c_t are respectively the real per capita values of one-period financial assets, money balances, and consumption chosen by the household for time t. n_t and π_t respectively denote population growth and the rate of inflation from $t - 1$ to t, and the real interest factor $(1 + r_{t-1})$ is equal to $(1 + R_{t-1})/(1 + \pi_t)$, where R_{t-1} denotes the nominal return on assets held from $t - 1$ to t. y_t is real per capita income from other sources.

Substituting the budget constraint and the specification about the relation between consumption services and purchases into (12.1), differentiating with respect to b_t and m_t, and rearranging yields the following first-order condi-

---

6. Although in the present paper we use a money in the utility function specification, we have also explored empirically, in previous work, a model with cash-in-advance constraints; see Eckstein and Leiderman (1988). On the functional equivalence of various specifications of the role of money, see Feenstra (1986).

7. See Singleton (1985); and Eichenbaum, Hansen, and Singleton (1988) for similar specifications.

tions for maximization of (12.1):

$$\beta E_t \left[\frac{U_2(t + 1)}{U_2(t)} \left[\frac{(1 + r_t)}{(1 + n_{t+1})} - \delta \right] \right]$$

$$+ \beta^2 \delta E_t \left[\frac{U_2(t + 2)}{U_2(t)} \frac{(1 + r_t)}{(1 + n_{t+1})} \right] - 1 = 0 \quad (12.3)$$

$$\frac{U_1(t)}{U_2(t)} + \beta E_t \left[\frac{U_2(t + 1)}{U_2(t)} \{[(1 + n_{t+1})(1 + \pi_{t+1})]^{-1} - \delta\} \right]$$

$$+ \beta^2 \delta E_t \left[\frac{U_2(t + 2)}{U_2(t)} [(1 + n_{t+1})(1 + \pi_{t+1})]^{-1} \right] - 1 = 0 \quad (12.4)$$

where $U_i(t + s)$ is the marginal utility with respect to the i'th argument ($i = 1, 2$) evaluated at time $t + s$ ($s = 0, 1, 2$).

Euler equation (12.3) is the standard condition for optimally allocating consumption between periods t and $t + 1$. It equates the marginal utility cost of giving up one unit of consumption in period t to the expected utility gain from shifting that unit to consumption in the next period. This equation, in alternative versions, has been the focus of numerous recent empirical studies of consumption (e.g. Hansen and Singleton [1982]). Equation (12.4) equates the expected utility costs and benefits of reducing current period consumption by one unit and allocating that unit to money holdings and then to consumption in the next period. From an empirical perspective, both these equations can be used to derive the model's restrictions on the comovements of consumption, money holdings, inflation and assets' return over time. Notice that in the special case in which the nominal return R_t is assumed to be known at the start of the period and $\delta = 0$, equations (12.3) and (12.4) can be combined to yield

$$\frac{U_1(t)}{U_2(t)} = \frac{R_t}{(1 + R_t)},$$

a nonstochastic relation between real-money balances, consumption, and the nominal interest rate. This equation can be viewed as a conventional demand for money in implicit form (see Lucas [1986]). In our framework, however, equations (12.3) and (12.4) cannot be combined to yield a nonstochastic relation.

In order to estimate the model and derive its implications for seigniorage and the welfare cost of inflation, we use the utility function

$$U(m_t, c_t^*) = \frac{[m_t^\gamma c_t^{*1-\gamma}]^\theta - 1}{\theta},\qquad(12.5)$$

where γ is a preference parameter between zero and one, and θ is a preference parameter that is less than one.[8] The parameter $1 - \theta$ represents both the coefficient of relative risk aversion and the inverse of the elasticity of intertemporal substitution. Accordingly, the marginal utilities appearing in equations (12.3) and (12.4) are expressed in terms of parameters and observables as follows:

$$U_1(t) = \gamma(m_t)^{\gamma\theta-1}(c_t + \delta c_{t-1})^{\theta(1-\gamma)},\qquad(12.6)$$

$$U_2(t) = (1 - \gamma)(m_t)^{\theta\gamma}(c_t + \delta c_{t-1})^{\theta(1-\gamma)-1}.\qquad(12.7)$$

When θ is equal to zero we attribute the marginal utilities in (12.6) and (12.7) to the log-utility specification $U(\cdot) = \gamma\log m_t + (1 - \gamma)\log c_t^*$.

Using these specifications, we next turn to the implications of the model for seigniorage revenue and the welfare cost of inflation—implications which are derived by comparing steady states of the model assuming different rates of inflation. We assume that per capita consumption and real-money balances grow in steady states at a constant rate $\phi > 0$, that population grows at a constant rate n, and that all real variables are invariant with respect to steady-state changes in the rate of inflation.[9] Accordingly, equation (12.4) can be rearranged to yield a steady-state "demand for money"

$$m = \frac{\left(\dfrac{\gamma}{1 - \gamma}\right)\left(1 + \dfrac{\delta}{(1 + \phi)}\right)c}{1 + \alpha_1 - \dfrac{\alpha_2}{(1 + \pi)}},\qquad(12.8)$$

where $\alpha_1 \equiv \beta\delta(1 + \phi)^{\theta-1}$, $\alpha_2 \equiv (1 + n)^{-1}(1 + \alpha_1)\beta(1 + \phi)^{\theta-1}$, and c and π denote the steady-state values of consumption per capita and rate of inflation. Being derived from an optimizing model, steady-state money demand is shown to depend on explicit preference parameters.

8. This function is analogous to the one used in different nonmonetary contexts by Kydland and Prescott (1982); and Eichenbaum, Hansen, and Singleton (1988).
9. We thus assume the same neutrality or invariance property as in Sidrauski (1967). See McCallum (1990) for a discussion of conditions under which this neutrality feature holds.

We compare below the seigniorage implications of the foregoing specification against those of a Cagan demand for money given by

$$m = c\zeta \exp\{-\omega[\pi/(1 + \pi)]\},$$

where ζ is a constant term and ω is a constant semi-elasticity of money demand with respect to $\pi/(1 + \pi)$.[10] This comparison is of interest because of the central role of this money-demand function in most previous research on seigniorage under high inflation.

Assuming that the parameters in equation (12.8) are invariant with respect to steady-state changes in the rate of inflation, we calculate from (12.8) the absolute value of the elasticity of money demand with respect to a steady-state change in the inflation rate as

$$\eta \equiv \left| \frac{\partial m}{\partial \pi} \frac{\pi}{m} \right| = \left[\left(1 + \pi\right)\left(1 + n\right) \right.$$
$$\left. \times \left(1 + \phi\right)^{1-\theta} \beta^{-1} - 1 \right]^{-1} \left(\frac{\pi}{1 + \pi}\right).$$

(12.9)

According to the model, the inflation elasticity of money demand depends on the underlying parameters and on the rate of inflation; the exact form of this dependence is explored below using values of estimated parameters. The elasticity of the semilogarithmic demand for money with respect to $\pi/(1 + \pi)$ is given by $\omega\pi/(1 + \pi)$, and the elasticity with respect to π is $\omega\pi/[(1 + \pi)^2]$.

In order to explore the present model's implications for seigniorage, notice that government's revenue from monetary base creation is given by

$$S_t = [(H_t - H_{t-1})/H_t][H_t/P_t],$$

where H is the monetary base. Seigniorage per capita, denoted by $\hat{S}$, can be written as

$$\hat{S}_t = \left(1 - \frac{H_{t-1}}{H_t}\right) h_t,$$

10. For a derivation of a Cagan-type demand for money from utility maximization see chapter 13 this vol. Notice that the inflation variable enters as $\pi/(1 + \pi)$ and not as π (as in many empirical studies).

where h denotes the monetary base in real per capita units. In the steady-state equilibrium considered here the gross rate of change of the monetary base (H_t/H_{t-1}) is equal to $(1 + n)(1 + \phi)(1 + \pi)$. Substituting for h, the derived demand for real monetary base from equation (12.8), and dividing by GNP per capita we get the following expression for the ratio of seigniorage to GNP in steady state (denoted by SR: seigniorage ratio):

$$SR = \left[1 - \frac{1}{(1 + n)(1 + \phi)(1 + \pi)} \right] \left[\frac{\left(\dfrac{\gamma}{1 - \gamma} \right)\left(1 + \dfrac{\delta}{1 + \phi} \right)\psi\kappa}{1 + \alpha_1 - \dfrac{\alpha_2}{(1 + \pi)}} \right],$$

$$\tag{12.10}$$

where ψ is the ratio of consumption to GNP and κ is the inverse of the money supply multiplier. When the inflation rate accelerates there are two conflicting forces operating on SR: the inflation-tax rate increases but at the same time there is a decrease in the tax base (i.e., in the demand for real balances). A sufficient condition for an increasing SR with respect to π is that $[1 - \beta(1 + \phi)^\theta] > 0$; a condition that is always met for configurations involving $\beta < 1$, $\phi \geq 0$, and $\theta \leq 0$.

For the Cagan specification of the demand for money, the steady-state ratio of seigniorage to GNP is computed by replacing the second set of squared brackets in the right hand side of (12.10) with the expression $\kappa\psi\zeta\exp\{-\omega[\pi/(1 + \pi)]\}$.

To calculate the welfare costs of various steady state levels of inflation we substitute equation (12.8) into (12.5) and compute the percentage decrease in consumption per capita that would generate the same welfare loss as that from moving from $\pi = 0$ to a given $\pi > 0$. This welfare loss, expressed as a percentage of GNP and denoted by *WL*, is given by

$$WL = \psi(\{[1 + \alpha_1 - \alpha_2(1 + \pi)^{-1}]/(1 + \alpha_1 - \alpha_2)\}^\gamma - 1). \tag{12.11}$$

Welfare cost calculations based on Cagan's demand for money generally measure the change in the area under the money-demand function due to a move from stable prices to a positive π.[11]

---

11. Den Haan (1990) shows that a welfare measure based on an expression such as equation (12.11) leads to very similar answers as the measure that calculates the area under the steady-state money-demand function of the structural model.

3. Estimation

From equations (12.3) and (12.4), we define the disturbances of the model as

$$d_{1t+2}(\sigma) = \beta \left\{ \frac{U_2(t+1)}{U_2(t)} \left[\frac{(1+r_t)}{(1+n_{t+1})} - \delta \right] \right\}$$
$$+ \beta^2 \delta \left[\frac{U_2(t+2)}{U_2(t)} \frac{(1+r_t)}{(1+n_{t+1})} \right] - 1 \quad (12.12)$$

$$d_{2t+2}(\sigma) = \frac{U_1(t)}{U_2(t)} + \beta \left(\frac{U_2(t+1)}{U_2(t)} \{ [(1+n_{t+1})(1+\pi_{t+1})]^{-1} - \delta \} \right)$$

$$+ \beta^2 \delta \left(\frac{U_2(t+2)}{U_2(t)} [(1+n_{t+1})(1+\pi_{t+1})]^{-1} \right) - 1. \quad (12.13)$$

Substituting into these equations our parameterization of marginal utilities (i.e., equations (12.6) and (12.7)) delivers the two-equation system to be estimated, whose parameter vector is $\sigma = (\beta, \gamma, \theta, \delta)$. Notice that the Euler equations (12.3) and (12.4) imply the orthogonality conditions $E[d_{it+2}(\sigma_0) \cdot z_{jt}] = 0$, for $i = 1, 2$, where z_{jt} is any variable that belongs to the information set at time t, and σ_0 is the true value of the parameter vector σ.

Based on these orthogonality conditions, we estimate the parameter vector by applying Hansen's (1982) Generalized Method of Moments (GMM) to quarterly data for Israel covering the period 1970:I to 1988:III. We impose the constraints that the weighting matrix is positive definite and that the disturbances follow a first-order moving average process (due to the presence of a two-period-ahead forecast error in the Euler equations).[12]

The aggregate time series used are as follows. Consumption is measured by total private consumption spending from the National Accounts. We also used a measure for purchases of nondurables and services as an alternative for the total measure. Money is defined as the standard M_1 or alternatively as the monetary base. All nominal variables are deflated by the relevant consumption deflators, and per-capita measures are obtained by dividing aggregates by the existing population. The nominal interest rate is the quarterly lending rate charged by banks; results for the average nominal return on indexed government bonds are discussed in note 15. The infla-

---

12. In estimating the weighting matrix, we apply the modified Durbin procedure developed by Eichenbaum, Hansen, and Singleton (1988: Appendix B). We thank Masao Ogaki for providing us the GMM program which we used along with Gauss v. 1.49.

Table 12.1

Estimates of the Model under Alternative Sets of Instruments. Israel, 1970:I–1988:III

Parameters	System 1				System 2			
	CM	CNM	CB	CNB	CM	CNM	CB	CNB
β	0.995	0.976	1.019	1.011	0.998	0.968	0.944	0.973
	(0.025)	(0.025)	(0.012)	(0.009)	(0.008)	(0.005)	(0.086)	(0.009)
γ	0.055	0.050	0.042	0.042	0.054	0.052	0.049	0.048
	(0.003)	(0.002)	(0.001)	(0.001)	(0.001)	(0.001)	(0.002)	(0.001)
θ	−5.631	−5.383	−2.336	−1.001	−1.529	0.241	1.034	−0.866
	(1.262)	(2.117)	(0.624)	(0.698)	(0.417)	(0.141)	(0.452)	(0.181)
δ	0.285	0.374	0.499	0.574	−0.006	−0.311	−0.753	−0.038
	(0.088)	(0.122)	(0.230)	(0.397)	(0.087)	(0.054)	(0.030)	(0.060)
J_T	4.844	15.022	5.072	10.460	22.251	4.547	30.279	4.653
	(0.304)	(0.005)	(0.280)	(0.033)	(0.014)	(0.919)	(0.001)	(0.913)
$\rho(d1, d2)$	0.783	0.746	0.346	0.176	0.590	0.611	0.918	0.516

Note: The data definitions are as follows. *CM*: aggregate consumption and M_1 per capita; *CNM*: aggregate consumption of nondurables and M_1 per capita; *CB*: aggregate consumption and monetary base per capita; *CNB*: aggregate consumption of nondurables and monetary base per capita. J_T is the value of the criterion quadratic function. Standard errors of estimates and probability values of J_T appear in parentheses. $\rho(d1, d2)$ is the correlation between the estimated residuals, defined as in equations (12.12) and (12.13) in the text.

System 1 corresponds to the $z1$ instrument set discussed in the text and System 2 to the $z2$ set of instruments.

tion rate is measured by the percentage change in the relevant consumer price deflator.[13]

In estimating the model, we first used the following vector of instrumental variables: $z1'_t = [1, c_t/c_{t-1}, m_t/m_{t-1}, (1 + r_{t-1})/(1 + n_t)]$. With these four instruments and two equations, there are eight orthogonality conditions. Since there are four parameters to be estimated, there are four overidentifying restrictions. In addition, we explored the impact of allowing an additional lag of our instruments by using the vector $z2'_t = [z1'_t, z1'_{t-1}]$.

Results are displayed in table 12.1. For each vector of instruments, we report four sets of estimates corresponding to two alternative definitions of consumption (total and nondurables plus services) and two alternative definitions of money (M_1 and the monetary base). In each case we report the minimal value of the objective function J_T which, as shown by Hansen (1982), is a chi-square test statistic for the validity of the model's overidentifying restrictions.[14]

The parameter estimates for β and γ are economically meaningful and are quite similar, and large relative to their estimated standard errors, across the different systems that were estimated. Most estimated values of β are below unity and most estimates of γ are around 0.05. It turns out that the estimates for θ and δ do vary across the eight systems that were estimated. Although some such variation arises from the alternative time series used for consumption and money, the main differences are due to the choice of instruments. Most of the estimated values for θ are negative and range from a low of -5.6 to a high of 1.03. The former points to a high relative risk aversion coefficient and to a low intertemporal elasticity of substitution; the latter implies nonconcave utility. While the estimated values of δ under the z_1 instrument vector are positive and range from 0.29 to 0.57, the parameter estimates under the $z2$ instrument vector are negative.

The J_T statistics for the model estimated with total consumption are small relative to the degrees of freedom for the $z1$ instrument vector, but large relative to the degrees of freedom for the $z2$ instrument vector. An opposite

13. The quarterly lending rate is the interest rate most widely used in Israel as an indicator of conditions in the money market and of the stance of monetary policy. Other interest rates have typically moved together with movements in this rate. The data source for the consumption quantity and price variables is the National Accounts publication by the Israeli Bureau of Statistics. The data on monetary aggregates and asset returns are from the data bank of the Bank of Israel.

14. Time trend regressions (with correction for first-order serial correlation) for the instrumental variables and the variables entering the Euler equations generally indicate lack of significant trends. This provides some indication of sample stationarity of these variables. The only exception is the $(1 + r_{t-1})/(1 + n_t)$ variable which has a trend coefficient of 0.0011 with a standard error of 0.00036.

pattern holds for estimates obtained under the nondurables-plus-services definition of consumption. In the case of four out of the eight estimated systems the J_T statistics indicate that the model's overidentifying restrictions are not rejected by the sample information at standard significance levels.[15] Overall, the extent to which the model's overidentifying restrictions are (or are not) rejected by the data depends on the definition of consumption and the choice of instruments. Hence, it is difficult to reach unambiguous conclusions regarding the empirical validity of the restrictions implied by the various specifications of the model implemented on the present sample.

4. Implications for Seigniorage and the Welfare Cost of Inflation

Based on the parameter estimates obtained in the previous section, we now explore the extent to which the model accounts for the observed stability of annual seigniorage in spite of large fluctuations in the annual rate of inflation. Then, we quantitatively assess the welfare cost of inflation. We do this by comparing, under the model's parameters, alternative hypothetical steady states under different rates of inflation.[16]

For our calculations of seigniorage and welfare cost of inflation we use the following parameter values:

$$\beta = 0.987 \mid \gamma = 0.05 \mid \psi = 0.61 \mid n = 0.0058 \mid \phi = 0.008,$$

where the parameter values for ω and γ are chosen from the estimates of the previous section and those for ψ, n, and ϕ correspond to the quarterly sample means of the share of consumption in GNP, the rate of change of population, and the rate of change of consumption per capita, respectively. Since the econometric results indicate that the estimated risk-aversion parameter θ is sensitive to the choice of instruments and data we experimented with three

15. The tables in the appendix provide evidence on the robustness of the results in relation to the asset return that is used in estimating the model: the interest rate used in table 12.1 against the return on government indexed bonds. Since we had data on the latter only up until 1986:IV, we reestimated System 1 of table 12.1 for this sample and compared the results with those with the alternative asset return. It turns out that the estimates of β and γ are quite insensitive to the asset return. Yet for θ and δ we obtain somewhat lower estimates (in absolute value) when the return on government indexed bonds is used. This return also results in lower J_T statistics thus providing more supporting evidence for the overidentifying restrictions of the model than when the interest rate of table 12.1 is used. All in all, we conclude that the results are not markedly sensitive to the choice of the asset return (among the two alternatives considered).

16. Clearly, there are limitations to comparisons restricted only to steady states. In many models the amount of seigniorage revenue that can be collected out of steady state markedly differs from that of a steady state. In future work, we plan to explore the implications of our framework for the dynamics of seigniorage out of steady state.

main values: -5.6, -1.5, and 0.0 (the latter corresponds to the case of log-utility). Similarly, our main calculations used $\delta = 0.3$, but we also checked the sensitivity of the results by using the alternative values $\delta = -0.3$, and $\delta = -0.7$.

Tables 12.2 and 12.3 report the results for seigniorage as a percentage of GNP, for the inflation rate elasticity of money demand, and for the welfare cost of inflation. Figure 12.1 depicts the implied seigniorage ratio for various rates of inflation and under three alternative values of the risk-aversion parameter θ. There are four main features of these seigniorage calculations.

First, as evident from tables 12.2 and 12.3, the ratio of seigniorage to GNP is an increasing function of the rate of inflation. That is, government can raise more revenue by increasing monetary base growth and inflation. This finding does not support the notion that inflation rates in Israel in the mid-eighties exceeded the revenue-maximizing rate.

Second, although the gains to government from increasing inflation from 0 to 10 percent per quarter are of about 1.5–2.0 percents of GNP, the gains from further increasing inflation are of a small order of magnitude. For example, shifting from a quarterly rate of inflation of 10 percent to 70 percent generally results in an increase in revenue of only 1 percent of GNP. As shown in figure 12.1, for low rate of inflation SR markedly increases with increases in π, but then SR rapidly reaches an asymptote. It is this flatness of SR with respect to π that accounts in our model for the observed stability of the seigniorage-to-GNP ratio despite wide fluctuations in the rate of inflation. The calculated values for SR under mild and high inflation correspond well with the actual figures, generally between 2 and 3 percent of GNP, observed in Israel in the first half of the eighties.

Third, the results for the seigniorage ratio are not very sensitive to the values chosen for the θ and δ parameters—namely, those parameters which were not precisely estimated in the econometric work. Thus, the calculated values of SR under a quarterly rate of inflation of 28 percent (as between 1980 to 1984 on average) reported in tables 12.2 and 12.3 range from a low of 2.4 percent of GNP to a high of about 3.0 percent. Notice that the higher the degree of relative risk aversion, the lower is the ratio of seigniorage to GNP (see figure 12.1), and the lower is the elasticity of money demand with respect to steady-state changes in the rate of inflation. Growth is clearly important for these effects; if there was no growth then the elasticity of money demand with respect to steady-state inflation would not be sensitive to a change in θ. Also, other things equal, lower values of δ result in lower values of SR.

Fourth, the model's implications for the relation between seigniorage and inflation markedly differ from those based on a Cagan semilog demand for money. Figure 12.2 plots, for the period from 1980 to 1986, the actual data

Table 12.2
Seigniorage Ratio, Money-Demand Elasticity, and Welfare Cost of Inflation

π (quarterly)	θ = −5.6			θ = −1.5			θ = 0.0		
	SR	η	WL	SR	η	WL	SR	η	WL
0.00	0.0064	0.00	0.0000	0.0116	0.00	0.0000	0.0166	0.00	0.0000
0.0123	0.0104	0.14	0.0046	0.0116	0.23	0.0082	0.0216	0.31	0.0113
0.0241	0.0132	0.24	0.0085	0.0196	0.36	0.0144	0.0240	0.45	0.0193
0.05	0.0174	0.37	0.0153	0.0233	0.52	0.0246	0.0268	0.61	0.0317
0.10	0.0219	0.50	0.0250	0.0266	0.63	0.0375	0.0289	0.70	0.0467
0.15	0.0243	0.56	0.0318	0.0281	0.67	0.0461	0.0299	0.72	0.0560
0.20	0.0258	0.58	0.0370	0.0290	0.67	0.0525	0.0304	0.72	0.0630
0.28	0.0274	0.58	0.0434	0.0298	0.66	0.0600	0.0309	0.70	0.0710
0.32	0.0279	0.58	0.0459	0.0301	0.65	0.0630	0.0310	0.68	0.0741
0.50	0.0294	0.55	0.0543	0.0308	0.60	0.0724	0.0314	0.62	0.0841
0.70	0.0302	0.50	0.0602	0.0312	0.54	0.0789	0.0316	0.55	0.0910
9E + 090	0.0325	0.00	0.1431	0.0323	0.00	0.1083	0.0322	0.00	0.1215

Note: SR denotes seigniorage as a percentage of *GNP*, η denotes the elasticity of money demand with respect to inflation, and *WL* is the welfare cost of inflation as a percentage of *GNP*. See text for further explanations.

The figures in this table were calculated under the following parameter values: $\beta = 0.987$; $\delta = 0.3$; $\gamma = 0.05$.

Table 12.3

Seigniorage Ratio, Money-Demand Elasticity, and Welfare Cost of Inflation: Additional Results

π (quarterly)	$\delta = -0.3$			$\delta = -0.7$			
	SR	η	WL	SR	η	WL	WLC
0.00	0.0062	0.00	0.0000	0.0056	0.00	0.0000	0.0000
0.0123	0.0100	0.14	0.0046	0.0091	0.14	0.0046	0.0013
0.0241	0.0127	0.24	0.0085	0.0116	0.24	0.0085	0.0022
0.05	0.0168	0.37	0.0153	0.0152	0.37	0.0153	0.0031
0.10	0.0211	0.50	0.0250	0.0192	0.50	0.0250	0.0106
0.15	0.0234	0.56	0.0318	0.0213	0.56	0.0320	0.0204
0.20	0.0249	0.58	0.0370	0.0226	0.58	0.0370	0.0310
0.28	0.0264	0.58	0.0434	0.0240	0.58	0.0434	0.0512
0.32	0.0269	0.58	0.0459	0.0244	0.58	0.0459	0.0519
0.50	0.0283	0.55	0.0543	0.0257	0.55	0.0543	0.0837
0.70	0.0291	0.50	0.0602	0.0264	0.50	0.0602	0.1021
9E + 090	0.0314	0.00	0.1430	0.0285	0.00	0.0873	0.1251

Note: See note to table 12.2. Here we set $\beta = 0.987$; $\theta = -5.6$; and $\gamma = 0.05$.

WLC is the welfare cost calculated from a Cagan-type money demand with an inflation rate semi-elasticity of -5.0.

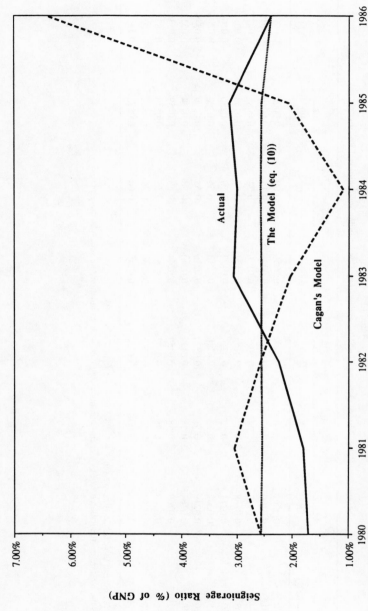

Figure 12.1   Seigniorage as a percentage of GNP under various rates of inflation and degrees of risk aversion. The plots depict the implications of the model for the seigniorage ratio (see eq. 12.10) for various rates of inflation and under three alternative values of the risk-aversion parameter θ. Other parameters are set at the values used in sect. 4 of the chapter.

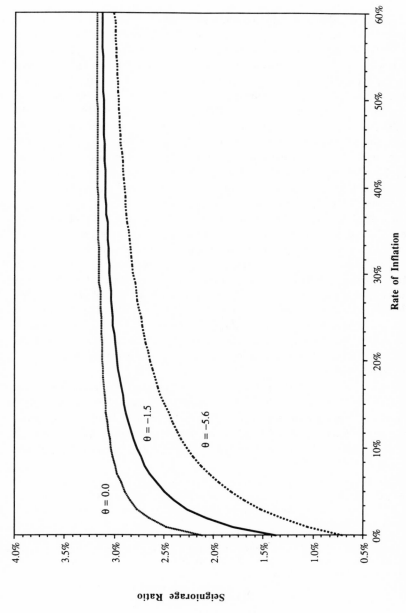

Figure 12.2   Actual and simulated values of seigniorage ratio. The figure plots the actual data on the ratio of seigniorage to GNP in Israel from 1980 to 1986 along with the seigniorage ratios predicted by the present model (i.e., eq. 12.10) and a Cagan-type model.

on seigniorage[17] along with the predictions of *SR* based on our model and a Cagan-type model. For the latter, we used a semi-elasticity of money demand of -5.0 which conforms well with estimates from previous empirical work on money demand in Israel and we normalized the constant term so as to give rise to the same *SR* for 1980 as our model's.[18] The simulation for *SR* under a semilog demand for money indicates that the ratio of seigniorage to GNP should have decreased from 1981 to 1984, as inflation accelerated, and should have sharply increased thereafter. In contrast, the actual figures for *SR* (plotted with solid lines in figure 12.2) indicate that it slightly increased from the early to mid-eighties and then decreased along with disinflation. In a broad sense, the relatively flat relation between *SR* and inflation that arises from the parameterization of our model (see figure 12.2) matches the actual data more closely than the semilog money-demand alternative.[19]

Tables 12.2 and 12.3 also report values of the inflation-rate elasticity of money demand that are implied by the various configurations of the underlying parameters. Notice that this elasticity first increases with the rate of inflation, reaches a maximum, and then decreases with further increases in inflation. For high inflation rates such as in the mid-eighties, the calculated elasticity is of about -0.6, which conforms quite well with available empirical findings.[20] By virtue of the underlying microfoundations of the present model, it is possible to relate the inflation-rate elasticity of money demand to a primitive parameter such as the degree of risk aversion. We find that the higher the degree of risk aversion, the lower is the inflation elasticity of money demand.

In order to provide some measure of the precision of the foregoing calculations for the seigniorage ratio and for the inflation-rate elasticity of money demand, we computed simulated standard errors for these variables assuming randomly generated values of θ and δ—namely, the two parameters that were quite imprecisely estimated in table 12.1. The simulated standard errors are

17. Since the discussion focuses on steady states, we express the figures on seigniorage as a five-year moving average of the actual data reported by Meridor (1988: table 3). That is, seigniorage at time t is the average of values from $t - 1$ to $t + 2$. This amounts to a smoothing of the seigniorage series.

18. Bruno (1986) also used in several of his calculations for seigniorage money demand semi-elasticities of about -5.0. We have checked this number by estimating, with our data, a Cagan demand for money in Israel for the period 1970:III to 1988:III. The estimated semi-elasticity is -5.04, with estimated standard error of 0.959.

19. As indicated in section 1, flatness of the seigniorage ratio with respect to changes in the rate of inflation is not unique to the case of Israel.

20. This value is quite close to the -0.5 elasticity of inventory (or transactions) models of the demand for money. In their study on money demand in Israel, Leiderman and Marom (1985) report a long-run inflation-rate elasticity of money demand of -0.41 for the period October 1978 to December 1981, using a semilog Cagan-type specification of money demand.

Table 12.4
Simulated Standard Errors for SR and η

π (quarterly)	S.E. for SR	S.E. for η
0.00	0.00062	0.0000
0.0123	0.00083	0.0148
0.0241	0.00091	0.0220
0.05	0.00092	0.0276
0.10	0.00080	0.0272
0.15	0.00067	0.0242
0.20	0.00057	0.0213
0.28	0.00046	0.0177
0.32	0.00041	0.0163
0.50	0.00029	0.0119
0.70	0.00021	0.0091
$9E + 090$	0.00011	0.0000

Note: Standard errors calculated through Monte Carlo simulations, using a normal distribution with means of $\theta = -5.6$ and $\delta = 0.3$ and standard errors of 1.262 and 0.1 respectively (see table 12.1) and 500 randomly generated observations.

given in table 12.4. We calculated them by using Monte Carlo methods to generate values for these two parameters using a normal distribution with means of $\theta = -5.6$ and $\delta = 0.3$ and standard errors of 1.262 and 0.1, respectively, (see table 12.2) and 500 randomly generated observations. Other parameter values are set as in tables 12.2 and 12.3. The simulated standard errors for the seigniorage ratio are quite low, and are generally no more than 10 percent of the value of *SR*. A similar finding holds for simulated standard errors of the inflation elasticity of money demand.

For each set of parameters the third column of tables 12.2 and 12.3 reports the welfare costs, as percents of GNP, associated with increasing inflation from zero to a positive rate. We use equation (12.11) to compute the decrease in per capita consumption (expressed as percent of GNP) that would generate the same welfare loss as that from increasing inflation from zero to a given rate in the tables. Notice that the welfare cost of inflation depends on the degree of risk aversion. Other things equal, the higher the degree of risk aversion, the lower is the welfare cost of inflation. From table 12.2 we see that a shift from zero inflation to an annual rate of inflation of 10 percent (i.e., 2.41 percent per quarter) results in a loss in utility equivalent to about 1 percent of GNP. This is more than double some of the estimates for the United States, such as the 0.28 percent of GNP estimate of McCallum (1989), the 0.3 and 0.45 percents of GNP figures reported by Fischer (1981) and Lucas (1981) respectively, and the 0.39 percent of GNP figure computed by Cooley and Hansen (1989).[21] The welfare cost of a rate of inflation of 168 percent per year (i.e., 28 percent per quarter), the average in Israel for the high-inflation period of 1980–84, reaches the sizable figure of about 5 percent of GNP.[22] The last column in table 12.3 indicates that a similar figure is obtained if the welfare cost is calculated from the area under a Cagan-type money demand such as the one used in figure 12.2. Notice, however, that for lower rates of inflation the welfare costs implied by the present structural model are higher than those implied by a Cagan-type model.

5. Concluding Remarks

In this paper, we found that the steady-state quantitative implications of a simple dynamic model of money in the utility function are generally compatible with the observed stability of seigniorage in Israel. That is, while inflation fluctuated in the sample between double-digit figures to 500 percent per year, the ratio of seigniorage to GNP remained between 2 and 3 percent. Although changes in inflation were not accompanied by marked fluctuations in seigniorage, they had a strong impact on welfare in the steady state. Based on the model's estimated parameters, the steady-state welfare cost of 10 percent inflation is about 1 percent of GNP, and the welfare cost of an inflation rate of 168 percent per year (the average in Israel between 1980 and 1984) is about 4 percent of GNP.

The analysis could be extended in several directions. First, our quantitative analysis of seigniorage and of the welfare cost of inflation was confined to steady states. It is well known that in episodes of high and volatile inflation, the actual levels of seigniorage revenue and of the welfare cost of inflation may well differ from steady-state levels. Thus, caution is suggested in regarding our quantitative findings as definitive, as it would be desirable to extend the analysis to take into account transitional factors which give rise to these differences.

Second, it seems plausible that the calculation of welfare costs of inflation may depend on the extent to which the distortions induced by other taxes are

21. Cooley and Hansen (1989) studied the effects of the inflation tax in the context of a real-business-cycle model in which money is introduced via cash-in-advance constraints. Notice that in their framework monetary velocity is invariant with respect to changes in the rate of inflation. Den Haan (1990); Gillman (1991); and Imrohoroglu and Prescott (1991) look at the welfare costs of inflation in models with considerably more substitution possibilities than Cooley and Hansen (1989) and consequently find higher welfare costs of inflation. The welfare cost calculations of McCallum (1989); Fischer (1981); and Lucas (1981) are directly based on the area under the demand curve for money. For a comparison of alternative measures of the welfare cost of inflation, see Gillman (1990).

22. All these calculations apply to comparisons of steady states. A more comprehensive assessment of the welfare costs of inflation would have to take into account the distortions and costs imposed by inflation out of steady state.

affected by changes in the inflation tax. Some progress on this issue has been made recently by Cooley and Hansen (1990), who explore in the context of a real-business-cycle model how the distortions associated with the inflation tax compare with the distortions arising from taxes on labor and capital income and on consumption.

Third, the analysis could be extended to allow for potential nonneutralities of money and inflation both in and out of steady states. Previous research indicates that changes in the rate of inflation may affect the allocation of time between work and leisure as well as the profitability of capital accumulation. Explicitly taking into account these effects may have a nonnegligible impact on the calculations of seigniorage and of the welfare cost of inflation that are based on the assumption of neutrality.

Appendix
Estimates under Alternative Asset Return*. Israel, 1970:I–1986:IV

Parameters	CM	CNM	CB	CNB
	Return: Bank's Lending Rate			
β	1.038	1.001	1.025	1.023
	(0.019)	(0.014)	(0.014)	(0.010)
γ	0.055	0.052	0.042	0.042
	(0.002)	(0.002)	(0.001)	(0.001)
θ	-4.270	-3.551	-2.609	-2.231
	(0.646)	(1.202)	(0.600)	(0.919)
δ	0.233	0.388	0.510	0.587
	(0.067)	(0.142)	(0.202)	(0.225)
J_T	7.472	10.931	4.811	7.591
	(0.113)	(0.027)	(0.307)	(0.108)
$\rho(d1, d2)$	0.706	0.533	0.300	0.273
	Return: Yield on Government Indexed Bonds			
β	0.997	1.000	1.012	0.984
	(0.004)	(0.005)	(0.004)	(0.007)
γ	0.049	0.043	0.041	0.034
	(0.004)	(0.003)	(0.003)	(0.024)
θ	1.061	-1.143	-0.831	-0.096
	(0.058)	(0.676)	(0.377)	(0.673)
δ	-0.394	0.149	0.150	0.239
	(0.264)	(0.103)	(0.071)	(0.168)
J_T	3.669	3.985	3.998	4.071
	(0.453)	(0.408)	(0.406)	(0.396)
$\rho(d1, d2)$	0.312	0.537	0.440	0.265

Note: See notes to table 12.1. The instrument set $z1$ was used in estimating the model. See also note 15.

228   *Chapter Twelve*

References

Bental, B., and Z. Eckstein. 1990. The Dynamics of Inflation with Constant Deficit under Expected Regime Change. *Economic Journal* 100:1245–60.

Blanchard, O. J., and S. Fischer. 1989. *Lectures on Macroeconomics*. Cambridge: MIT Press.

Bruno, M. 1986. Israel's Stabilization: The End of the "Lost Decade"? Working paper. Jerusalem: M. Falk Institute, June.

Bruno, M., and S. Fischer. 1990. Seigniorage, Operating rules, and the High Inflation Trap. *Quarterly Journal of Economics* 105:353–74.

Cooley, T. F., and G. D. Hansen. 1989. The Inflation Tax and the Business Cycle. *American Economic Review* 79:733–48.

———. 1990. Tax Distortions in a Neoclassical Monetary Economy. Working paper. University of Rochester, August.

Den Haan, W. J. 1990. The Optimal Inflation Path in a Sidrauski-Type Model with Uncertainty. *Journal of Monetary Economics* 25:389–409.

Drazen, A., and E. Helpman. 1990. Inflationary Consequences of Anticipated Macroeconomic Policies. *Review of Economic Studies* 57:147–64.

Eckstein, Z., and L. Leiderman. 1988. Estimating Intertemporal Models of Consumption and Money Holdings and Their Implications for Seigniorage and Inflation. Working paper. Tel Aviv University.

Eichenbaum, M. S., L. P. Hansen, and K. J. Singleton. 1988. A Time Series Analysis of Representative Agent Models of Consumption and Leisure Choice under Uncertainty. *Quarterly Journal of Economics* 103:51–78.

Feenstra, R. C. 1986. Functional Equivalence between Liquidity Costs and the Utility of Money. *Journal of Monetary Economics* 16:271–91.

Finn, M. G., D. L. Hoffman, and D. E. Schlagenhauf. 1990. Intertemporal Asset Pricing Relationships in Barter and Monetary Economies: An Empirical Analysis. *Journal of Monetary Economics* 25:431–52.

Fischer, S. 1981. *Towards an Understanding of the Costs of Inflation*. Carnegie-Rochester Conference Series on Public Policy 15:5–41.

Gillman, M. 1990. Standardizing Estimates of the Welfare Costs of Inflation. Working paper. Emory University, December.

———. 1991. The Welfare Costs of Inflation in a Cash-in-Advance Economy with Costly Credit. Working paper. Emory University.

Hansen, L. P. 1982. Large Sample Properties of Generalized Method of Moment Estimators. *Econometrica* 50, 1029–54.

Hansen, L. P., and K. J. Singleton. 1982. Generalized Instrumental Variables Estimation of Nonlinear Rational Expectations Models. *Econometrica* 50:1269–86.

Imrohoroglu, A., and E. C. Prescott. 1991. Evaluating the Welfare Effects of Alternative Monetary Arrangements. *Federal Reserve Bank of Minneapolis Quarterly Review* (Summer):3–10.

King, R. G., and C. I. Plosser. 1985. *Money, Deficits, and Inflation*. Carnegie-Rochester Conference Series on Public Policy 22, 147–96.

Kydland, F. E., and E. C. Prescott. 1982. Time to Build and Aggregate Fluctuations. *Econometrica* 50:1345–70.

Leiderman, L., and A. Marom. 1985. New Estimates of the Demand for Money in Israel. *Bank of Israel Economic Review* 13:17–33.

Lucas, R. E., Jr. 1981. *Discussion of: Stanley Fischer: Towards an Understanding of the Costs of Inflation* (II). Carnegie-Rochester Conference Series on Public Policy 15, 43–52.

Lucas, R. E., Jr. 1986. Models of Business Cycles. Yrjo Jahnsson Lectures. Helsinki.

Marshall, D. A. 1988. Inflation and Asset Returns in a Monetary Economy—Empirical results. Working paper. Northwestern University, November.

McCallum, B. T. 1989. *Monetary Economics: Theory and Policy.* (New York: Macmillan).

————. 1990. Inflation: Theory and Evidence. In *Handbook of Monetary Economics,* Vol. II, ed. B. M. Friedman and F. H. Hahn. (Amsterdam, North Holland).

Meridor, L. 1988. The Role of the Public Sector in the Israeli Economy 1960–1986: Facts, Causes and Implications. Working paper. Program for the Study of the Israeli Economy, MIT, February.

Ogaki, M. 1987. Do Monetary Distortions Exist in Relative Prices? Working paper. University of Chicago, December.

Poterba, J. M., and J. Rotemberg. 1987. Money in the Utility Function: An Empirical Implementation. In *New Approaches to Monetary Economics,* ed. W. A. Barnett and K. J. Singleton. Cambridge: Cambridge University Press.

Sargent, T. J. 1987. Dynamic Macroeconomic Theory. Cambridge: Harvard University Press.

Sargent, T. J., and N. Wallace. 1973. Rational Expectations and the Dynamics of Hyperinflation. *International Economic Review* 14:328–50.

————. 1987. Inflation and the Government Budget Constraint. In *Economics in theory and practice,* ed. A. Razin and E. Sadka. New York: Macmillan.

Sidrauski, M. 1967. Rational Choice and Patterns of Growth in a Monetary Economy. *American Economic Review* 57:534–44.

Singleton, K. J. 1985. Testing Specifications of Economic Agents Intertemporal Optimum Problems in the Presence of Alternative Models. *Journal of Econometrics* 30:391–413.

13

Optimal Inflation Tax under Precommitment: Theory and Evidence

I. Introduction

The notion that optimal fiscal policy entails the smoothing of tax rates over time has received growing attention since Barro's (1979) important contribution. Recent work has extended Barro's framework to consider government's use of the inflation tax, along with other taxes, as a source of revenue. A first-order condition for optimal policy in the extended model is that the marginal social costs of raising revenue through direct taxation and through seigniorage are equated at each point in time. Thus, other things equal, the model implies that tax rates should move together with the rate of inflation and nominal interest rates. This implication of the theory has been the subject of recent empirical work by Mankiw (1987) and Poterba and Rotemberg (1990) who reported mixed results about its empirical validity. While Mankiw found that the inflation rate and the nominal interest rate are indeed positively correlated with the average tax rate in the postwar U.S., the evidence on France, Germany, and the United Kingdom reported by Poterba and Rotemberg does not conform well with the theory.

In addition to the foregoing static implication, the theory has intertemporal implications for the determination of tax rates. First-order conditions for optimal policy generally imply equality between the expected marginal social costs of taxation in any two periods, and this is precisely the foundation for the tax-smoothing hypothesis. Since inflation is another form of taxation, the theory implies some type of smoothing for the rate of inflation. In fact, Mankiw (1987) and Grilli (1988) have elaborated on the restrictive case in which the rate of inflation should follow a martingale, and Obstfeld (1988) reported evidence against this hypothesis based on data

Reprinted with permission from *American Economic Review* 82 (March 1992): 179–94.

for the U.S. and U.K. for the period between 1871 and 1986. Grilli has tested the even more restrictive hypothesis that seigniorage follows a martingale, and his evidence seems to reject this hypothesis in at least five European countries.

An important characteristic of most of the above-mentioned studies is that the specification of the demand for money is taken from outside the model and has thus no impact on government's objective (social loss) function. In contrast, traditional analysis of the welfare costs of inflation has emphasized how these costs do depend on the form of the money-demand function (e.g., Bailey [1956]). Accordingly, the first objective of the present paper is to develop and estimate a model of the optimal intertemporal determination of the inflation tax in which the demand for money is derived from first principles and thus there is an explicit link between its functional form and the social costs of inflation. Specifically, we assume an objective function such that at the optimum it results in the widely used Cagan semilog demand for money. Our analysis shows how the (time-varying) Cagan semi-elasticity of money demand is related to primitive parameters governing the marginal utilities of consumption and real-money balances and how these parameters affect government's optimal determination of inflation. We express the inflation-rate smoothing implications of our model in the form of an empirically testable orthogonality condition which differs from the conditions that have been derived from previous investigations.

The very few available empirical studies on the tax-smoothing model have used data for industrialized countries whose inflation rates have been relatively stable at low levels. Moreover, by all accounts seigniorage has not been used in these countries as a main source of government revenue. Thus, the second objective of our paper is to focus attention on some high-inflation developing countries where the inflation tax has been widely used by government. We examine here data for Argentina, Brazil, and Israel which exhibit wide fluctuations in inflation, money creation, and government budget deficits and thus potentially constitute a useful territory within which to test the intertemporal implications of the model.

The paper is structured as follows. Section II sets up the basic model and derives the dynamic first-order condition that implicitly determines the relation between optimal inflation rates for any two consecutive time periods. This Euler equation is expressed in the form of a testable orthogonality condition in section III. The section provides results of estimating and testing this condition by GMM (Generalized Method of Moments) on quarterly data for three countries: Argentina (1963:4–1986:4), Brazil (1975:4–1988:2), and Israel (1971:1–1988:3). Section IV provides extensions of the main analysis, and section V concludes the paper.

II. The Basic Model

A. Individuals

We assume the existence of a representative individual whose utility at time 0, say, can be expressed as the mathematical expectation of an infinite sum

$$\sum_{t=0}^{\infty} \beta^t [u(c_t) + v(m_t)], \tag{13.1}$$

where c and m are, respectively, per capita consumption and real monetary balances, and $\beta(<1)$ is the (constant) subjective discount factor. The functions u and v are defined on the positive real line, and are strictly concave and twice-continuously differentiable everywhere.

The representative individual's budget constraint in period t is

$$b_t = b_{t-1}R_{t-1} + y_t - c_t - x_t + \frac{M_{t-1} - M_t}{P_t} + g_t, \tag{13.2}$$

where b is the stock of (default-free) bonds in terms of (homogeneous) output; bonds are indexed to the money price of output P (i.e., the price level), and at the beginning of period t yield interest equal to $(R_{t-1} - 1)$. (Thus, in other words, the interest factor between periods $t - 1$ and t is denoted by R_{t-1}).[1] Moreover, y stands for exogenous labor income in terms of output, M is the stock of (non-interest-bearing) money, g denotes government real lump-sum transfers, and x is the real value of net taxes.[2] Real monetary balances, m, are defined by

$$m_t = M_t/P_t. \tag{13.3}$$

Furthermore, we define

$$\Pi_t = P_t/P_{t-1}. \tag{13.4}$$

---

1. The use of indexed bonds in the model is justified by the fact that in the countries whose data are used in the empirical analysis both indexation and floating interest rates are common. The analysis can be extended to incorporate nominal bonds, in which case a surprise increase in inflation from t to $t + 1$ reduces the real value of every nominal bond that matures after period $t + 1$.

2. The model can be extended to account for optimal determination of conventional distortionary taxes, and this would require providing microfoundations for the welfare losses from these taxes (see Calvo and Guidotti [1989]). We do not pursue this extension here because of the lack of meaningful quarterly tax data for the countries presently studied and of our interest in focusing on the time path of the inflation tax under optimal seigniorage.

Thus, Π_t is the inflation factor between periods $t - 1$ and t (i.e., Π_t is 1 plus the inflation rate between periods $t - 1$ and t). Using the notation introduced in equations (13.3) and (13.4), the budget constraint for period t can now be expressed in the following more convenient way:

$$b_t = b_{t-1}R_{t-1} + y_t - c_t - x_t + \frac{m_{t-1}}{\Pi_t} - m_t + g_t. \qquad (13.5)$$

At the beginning of period t, the individual is assumed to know all the variables whose time subscript is smaller than or equal to t.[3] In addition, for empirical tractability we assume that in period t the consumer knows Π_{t+1}. This assumption allows us to derive expressions that can be directly estimated by a nonlinear instrumental-variables technique. The more realistic case of stochastic inflation and its relation to the results of this section are discussed in section IVB below. Furthermore, the consumer is assumed to know the rules governing monetary and fiscal policy, as to be able to rationally derive the probability distribution of all the relevant variables.

Our representative individual maximizes the expected value of his utility (13.1), subject to (13.5): Thus, assuming that the solution is interior, we get the following familiar first-order conditions (see, for example, Sargent [1988]; Eckstein and Leiderman [1989]):[4]

$$u'(c_t) = \beta R_t E_t u'(c_{t+1}), \text{ and} \qquad (13.6)$$

$$v'(m_t) = u'(c_t) \left[1 - \frac{1}{R_t \Pi_{t+1}} \right], \qquad (13.7)$$

where E_t is the mathematical expectations operator taking into account the information available to the consumer at the beginning of period t. Notice that

$$R_t \Pi_{t+1} = 1 + i_t, \qquad (13.8)$$

where i_t is the nominal rate of interest between periods t and $t + 1$.[5] Hence, equation (13.7) can be expressed in the more familiar form

$$v'(m_t) = u'(c_t) \frac{i_t}{1 + i_t}. \qquad (13.9)$$

3. The assumption that R_t is nonstochastic from the perspective of period t can be relaxed without serious analytical consequences.
4. Unless explicitly stated, the analysis will assume away corner solutions.
5. Under the above assumptions the risk premium is zero, because both the real interest and inflation factors (R_t and Π_{t+1}) are not stochastic.

The next step is to specialize $v(m)$ so that it gives rise to a Cagan-type demand for money (under the separability conditions imposed by expression 13.1).[6] Thus, we assume

$$v_t(m_t) = m_t(B_t - D_t \ln m_t), \qquad (13.10)$$

where B and D are positive time-varying parameters, and ln denotes the natural-logarithm function. Hence, by equations (13.9) and (13.10), we get:

$$m_t = A_t e^{-\alpha_t \omega_t}, \qquad (13.11)$$

where

$$A_t = \exp(B_t/D_t - 1), \qquad (13.12a)$$

$$\alpha_t = u'(c_t)/D_t, \qquad (13.12b)$$

and

$$\omega_t = i_t/(1 + i_t). \qquad (13.12c)$$

Notice that equation (13.12b) provides micro foundations for money demand's semi-elasticity by expressing the latter as a function of primitive parameters, such as those governing the marginal utility of consumption and the utility from real-money balances. In this context, the constancy of α, assumed in many empirical studies of money demand, requires the D_t moves in unison with $u'(c_t)$.[7] Furthermore, the opportunity cost of holding money is ω and not i as is usually assumed in estimations of the Cagan equation.[8]

B. Government

The problem faced by the government is as follows. Its budget constraint for period t is given by

$$z_t = z_{t-1} R_{t-1} + x_t + (M_t - M_{t-1})/P_t - g_t, \qquad (13.13)$$

6. More general utility functions and the case of iso-elastic demand for money are discussed in appendix B.
7. This dependency between α and c might not hold if the demand for money is derived from an instantaneous utility function that is homothetic in c and m. However, we have not yet been able to obtain a simple characterization of homothetic utility functions that give rise to a Cagan demand for money.
8. In continuous time $\omega = i$. However, in discrete time these two concepts could be very different. For example, by (13.12c), as i tends to infinity, ω converges to unity (not to infinity!).

where z_t is the stock of real assets held by government at the beginning of period $t + 1$. Thus, recalling equations (13.3) and (13.4) we have

$$z_t = z_{t-1}R_{t-1} + x_t + m_t - m_{t-1}/\pi_t - g_t. \tag{13.14}$$

Notice that we have identified m with the demand for real monetary balances. This is consistent with our model, because we will assume that at the beginning of period t the government announces the inflation factor from t to $t + 1$ (i.e., Π_{t+1}), and supplies enough money (in exchange for output) as to satisfy demand given the initial price level, P_t.

The government's objective is to maximize social welfare as given by the expected value of expression (13.1), subject to its budget constraint (13.14) and, most importantly, subject to the private sector's demand for money (13.11). At the beginning of period t, the government, like the representative consumer, knows all variables with time subindex smaller than or equal to t, and determines the inflation factor for the periods t to $t + 1$, Π_{t+1} (recall note 4).

We will now derive the Euler equations characterizing the optimal government inflation policy. Using equation 13.14, we get

$$z_{t+2} = m_{t+2} - m_{t+1}/\Pi_{t+2} + x_{t+2} + R_{t+1}\{m_{t+1} - m_t/\Pi_{t+1} + x_{t+1} \\ + R_t[m_t - m_{t-1}/\Pi_t + x_t + z_{t-1}R_{t-1} - g_t] - g_{t+1}\} - g_{t+2}. \tag{13.15}$$

Recalling equations (13.8), (13.9), and (13.12c), equation (13.15) can be written as follows:

$$z_{t+2} = R_{t+1}[\omega_{t+1}m_{t+1} + R_t\omega_t m_t] \\ + \text{ terms involving only } x\text{'s, } g\text{'s, } R\text{'s and } z_{t-1}. \tag{13.16}$$

By assumption, R_t is known in period t. To derive the relevant Euler equation, we study the impact on welfare of changing ω_t and adjusting ω_{t+1} in period $t + 1$, based on the new information available in period $t + 1$, so as to keep z_{t+2} constant for each state of nature. At optimum, the impact on government's objective function should be nil. By (13.11), the demand for money depends on ω, and this dependency must be taken into account in the government optimization problem. In fact, by (13.11),

$$\omega_t = \ln(A_t/m_t)/\alpha_t \equiv \hat{h}(m_t; B_t, D_t, c_t) \equiv h(m_t; t). \tag{13.17}$$

With this notation, we now express the square-bracketed expression in (13.16) as follows:

$$h(m_{t+1}; t + 1)m_{t+1} + R_t h(m_t; t)m_t. \tag{13.18}$$

Since in the present setup consumption and the real interest factor are independent of monetary policy (see appendix A), the above-mentioned conjectural variation implies that for each state of nature revealed in period $t + 1$ we have

$$[\omega_{t+1} + m_{t+1}h'(m_{t+1}; t + 1)]dm_{t+1}$$
$$+ R_t[\omega_t + m_t h'(m_t; t)]dm_t = 0, \qquad (13.19)$$

where $h' \equiv \partial h/\partial m$. Equation (13.19) captures the effects associated with the variation of ω in periods t and $t + 1$. Moreover, by (13.17),

$$h'(m_t; t)m_t = -1/\alpha_t, \qquad (13.20)$$

and, consequently, for each state of nature revealed in period $t + 1$, we have the following implicit derivative:

$$\partial m_{t+1}/\partial m_t = -R_t(1/\alpha_t - \omega_t)/(1/\alpha_{t+1} - \omega_{t+1}). \qquad (13.21)$$

As previously discussed, a conjectural variation like the one performed above would not affect total welfare. Thus, by (13.1), at a government optimum we have

$$v'(m_t) + \beta E_t v'(m_{t+1})\partial m_{t+1}/\partial m_t = 0. \qquad (13.22)$$

In order to evaluate the above expression, we first note that, by equations (13.9) and (13.12c),

$$v'(m_t) = u'(c_t)\omega_t. \qquad (13.23)$$

Hence, by (13.22) and (13.23),

$$u'(c_t)\kappa_t = \beta R_t E_t u'(c_{t+1})\kappa_{t+1}, \qquad (13.24)$$

where

$$\kappa_t = \frac{\omega_t}{1/\alpha_t - \omega_t}. \qquad (13.25)$$

Equation (13.24) is the focal object for our empirical work, to be discussed in the next section. The equation represents the first-order condition (or Euler equation) for government's optimal choice of ω for any two consecutive time periods. It implies that at optimum the expected marginal cost of raising revenue through seigniorage should be the same, irrespective of the period in which seigniorage is raised. Thus, the equation embodies an element of inflation-tax smoothing of optimal government policy. To the extent that $u'(c)$ is constant through time and $\beta R_t = 1$ for all t, the following simple martingale characterization is derived:

$$\kappa_t = E_t \kappa_{t+1}. \tag{13.26}$$

Exression (13.26) implies a smoothing of κ over time. Notice that both equations (13.24) and (13.26) imply different restrictions on data than the martingales in the rate of inflation (i.e., $\Pi - 1$) that are stressed in Mankiw (1987) and Grilli (1988). If, in addition, the optimization problem is enriched by allowing the government to choose the time profile of taxes, then there would be a first-order condition linking conventional taxes with the inflation tax at each point in time. Such condition has been the focus of the empirical investigations by Mankiw (1987) and Poterba and Rotemberg (1990). It should be noted, however, that in our model the marginal cost of raising revenue from inflation is, as argued above, a function of the interest-rate semi-elasticity of the demand for money (through the κ term). Therefore, the relevant intratemporal condition implied by such an extension could be much different from the specifications used in previous empirical studies.

III. Empirical Implementation

As indicated above, we focus our empirical work on equation (13.24). For empirical purposes, it is convenient to divide through equation (13.24) by the first-order condition for optimal choice of consumption by the individual, equation (13.6), and to rearrange, thus yielding

$$\kappa_t = \frac{E_t u'(c_{t+1}) \kappa_{t+1}}{E_t u'(c_{t+1})}. \tag{13.27}$$

Multiplying both sides of this equation by $E_t u'(c_{t+1})$, dividing by $\kappa_t u'(c_t)$, and rearranging delivers

$$E_t \left[\frac{u'(c_{t+1})}{u'(c_t)} \left(\frac{\kappa_{t+1}}{\kappa_t} - 1 \right) \right] = 0, \tag{13.28}$$

where variables dated t or earlier are assumed to be part of the information set at time t.

Equation (13.28) is an orthogonality condition. It implies that at government's optimum, the information set has no predictive power for the object that follows the conditional expectation E_t. In what follows we use three alternative specifications of this condition, depending on the type of data being used. Version 1 of the model assumes that $u'(c_t)$ and α_t are constant through time. In this case, the orthogonality condition is

$$E_t\left(\frac{\kappa_{t+1}}{\kappa_t} - 1\right) = 0; \qquad (13.29)$$

i.e., κ_t follows a martingale. Version 2 relaxes the assumption that $u'(c_t)$ is constant, but maintains the hypothesis that α_t is constant. As discussed earlier, this implies that D_t moves in unison with $u'(c_t)$. To implement this version it is required to parameterize marginal utility of consumption. We do this by assuming that the function $u(c_t)$ is logarithmic and hold this as a maintained hypothesis. Consequently, the relation pertinent to this version is

$$E_t\left[\frac{c_t}{c_{t+1}}\left(\frac{\kappa_{t+1}}{\kappa_t} - 1\right)\right] = 0. \qquad (13.30)$$

Last, Version 3 allows for time variation in both $u'(c_t)$ and α_t. Recalling that $\alpha_t = u'(c_t)/D_t$, we now adopt a simple and tractable parameterization of D_t as

$$D_t = \frac{\delta}{y_t}, \qquad (13.31a)$$

where y_t is a measure of income or output. This specification implies that individual's utility from holding real-money balances increases with the level of y_t. In terms of α, this implies

$$\alpha_t = \frac{y_t}{\delta c_t}. \qquad (13.31b)$$

This formulation is consistent with the view that money balances held against consumption purchases are less interest-rate sensitive than those held against other uses (e.g., investment or production). This would be the case in an environment in which consumers are subject to a cash-in-advance constraint while firms have access to a wider menu of financial instruments. Notice the similarity between Versions 2 and 3 in the modeling of the preference parameter D_t (see equation (13.31a) for Version 3 and recall that $D_t = 1/(\alpha c_t)$ for Version 2). The versions are similar in that both imply that a drop in consumption or income, as in a recession, is associated with increased concavity of $v(\cdot)$. In principle, other parameterizations of D_t could be considered and the orthogonality conditions would have to be changed accordingly. Under assumption (13.31b), however, the orthogonality condition becomes:

$$
E_t\left[\frac{c_t}{c_{t+1}}\left(\frac{\left\{\dfrac{\omega_{t+1}}{\delta(c_{t+1}/y_{t+1}) - (\omega_{t+1})}\right\}}{\left\{\dfrac{\omega_t}{\delta(c_t/y_t) - \omega_t}\right\}} - 1\right)\right] = 0. \quad (13.32)
$$

We used orthogonality conditions (13.29), (13.30), and (13.32) to obtain estimates of α and δ and to test the overidentifying restrictions of the model. Our empirical investigation used quarterly data from three relatively high-inflation countries: Argentina, Brazil, and Israel. The fact that inflation, money growth, seigniorage and government budget deficits have shown considerable fluctuations through time in these countries makes them a challenging territory within which to implement the model. The data set consists of quarterly time series on the rate of inflation (measured by the rate of change of the CPI), private consumption spending, and gross domestic product.[9] The sample periods for estimation vary across countries depending on the availability of data on these three series.

In estimating the orthogonality conditions, we used Hansen's (1982) Generalized Method of Moments (GMM). Given a chosen set of n instrumental variables which are assumed to be included in government's information set, it is possible to form n orthogonality conditions for each one of the first-order conditions considered here (i.e., equations (13.29), (13.30), and (13.32)). GMM chooses the estimate of the α (or δ) parameter such that a weighted combination of these n orthogonality conditions is being minimized. The minimized value of this method's objective function converges in distribution to a chi-square random variable with degrees of freedom equal to $n - 1$, and can thus be used to test the model's overidentifying restrictions.

The estimates are displayed in table 13.1. For instruments we used a constant along with the following ratios: ω_t/ω_{t-1}, c_t/c_{t-1}, and y_t/y_{t-1}. In implementing a GMM estimator we assume that the instrumental variables and the objects entering the Euler equations form a stationary vector stochastic process. The instrumental variables used in the analysis are in the form of ratios which do not exhibit marked trends over the sample period; the same applies

9. The data source for the CPI is International Financial Statistics. For consumpion and GDP data we used country sources: FIEL Data Bank (for Argentina), Cojunctura Economica (For Brazil) and the Israel Bureau of Statistics (for Israel).

Table 13.1
Estimated Versions of the Model

| | | Model's Version | | |
Country	Estimates	1	2	3
Argentina	α	3.242	3.243	
(73:4–86:4)		(0.031)	(0.0364)	
	δ			0.270
				(0.0038)
	J_T	3.498	3.511	1.526
		(0.321)	(0.319)	(0.676)
Brazil	α	4.760	4.758	
(75:4–88:2)		(0.092)	(0.092)	
	δ			0.222
				(0.0064)
	J_T	4.840	4.963	4.367
		(0.184)	(0.175)	(0.225)
Israel	α	3.343	3.350	
(71:1–88:3)		(0.108)	(0.114)	
	δ			0.486
				(0.0024)
	J_T	7.910	8.079	5.555
		(0.048)	(0.044)	(0.135)

Note: See text for specifications under the alternative versions. J_T is the statistic for testing the overidentifying restrictions of the models. It is distributed chi square with 3 degrees of freedom. Standard errors of the estimates and marginal significance levels (for J_T) are given in parentheses.

to the ratios appearing in the Euler equations. To obtain initial values for estimation, we estimated at a first stage simple versions of equation (13.11), money demand, using least squares and instrumental variables. The latter were a constant and four lagged values of ω. The estimated values of α were as follows: 3.18 for Argentina, 4.9 for Brazil, and 3.77 for Israel. These values conform quite well with confidence intervals for estimated semi-elasticities found in previous money-demand studies for these countries.

It can be seen in table 13.1 that α is estimated quite precisely in Versions 1 and 2, and the same applies to the utility function parameter δ in Version 3. The values of α implied by the estimated δ's in Version 3, evaluated at the sample means of y_t/c_t, are quite close to those obtained in the first two versions: 4.13 for Argentina, 4.54 for Brazil, and 3.31 for Israel. For Argentina and Brazil, the J_T statistics reported in the table are generally small relative to the degrees of freedom thus indicating that the model's overidentifying restrictions are not rejected by the sample information at a standard significance level of 10 percent. The results for Israel are less favorable for the model. That is, the overidentifying restrictions imposed by Versions 1 and 2 are rejected at the 10 percent significance level. In all cases it appears that shifting from the first two versions toward Version 3 enhances the conformity of the model with the sample information.[10]

In an attempt to compare the orthogonality conditions of our model with those derived in previous work, it seems appropriate to treat the latter as implying the condition $E_t[(\Pi_{t+1}/\Pi_t) - 1] = 0$ which embodies the martingale property of these models. We have tested this condition by projecting the term in square brackets on a constant and one lagged value of Π_{t+1}/Π_t and then testing that the coefficients on these instruments are all zero. Values for the chi-square statistic for testing this hypothesis are (with marginal significance levels in parentheses): 5.40 (0.067) for Argentina, 2.92 (0.23) for Brazil, and 8.68 (0.013) for Israel. Thus, the hypothesis is rejected at the 10 percent significance level for Argentina and Israel. Coupling this finding with the results in table 13.1 indicates that the data for Argentina and Israel can distinguish between the specifications derived in this paper and those used in previous work.

While some of the findings discussed thus far provide support for the present specifications, a careful examination of the data reveals a specific limitation of the model. When the estimated α's, which as stated previously conform well with values previously estimated in money demand studies, are used to calculate κ_t (see equation (13.25)) within the sample period it turns out that there are several observations for which these calculated κ's are negative. Put differently, inflation rates were "too large" at some data points relative to what is predicted by the model; i.e., these points appear to be in the inefficient region of the Laffer curve for the inflation tax. Not surprisingly, and using α values from Version 1 of table 13.1, this occurs at data points in which inflation sharply accelerated such as the period from late 1983 to early 1985 in Israel, from late 1975 to mid-1976 and then from 82:4 to 85:2 in Argentina, and for 83:2−86:1 and 87:1−88:2 in Brazil.

It thus appears that in order to fully account for these observations it is necessary to relax some of the restrictive assumptions made in the foregoing analysis. Extensions of the model in this direction are discussed in the next section.

IV. Extensions

In discussing extensions of the model that could account for the "anomalous" data points discussed above, we first consider the role of competitive banks.

---

10. Estimation of the various versions of the model under a shorter list of instruments which included a constant and the ratio ω_t/ω_{t-1} yields very similar qualitative results and parameter estimates to those of table 13.1. In this case, the J_T statistics indicate rejection of the model's overidentifying restrictions at the 10 percent significance level for Israel's Versions 1 and 2, as in table 13.1, and for Brazil's Version 1 (the marginal significance levels for these statistics are 0.004 and 0.0054 for Israel and 0.077 for Brazil, respectively).

This is especially relevant for the analysis of economies, such as Argentina, which have undergone financial and banking reforms during the sample period. Second, we explore some of the implications of relaxing the assumption that inflation is determined independently of the state of nature, and, finally, we elaborate on the possible role of time inconsistency in government's optimal choices of inflation.

A. Competitive Banks

Here we follow the approach of Bailey (1956) and Calvo and Fernandez (1982), and discuss the potential effects of financial liberalization. For the sake of simplicity, we assume that the private sector uses only deposits, while banks are the only holders of high-powered money.

The individuals' budget constraint is now given by

$$b_t = b_{t-1}R_{t-1} + y_t - c_t - x_t + \frac{\tilde{m}_{t-1}(1 + \iota_{t-1})}{\Pi_t} - \tilde{m}_t + g_t, \quad (13.5')$$

where $\tilde{m}$ stands for individuals' stock of bank deposits, and ι stands for the interest rate on those deposits.

In line with the previous analysis, we denote by $v(\tilde{m})$ the utility from deposits. Accordingly, by (13.5'), first-order condition (13.9) now becomes

$$v'(\tilde{m}_t) = u'(c_t) \frac{i_t - \iota_t}{1 + i_t}. \quad (13.9')$$

In this expression, the opportunity cost of holding deposits is $(i - \iota)/(1 + i)$. To the extent that the interest rate paid on deposits, ι, is equal to zero, the above expression becomes identical to equation (13.9). This is to be expected, because the analysis leading to equation (13.9) relied on the assumption that individuals could only hold non-interest-bearing money.

Assuming that banks are perfectly competitive, and that bank operating costs are negligible, it follows that the interest rate paid on deposits, ι, satisfies: $\iota_t = (1 - 1/k)i_t$, where k is the inverse of the required reserves ratio; thus, k is the high-powered-money multiplier, and in equilibrium $\tilde{m} = km$. Therefore, in equilibrium equation (13.9') implies

$$v'(k_t m_t)k_t = u'(c_t)\omega_t, \quad (13.33)$$

which is the present counterpart of equation (13.23). Further, if we replace (13.10) by

$$v(m_t k_t) = m_t k_t (B_t - D_t \ln k_t m_t), \quad (13.34)$$

we get

$$m_t k_t = A_t e^{-\alpha_t \omega_t / k_t}, \tag{13.35}$$

where A and α are defined as in 13.12a and 13.12b. In this case, $\omega_t < (k_t/\alpha_t)$ is the condition for being on the efficient region of the inflation-tax Laffer curve.

Consider now the effects of a financial liberalization resulting in an increase in the high-powered-money multiplier k_t. Clearly, it is now possible for ω_t to increase markedly without yet violating the efficiency condition of above. This could possibly explain some of the high-inflation observations for Argentina, discussed at the end of section III, for the period after 1977:4, a time at which a wide financial liberalization was implemented. To explore this possibility, we reestimated Version 1 of the model for Argentina replacing the $1/\alpha_t$ term in the Euler equation (13.29) by k_t/α_t, with k_t measured by the ratio of money plus quasi-money to high-powered money (calculated from data from International Financial Statistics). The estimated value of α decreased to 2.77 with a standard deviation of 0.05. With this estimate, the efficiency condition $\omega_t < (k_t/\alpha_t)$ now holds for all the observations after the financial liberalization of late 1977. Thus, what appeared to be violations of the efficiency condition for inflation-tax collection in the basic analysis need not be so in a richer framework that explicitly allows for changes in the monetary institutional setup. Admittedly, this is only a first and simple attack on this issue; more complex and realistic specifications of banking-system behavior would be required before one can take a decisive stand on the effects of such a system on the optimal intertemporal smoothing of the inflation tax. In addition, the fact that the efficiency condition is still violated for the 75:3 to 76:2 and 76:4 to 77:1 preliberalization observations remains to be explained in a more complete analysis which incorporates, for example, the possibility of random inflation and time inconsistency.

B. State-Contingent Inflation

A reformulation of the model to account for state-contingent inflation commitments by the policymaker proceeds as follows. Assume now that the rate of inflation from t to $t + 1$ is not known with certainty by the representative individual, who now treats Π_{t+1} as a random variable. In this case, the first-order condition associated with the optimal choice of m_t satisfies:

$$v'(m_t) = \beta E_t(R_t - \theta_{t+1}) u'(c_{t+1}), \tag{13.36}$$

where $\theta_t = 1/\Pi_t$ and E_t denotes expectations conditional on the state at time t. The semilog demand for money is now given by

$$\ln m_t = \ln A_t - \beta E_t(R_t - \theta_{t+1}) u'(c_{t+1})/D_t. \tag{13.37}$$

Let us express the state of nature by a vector $(s_0, s_1, \ldots)$, and assume that at time t the individual knows $(s_0, s_1, \ldots, s_t)$ which we denote $_ts$. (Thus, E_t denotes expectations conditional on $_ts$.) Upon noting that, with this notation, knowledge in period t could also be expressed as $(_{t-1}s, s_t)$, we could write the optimal policy response in period t as a function of $_ys$, as e.g. $\theta_t = \phi(_ts)$. Hence, equation (13.16) can now be written as follows:

$$z_{t+2} = R_{t+1}m_t[R_t - \phi(_{t+1}s)] \tag{13.38}$$
$$+ m_{t+1}[R_{t+1} - \phi(_{t+1}s, s_{t+2})] + \text{other terms.}$$

As shown in appendix C, equation (13.38) and the first-order conditions of individuals' optimization can be used to derive the following orthogonality condition, which is the present counterpart to equation (13.24) above:

$$E_t\left\{\omega_t u'(c_{t+1}) - \beta R_{t+1}E_{t+1}\omega_{t+1}u'(c_{t+2}) \frac{1/\alpha_t - \omega_t}{1/\alpha_{t+1} - \dfrac{E_{t+1}\omega_{t+1}u'(c_{t+2})}{E_{t+1}u'(c_{t+2})}}\right\} = 0 \tag{13.39}$$

To the extent that ω_t is nonrandom from the perspective of the planner in period t, then equation (13.39) becomes identical to equation (13.24). Furthermore, in the special case in which $\beta = R = u'(c) = 1$, we obtain the counterpart of martingale condition (13.26) which is given by:

$$E_t\left\{\omega_t - E_{t+1}\omega_{t+1} \frac{\omega_t - 1/\alpha_t}{E_{t+1}\omega_{t+1} - 1/\alpha_{t+1}}\right\} = 0, \tag{13.40}$$

where $\alpha_t = 1/D_t$.

The main implication of this extension of the model is that, contrary to the case studied in the previous sections, when inflation is contingent on the state of nature the rate of inflation is not constrained to be below a certain critical level (see also Calvo and Guidotti [1989]). Unfortunately, however, the orthogonality conditions that emerge from this alternative model—close as they are to the ones earlier derived—do not lend themselves to direct estimation by GMM; thus, their implementation will have to await further statistical research.

C. Time Inconsistency

Term m_{t-1}/Π_t in equation (13.14) and the welfare criterion (13.1) show that, unless $m_{t-1} = 0$, the government will be tempted to increase Π_t whenever taxes are positive, or to decrease it if taxes are negative. In a world of homogeneous individuals this may turn out to be a serious problem, because the government at t could actually improve the representative individual's utility by departing from previously announced inflation for period t, i.e., by changing Π_t in period t. Obviously, if the public was aware that the government could revise Π_t in period t, then no inflation announcement would be credible unless we are in the special, and factually uninteresting, case in which total conventional distorting taxes are zero. Thus, in equilibrium, the optimal rate of inflation may well lie on the inefficient side of the inflation-tax Laffer curve (see Calvo [1978], and Calvo and Guidotti [1989]).

This credibility problem has been recently reexamined by Persson, Persson and Svensson (1987), PPS, who suggested that the problem would go away if the government had nominal assets whose real present value equaled m_{t-1}. The intuition is that, given the path of interest rates, a change in Π_t would, under the PPS condition, result in no net fiscal gain for the government. The problem with this conjecture is that, in general, interest rates are affected by government policy and, thus, the PPS condition cannot be ensured to hold in general. One case where it still guarantees time consistency (see Calvo and Obstfeld [1990]), however, is that in which the interest rate factor R is exogenous and all nominal government debt matures in one period (or, in continuous time, if nominal debt matures instantaneously, like NOW accounts). Hence, in the previous section's framework credibility could be ensured through the PPS device if nominal debt has one-period maturity.

As stated above, the PPS device requires the government to have nominal assets of similar value as the stock of high-powered money. Thus, the question arises, what are those assets? We submit that in practice an important component of those assets are fiscal obligations of the private sector, for example, last-period taxes. Normally, there is a lag between the time a tax is due and the time the payment is actually made; furthermore, taxpayers are normally not penalized for relatively short payment delays.[11] At any point in time, therefore, there is a stock of nominal obligations from the private sector to the government which, therefore, contributes to satisfying the PPS condition. Under these circumstances, for example, the incentives for surprise inflation are attenduated by the associated fiscal revenue loss. To illustrate the possible importance of these implicit nominal government assets, consider the case in which total taxes represent 30 percent of (annual) GNP, m is about 10 percent of GNP, and the tax-collection lag is about 3 months. This means that the fiscal government assets at any point in time represent about 9 percent of

---

11. Several authors have stressed the importance of these tax-collection lags. See, for example, Lovell (1963), Olivera (1967), Dutton (1971), Aghevli and Kahn (1977) and Tanzi (1977).

GNP, which compares favorably with *m*. Thus, if government debt is fully indexed to the price level, the incentives to depart from previous inflation announcements may be insignificant.

This should not be taken to imply that in practice time inconsistency is not a problem in a monetary economy. The above economy could easily bring about conditions under which credibility would be seriously impaired by, for example, generating a nominal government debt in the order of 50 to 100 percent of GNP.[12] Under those circumstances, other "costs" of inflation must play a significant role to ensure credibility. These costs will, however, change the above-mentioned first-order conditions, and, therefore, will not be discussed here at any length. However, we would like to mention at this juncture that the costs of surprise inflation are likely to be very different from those modeled by *v*(*m*), since surprise-inflation costs have to do with issues such as income distribution, money-demand lags, etc.[13] Consequently, testing for the presence of time inconsistency under the assumption that costs of anticipated and unanticipated inflation are the same could involve serious specification errors.[14]

V. Conclusions

This paper has derived and tested the restrictions implied by an intertemporal optimizing model on the time path of the inflation tax. A key feature that distinguishes our work from previous research on inflation-tax smoothing is that here the welfare loss from inflation, the money-demand function, and the time path of the rate of inflation are jointly derived under the assumption that the policymaker attempts to maximize the welfare of the representative individual. The resulting implications for the time-series properties of the inflation tax turn out to differ from the inflation-rate martingale conditions emphasized in previous work. Another distinguishing feature is that we implemented the model on time-series data for three high-inflation countries (Argentina, Brazil, and Israel) in which seigniorage, inflation, and government budget deficits have shown wide variation over time. Interestingly, the evidence indicates that the distinction between the specifications used in this paper and those used in previous work has empirical content.

Our empirical analysis produced mixed results. Although the model's overidentifying restrictions are not rejected by the data (at standard significance

12. These kinds of numbers are not unheard of, as the recent experience in Brazil and Italy demonstrate.

13. For some discussion and examples of money-demand lags, see Calvo (1988), Calvo and Obstfeld (1990), Persson, Persson, and Svensson (1989), and Calvo and Guidotti (1989).

14. See Poterba and Rotemberg (1990).

levels) for most of the specifications considered, we found several data points that do not satisfy the model's postulates. These are observations which feature inflation rates that are excessively (and inefficiently) high from the standpoint of government's optimal policy under precommitment. Thus, a section in the paper was devoted to explore three possible extensions and explanations for these somewhat "anomalous" observations. First, we discussed how during periods of financial liberalization which result in an increase in the money multiplier it is possible for the rate of inflation to increase markedly without yet necessarily violating the underlying efficiency condition. Then, we modified the model to account for state-contingent inflation commitments by the policymaker. Under this extension, and at variance with the basic model of section II, the rate of inflation is not constrained to be below a certain critical level. Last, we discussed the possible role of time inconsistency in giving rise to rates of inflation that are well above the rates implied by standard efficiency considerations. A common theme in these extensions is that what appeared to be violations of the efficiency condition for inflation tax collection in the basic analysis, or "anomalous" observations, need not be so in richer frameworks which e.g. allow for financial reform, for state-contingent inflation, and for time inconsistency.

In any case, and even if the foregoing considerations give rise to a more satisfactory explanation of the evidence, the fact that our analysis relied on several restrictive assumptions suggests that the empirical results should be interpreted with caution. For example, it is likely that in the countries under study there have been inflationary episodes that were motivated by factors other than seigniorage needs, such as government's concern with employment, income distribution, and other goals.

Along the paper we suggested several possible extensions of the analysis which could be undertaken in future work, such as taking into account distortionary conventional taxes, nominal bonds, and the structure of the banking sector among others. A particularly promising line of research, in our view, is to allow for imperfect policy precommitment and to look for ways to empirically distinguish between periods in which policy precommitment was possible, or effective, from those in which it was not. This is of relevance because, as is well understood by now, the nature of optimal policy is strongly dependent on the ability to make credible commitments. Put differently, it would be useful to develop a framework tractable and general enough to enable an assessment of the relative empirical importance of the two main approaches that exist on this subject: the discretionary policy approach and the inflation-smoothing approach; (see Obstfeld [1988] who used these terms and developed a dynamic model that synthesizes elements of both these approaches). While we have been able to make some progress in this direction, it is still too early to report any definitive results.

Appendix A

Intertemporal first-order conditions in the text were obtained under the assumption that monetary policy does not affect the representative-individual optimal consumption plan. We show here that such a property follows from our assumptions that (a) monetary policy is not used to increase or decrease government expenditure on goods and services, and (b) that the instantaneous utility index is separable in c and m.

The proof is straightforward. Let us define

$$n_t = b_t + z_t. \tag{A13.1}$$

Thus, n stands for *net* foreign assets in the hands of the public and the government. Moreover, by (13.5), (13.13), and (A13.1), we have

$$n_t = n_{t-1}R_{t-1} + y_t - c_t, \tag{A13.2}$$

which implies that net asset accumulation is entirely independent of monetary policy (a critical assumption for this result is that monetary policy is invariant with respect to changes in government expenditure on goods and services, i.e., point [a] above).

Consider the small open-economy case in which n could be different from zero (but is subject to some inequality constraints or transversality conditions), and in which the country takes as given the path of R_t. By (13.1) a central planner would choose the path of c so as to maximize

$$\sum_{t=0}^{\infty} \beta^t u(c_t) \tag{A13.3}$$

subject to (A13.2), initial n and boundary conditions. Since m does not affect the marginal utility of c, then the first-order conditions are independent of monetary policy, and satisfy equation (13.6). The consumption plan is feasible for the economy as a whole and, therefore, it is also feasible for the representative consumer. Since, in addition, the planner's optimal c path satisfies the same first-order conditions that are relevant for the consumer, the planner's optimum coincides with that of the individual. Consequently, the equilibrium consumption path is independent of monetary policy as asserted in the text. Furthermore, by assumption the interest rate factor is also independent of monetary policy. Thus, the conjectural variation in the text follows. As is well known, the independence of the equilibrium path of c and R with respect to monetary policy can also be shown to hold in a Sidrauski-type closed economy.

Appendix B

In this appendix we consider more general utility functions. Extensions to the general separability case are straightforward. Expression (13.17), without the middle section which applies only when (13.10) holds, can be derived from (13.23) if c_t is exogenous with respect to monetary policy. The latter is, in fact, true with separability of c and m in the utility function, and exogeneity of R (see appendix A). Therefore, condition (13.19) still applies and, together with (13.23), it can be used to show:

$$u'(c_t) \frac{\omega_t}{\omega_t + m_t h'(m_t; t)}$$
$$= R_t \beta E_t u'(c_{t+1}) \frac{\omega_{t+1}}{\omega_{t+1} + m_{t+1} h'(m_{t+1}; t+1)}. \qquad (A13.4)$$

The expressions on both sides of the equation have a straightforward interpretation. For example, the numerator of the left-hand-side expression is the marginal utility of an additional unit of real monetary balances, while the denominator is the corresponding marginal revenue (in terms of output). Thus equation (A13.4) implied that at an optimum the government should equate the marginal cost of collecting one unit of output through seigniorage at time t to the marginal cost of raising R_t units through seigniorage in period $t + 1$. In other words, (A13.4) is a special case of the general optimality principle according to which at an (interior) optimum the marginal cost of collecting one unit of present output must be the same irrespective of the tax instrument that is being used.

As an application of (A13.4), consider the case in which the demand for money is iso-elastic with respect to ω. This function corresponds to the utility function

$$v(m) = \frac{m^{1-\gamma}}{1-\gamma} N, \qquad (A13.5)$$

where γ and N are some positive (possibly time-varying) parameters. In this case, however, if ω is positive for t and $t + 1$, condition (A13.4) would require

$$\frac{u'(c_t)}{1-\gamma_t} = \beta R_t E_t \frac{u'(c_{t+1})}{1-\gamma_{t+1}}. \qquad (A13.6)$$

Since c is exogenous, the equation will not hold in general. This implies that, in general, seigniorage will only be collected at one point in time.

The above becomes more transparent when γ is nonstochastic. In that case γ could be pulled outside the expectations operator in equation (A13.6). Hence, by (13.6) and (A13.6), we get $\gamma_t = \gamma_{t+1}$. This means that if γ is constant over time, the monetary authority will be indifferent as to when seigniorage is collected. But, on the other hand, if the γ's differ, seigniorage will be collected at only one point in time. This is a counterfactual implication that could be used to rule out, in the present context, iso-elastic demand-for-money functions.

Appendix C

Here we discuss the derivation of the orthogonality condition for the case of state-contingent inflation; i.e., equation (13.39). Starting with equation (13.38), we perturb an optimal solution by increasing m_t by one unit, by changing *all* values of θ_{t+1} by the same fixed amount $d\theta_{t+1}$ (i.e., $d\theta_{t+1}$ is a constant independent of the state of nature). Recalling equation (13.37), this perturbation changes the first term of (13.38) by:

$$R_{t+1}[R_t - \phi(_{t+1}s) - D_t/E_t\beta u'(c_{t+1})] \equiv J. \qquad (A13.7)$$

This quantity is unknown in period t because s_{t+1} has not yet been revealed. However, expression (A13.7) is fully known by the planner in period $t + 1$. We will examine the possibility of compensating the increase in the budget surplus given by (A13.7) by correspondingly changing the second term in equation (13.38) through a change in m_{t+1}. The problem faced by the planner in $t + 1$ is that he does not know the full implications of modifying m_{t+1}, because he does not know s_{t+2}.

Let $\partial\theta_{t+2}(x_{t+2})/\partial m_{t+1}$ denote the variation in θ_{t+2} (chosen in period $t + 2$) around its optimal value per unit of change in m_{t+1} in order to make the total variation of expression (13.38) equal to zero, for every s_{t+2}. This is equivalent to saying that, for each s_{t+2}, we must have (recall 13.38):

$$J + [R_{t+1} - \theta_{t+2} \qquad (A13.8)$$
$$+ m_{t+1}\,\partial\theta_{t+2}(s_{t+2})/\partial m_{t+1}]\,\partial m_{t+1}(_{t+1}s)/\partial m_t = 0,$$

where $\theta_{t+2} = \phi(_{t+2}s)$. Note that $_{t+1}s$ is in the expression $\partial m_{t+1}(_{t+1}s)/\partial m_t$ to stress the fact that the change in m_{t+1} is made on the basis of information available in $t + 1$ (but not necessarily in t). Hence, multiplying both sides of (A13.8) by $u'(c_{t+2})$ and taking expectations as of period $t + 1$, we get

$$JE_{t+1}u'(c_{t+2}) + \{E_{t+1}(R_{t+1} - \theta_{t+2})u'(c_{t+2})$$
$$+ m_{t+1}\,\partial[E_{t+1}u'(c_{t+2})\theta_{t+2}(s_{t+2})]/\partial m_{t+1}\}\partial m_{t+1}(_{t+1}s)/\partial m_t = 0 \qquad (A13.9)$$

where, once again, we assume that c_{t+2} is not affected by monetary policy (for a proof, see appendix A).

By (13.37), we have

$$m_{t+1} \frac{\partial E_{t+1} u'(c_{t+2})\theta_{t+2}}{\partial m_{t+1}} = -D_{t+1}/\beta. \qquad (A13.10)$$

Furthermore, using (A13.10) in (A13.9) and solving for $\partial m_{t+1}(_{t+1}s)/\partial m_t$, we get:

$$\frac{\partial m_{t+1}(_{t+1}s)}{\partial m_t} = \frac{-J E_{t+1} u'(c_{t+2})}{E_{t+1}[R_{t+1} - \phi(_{t+2}s)]u'(c_{t+2}) - D_{t+1}/\beta}. \qquad (A13.11)$$

Once again, at individual optimum we have

$$u'(c_t) = \beta R_t E_t u'(c_{t+1}). \qquad (A13.12)$$

Hence, using (A13.12) in (A13.11), and recalling that $\omega_t = 1 - \theta_{t+1}/R_t$, we have:

$$\frac{\partial m_{t+1}(_{t+1}s)}{\partial m_t} = -R_t \frac{1/\alpha_t - \omega_t}{1/\alpha_{t+1} - \dfrac{E_{t+1}\omega_{t+1} u'(c_{t+2})}{E_{t+1} u'(c_{t+2})}} \qquad (A13.13)$$

where, as before, $\alpha_t = u'(c_t)/D_t$.

We can write equation (13.36) as follows:

$$v'(m_t) = \beta R_t E_t \omega_t u'(c_{t+1}). \qquad (A13.14)$$

Consequently, equation (13.39) is the orthogonality condition that replaces now equation (13.24) of the previous analysis. Notice that since ω_t is now random, $E_t\omega_t$ denotes the rational-expectations expected value of ω_t when calculated in period t.

References

Aghevli, Bijan B., and Mohsin S. Kahn. 1977. Inflationary Finance and the Dynamics of Inflation: Indonesia, 1951–72. *American Economic Review* 67 (June):390–403.
Bailey, Martin J. 1956. The Welfare Cost of Inflationary Finance. *Journal of Political Economy* 64 (April):93–110.

Barro, Robert J. 1979. On the Determination of Public Debt. *Journal of Political Economy.* 87 (October):940–71.

Calvo, Guillermo A. 1978. On the Time Consistency of Optimal Policy in a Monetary Economy. *Econometrica* 46 (November):1411–28.

———. 1988. Controlling Inflation: The Problem of Non-Indexed Debt. In *Debt, Adjustment and Recovery: Latin America's Prospect for Growth and Development,* ed. Sebastian Edwards and Felipe Larraín. New York: Basil Blackwell.

Calvo, Guillermo A., and Roque B. Fernandez. 1982. Competitive Banks and Inflation Tax. *Economic Letters* 12 (December):313–17.

Calvo, Guillermo A., and Pablo E. Guidotti. 1989. On the Level and Variability of the Inflation Tax. Manuscript. International Monetary Fund, Washington, D.C., October.

Calvo, Guillermo A., and Maurice Obstfeld. 1990. Time Consistency of Fiscal and Monetary Policy: A Comment. *Econometrica* 58 (September):1245–47.

Dutton, D. S. 1971. A Model of Self-Generating Inflation. *Journal of Money, Credit and Banking* 3 (May):245–62.

Eckstein, Zvi, and Leondardo Leiderman. 1989. Estimating an Intertemporal Model of Consumption, Money Demand, and Seigniorage. Unpublished. (Tel Aviv University, July).

Grilli, Vittorio. 1988. Seigniorage in Europe. Working Paper no. 2778. NBER, Cambridge, November.

Hansen, Lars P. 1982. Large Sample Properties of Generalized Method of Moment Estimators. *Econometrica* 50 (July):1029–54.

Lovell, M. C. 1963. A Keynesian Analysis of Forced Savings. *International Economic Review* (September):247–64.

Mankiw, N. Gregory J. 1987. The Optimal Collection of Seigniorage: Theory and Evidence. *Journal of Monetary Economics* 20 (September):327–41.

Obstfeld, Maurice. 1988. Dynamic Seigniorage Theory: An Exploration. Unpublished. (University of Pennsylvania and NBER, December.)

Olivera, Julio H. G. 1967. Money, Prices and Fiscal Lags: A Note on the Dynamics of Inflation. *Banca Nazionale del Lavoro Quarterly Review* (September):258–67.

Persson, Mats, Torsten Persson, and Lars E. O. Svensson. 1987. Time Consistency of Fiscal and Monetary Policy. *Econometrica* 55 (November):1419–32.

———. 1989. A Reply. Seminar Paper no. 427. Institute for International Economic Studies, Stockholm, Sweden, January.

Poterba, James M., and Julio J. Rotemberg. 1990. Inflation and Taxation with Optimizing Governments. *Journal of Money, Credit, and Banking* 22 (February):1–18.

Sargent, Thomas J. 1987. *Dynamic Macroeconomic Theory.* Cambridge: Harvard University Press.

Tanzi, Vito. 1977. Inflation, Lags in Collection, and the Real Value of Tax Revenue. *IMF Staff Papers* 24 (March):154–67.

Part IV: Relative Price Variability

14

Overview

The main objective for the work in part IV was to examine the extent to which the acceleration of inflation in Israel was accompanied by a marked change in the variability of relative prices. While textbook-type monetary inflation is regarded as neutral with respect to the structure of relative prices, there was the perception in Israel and in other high-inflation countries that increases in the overall rate of inflation were accompanied by a rise in the variability of relative price change across different sectors. If true, this relation would imply different consequences of inflation for the allocation of resources across sectors and for welfare than those of frameworks where increases in inflation have no impact on the structure of relative prices.

Previous research in macroeconomics has provided two main classes of models that are capable of explaining a positive comovement between the rate of inflation and the cross-section variability of relative price change. First, models of incomplete information based on agents' confusion between aggregate and relative price movements imply that relative-price variability is affected by unanticipated aggregate shocks. Second, models that embody contractual rigidities and/or staggering of wages and prices imply differential prices responses in the short run across sectors in response to a common aggregate shock. See Cukierman (1983) for a useful survey of these and other models.

Part IV begins with theoretical and empirical analysis of an extension of imperfect information models that is important for the case of Israel as well as several other economies. Namely, the case in which some prices in the economy are directly set by government or regulated by it. It is the case in countries such as Israel, Argentina, and Brazil, to name a few, that prices of basic foodstuffs, electricity, public transportation, and other items are determined by government. The fact that adjustments of these prices are widely publicized implies that in analyzing these economies the information structure of incomplete information models has to be modified. Accordingly, chapter 15 explores the implications of this modified information structure for the variability of relative prices. A major result was that the extent to which the average price of controlled goods is not aligned with the nominal supply of money can have an impact, beyond that of unanticipated aggregate shocks, on relative price variability within the free sector of the economy. Econometric results based on monthly data from 1966 to 1980 indicated that the proposed mechanism for nonneutral effects of controlled prices has significant explanatory power for relative price variability within free goods. That is, government pricing policy had an impact not only on overall relative price variability but also on relative price variability within that sector of the economy whose prices are not regulated by the authorities.

While the foregoing analysis was confined to a specific framework within the class of imperfect information models, the remainder of this part is devoted to a relatively more model-free examination of the empirical links between the rate of inflation, its variability, and the variability of relative inflation rates across sectors. The data set for this part consists of monthly observations of the price level, of sectoral prices, and of other variables from 1966 to 1988. This work documents a positive significant relation between the rate of inflation, its variance over time, and the variability of relative inflation rates. It is shown that unexpected and expected inflation are both positively related to relative price variability, but the former relation is the stronger one statistically. Variance decompositions indicate that most of the observed variability in relative inflation rates can be attributed to inflation variability within the free-goods sector. Yet, inflation variability within the set of controlled goods accounts for a nonnegligible portion of overall relative inflation variability.

Last, I examined these relations after 1985 along the path to stabilization. The evidence indicates that disinflation was accompanied by a sharp drop in both the variability of inflation rates across sectors and the time variability of the overall rate of inflation. Thus, disinflation probably attenuated important elements of "noise" in relative prices and of inflation uncertainty that prevailed under high inflation.

References

Cukierman, Alex. 1983. Relative Price Variability and Inflation: *A Survey and Further Results*. Carnegie-Rochester Conference Series on Public Policy 19:105–66.

15

Price Controls and the Variability
of Relative Prices

1. Introduction

Recent literature that explains relative price variability within a partial information multimarkets framework typically assumes that prices in *all* markets are determined by market clearing.[1] However, in many countries a certain number of prices is either directly set by the government or regulated by it. In Israel, for example, the government is directly involved in setting the prices of some basic foodstuffs, fuels, electricity, public transportation, and a number of other items.[2] Adjustments in the prices of these goods are made at discrete intervals and are widely and instantaneously disseminated by the media. As a result individuals in all markets have up-to-date information on that component of the general price level which is set by the government. In terms of the "islands" paradigm this means that the component of the general price level which is confused with relative price movements is smaller than the same component in an economy in which all prices are freely determined by the market.

The purpose of this article is to explore the implications of this modified information structure for relative price variability within a partial information framework and to test some of those implications using Israeli data. The Israeli economy is characterized by a wide range of fluctuations in the rate of inflation (from a level of almost zero in 1968 to a rate of 133 percent in 1980)

Reprinted with permission from *Journal of Money, Credit, and Banking* 16 (August 1984):271–84.

1. Examples are Barro (1976); Parks (1978); Cukierman (1979b); and Hercowitz (1981). See also Fischer (1981).

2. The government uses the setting of these prices as a policy tool whose target is to maintain the cost of some basic basket below some (usually changing) level. In the last few years, the setting of these prices has also been influenced by an attempt to change the path of inflation over time.

258   *Chapter Fifteen*

as well as in relative price variability. It therefore provides a potentially useful environment for testing various hypotheses about inflation and relative price variability.

Using Theil's (1967) variance decomposition, the variance of relative prices can be attributed to terms involving the variance of relative prices within the group of free goods, the variance of relative prices within the group of goods whose prices are controlled, and the variance between the two groups.[3] The last two variances are obviously directly affected by governmental price setting policy in the controlled segment of the economy. The main interest of this paper, however, is in possible effects of controls on relative price variability *within* the free or market segment of the economy. We therefore lump all the goods in the controlled or administered sector of the economy into one single aggregate, whose price is set by the government, and focus on the effects of the price of this aggregate on relative price variability within the free segment of the economy.[4] Throughout the paper we refer to the composite good whose price is set by the government as the controlled part of the economy and to its price as the price of the controlled good. This connotes, at least to American readers, the type of price controls imposed by Nixon in the years 1971–74. However, the price controls we consider are different in two important respects. First, they are a permanent institution and not, as during 1971–74 in the United States, a temporary device for slowing inflation down. Second, they involve direct subsidization and price setting by the government.[5]

A major result is that in addition to aggregate unanticipated shocks, relative price variability within the free part of the economy is also affected by the extent to which the price of the controlled good is not synchronized with the nominal supply of money. This effect is perfectly anticipated and arises because of divergences in supply and demand elasticities among markets within the free sector of the economy. Empirical testing of this hypothesis using Israeli monthly data between 1966 and 1980 reveals that relative price variability is significantly affected by both factors.[6]

The conceptual framework also makes it possible to investigate the effect

3. See Blejer and Leiderman (1982) for an application of this decomposition to the traded and nontraded sectors of an open economy.
4. Explanation of relative-price variability within the group of controlled goods and between groups requires a theory of government's behavior that is beyond the scope of this paper.
5. A fuller description of the institutional details of price setting by the government in Israel can be found in Shapira (1980).
6. By contrast Hercowitz (1981, 1982) finds that unanticipated monetary shocks affected relative-price variability during the hyperinflation in Germany, but not during the postwar period in the United States.

of the existence of a controlled sector on the Lucas-type tradeoff coefficient (Lucas 1973). In particular, it is shown that as the size of the controlled sector increases, the tradeoff coefficient between unanticipated shocks and output in the free sector also increases.

The model and the main analytical results are presented in section 2. An expression for the variance of relative price change within the free sector is derived and evaluated. Empirical results that are based on this equation are presented in section 3. This is followed by concluding remarks.

2. The Model

A. Structure and Solution

The economy consists of two distinct segments. A composite controlled good whose price is determined by the government and a free goods segment whose prices are determined by market clearing as in recent multimarkets rational expectations models (see Lucas 1973; Barro 1976; Cukierman and Wachtel 1979; Hercowitz 1981). Individuals in the free segment of the economy do not have full current information about the general price level since they operate in markets across which information does not flow instantaneously. However, individuals have information about the current value of the price of the good that is traded in the market in which they currently operate. In addition individuals in all markets have up-to-date information on the current price of the controlled good. This informational assumption is designed to approximate the situation in countries such as Israel in which any changes in the prices of a small group of controlled goods are immediately and widely disseminated to the public through all the channels of the media.

Demand for free good v assumes the log-linear form

$$y_t^d(v) = -\psi(v)[p_t(v) - Q_t^*(v)]$$
$$+ \alpha[x_t - Q_t^*(v)] + w_t^d(v), \quad \psi(v) > 0, \quad (15.1)$$

where $y_t^d(v)$ and $p_t(v)$ are, respectively, the logarithms of the quantity demanded and the price of the good in market v. $Q_t^*(v)$ is the perception of the logarithm of the current general price level as formed by individuals in market v given the information they have at time t. x_t is the quantity of a nominal stock and $w_t^d(v)$ is a random shock to demand in market v. For each free good v, the term $p_t(v) - Q_t^*(v)$ is the locally perceived relative price and $-\psi(v)$ is the (negative) elasticity of demand with respect to this relative price. This demand elasticity is allowed to vary across markets.

Demand is also influenced by the term $x_t - Q_t^*(v)$, which reflects a real balance effect.

Supply of free good v is given by

$$y_t^s(v) = \gamma(v)[p_t(v) - Q_t^*(v)] + w_t^s(v), \ \gamma(v) > 0, \qquad (15.2)$$

where $y_t(v)$ is the logarithm of the quantity supplied in market v and $w_t^s(v)$ is a random shock to supply in this market. $\gamma(v)$ is the (positive) elasticity of supply with respect to the locally perceived relative price and is allowed to differ among markets. The relative excess demand shock $w_t(v) \equiv w_t^d(v) - w_t^s(v)$ has a normal distribution that is given by

$$w_t(v) \sim N(0, \sigma_w^2) \qquad \text{for all } v. \qquad (15.3)$$

$w_t(v)$ is also uncorrelated over time and across markets. The rate of change of the nominal stock, x_t, obeys

$$\Delta x_t \equiv x_t - x_{t-1} = E_{t-1}\Delta x_t + \varepsilon_t \equiv \delta_t + \varepsilon_t. \qquad (15.4)$$

$\delta_t \equiv E_{t-1}\Delta x_t$ is that part of Δx_t which is perfectly predictable on the basis of aggregate information up to and including period $t - 1$. In period t this information is known by individuals in all markets of the economy. ε_t is the innovation to the rate of change of the nominal stock and is not known with certainty in period t. It is serially uncorrelated, independent of $w_t(v)$, and possesses a distribution

$$\varepsilon_t \sim N(0, \sigma_x^2). \qquad (15.5)$$

δ_t can be considered as the prior expectation about the rate of growth of the nominal stock. The posterior is formed using the additional information conveyed by the local market price since this price partially reflects movements in ε_t. However, since the local price also reflects (differing across markets) relative excess demand shocks, the posterior expectation of x_t varies across markets making the perception of the current general price level different across markets as well.

The model's specification follows the tradition of recent multimarkets models in that it does not impose an economy-wide budget constraint. Such a constraint implies that given the levels of demand in all markets but one, the level of demand in this market cannot be specified independently. In our case specification of independent demand equations for each of the free goods implies that the demand for the controlled good will depend through the economy-wide budget constraint on the demands for the free goods. But we do not need to impose this dependence explicitly since the focus of the paper is on relative price variability within the free segment of the economy, which is affected in turn by the controlled sector only through the price of the controlled good. Since in the present framework government does not set the price of this good in response to market forces, there is no need to impose an economy-wide budget constraint explicitly.[7]

Equating demand and supply in a typical free market and using equation (15.4),

$$p_t(v) = \alpha\lambda(v)(x_{t-1} + \delta_t) + (1 - \alpha\lambda(v))Q_t^*(v)$$
$$+ \lambda(v)(\alpha\varepsilon_t + w_t(v)), \quad (15.6)$$

where $\lambda(v) \equiv 1/(\gamma(v) + \psi(v))$ is the inverse of the sum of the absolute values of demand and supply elasticities in market v.

The general price level is a weighted (geometric) average of all prices including in particular prices of free goods and of controlled goods. The logarithm of the general price level is

$$Q_t = \sum_v u(v)p_t(v) + u(c)p_t(c), \qquad \sum_v u(v) + u(c) = 1, \quad (15.7)$$

where $u(v) \geq 0$ is the weight of the vth free good in the general index and $u(c) > 0$ is the weight of the controlled good in the general index.

Equations (15.6) and (15.7), together with the rationality of expectations, imply that individual prices in the free goods sector and the actual and perceived values of the general price level are all determined simultaneously. Since the model is log linear, we hypothesize the log linear solution

$$Q_t = \Pi_1\delta_t + \Pi_2 x_{t-1} + \Pi_3\varepsilon_t + \Pi_4 p_t(c) \quad (15.8)$$

for the general price level, where $\Pi_i (i = 1, \ldots, 4)$ are unknown coefficients to be determined. The rational perception of Q_t in free market v is from (15.8):

$$Q_t^*(v) \equiv E[Q_t \mid I_t(v)]$$
$$= \Pi_1\delta_t + \Pi_2 x_{t-1} + \Pi_3 E[\varepsilon_t \mid I_t(v)] + \Pi_4 p_t(c), \quad (15.9)$$

7. At least not for the questions investigated in this article.

where $I_t(v)$ is the information set available to individuals in market v at time t. This information set includes δ_t, x_{t-1}, the current values of the individual price, $p_t(v)$, and the price $p_t(c)$, of the controlled good. In addition all individuals in the economy know α, σ_x^2, σ_w^2, the value of λ in their own market, and the (nonstochastic) weighted mean and variance of λ over all free markets of the economy. In other words, individuals have perfect knowledge about the sum of supply and demand elasticities in their own markets and only some aggregate knowledge about the distribution of those sums over free markets in the economy.

Using the method of undetermined coefficients and the optimal forecast (in the mean square sense) of ε_t given $I_t(v)$, the solution for equilibrium price in free market v is[8]

$$
\begin{aligned}
p_t(v) = \bar{Q}_t &+ \frac{\alpha\lambda(v)u(c)}{\alpha k\lambda_m + u(c)}\,(x_{t-1} + \delta_t - p_t(c)) \\
&+ \frac{(1 - k\theta)\lambda(v) + k\theta\lambda_m}{1 - k\theta + \alpha k\theta\lambda_m}\,(\alpha\varepsilon_t + w_t(v)),
\end{aligned}
\tag{15.10}
$$

where $k \equiv \Sigma_v u(v) < 1$ is the sum of the weights of the free goods and $\lambda_m \equiv (1/k)\Sigma_v u(v)\lambda(v)$ is the weighted mean value of λ within the group of free goods.

B. Relative Price Variance and the Effect of Controls

It is intuitively obvious that a *ceteris paribus* change in the price of the controlled good will affect relative price variability by changing the price ratio between controlled and noncontrolled goods. What is less clear is the effect of a *ceteris paribus* change in the price of the controlled good on relative price variability *within* the group of free goods. We now turn to the investigation of this question. A formal measure of relative price variability within the group of free goods is provided by

$$
\tau_{Ft}^2 \equiv E_w \sum_v \frac{u(v)}{k}\,[p_t(v) - Q_{Ft}]^2,
\tag{15.11}
$$

---

8. The details of the solution appear in an unpublished appendix to this article, which is available upon request from the authors. Note that it is hypothesized in equation (15.8) that individual relative excess demand shocks do not affect the general price level. Conditions under which this restriction is satisfied are also discussed in this appendix. $\bar{Q}_t$ is that part of the perception of Q_t which depends only on publicly available information as of time t and is equal to $[\alpha k\lambda_m(x_{t-1} + \delta_t) + u(c)p_t(c)]/(\alpha k\lambda_m + u(c))$.

where

$$Q_{Ft} \equiv \sum_v \frac{u(v)}{k} \, p_t(v) \tag{15.12}$$

is the mean (log of the) price level within the group of free goods. The w under the expected value sign in equation (15.11) indicates that the expected value is over the distribution of relative excess demand shocks. Substituting (15.10) into (15.12), subtracting the resulting expression from (15.10), and rearranging,[9] we obtain the following expression for a typical relative price within the group of free goods:

$$
\begin{aligned}
p_t(v) - Q_{Ft} &= \frac{\alpha u(c)\tilde{\lambda}(v)}{\alpha k \lambda_m + u(c)} (x_{t-1} + \delta_t - p_t(c)) \\
&+ \frac{\alpha(1 - k\theta)\tilde{\lambda}(v)}{1 - k\theta + \alpha k \theta \lambda_m} \varepsilon_t \\
&+ \frac{(1 - k\theta)\lambda(v) + k\theta\lambda_m}{1 - k\theta + \alpha k \theta \lambda_m} w_t(v)
\end{aligned}
\tag{15.13}
$$

where $\tilde{\lambda}(v) \equiv \lambda(v) - \lambda_m$ is the deviation of the value of λ in market v from its mean value within the group of free goods.

The main novelty of this paper is captured by the first term on the right hand side of equation (15.13). This term implies that in the presence of a controlled sector and some disparity in elasticities across free goods, lack of synchronization between the certain part of the nominal stock $(x_{t-1} + \delta_t)$ and the price of the controlled good will affect relative prices even within the group of free goods. When the government sets $p_t(c)$ in each period so as to make it equal to $x_{t-1} + \delta_t$, this effect vanishes.

Thus when $p_t(c)$ is chosen so as to equal $p_t^*(c)$, where

$$p_t^*(c) \equiv x_{t-1} + \delta_t, \tag{15.14}$$

the effects that the existence of a controlled sector may have on relative price variability are neutralized. We therefore refer to $p_t^*(c)$ as the neutralizing level of $p_t(c)$. In general, $p_t(c)$ need not be set at its neutralizing level. In such cases $d_t \equiv p_t^*(c) - p_t(c)$ is nonzero and the levels chosen for the price of controlled good and for the nominal stock affect relative prices even within

9. Detailed calculations appear in part A of the appendix.

the group of free goods. In particular, a positive value of d_t will increase (decrease) the relative price of goods with lower (higher) than average sums of demand and supply elasticities.

An elicit expression for the variance of relative prices within the group of free goods is obtained by substituting (15.13) into (15.11), using (15.3), and rearranging:

$$\tau_{Ft}^2 = C_0 + C_1\varepsilon_t^2 + C_2(p_t(c) - p_t^*(c))^2$$
$$+ C_3(x_{t-1} + \delta_t - p_t(c))\varepsilon_t, \qquad (15.15)$$

where

$$C_0 \equiv \frac{[\lambda_m^2 + (1 - k\theta)^2 V(\lambda)]\sigma_w^2}{[1 - \theta k(1 - \alpha\lambda_m)]^2} \qquad (a)$$

$$C_1 \equiv \frac{\alpha^2(1 - k\theta)^2 V(\lambda)}{[1 - \theta k(1 - \alpha\lambda_m)]^2} \qquad (b)$$

$$C_2 \equiv \left[\frac{\alpha u(c)}{\alpha k\lambda_m + u(c)}\right]^2 V(\lambda) \qquad (c)$$

$$C_3 \equiv \frac{2\alpha^2 u(c)(1 - \theta k)V(\lambda)}{[\alpha k\lambda_m + u(c)][1 - \theta k(1 - \alpha\lambda_m)]} \qquad (d)$$

$$V(\lambda) \equiv \sum_v \frac{u(v)}{k}(\tilde{\lambda}(v))^2 \qquad (e). \qquad (15.16)$$

$V(\lambda)$ is the nonstochastic weighted variance of λ within the free goods sector. Equation (15.15) says that the variance of relative prices within the group of free goods has several sources.[10] First, it naturally depends positively through C_0 on the variance σ_w^2 of relative excess demand shocks. The effect of a given σ_w^2 on τ_F^2 is stronger (see [15.16a]) the larger $V(\lambda)$ and the lower the average level of supply and demand elasticities (high λ_m^2) in the free goods sector. Second, it depends (through $C_1\varepsilon_t^2$) on the level of the current unanticipated nominal shock. This is the effect discussed by Hercowitz (1981). The third effect is related to the divergence of the price of the controlled good from its neutralizing level $p_t^*(c)$. Any increase in the absolute value of this divergence increases the dispersion of relative prices within the group of free goods. The

---

10. Note that $C_i > 0$ for all i including in particular the coefficient C_3 of the interaction term (since $\theta k < 1$).

difference $|p_t(c) - p_t^*(c)|$ measures, in effect, the degree of nonneutrality induced by the pricing policy chosen for the controlled good. The last effect in equation (15.15) is related to interaction between the unanticipated nominal shock and the degree of nonneutrality induced by the choice of $p_t(c)$. Obviously when $p_t(c) = p_t^*(c)$, the effect of the last two terms on the right-hand side of (15.15) vanishes. However, the government need not set $p_t(c)$ at its neutralizing level, and as the case of Israel suggests it usually does not do that. It can be seen from (15.16) that a given degree of nonneutrality as measured by the absolute value of the difference, $p_t(c) - p_t^*(c)$, causes more relative price dispersion within the free goods' sector the higher the divergence in elasticities across goods in this sector, as measured by $V(\lambda)$. As a matter of fact, when $V(\lambda) = 0$, which is the case when supply and demand elasticities do not vary across markets in the free sector, the last three components of relative price variability vanish identically (i.e., even if $d_t \neq 0$). This suggests that a nonneutral choice of the price of the controlled good will affect relative price variability within the free sector only if some elasticities differ among markets in this sector.

A choice of a nonneutralizing level for $p_t(c)$ will generally also have consequences for real output in the free segment of the economy. In particular if $p_t(c)$ is set below its neutralizing level, so that $p_t^*(c) - p_t(c) > 0$, output in the vth free market is larger than in the case $p_t(c) = p_t^*(c)$. Thus by delayed adjustments of $p_t(c)$ to its neutralizing level, the government can cause an expansion of output in the free segment of the economy.[11] Intuitively, when $p_t(c)$ is set below its neutralizing level, real balances are higher and demand for all goods is higher. This pushes up the relative prices of free goods and causes an expansion in the output of the free sector.

Essentially, a nonneutralizing choice of $p_t(c)$ triggers a wealth effect in all free markets whose influence on relative prices and outputs varies in accordance with the magnitudes of supply and demand elasticities in these markets.

C. Relative Price Change Variability and Controls

Since the focus of the discussion is on the short-run effects of price controls and incomplete information on relative price variability, the model is tested by using the variance of relative price change within the free sector.[12] This

---

11. This statement is based on the fact that the coefficient of $p_t^*(c) - p_t(c)$ in the solution for $y_t^s(v)$ is given by $\alpha u(c)\gamma(v)/[(\gamma(v) + \psi(v))(\alpha k\lambda_m + u(c))]$, which is positive. Note that this effect is stronger the larger the effect of real balances on demand (higher α) and the larger the size of the controlled sector (higher $u(c)$). In addition, both $p_t^*(c) - p_t(c)$ and ε_t have stronger effects on output in markets with larger supply elasticities.

12. Taking first differences eliminates long-run trends that are not explicitly modeled here. This procedure is used in most of the recent empirical work on relative price variability. See

variance is defined as

$$V_{Ft}(RPC) = E_w \sum_v \frac{u(v)}{k} [RPC_t(v)]^2. \tag{15.17}$$

$V_{Ft}(RPC)$ measures the nonproportionality of price movements within the economy's free sector. If all free prices change at the same rate, V_{Ft} is equal to zero; and it increases with the dispersion of price changes across free goods and services (see Theil 1967, chap. 5). Taking the first difference of equation (15.13), substituting the resulting expression into (15.17), using (15.3), and rearranging yields

$$V_{Ft}(RPC) = 2C_0 + C_1(\varepsilon_t - \varepsilon_{t-1})^2 + C_2(\delta_t + \varepsilon_{t-1} - \Delta p_t(c))^2$$
$$+ C_3(\delta_t + \varepsilon_{t-1} - \Delta p_t(c))(\varepsilon_t - \varepsilon_{t-1}), \tag{15.18}$$

which is the equation that is estimated in the empirical section. (The C_i coefficients have been defined in eq. (15.16) above.) When there are no controlled prices in the economy, $u(c) = 0$ so that $C_2 = C_3 = 0$, and this equation reduces to that estimated by Hercowitz (1981) for Germany during the hyperinflation. If in addition there is no disparity in elasticities across markets in the free sector, the variance of relative price change simply equals to $2C_0$, which is qualitatively analogous to the expression obtained for relative price variability in Barro (1976), Cukierman (1979b), and Cukierman and Wachtel (1982).[13]

D. The Size of the Controlled Sector and the Lucas Effect

Before concluding this section, it is interesting to investigate the effects of the existence of a sector in which prices are controlled on the relationship be-

---

Vining and Elwertowski (1976); Parks (1978); Fischer (1981); Hercowitz (1981); and Cukierman and Wachtel (1982).

13. In all three papers, relative price variability is found to be an increasing function of monetary uncertainty. Here, with different elasticities among markets, C_0 will be an increasing function of σ_x^2 if $\alpha \leq 1$ and $\gamma(v) + \psi(v) \geq 1$ for all v's. It is interesting to note that if the government sets the price of the controlled good at a constant percentage discount (premium) below (above) its neutralizing level, this contributes to relative price level variability but not to the variance of relative price change. This follows directly from the fact that relative price *level* dispersion is affected by $(p_t(c) - p_t^*(c))^2$ and relative price *change* dispersion is affected by $(\Delta p_t(c) - \Delta p_t^*(c))^2$ (compare eq. (15.15) with (15.18)). Thus if the government sets the price of the controlled good at a constant percentage below $p_t^*(c)$, in effect indexing it to some percentage of its neutralizing level, the variance of relative price change is not affected. This variance is affected only by *changes* over time in the percentage subsidy implicit in the price of the controlled good.

tween unanticipated nominal shocks and output within the free sector. The solution for equilibrium output in free market v is [14]

$$y_t^s(v) = \gamma(v)\lambda(v)\left[\frac{u(c)}{\alpha k\lambda_m + u(c)}(p_t^*(c) - p_t(c))\right.$$

$$\left. + \frac{\alpha(1 - k\theta)}{1 - k\theta(1 - \alpha\lambda_m)}\varepsilon_t\right]$$

$$+ \frac{(1 - k\theta)\gamma(v)\lambda(v)}{1 - k\theta(1 - \alpha\lambda_m)}w_t^d(v)$$

$$- \frac{(1 - k\theta)(1 + \gamma(v)\lambda(v)) + \alpha k\theta\lambda_m}{1 - k\theta + \alpha k\theta\lambda_m}w_t^s(v).$$

(15.19)

Since $k\theta < 1$, the effect of the unanticipated shock, ε_t, on output in a typical free market is positive. It can be shown that the coefficient of ε_t in equation (15.19) is a decreasing function of σ_z^2. This is the usual Lucas (1973) effect.

In order to determine the effect that the size of the controlled sector has on the tradeoff between output and unanticipated shocks, differentiate the coefficient of ε_t partially with respect to k. The sign of this partial derivative is the same as the sign of $-\alpha\theta\lambda_m$, which is negative. It follows that the larger the size of the sector in which the government sets prices, the larger the tradeoff coefficient within the free sector of the economy. At first sight, this result seems counterintuitive since when $u(c)$ goes up there is, in a sense, better information about the general price level and this should decrease the tradeoff coefficient. The resolution of this apparent puzzle is as follows: as the weight $u(c)$ goes up, the general price level is less influenced by unanticipated nominal shocks since a larger fraction of prices is directly set by the government. Knowing this fact individuals, when forming their perception about the current general price level, attribute less importance to the observations on individual market prices. As a result they are led to interpret any given change in individual prices more as relative price changes when $u(c)$ is higher. This causes a stronger output response to any given realization of ε_t, the higher $u(c)$. This result contrasts with the general notion that when individuals have additional information on some economy-wide variable, the tradeoff between real variables and unanticipated shocks decreases and may even, in Lucas's words, "eliminate the real part of the cycle altogether." [15]

14. It is shown in part A of the appendix that $Q_t^*(v) = \bar{Q}_t + [k\lambda_m\theta/(1 - k\theta + \theta\alpha k\lambda_m)] \cdot (\alpha\varepsilon_t + w_t(v))$. Equation (15.19) is obtained by substituting this expression and equation (15.10) into equation (15.2) and by rearranging.

15. See Lucas (1975:1138). Cukierman (1979a) shows that as the number of individual prices that any given individual is allowed to sample in the current period increases, the tradeoff

The reason for this divergence in results is that in all previous cases the additional aggregate information helps sharpen the forecast of ε_t. By contrast here as the size of the controlled sector increases, the need to use the forecast of ε_t decreases without helping to improve this forecast.

3. Empirical Results

The main goal of our empirical investigation is to estimate equation (15.18). This equation states that the variability of relative price change within the economy's free sector depends on three variables: unexpected money growth, the divergence of actual controlled good's inflation from its neutralizing level, and an interaction term. Here we use monthly data on the Israeli economy covering the period from 1966 to 1980. Israel is a potentially interesting case study for the present model because of two main reasons. First, its economy has experienced relatively wide variations in both inflation and relative price variability during the sample period. Second, and perhaps more importantly, controlled goods and services have a weight of approximately 40 percent in the CPI. Thus, there is potential room for important effects of government direct price setting on the behavior of relative prices in the economy. These price controls take in practice several forms. The price of bread, for example, is set by the government, which also subsidizes bread production; on the other hand, the price of stamps is directly set by the governmental post office.

The estimation of equation (15.18) requires price and money data. Our price data are based on the CPI figures published by the Israeli Central Bureau of Statistics in its publication *Price Statistics Monthly* (various issues). For the present purposes, we used a subdivision of the CPI into 23 components. Each one of these components, in turn, was classified as pertaining to either the controlled or the free group of goods and services.[16] During the sample period the weights of the CPI components were changed twice, at the beginning of 1974 and 1977, to adjust for changes in the consumption patterns of the population. These changes have been explicitly taken into account in our

---

coefficient decreases. Barro (1980) considers a model in which individuals in all markets have information on an economy-wide interest rate. This additional information also decreases the size of the tradeoff coefficient in comparison to a situation in which no observation on the interest rate is available.

16. Specifically, free goods and services include furniture, clothing and textiles, shoes, ferrous products, construction and housing, entertainment, meat and poultry, personal services, other services, other industries, and business services. Controlled goods and services include milk and dairy products, bread, flour and baking products, taxes and insurance, education, medical services, electricity, fishing products, canned fish and meat, other food, chemical products, mail, and transportation. The weights of controlled goods and services in the overall CPI used here are 0.42 (1966–69), 0.44 (1970–76), and 0.39 (1977–80). This classification follows along broad lines the one presented in the 1974 *Annual Report* of the Bank of Israel (p. 194).

calculations. Regarding money data, we used the M_1 (currency + demand deposits) figures reported by the Bank of Israel in its *Annual Report* (various issues).

The index of relative price change dispersion used here is the one discussed in the previous section of the paper:

$$V_{Ft}(RPC) = \sum_v \frac{u(v)}{k} [\Delta p_t(v) - \Delta Q_{Ft}]^2,$$

where v indexes the goods and services of the free sector, $u(v)$ is the weight of good v in the overall CPI, and k is the weight of the free sector in the CPI.[17]

To estimate equation (15.18), it is necessary to decompose actual money growth (Δx_t) into expected and unexpected components (δ_t and ε_t, respectively); see equation (15.4) above. Here we assumed that money growth follows an AR(6) process.

$$\Delta x_t = \sum_{i=0}^{5} \phi_i L^i \Delta x_{t-1} + \phi_6 + \varepsilon_t, \tag{15.20}$$

where Δx_t is the logarithmic first difference of M_1 and L is the lag operator (i.e., $L^i \Delta x_t = \Delta x_{t-i}$).[18]

With these specifications, joint estimation of equations (15.18) and (15.20) by maximum likelihood yields the following results:

$$\Delta x_t = 0.010 + (-0.172 + 0.068L + 0.187L^2 + 0.136L^3$$
$$\quad (0.004) \quad\quad (0.073) \quad (0.075) \quad\quad (0.073) \quad\quad (0.076)$$

$$- 0.018L^4 + 0.372L^5)\Delta x_{t-1} \tag{15.20'}$$
$$(0.076) \quad\quad (0.072)$$

$$\rho^2 = 0.19$$

$$V_{Ft}(RPC) = 0.0003 \quad + \quad 0.085 \, (\varepsilon_t - \varepsilon_{t-1})^2$$
$$(0.00007) \quad\quad (0.023)$$
$$+ \quad 0.153 \, [\delta_t + \varepsilon_{t-1} - \Delta p_t(c)]^2$$
$$(0.022)$$
$$+ \quad 0.141 \, (\varepsilon_t - \varepsilon_{t-1})[\delta_t + \varepsilon_{t-1} - \Delta p_t(c)].$$
$$(0.052)$$

$$\rho^2 = 0.19$$

17. ΔQ_{Ft} is the inflation rate of the free sector as a whole and is defined as $\Delta Q_{Ft} = \Sigma_v[u(v)/k]\Delta p_t(v)$.

18. Use of broader monetary aggregates than M_1 and inclusion of additional regressors in equation (15.20), such as controlled inflation rates and lagged values of V_F, yielded similar (though less precise) findings for equation (15.18) than those that are reported below.

270   *Chapter Fifteen*

Figures in parentheses below regression coefficients are estimated standard errors. ρ^2 is the squared correlation coefficient between actual and fitted values. The sample period for the dependent variables is October 1966 through December 1980. Equation (15.20') is the estimated money growth process. This specification yielded white noise residuals and thus an operational measure for $\delta(\delta_t = \Delta x_t - \varepsilon_t)$. The estimated relative price change dispersion equation is given in (15.18'). All the estimated parameters obtain the hypothesized signs and are significantly different from zero.

To test the marginal contribution of the price-control terms to the explanatory power of the estimated two-equation system, it is appropriate to compare the above system with one in which the last two coefficients on the right-hand side of (15.18') are constrained to be equal to zero. In the latter case, the system's log of likelihood function turns out to be equal to 1,290.89; for equations (15.18') and (15.20') it is 1,309.32. These systems can be formally compared by using the likelihood ratio statistic, which is calculated as $LR = -2 \log(L_R/L_u)$, where L_R is the maximal value of the likelihood function under the restrictions and L_u is its value under no such restrictions. In the present case, LR is equal to 36.86, and this is higher than the critical chi-square value (with 2 degrees of freedom) for a significance level of 0.001.

These results support the notion that the existence of a controlled sector may have important implications for relative price variability within the economy's free sector through the channel suggested in this investigation. However, it is also well to point out that the model's explanatory power for V_{Ft} is not impressively high. This suggests that in order to fully account for the *monthly* variation in V_{Ft}, is is necessary to include in the analysis additional variables to those implied by the present imperfect-information model.

4. Concluding Remarks

This paper has presented and tested a theory of relative price variability for market-determined prices in the presence of a sector whose prices are directly set by the government and disseminated promptly and widely throughout the economy. The empirical evidence supports a key implication of the theory; namely, that relative price variance within the free segment of the economy is positively affected by both unanticipated monetary shocks and the divergence of the price of the controlled good from its neutralizing level.

More generally, the implications for relative price behavior of the partial information island paradigm are supported, in a nonnegligible manner, by the present Israeli data, as they are by the German hyperinflation data (Hercowitz 1981). Coupling these findings with the fact that unanticipated money growth fails to provide significant explanation for relative price variability in the United States, Hercowitz (1982) seems to suggest that the implications of partial information models stand a better chance of being detected in countries with high and variable inflation.[19]

Although the data sustain the implications of the theory, the model does not fully account for the monthly fluctuations in the variance of relative price change. This suggests, in our view, that other factors besides partial information, such as the existence of contracts and costs of price adjustment, are also responsible for part of the variability in relative prices.[20] A merging of these two approaches seems to be a potentially fruitful avenue for research in the area of relative price change and inflation.

References

Barro, Robert J. 1976. Rational Expectations and the Role of Monetary Policy. *Journal of Monetary Economics* 2 (January):1–32.

———. 1980. A Capital Market in an Equilibrium Business Cycle Model. *Econometrica* 48 (September):1393–417.

Blejer, Mario I., and Leonardo Leiderman. 1982. Inflation and Relative Price Variability in the Open Economy. *European Economic Review* 18 (July):387–402.

Bordo, Michael D. 1980. The Effects of Monetary Change on Relative Commodity Prices and the Role of Long-Term Contracts. *Journal of Political Economy* 88 (December):1088–1109.

Cukierman, Alex. 1979a. Rational Expectations and the Role of Monetary Policy: A Generalization. *Journal of Monetary Economics* 5 (April):213–29.

———. 1979b. The Relationship between Relative Prices and the General Price Level: A Suggested Interpretation. *American Economic Review* 69 (June):444–47.

Cukierman, Alex, and Paul A. Wachtel. 1979. Differential Inflationary Expectations and the Variability of the Rate of Inflation: Theory and Evidence. *American Economic Review* 69 (September):595–609.

———. 1982. Relative Price Variability and Nonuniform Inflationary Expectations. *Journal of Political Economy* 90 (February):146–57.

Fischer, Stanley. 1981. Relative Shocks, Relative Price Variability, and Inflation. *Brookings Papers on Economic Activity* 2:381–442.

Hercowitz, Zvi. 1981. Money and the Dispersion of Relative Prices. *Journal of Political Economy* 89 (April):328–56.

———. 1982. Money and Price Dispersion in the United States. *Journal of Monetary Economics* 10 (July):25–38.

Lucas, Robert E., Jr. 1973. Some International Evidence on Output Inflation Trade-offs. *American Economic Review* 63 (June):326–35.

19. The level and the variance of inflation are usually positively correlated and Israel is no exception to this regularity. See table 16.3.

20. See, for example, Sheshinski and Weiss (1977); Taylor (1981); and Bordo (1980) for discussions along these lines.

————. 1975. An Equilibrium Model of the Business Cycle. *Journal of Political Economy* 83 (December):1113–44.

Parks, Richard W. 1978. Inflation and Relative Price Variability. *Journal of Political Economy* 86 (February):79–95.

Shapira, Ehud. 1980. The Inflationary Process and Relative Price Changes: The Israeli Case. Ph.D. dissertation, Graduate School of Business Administration, New York University.

Sheshinski, Eytan, and Yoram Weiss. 1977. Inflation and Costs of Price Adjustment. *Review of Economic Studies* 44 (June):287–303.

Taylor, John B. 1981. On the Relation between the Variability of Inflation and the Average Inflation Rate. In *The Costs and Consequences of the Inflation,* ed. Karl Brunner and Allan H. Meltzer, 57–85. Carnegie-Rochester Conference Series on Public Policy, vol. 15. Amsterdam: North-Holland.

Theil, Henri. 1967. *Economics and Information Theory.* Chicago: Rand McNally.

Vining, Daniel R., and C. Thomas Elwertowski. 1976. The Relationship between Relative Prices and the General Price Level. *American Economic Review* 66 (September):699–708.

16

Relative Price Variability and Inflation in the Israeli Economy

A basic paradigm of economic theory is that relative prices and the general price level are independent. However, with the advent of high inflation in Israel and elsewhere it became clear that inflation and relative prices are not unrelated. This stimulated a substantial body of empirical work as well as the development of a number of theories designed to explain the observed relationships between some of the dimensions of the inflationary process and relative price variability. Some of these theories offer competing explanations of these interactions and controversies on the subject have not yet been definitely resolved.

While previous empirical studies have focused on low or mild inflation countries, we here study the case of a high-inflation economy, Israel 1966–79. This sample of Israeli data is a potentially rich one for studying inflation and relative price variability; the average monthly inflation rate at the end of our sample period is more than ten times that prevailing at its start.

The main purpose of this paper is to investigate empirically the relationships between relative price variability and inflation in Israel and to describe the similarities and differences in the behavior of individual relative prices. Since the focus is on the discovery of empirical regularities the paper is not wedded to any particular theory. However, some of the implications of the major alternatives are surveyed briefly in order to provide a background for the results. This is done in section 1. Data description and basic computations appear in section 2. Section 3 presents, analyzes, and compares the behavior of individual relative prices over time. In particular the similarities and differences in the behavior of the prices of controlled and free commodities are discussed. Empirical evidence on the relationship between relative price variability, on the one hand, and on the other, various aspects of inflation (such as actual inflation, expected and unexpected inflation, the

Reprinted with permission from *Bank of Israel Economic Review* 59 (1987):47–63.

variance of inflation and the variance of the error of forecast of inflation) is presented in section 4, which also presents a decomposition of relative price variability into within-group and between-group variability for free and controlled commodities. It also reports on Granger-type causality tests between relative price variability and various dimensions of the inflationary process.

1. Alternative Models Dealing with Inflation and Relative Price Variability

The recent literature presents a number of competing, or at times complementary, hypotheses to explain observed relationships between the distributions of general inflation and relative prices. Methodologically speaking, these hypotheses can be classified as follows: (a) equilibrium *versus* disequilibrium theories; (b) hypotheses based primarily on imperfect information as opposed to those which are not. This leads to a fourfold classification of theories:

1. Imperfect information cum equilibrium
2. Imperfect information cum disequilibrium
3. Perfect information cum equilibrium
4. Perfect information cum disequilibrium.

The most explicit models belong to group 1. These include multimarket equilibrium models based on the aggregate-relative confusion (Lucas 1973; Barro 1976; and Cukierman and Wachtel 1979) as well as multimarket models based on the permanent-transitory confusion. In both types of model the economy is viewed as neutral to monetary impulses under full information. In the first class of model information is imperfect in that the current general price level is not known, thereby inducing a positive relationship between relative-price variability and unexpected nominal shocks (Parks 1978; Hercowitz 1981) or the variability of inflation (Cukierman 1979). Even when the current price level is perfectly known a positive relationship emerges between relative price variability and the variability of inflation provided that people are not certain about the permanence of current shocks and provided that production takes time (Cukierman 1982).

A model of the aggregate-relative confusion variety which includes a controlled goods sector is developed and estimated with data for Israel in chapter 15. A major point of this paper is that unsynchronized choice of the money supply and the price level in the controlled goods sector contributes an additional element of relative price variability within the free goods sector.

The most important models in group 2 (imperfect information cum dis-equilibrium) belong to the contract approach. For staggered contracts of exogenously specified duration this approach also predicts a positive relationship between relative price variability and the variance of inflation (Taylor 1981).

Even under full information the existence of price adjustment costs makes it profitable to adjust nominal prices discontinuously. Sheshinski and Weiss (1977) show that in these circumstances an increase in expected inflation causes an increase in the magnitude of price adjustments at the level of the firm. Under plausible conditions this increase creates a positive relationship between relative price variability and the level of expected inflation. This type of hypothesis belongs to group 3.

The fourth group of hypotheses which is associated with Schultze (1959), asserts that (because of temporary downward price stickiness) an upward change in an important relative price triggers a policy response which tends to increase inflation. This type of hypothesis implies that the direction of causality is from relative-price variability to general inflation; real changes in relative prices alter the rate of inflation through the government's policy response. Further discussion of some of these issues appears in Fischer (1981). An extensive survey within the framework of equilibrium models with imperfect information appears in Cukierman (1983a).

2. Data and Methods

The Consumer Price Index (CPI) was broken down into 22–23 major industry groups which we refer to as commodities (see table A16.1). Their prices and weights were collected monthly from January 1966 to December 1979 (inclusive).[1] Thus the period analyzed covers the low inflation of the 1966–68 recession as well as the high and variable inflation of the late 1970s.

These basic data were used in order to compute both cross-sectional and time indexes of the variability of relative prices. The cross-sectional indexes were obtained by computing for each month the weighted variance of relative prices round the mean (which is the general level of the CPI) and the weighted variance of monthly rate of price change around the rate of change of the mean. We refer to the first variance as the cross-sectional variance of relative-price *levels* and denote it by τ_t^2, and to the second as the cross-sectional variance of relative price *change* (or inflation) and denote it by $V_t(\pi^R)$, where

---

1. However, the econometric evidence of section 4 is based on the period January 1966–December 1980.

t is a monthly time index. The over time variability of each commodity is measured by the fluctuations in the natural logarithm of the ratio of the price index of commodity *i* to the average CPI. This measure of relative price variability is approximately equal to the percentage deviation of the price of good *i* from the CPI. It does not therefore depend on the general level of prices; a *ceteris paribus* increase in all prices does not affect this percentage deviation. This measure is denoted by $Rp_t(i)$.

In addition to these basic computations the components of the CPI were classified as controlled commodities (C), whose prices are determined by the government and its agencies, and free commodities (F) whose prices are determined by market forces.[2] A monthly price index was computed for each group. The cross-sectional variances of relative price levels and relative inflation were also computed for each group. The total cross-sectional variance of relative price levels was decomposed into (a) the within-group cross-sectional variance of relative price levels of free commodities, τ_{Ft}^2; (b) the within-group cross-sectional variance of relative price levels of controlled commodities, τ_{Ct}^2; and (c) the between-group cross-sectional variance of relative price levels, τ_{FCt}^2.

3. The Behavior of Individual Relative Prices Over Time

An important feature of the Israeli economy is that some prices are controlled by the government while others are determined by market forces. Thus the average price index of the controlled group reflects the policy of the government and the average price index of the free group is set in the market. In this section we present evidence on relative-price developments for the controlled commodities group and for individual free and controlled commodities.

The Relative Price of Controlled and Free Goods, 1966–79

Free commodities usually account for between 65 and 70 percent of the CPI and the rest is controlled goods. We define the general level of the CPI in period *t* as

$$Q_t \equiv \sum_i u(i)p_t(i), \tag{16.1}$$

---

2. The classification of the CPI components into free and controlled commodities follows broadly that presented in Bank of Israel, *Annual Report 1974*, p. 233. The detailed classification is shown in table A16.1.

where $p_t(i)$ is the natural logarithm of the price of commodity i in period t and $u(i)$ is its weight in the CPI.[3] Similarly the price levels of controlled and free goods in period t are defined as respectively

$$Q_{Ct} \equiv \sum_{i \in C} \frac{u(i)}{\beta(C)} p_t(i) \qquad (16.2)$$

and

$$Q_{Ft} \equiv \sum_{i \in F} \frac{u(i)}{\beta(F)} p_t(i) \qquad (16.3)$$

where

$$\beta(C) \equiv \sum_{i \in C} u(i); \quad \beta(F) \equiv \sum_{i \in F} u(i); \; \beta(C) + \beta(F) \equiv \sum_{i} u(i) \equiv 1, \qquad (16.4)$$

since the sum of the weights of all commodities entering the CPI is unity by definition. The relative price of the group of controlled (C) or free (F) commodities at time t is defined as

$$Rp_t(X) \equiv Q_{Xt} - Q_t \qquad X = C, F. \qquad (16.5)$$

Since Q_t, Q_{Ct}, and Q_{Ft} all have logarithmic dimensions, the $Rp_t(X)$ approximate the percentage deviation from the CPI of the respective indexes. The time paths of these deviations appear in figures 16.1 and 16.2. The figures suggest that until after the Yom Kippur War (1973) there is a secular decline in the relative price of controlled commodities and a complementary secular increase in the relative price of free goods. The relative price of controlled goods is adjusted upward during 1974 and it then declines until the beginning of 1977, when there is again a sharp upward adjustment, which is eroded by the rapid inflation of 1978 until the next substantial upward adjustment, in the first half of 1979. The path of the relative price of free commodities in figure 16.2 is more or less a mirror image of the path for controlled com-

3. Note that (a) the general price level is defined as a geometric average and not as an arithmetic average as done by the Central Bureau of Statistics. This definition facilitates the analytical discussion of relative prices that follows; (b) the weight $u(i)$ also changes, albeit discretely, over time; for notational simplicity no time index is attached to $u(i)$. However, the computation presented below incorporates the periodic updating of the weight structure.

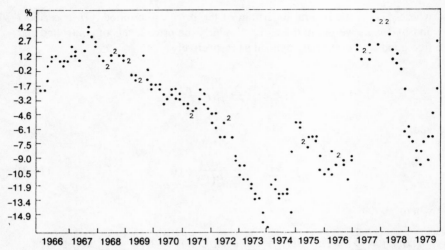

Figure 16.1   The relative price of controlled goods, 1966–79. Note: Here and in figures 16.2, 16.3, 16.4 the relative price of commodity group X is approximated by $Rp_t(X)$; see eq. 16.5 and the accompanying text. The numeral 2 indicates a closely similar pair of observations in adjacent months.

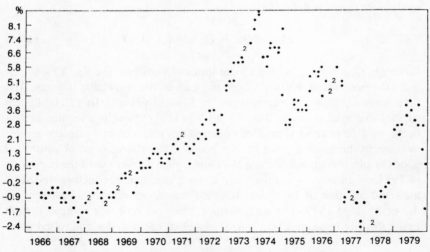

Figure 16.2   The relative price of free goods, 1966–79. See note to figure 16.1.

modities in figure 16.1. In general the figures suggest that the period between 1966 and 1979 falls into two subperiods as far as the government's pricing of controlled goods is concerned. Until the end of 1973 the government allowed inflation to erode the real price of controlled goods. From 1974, controlled prices were adjusted periodically. As a result the real price of controlled commodities fluctuates more in the second period. It is interesting that 1974–79, when inflation was much higher than in 1966–73, is also a period in which the government made a serious attempt to maintain the real price of controlled goods. (A more detailed year-by-year institutional discussion of adjustments in the prices of controlled goods can be found in Shapira [1980:62–75].)

The Relative-Price Behavior of Free Commodities

Broadly speaking, the relative price of the following free commodities rose in 1966–79: fruit & vegetables, furniture, chemicals, iron and steel products, and other industries. The relative price of fish, textiles & clothing, footwear, and entertainment decreased. The relative prices of housing services and meat & poultry did not show any significant upward or downward drift.[4] However, until the beginning of 1975 the relative price of housing services displayed a systematic upward drift which was followed by a very large decrease from 1975 to roughly mid-1978, when it started to increase again. Behind these general tendencies can be identified two distinct types of relative-price behavior. The relative prices of such items as fruit & vegetables, fish, and meat & poultry tend to fluctuate considerably over short periods. On the other hand, the relative prices of commodities such as housing services, furniture, chemicals, iron & steel products, and entertainment display more short-run stability. However, these commodities are characterized by long-run relative-price cycles. The first type of behavior is illustrated by fruit & vegetables in figure 16.3 and the second by housing services in figure 16.4.[5]

The commodities also differ in the variability of relative prices over time, as shown in table 16.1, in which they are ranked by residual variance. The table suggests that even after controlling for changes in the trend of relative prices, housing services and other industries remain the sectors with the most volatile relative prices.

The Relative-Price Behavior of Controlled Commodities

The relative prices of most controlled commodities follow the pattern displayed by the group average in figure 16.1. However, there are notable excep-

---

4. These statements are based on the significance and the sign of the β_i in regressions of the form $Rp_t(i) = \alpha_i + \beta_i t$.

5. Similar figures showing the relative-price behavior of other commodities are available from the authors on request.

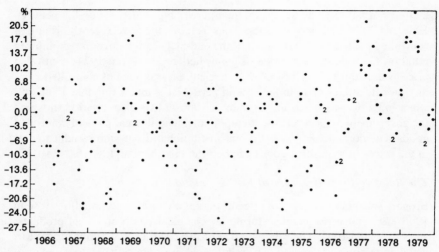

Figure 16.3   The relative price of fruit and vegetables (free), 1966–79. See note to figure 16.1.

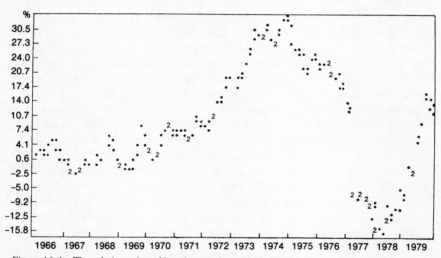

Figure 16.4   The relative price of housing services, 1966–79. See note to figure 16.1.

tions such as canned meat, bread, and other food. But even these outliers share with the other controlled commodities the dramatic upward relative-price adjustment that took place some time in or around 1974. In general the relative prices of individual controlled commodities display sharp increases followed by a fairly long period of decline (see figure 16.1).

Among the controlled commodities whose relative-price behavior is similar

Table 16.1
Residual Variance Over Time of Relative Prices

Free Commodities	%	Controlled Commodities	%
Housing services	13	Educational services	14
Other industries	11	Taxes & insurance	13
Furniture & wood products	11	Milk & dairy products	11
Fruit & vegetables	10	Health services	10
Chemical products	10	Electricity & water	10
Entertainment	9	Bread etc.	9
Metal products	8	Meat & canned fish	7
Clothing & textile products	7	Other food	6
Meat & poultry	6	Postal services & transport	4
Footwear etc.	6		
Fish & livestock	5		

to that of the group average there are still differences in the timing and intensity of adjustments. For example the relative price of bread, flour, and bakery products was adjusted strongly upwards during 1970 when the relative prices of most other controlled goods were sliding down. The 1979 upward adjustment was shared by all controlled commodities except medical services.

For the period as a whole (1966–79), the following controlled commodities show a strong rise in relative price: meat & canned fish; bread, flour & bakery products; other food; and electricity. However, the relative price of milk & dairy products, postal services & transport, taxes & insurance, and education declined strongly. There was no significant trend in the relative price of medical services.

Like the free commodities, the controlled commodities differ in the variability over time of relative prices, as can be seen in the second column of table 16.1.

4. The Empirical Evidence

Empirical evidence from some western countries suggests that when the rate of inflation and its variance go up so does the cross-sectional variability of relative prices.[6] The large swings in the rate of inflation in Israel during the

6. Work by Vining and Elwertowski (1976) and Fischer (1981) for the United States and by Padoa Schioppa (1979) for Italy suggests the existence of a positive relationship between relative price variability and inflation variance. Table 6 of Kleiman (1977) displays a positive correlation between relative price variability and the rate of inflation in Israel during the period 1964–75. However, table 2 of Jaffee and Kleiman (1977), using data from various countries until the early 1970s, implies no relationship between relative price variability and the rate of inflation. This finding conflicts with those of Kleiman (1977) and Vining and Elwertowski as well as with those presented below. This may be due, in our opinion, to bias caused by the statistical procedure used in Jaffee and Kleiman.

latter part of the 1970s make it possible to determine whether this relationship persists when the rate of inflation approaches and reaches the three-digit level. These issues are investigated in the present section, both informally and through formal econometric tests.

Review of the Data

As noted in section 2 the cross-sectional variability of relative prices is characterized by the variance of relative prices, τ_t^2, and the variance of relative inflation rates, $V_t(\pi^R)$. The formal definition of these two concepts is given by

$$\tau_t^2 \equiv \sum_i u(i)[Rp_t(i)]^2 \qquad (16.6)$$

and

$$V_t(\pi^R) \equiv \sum_i u(i)[Rp_t(i) - Rp_{t-1}(i)]^2, \qquad (16.7)$$

where τ_t measures the average percentage deviation of individual prices from the general price level in period t. The square root of $V_t(\pi^R)$ measures the average percentage deviation of the rate of inflation of commodity i from the general rate of inflation as measured by $Q_t - Q_{t-1}$. In order to determine whether there is a systematic relationship between relative price variability and the variability of inflation it is necessary to have some measure of the variability of inflation. Here, we use the variance of monthly inflation rates within a year. Formally, let

$$\pi_t \equiv Q_t - Q_{t-1} \qquad (16.8)$$

be the rate of inflation in month t. The variance of the rate of inflation for a given year is defined as the variance of the twelve monthly π_t. The data on average yearly figures for π_t, τ_t, $[Vt(\pi^R)]^{1/2}$ and the within-year variance, $[V(\pi)]^{1/2}$, of the rate of inflation are summarized in table 16.2. A quick glance at the table suggests that the variables were on the whole positively related during the period. More often than not, an increase in the rate of inflation and its variance is accompanied by an increase in both the variance of relative-price levels and the variance of relative inflation rates. Note also that at low rates of inflation the standard deviation of cross-sectional relative inflation rates is substantially higher than the monthly general rate of inflation; this implies that changes in relative prices dominate the scene. However, at high rates of inflation the monthly general rate of inflation is

Table 16.2
Inflation, Relative Prices, and Their Variability
(monthly rates, %)

	$\bar{\pi}$	$[V(\pi)]^{1/2}$	τ	$[V(\pi^R)]^{1/2}$
1966	0.56	0.96	6.6	2.4
1967	0.01	0.69	7.3	2.2
1968	0.16	0.68	8.5	2.4
1969	0.31	0.96	8.5	3.2
1970	0.85	1.01	5.3	2.0
1971	1.00	1.04	6.6	2.6
1972	0.95	1.14	10.1	3.2
1973	1.80	1.10	15.5	2.8
1974	3.79	3.57	18.4	4.8
1975	1.77	1.75	19.3	3.0
1976	2.71	1.81	17.9	3.3
1977	3.19	2.71	7.4	3.6
1978	3.23	1.65	11.1	3.3
1979	6.20	2.14	12.0	4.9

[a]The rate of inflation, $\bar{\pi}$, is an unweighted arithmetic mean of the monthly figures.

higher than the standard deviation of cross-sectional relative rates of inflation $[V(\pi^R)]^{1/2}$.

Note that the view that it is the *acceleration* of inflation that is closely associated with increases in $V(\pi^R)$ receives some support from the data. Indeed, peak values for $V(\pi^R)$ were obtained in 1974 and 1979, when inflation accelerated sharply.

Table 16.3 presents some summary statistics for free and controlled commodities. The picture within each group is similar to that for the two combined; as the within-group rate of inflation goes up, the within-group cross-sectional variability of relative prices goes up as well. It can also be seen that the variances of relative price levels of free and controlled commodities move rather closely together. Both go up and down at roughly the same time and their magnitude is on the whole similar.

To summarize, the preliminary evidence presented here supports the view that as the rate of inflation and its variance go up, so does the variability of relative prices. This relationship is explored more precisely below.

Decomposition of the Cross-Sectional Variance of Relative Prices

It is instructive to find out how much of the cross-sectional variability of relative prices is due to within-group relative-price variability and how much is due to between-group variability. The within-group variability of free commodities can be regarded as 'natural' variability of relative prices, while

Table 16.3
Inflation and Relative Prices
(monthly rates, %)

	Free Commodities		Controlled Commodities	
	$\tilde{\pi}_F$	τ_F	$\tilde{\pi}_C$	τ_C
1966	0.44	6.4	0.82	6.8
1967	−0.05	6.9	0.14	7.5
1968	0.22	8.8	0.05	7.7
1969	0.42	8.7	0.07	8.1
1970	0.92	5.7	0.72	2.8
1971	1.08	6.5	0.87	5.2
1972	1.19	9.6	0.52	7.0
1973	2.10	13.0	1.24	10.7
1974	3.29	17.1	4.72	14.0
1975	2.01	17.2	1.33	20.3
1976	2.67	15.7	2.81	17.6
1977	3.08	7.6	3.45	5.7
1978	3.61	10.9	2.36	10.5
1979	5.89	9.9	6.91	13.2

the within-group variability of controlled commodities reflects government policy. The between-group variance is influenced by both government policy with respect to the prices of controlled commodities and by the pricing practices of the private sector.

To find how much of total relative price variability is due to each of the above components we use the following variance decomposition.[7]

$$\pi_t^2 = \beta(F)\tau_{Ft}^2 + \beta(C)\tau_{Ct}^2 + \tau_{FCt}^2, \qquad (16.9)$$

where

$$\tau_{Ft}^2 = \sum_{i \in F} \frac{u(i)}{\beta(F)} [p_t(i) - Q_{Ft}]^2 \quad (a)$$

$$\tau_{Ct}^2 = \sum_{i \in C} \frac{u(i)}{\beta(C)} [p_t(i) - Q_{Ct}]^2 \quad (b) \qquad (16.10)$$

$$\tau_{FCt}^2 = \sum_{i \in F,C} \beta(i)(Q_{it} - Q_t)^2, \quad (c)$$

7. A similar decomposition is applied to tradables and nontradables in Mexico by Blejer and Leiderman (1982).

where τ_{Ft}^2 and τ_{Ct}^2 are the within-group variances of relative prices of free and controlled commodities respectively; τ_{FCt}^2 is the between-group variance of relative prices. Equation (16.9) decomposes total relative-price variability into the within-group variances of (a) free and (b) controlled commodities, where $\beta(F)$, $\beta(C)$ are the respective CPI weights, and (c) the variance between the average price levels of the two groups.

The share of $\beta(C)\tau_{Ct}^2$ in the total cross-sectional variance of relative prices is usually substantially below half and that of $\beta(F)\tau_{Ft}^2$ is usually above half. The rest of the variability of relative prices is due to the between-group variation. However, as can be seen in table 16.4, there are substantial fluctuations in these percentages over time. Note first that most of the variance in relative price levels is due to within-group rather than between-group variability. The within-group variance is responsible for most of the relative-price variability at the beginning of the sample period. Its share then drops to a minimum in 1972–74 and rises again towards the end of the period but to a level below the initial share. The increase in the share of between-group variance in 1972–74 reflects the government's attempts to adjust the real prices of controlled goods in 1973 and 1974. As can be seen from figure 16.1, substantial upward adjustments were made in the real prices of controlled commodities after a continuous and prolonged decline. Second, when the share of the within-group variances declines, it usually does so in both groups. However, the decline is stronger for controlled commodities. This probably reflects the fact that once it has decided to adjust their prices, the government does it across the board, at fairly similar rates. By contrast, the dispersion in the adjustment of individual controlled prices was greater in 1978–79. In general it seems that when the relative price, $Q_{CT} - Q_t$, of controlled commodities goes down, the contribution of relative price variance within this group to τ^2 goes up, and vice versa.

Table 16.4
Decomposition of the Variance of Relative Prices*

	% τ^2 due to		
	Controlled Goods $\beta(C)\tau_C^2/\tau^2$	Free Goods $\beta(F)\tau_F^2/\tau^2$	Between-Group Variance τ_{FC}^2/τ^2
1966–68	34	63	3
1969–71	22	67	11
1972–74	19	52	29
1975–77	30	58	12
1978–79	31	57	12

*Period averages.

Relative Inflation Variability: Econometric Results

This section reports econometric evidence on the association between $V(\pi^R)$ and various parameters of the inflationary process such as the rate of inflation (actual, expected, and unexpected), the variance of inflation over time, the acceleration of inflation, and the variance of the error of forecast of inflation. The equations presented here are intended to capture key elements embodied in the alternative models discussed in section 1. However, it is as well to emphasize that these equations (in their present form) are mainly presented for descriptive-indicative purposes; and they do not make possible any definitive test of one set of models against another.

Let us first turn to the results of estimating an equation for $V(\pi^R)$ as a function of π^2 (sample period: 8/1966–12/1980)

$$V(\pi^R) = \underset{4.04}{0.0003} + \underset{19.44}{0.46\pi^2} \qquad \begin{aligned} R^2 &= 0.69 \\ DW &= 1.97 \end{aligned}$$

(small numerals are t statistics).

According to this equation an increase in the inflation rate is accompanied by a significant increase in relative inflation variability. Interestingly, the DW statistic is consistent with absence of first-order serial correlation. Is the coefficient of π^2 invariant through time? The answer is no. For 1966–69 it is 2.62 ($t = 2.87$); for 1970–73 it is 0.51 ($t = 5.24$); and for 1974–80 it is 0.45 ($t = 12.0$). Thus it appears to have been declining in the course of time (and as inflation accelerated). Although these results are informative they do not reveal whether the positive association between $V(\pi^R)$ and inflation is due only to the effect of unexpected inflation on $V(\pi^R)$ or also to a direct effect of expected inflation on relative price variability.[8]

To test this hypothesis, we first constructed an expected inflation ($E\pi$) series with the following estimated sixth-order autoregressive inflation process.

$$E\pi_t = \underset{1.32}{0.003} + \underset{5.46}{0.42\pi_{t-1}} - \underset{0.23}{0.02\pi_{t-2}} + \underset{1.78}{0.15\pi_{t-3}} + \underset{0.49}{0.04\pi_{t-4}}$$
$$+ \underset{2.17}{0.18\pi_{t-5}} + \underset{1.88}{0.15\pi_{t-6}}$$

$$\begin{aligned} R^2 &= 0.55 \\ DW &= 2.03 \end{aligned}$$

8. The first effect is implied by the Lucas-type confusion between aggregate and relative shocks (see Hercowitz [1981]; Cukierman [1984: ch. 6]). The second is implied by the existence of costs of price adjustment (Sheshinski and Weiss 1977).

(Only one equation was used for the entire sample period—7/1966–12/ 1980—because the hypothesis that the coefficients of this equation were stable throughout the period could not be rejected at usual significance levels.) Unexpected inflation is then given by $(\pi_t - E\pi_t)$.

Using expected inflation and unexpected inflation as regressors, the following equation is obtained for the entire period:

$$V(\pi^R) = \underset{2.92}{0.0002} + \underset{13.35}{0.82}(\pi_t - E\pi_t)^2 + \underset{7.60}{0.36}(E\pi_t)^2. \qquad \begin{array}{l} R^2 = 0.60 \\ DW = 1.86 \end{array}$$

Unexpected inflation (squared) has a stronger and more significant effect on $V(\pi^R)$ than expected inflation (squared). Note that the coefficient of the latter is significantly different from zero, a finding that is in conflict with theories predicting that *only* the unexpected portion of π_t affects $V(\pi^R)$. Thus for 1966– 69, 1970–73, and 1974–80, respectively, the coefficient of $(\pi_t - E\pi_t)^2$ is 0.77 ($t = 1.3$); 1.08 ($t = 5.17$); and 0.81 ($t = 8.9$). For $(E\pi_t)^2$ the respective coefficients are 1.28 ($t = 1.3$); -0.03 ($t < 1$), and 0.34 ($t = 4.09$). Thus, while the results for the unexpected inflation coefficient seem to be stable over time, the coefficient of $(E\pi_t)^2$ falls sharply at the end of the period.

Additional regressions were run for $V(\pi^R)$ as a function of two alternative measures of inflation variability: the moving (6-month) variances of the inflation rate $[V(\pi)]$ and of unexpected inflation $[V(\pi - E\pi)]$. The results are

$$V(\pi^R) = \underset{4.44}{0.0005} + \underset{5.10}{1.33}V(\pi) \qquad \begin{array}{l} R^2 = 0.14 \\ DW = 1.43 \end{array}$$

$$V(\pi^R) = \underset{4.64}{0.0006} + \underset{4.42}{1.00}V(\pi - E\pi) \qquad \begin{array}{l} R^2 = 0.11 \\ DW = 1.42 \end{array}$$

The two equations give quite similar results, indicating a positive and significant association between the two measures of inflation variance and relative price variability. This is consistent with theoretical implications of models featuring the aggregate-relative confusion, as well as with empirical results for the United States (see Cukierman 1984: chapter 4). Theoretically, although inflation variance and inflation uncertainty as measured by $V(\pi - E\pi)$ are not identical, they tend to be positively associated.

The coefficient of $V(\pi)$ seems to have declined, from 3.13 in the first subperiod to 0.76 in the last. The coefficient of the variance of unexpected inflation, however, shows a less clear pattern; it increases in the 1970–73 sample and then decreases during 1974–80.

Last, we turn to an equation that attempts to capture any asymmetries in the response of $V(\pi^R)$ to increases and decreases in inflation (1966–80),

$$V(\pi^R) = \underset{0.82}{-0.00007} + \underset{9.89}{0.03\pi} + \underset{5.76}{0.02D\pi} + \underset{4.20}{0.02|D\pi|}, \qquad R^2 = 0.71$$
$$DW = 1.92$$

where $D\pi$ is the acceleration of the inflation rate, and $|D\pi|$ is its absolute value. If the acceleration of inflation has no effect on $V(\pi^R)$ the coefficients of both $D\pi$ and $|D\pi|$ should be zero. If there is such an effect and if the effect of changes in the rate of inflation on $V(\pi^R)$ is symmetrical, the coefficient of $|D\pi|$ should be nonzero and that of $D\pi$ should be zero, and in the presence of asymmetry both coefficients should differ significantly from zero. The empirical evidence is consistent with the last case: $V(\pi^R)$ increases more when inflation increases than when it decreases. As a matter of fact, since the coefficients of $D\pi$ and $|D\pi|$ are equal the estimated equation is consistent with the view that only acceleration (as opposed to deceleration) of inflation affects relative price variability. Evidence for the subperiods considered indicates that this asymmetry is more typical of the end of the sample period than of its beginning.

These results hold in most cases for contemporaneous relationships between the variables of interest. In principle, though, relationships may involve lags. To check for this possibility, we ran Granger causality tests involving six lagged values of the 'caused' and potentially 'causal' variables. This was done by estimating bivariate autoregressive processes in each of which $V(\pi^R)$ was regressed on six of its own lagged values and on six lagged values of X (X is an inflation-related variable). Similarly X was regressed on six of its own lagged values and on six lagged values of $V(\pi^R)$. This bivariate structure was estimated with six alternative measures (X) of inflation: π, π^2, $(\pi - E\pi)$, $(\pi - E\pi)^2$, $V(\pi)$ and $V(\pi - E\pi)$. In every case the statistical tests indicated that there is no Granger causality—in either direction—between relative price variability and measures of general inflation. The inflationary process does not seem to precede relative-price variability; nor does the latter precede the inflationary process. This result is at variance with the results obtained by Fischer (1981; 1982) for the United States and Germany, probably because of Israel's much higher rate of inflation and its much more comprehensive system of indexation. These factors probably combine to eliminate any lagged interactions between relative price variability and inflation, thus leaving only the contemporaneous effects as the main element of interaction.

To sum up, we have found significant contemporaneous relations between $V(\pi^R)$ and other inflation-related variables. In our opinion, these relations reveal interesting regularities characterizing the economy of Israel. In general, the results support elements of many of the theories discussed in section 1. To determine which is the most compatible with the data, however, one would have to perform more detailed tests than those reported here, a task worthy of future attention.

Appendix

Table A16.1

CPI Basket Weights, Classified into Free and Controlled Commodities, 1966–79[a] (%)

	1966–69	1970–76	1977–79
Free commodities			
Fruit and vegetables	7.46	6.89	5.81
Fish and livestock	3.02	2.39	1.82
Meat and poultry	5.59	4.11	3.32
Furniture and wood products	3.72	2.69	2.69
Clothing and textile products	8.01	7.82	7.39
Footwear, leather, rubber & plastics	2.91	2.84	2.69
Chemical and petroleum products	3.03	3.31	4.86
Metal products	6.77	6.04	8.31
Other industries	2.68	3.02	2.95
Housing and construction services	15.84	14.65	20.72
Entertainment	1.86	2.08	1.06
Personal services	6.12	4.74	3.95
Hotels, restaurants, etc.	—	4.06	3.63
Business services	—	0.19	0.64
Other services	0.51	—	—
Controlled commodities			
Milk and dairy products	3.11	3.04	2.91
Meat and canned fish	1.82	1.34	1.08
Bread, flour, bakery products	3.64	3.63	3.18
Other food	7.87	7.86	6.89
Electricity and water	2.04	2.24	2.51
Postal services and transport	4.69	5.56	4.79
Taxes and insurance	2.61	3.85	3.12
Educational services	3.00	3.71	2.54
Health services	3.70	3.94	3.16
Total	100.00	100.00	100.00

[a] Based on the industrial classification of the Central Bureau of Statistics (see e.g., *Statistical Abstract of Israel 1983*, p. 270). The Classification was changed in 1970; in particular, 'hotels and restaurants' and 'business services' were not previously listed, and 'other services' was abolished. However, the number and identity of the commodities entering the computation of τ^2 and $V(\pi)$ are only marginally affected.

References

Barro, Robert J. 1976. Rational Expectations and the Role of Monetary Policy. *Journal of Monetary Economics* 2, no. 1 (January):1–32.

Blejer, Mario I., and Leonardo Leiderman. 1982. Inflation and Relative-Price Variability in the Open Economy. *European Economic Review* 18, no. 3 (July):387–402.

Cukierman, Alex. 1979. The Relationship between Relative Prices and the General Price Level: A Suggested Interpretation. *American Economic Review* 69, no. 3 (June):444–47.

————. 1982. Relative Price Variability, Inflation and the Allocative Efficiency of the Price System. *Journal of Monetary Economics* 9, no. 2 (March):131–62.

————. 1983a. Relative Price Variability and Inflation: A Survey and Further Results. Carnegie-Rochester Conference Series on Public Policy 19: *Variability in Employment, Prices, and Money* (Autumn):103–158.

————. 1983b. Reply to Parks and Cutler "A Comment on the Cukierman Paper." Carnegie-Rochester Conference Series on Public Policy 19: *Variability in Employment, Prices, and Money* (Autumn):167–69.

————. 1984. *Inflation, Stagflation, Relative Prices and Information*. Cambridge: Cambridge University Press.

Cukierman, Alex, and Paul Wachtel. 1979. Differential Expectations and the Variability of the Rate of Inflation: Theory and Evidence. *American Economic Review* 69, no. 4 (September):595–609.

Fischer, Stanley. 1981. Relative Shocks, Relative Price Variability, and Inflation. *Brookings Papers on Economic Activity* 2:381–431.

————. 1982. Relative Price Variability and Inflation in the United States and Germany. *European Economic Review* 18, no. 1/2 (May/June):171–96.

Hercowitz, Zvi. 1981. Money and the Dispersion of Relative Prices. *Journal of Political Economy* 89, no. 2 (April):328–56.

Jaffee, Dwight M., and Ephraim Kleiman. 1977. The Welfare Implications of Uneven Inflation. In *Inflation Theory and Anti-Inflation Policy*, 285–307 ed. Erik Lundberg. (International Economic Association Series Vol. 2.) London: Macmillan.

Kleiman, Ephraim. 1977. Indexation, Risk, and Relative Prices in Israel: 1964–1975. Discussion Paper No. 7713. Jerusalem: Falk Institute.

Lucas, Robert E., Jr. 1973. Some International Evidence on Output-Inflation Trade-offs. *American Economic Review* 63, no. 3 (June):326–34.

Padoa-Schioppa, F. 1979. Inflazione e Pressi-Relativi. *Moneta e Credito* 32, no. 128.

Parks, Richard W. 1978. Inflation and Relative Price Variability. *Journal of Political Economy* 86, no. 1 (February):79–95.

Schultze, Charles L. 1959. *Recent Inflation in the U.S.* Study Paper No. 1, Prepared for the Joint Economic Committee, U.S. Congress.

Shapira, E. 1980. The Inflationary Process and Relative Price Changes: The Israeli Case. Unpublished Ph.D. thesis, Graduate School of Business Administration, New York University.

Sheshinski, Eytan, and Yoram Weiss. 1977. Inflation and Costs of Price Adjustment. *Review of Economic Studies* 44, no. 2 (June):287–303.

Taylor, John B. 1981. On the Relation between the Variability of Inflation and the Average Inflation Rate. Carnegie-Rochester Conference Series on Public Policy 15: *The Costs and Consequences of Inflation* (Autumn):57–85.

Vining, Daniel R., Jr., and Thomas C. Elwertowski. 1976. The Relationship between Relative Prices and the General Price Level. *American Economic Review* 66 (September):699–708.

17

Relative Price Variability under High Inflation and Disinflation

In what follows, I present a brief update of the evidence reported in the preceding chapter regarding developments of the rate of inflation, its variability over time, and the cross-sectional variability of relative prices for the high-inflation period of the early to mid-eighties and for the period of disinflation thereafter. The data, variable notation and definitions correspond to those of the preceding chapter.

Table 17.1 provides the updated evidence for the average monthly rate of inflation, its variability, and the cross-sectional variability of relative rates of inflation. It can be seen that inflation accelerated rapidly in the early eighties and reached a peak of about 14 percent per month in 1984. Along with this trend, there was a strong rise in the cross-sectional variability of relative rates of inflation and in the variability of the rate of inflation through time. The peak value for the standard deviation of the variability of relative inflation rates was reached in 1984. This value was double the value of this variable in the very early eighties, and about six times the value of this variable in the late sixties and early seventies. For the standard deviation of the rate of inflation, the peak value obtained in the first half of 1985, at a level that was about three times the level in the early eighties and six times the level of the late sixties and early seventies.

The evidence for the period after the inflation-stabilization program of 1985 indicates that both these variabilities decreased rapidly with disinflation. In fact, by 1987 and 1987 the variability of inflation and the cross-section variability of relative rates of inflation reached figures lower than their values in the earlier low-inflation periods of the late sixties and early seventies. Especially interesting is the fact that despite government's implementation of selective price controls and of a fixed exchange rate with respect to the U.S. dollar during the first phase of the inflation-stabilization program, which presumably affected differently various sectors, there was a sharp drop in relative inflation-rate variability.

Table 17.1
Relative Price Variability under Inflation and Disinflation

Year	$\bar{\pi}$	$[V(\pi)]^{.5}$	$[V(\pi^R)]^{.5}$
1966–69	0.26	0.82	2.55
1970–73	1.15	1.07	2.65
1974	3.79	3.57	4.80
1975–78	2.73	1.98	3.30
1979	6.20	2.14	4.90
1980	7.07	2.06	7.29
1981	5.72	1.96	5.99
1982	6.97	1.42	7.04
1983	9.77	4.20	10.53
1984	14.09	4.72	14.71
1985a	12.95	6.06	14.15
1985b	2.61	1.58	3.02
1986	1.51	1.13	1.87
1987	1.24	0.54	1.34
1988	1.25	0.85	1.50

Note: $\bar{\pi}$ is the arithmetic mean (in percentage) of monthly rates of inflation; $V(\pi)$ is the variance of monthly inflation rates within a given year or
time period; $V(\pi^R)$ is the within year (or within period) average of relative
inflation variability. All variables are defined as in chapter 16. For the periods
after 1980, the CPI weights appearing in table 16A.1 have been updated
based on publication of new weights by the Israeli Central Bureau of Statistics. These weights are available from the author upon request. Last, 1985a
and 1985b indicate January–July and August–December of that year.

Table 17.2 provides updated evidence on the average rates of inflation
within the free-goods and the controlled-goods sectors of the economy, and
on the decomposition of relative inflation-rate variability into variability
within free goods, variability within controlled goods, and variability between
these two sets of goods (all these defined as in the preceding chapter).

Throughout the period of accelerating inflation there was a relatively strong
comovement between the rates of inflation of free goods and of controlled
goods. However, in the first half of 1985, right before the stabilization program, the rate of inflation of controlled goods was much higher than that of
free goods. This, in part, reflected the government's upward adjustment of
controlled goods' prices in anticipation of a subsequent period with more
limited price adjustments. Indeed, in the second half of 1985 the inflation rate
of controlled goods was lower than that of free goods, reflecting a key role of
price controls along with a fixed exchange rate in the disinflation process.
From 1986 on, there was again a high degree of comovement between these
rates of inflation.

As far as variance decompositions are concerned, there was a remarkable stability of the various shares for most periods during the episode of accelerating inflation. Most of the variability in relative rates of inflation (i.e., about 65 percent) could then be attributed to variability within the free-goods sector of the economy. Relative inflation rate variability within controlled goods accounted for about 30 percent of overall relative inflation-rate variability. This pattern appears to have changed after disinflation. While the share of variability within controlled goods has remained approximately the same as before, there has been a drop in the fraction of overall relative inflation-rate variability that can be attributed to variability within the free-goods sector. Thus, the share of between-groups variability has increased accordingly and it reached about 10–15 percent of overall variability in the late eighties. Whether this is a permanent change or not is something to be determined only as more data become available.

Overall, the updated evidence in this chapter supports the view that the close relation between the rate of inflation, the variance of inflation, and the

Table 17.2
Decomposition into Free and Controlled Goods

Year	$\bar{\pi}_F$	$\bar{\pi}_C$	Free Goods	Controlled Goods	Between Groups
			% of $V(\pi^R)$ Due to:		
1966–68	0.20	0.34	63	34	3
1969–71	0.81	0.55	67	22	11
1972–74	2.19	2.16	52	19	29
1975–77	2.59	2.53	58	30	12
1978–79	4.75	4.64	57	31	12
1980	6.83	7.60	60	37	3
1981	6.27	4.62	68	27	5
1982	6.81	7.30	56	40	4
1983	9.77	9.75	64	34	2
1984	14.38	13.47	66	31	3
1985a	11.03	16.52	43	51	6
1985b	3.85	0.52	76	3	21
1986	1.63	1.68	52	30	18
1987	1.27	1.18	50	38	12
1988	1.30	1.13	52	33	15

Note: $\bar{\pi}_F$ and $\bar{\pi}_C$ are the arithmetic averages of the monthly inflation rates (in percentages) of free and controlled goods. The classification of goods into free and controlled is as in chapter 16. Data after 1980 take into account updated weights for the various items in the CPI which have been published by the Israeli Central Bureau of Statistics. Thus, different weights apply to the periods 1980–84, 1985–86, and 1987–88. The weights for earlier periods appear in table A16.1. 1985a and 1985b indicate the periods January–July and August–December, respectively, of that year.

cross-section variability of relative inflation rates that we found in the previous two chapters works both ways. The acceleration of inflation in the early and mid-eighties was accompanied by a clear rise in the variabilities of inflation both over time and across sectors. And the evidence under the 1985 inflation-stabilization program points to a sharp drop in both these variabilities along with the rapid decrease in the rate of inflation.

Part V: Effects of Government Budget Policies

18

Overview

The Ricardian-neutrality notion that for a given path of government expenditures substitution of debt for taxes (or vice versa) does not affect private-sector wealth and consumption has been the source of wide controversy in modern macroeconomic policy analysis. This notion is in sharp contrast to the common Keynesian proposition that debt-financed tax cuts stimulate private consumption spending and aggregate demand. According to the Ricardian-neutrality proposition, it actually makes no difference to the level of aggregate demand if the government finances its outlays by debt or by taxation. Put differently, it is economically equivalent for the government to maintain a balanced budget or to run a debt-financed deficit.

Previous analytical research has made it clear that Ricardian results emerge only under a restrictive set of assumptions. Factors such as imperfect capital markets and liquidity constraints, distortionary taxes, uncertainty about future taxes, and finite horizons have been shown to produce deviations from Ricardian neutrality. Along with these various theoretical possibilities, the large body of empirical work on Ricardian neutrality that has accumulated over recent years yields conflicting and inconclusive evidence on the empirical validity of this proposition; see for example, the work surveyed by Leiderman and Blejer (1988).

While most previous empirical work relied on data for industrialized countries, where there have been moderate fluctuations in government budget aggregates, in this part I turn to evidence based on the case of Israel where there is a large public sector and where there have been sizable movements in government spending, taxes, and the budget deficit. These circumstances may provide fertile ground on which to test the hypothesis of Ricardian neutrality. To anticipate the econometric results of chapter 19 it is useful to examine first the general trends exhibited by the data. Figure 18.1 depicts the national saving rate as well as its two components: the saving ratio of the private sector and the saving ratio of the public sector. Each one of these is expressed as the

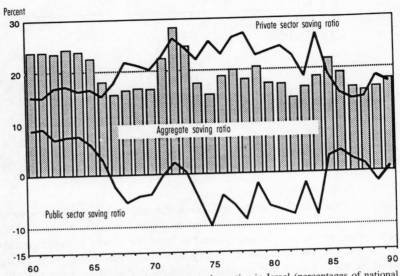

Figure 18.1   Private, public, and aggregate saving ratios in Israel (percentages of national income). Source: Bank of Israel, *Annual Report 1990*.

ratio of saving to the economy's national income, where the latter includes gross national product plus unilateral transfers from abroad.

It can be seen from figure 18.1 that the long-run behavior of the aggregate saving ratio does not exhibit a clear-cut trend from the late sixties and it has stayed at about 17 percent of national income. Despite this, there have been subperiods with marked cycles in the saving ratio. In particular, there were noticeable drops in the aggregate saving ratio in the mid-seventies, early eighties, and late eighties, and this ratio increased in the early and late seventies and in the mid-eighties.

This relatively trendless behavior of the aggregate saving ratio over several years was accompanied by a few episodes in which private-sector and public-sector saving behaved as mirror images of each other, much as predicted by the Ricardian neutrality hypothesis. Throughout the decade of the sixties the private saving ratio exhibited an upward trend and the public saving ratio showed a strong downward trend. This pattern was reversed in the early to mid-eighties, and it reappeared in the late eighties. Notice the quite sizable magnitude of these fluctuations, which ranged from -10 percent to $+10$ percent for the public savings ratio, and from 15 percent to 27 percent for the private saving ratio.

Of particular interest in this context is a comparison of public-sector and private-sector saving rates before and after the 1985 inflation-stabilization

program. It can be seen in table 18.1 that the aggregate saving rate did not
change much from 1981–85 to 1986–90 and remained in the order of 17
percent of national income. However, the public-sector saving ratio increased
sharply from −4.7 percent to 1.1 percent of national income. This increase
reflects an important degree of fiscal adjustment in the context of the stabilization plan, in that the public sector raised taxes and reduced spending in
order to balance the budget. As indicated in chapter 1, this element of fiscal
discipline after 1985 was a key factor for the success of the disinflation program. At the same time, there was a decrease in the saving ratio of the private
sector almost fully offsetting the increase in public-sector savings. The
private-sector saving ratio decreased from 22.3 percent of national income in
1981–85 to 16 percent in 1986–90. Interestingly, although the restrictive assumption behind the Ricardian neutrality hypothesis may not be fully met in
reality, the broad evidence of offsetting behavior by private and public saving
ratios, in figure 18.1 and table 18.1, conforms well with this hypothesis.

To formally test Ricardian neutrality, however, more structure is required.
This is the motivation for the next chapter, which develops an explicit stochastic framework in which the implications of Ricardian neutrality can be
tested with time-series data. What mainly distinguishes this approach from
earlier empirical investigations, besides the data used, is the fact that the tests
to be presented are not based on unrestricted reduced forms. Instead, the tests
focus on the cross-equation restrictions imposed by the Ricardian hypothesis
in the context of an intertemporal framework of consumers' optimization. The
model used allows for two sources of deviation from the benchmark case of
Ricardian neutrality: the existence of consumers' finite horizon and of liquidity constraints. The main findings indicated that the restrictions implied
by the Ricardian neutrality hypothesis are not rejected by the sample information. Thus, these econometric results tend to support the broad evidence
discussed here indicating that private consumption spending in Israel is in-

Table 18.1
Saving Ratios in Israel

Saving Ratios	1981–85	1986–90
Aggregate	17.6	17.1
Public sector	−4.7	1.1
Private sector	22.3	16.0

Note: The figures are yearly averages expressed as percentages of
national income. The latter is equal to gross national product plus
unilateral transfers from abroad. The data source is *Annual Report
1990*, Bank of Israel, Jerusalem.

variant with respect to changes in the financing of a given stream of government expenditures, whether by conventional taxes or public debt.

References

Leiderman, Leonardo, and Mario I. Blejer. 1988. Modeling and Testing Ricardian Equivalence. *IMF Staff Papers* 35 (March): 1–35.

19

Testing Ricardian Neutrality with an Intertemporal Stochastic Model

The impact of government budget variables on private-sector consumption is a key issue in assessing the implications of fiscal and monetary policy on the real side of the economy. In fact there are sharp controversies on this topic, most of which center around the Ricardian-equivalence proposition.[1]

The purpose of this paper is to develop and estimate a stochastic-intertemporal model of consumption behavior and to use it for testing a version of the Ricardian-equivalence proposition with time-series data. Our framework allows for two channels that may give rise to deviations from Ricardian neutrality: finite horizons and liquidity constraints. In addition, it incorporates explicitly the roles of taxes, substitution between public and private consumption, and different degrees of consumption durability.

The standard approach in empirical studies of the neutrality hypothesis is based on directly specifying regression equations linking consumption to disposable income, measures of nonhuman wealth, government spending, taxes, government transfers, etc. (see, for example, Kochin 1974; Tanner 1979; Feldstein 1982; Seater 1982; Kormendi 1983; Reid 1985). While the results from applying this approach are informative, a limitation, which makes the interpretation of the results ambiguous, is that the connection between the estimated equations and the underlying theoretical model is not specified explicitly. Although the theoretical model typically specifies that current consumption is influenced by current *and* expected future changes in labor income, taxes, etc., most of the empirical applications focus mainly on current explanatory variables and ignore expected future ones. Therefore, the estimated coefficients of a given explanatory variable (such as current government spending or taxes) in a consumption equation may reflect not only direct

Journal of Money, Credit, and Banking (February 1988): 1–21.
1. See Barro (1974).

effects of this variable, but also its effects as a predictor of future relevant variables. Moreover, these results cannot be used to assess the effects of policy changes, as, for example, a change in taxation, on consumption (Lucas's [1976] critique).[2] In contrast, the present study adopts an intertemporal optimizing framework whose implications, derived explicitly in the analysis, are the subject of empirical tests.

Since the seminal contribution of Hall (1978), numerous studies have applied the intertemporal optimizing approach to examine consumption behavior. However, almost none of these studies focus on the comovements of consumption and government-budget variables.[3] Moreover, these studies typically assume an infinite-horizon representative consumer. This assumption restricts the economic channels through which government-budget finance exerts its effects on consumption, resulting in an extreme case in which the model exhibits Ricardian properties. To move away from this case, Blanchard (1985) extended the intertemporal framework by relaxing the infinite-horizon assumption. His formulation allows for a richer set of interactions between government-budget-deficit variables and consumption, with Ricardian implications emerging only as a special case.[4] Another factor that may give rise to deviations from Ricardian neutrality is the existence of liquidity constraints that prevent some consumers from free access to capital markets (see the early work by Tobin and Dolde [1971], and the more recent contributions by Hayashi [1985] and Hubbard and Judd [1986]). In the present study, we develop a testable model which allows for deviations from neutrality through both these channels.

By virtue of the assumption of rational expectations, our framework results in a set of cross-equation restrictions. These restrictions are taken into account in the joint estimation of the consumption-behavior parameters and those of the stochastic processes governing the evolution of the forcing variables. We implement the model on monthly time-series data for Israel covering the 1980–1985 period. This case is of particular interest in testing the Ricardian-equivalence hypothesis because of the high volatility of movements in the budget deficit, taxes, and private consumption in an economy with unusually high government budget deficits, amounting to 15 percent of aggregate output, on average, during this period. The sizable deficits have resulted in a relatively large government debt, which was twice the size of GNP at the end of the period. These characteristics differ from those of the more stable envi-

---

2. For a recent survey of empirical tests of Ricardian equivalence, see Leiderman and Blejer (1988).

3. For an exception, see Aschauer (1985).

4. For analysis of effects of fiscal policy in open economies using this type of model, see Frenkel and Razin (1986). For an empirical implementation motivated by a model of this type, see van Wijnbergen (1985).

ronments studied in previous empirical works. They, therefore, enable a potentially more powerful test of hypotheses related to the comovements of private-sector consumption and taxes and public-sector spending.

Section 1 of this paper outlines the model. Empirical specifications and implementation of the model are presented in section 2. Section 3 extends the basic model to account for direct effects of public consumption on private consumption. Last, section 4 concludes the paper.

1. Theoretical Framework

We assume that there are overlapping generations of rational agents that have finite horizons. Specifically, there is a probability γ, smaller than unity, that individuals living in the present period will survive to the next period. A small open economy is considered, one that takes as given the world interest rate. We begin by considering the choice problem of an individual consumer.

1. Individual Consumer

The consumer is assumed to face a given safe interest factor R (where $R = (1 + r)$ and r denotes the safe rate of interest), but due to lifetime uncertainty the effective (risk-adjusted) interest factor is R/γ.[5] Disposable income is assumed to be stochastic and is denoted by y. Viewed from the standpoint of period t, consumer's utility from his stock of consumption goods during period $t + \tau$, $c_{t+\tau}$, is given by $\delta^\tau U(c_{t+\tau})$, where δ is the subjective discount factor. The probability of survival from period t through period $t + \tau$ is γ^τ, and therefore expected lifetime utility as of period t is

$$E_t \sum_{\tau=0}^{\infty} (\gamma\delta)^\tau U(c_{t+\tau}), \qquad (19.1)$$

where E_t is the conditional expectations operator. Individuals are assumed to maximize (19.1) subject to

$$c_t = (1 - \phi)c_{t-1} + x_t, \qquad (19.2a)$$

$$x_t = b_t + y_y - \left(\frac{R}{\gamma}\right)b_{t-1}, \qquad (19.2b)$$

5. See Blanchard (1985). Throughout we use the assumption of a constant real rate. While this is a restrictive assumption, it need not be very unrealistic in an economy with widespread indexation in financial markets.

and the solvency condition $\lim(\gamma/R)^t b_t = 0$. The variable x_t denotes the

$$t \to \infty$$

flow of consumption purchases, c_t denotes the stock of consumer goods, and ϕ denotes the rate of depreciation of this stock. The variable b_t is the one-period debt issued in period t. Consolidating equations (19.2a) and (19.2b), the expected value of the lifetime budget constraint is given by

$$\left[1 - \left(\frac{\gamma}{R}\right)(1 - \phi)\right] E_t \sum_{\tau=0}^{\infty} \left(\frac{\gamma}{R}\right)^{\tau} c_{t+\tau} = E_t \sum_{\tau=0}^{\infty} \left(\frac{\gamma}{R}\right)^{\tau} y_{t+\tau}$$

$$- \left(\frac{R}{\gamma}\right) b_{t-1} + (1 - \phi)c_{t-1} \equiv E_t w_t,$$

where $E_t w_t$ is (a specific definition of) expected wealth. This consolidated budget constraint is implied from the equality of the expected value of the discounted sum of the flow of consumption purchases and the corresponding discounted sum of the flow of disposable income, minus initial debt commitment.

With a view towards empirical implementation, we specify the utility function to be quadratic. That is,

$$U(c_t) = \alpha c_t - \frac{1}{2} c_t^2, \tag{19.3}$$

where $\alpha > 0$ and $c_t < \alpha$.

It is shown in the appendix that the solution to the optimization problem is

$$c_t = \beta_0 + \beta_1 E_t w_t, \tag{19.4}$$

where

$$\beta_0 = \gamma\alpha \frac{1 - \delta R}{\delta R(R - \gamma)},$$

and

$$\beta_1 = 1 - \frac{\gamma}{\delta R^2}\left[1 - \left(\frac{\gamma}{R}\right)(1 - \phi)\right]^{-1}.$$

Equation (19.4) is a linear consumption function, relating the stock of consumer goods c_t to the expected value of wealth, where β_1 is the marginal propensity to consume out of wealth.

2. Aggregate Consumption

The economy consists of overlapping generations. The size of each cohort is normalized to 1, there are γ^a individuals of age a, and the size of population is constant at the level $1/(1 - \gamma)$.

From equation (19.4), the consumption of an individual of age a at time t is

$$c_{t,a} = \beta_0 + \beta_1 \left[E_t \sum_{\tau=0}^{\infty} \left(\frac{\gamma}{R}\right)^{\tau} y_{1+\tau} - \frac{R}{\gamma} b_{t-1,a-1} \right. \tag{19.5}$$
$$\left. + (1 - \phi)c_{t-1,a-1} \right].$$

Aggregating consumption over all cohorts and dividing by the size of population, yields per capita aggregate consumption, C_t, as

$$C_t = (1 - \gamma) \sum_{a=0}^{\infty} \gamma^a c_{t,a} = \beta_0 + \beta_1 \left[E_t \sum_{\tau=0}^{\infty} \left(\frac{\gamma}{R}\right)^{\tau} y_{t+\tau} \right. \tag{19.6}$$
$$\left. - RB_{t-1} + \gamma(1 - \phi)C_{t-1} \right].$$

where B_{t-1} is aggregate per capita debt issued in period $t - 1$.

It is shown in the Appendix that equation (19.6) can be rearranged as follows:

$$C_t = \gamma\alpha(R - 1) \frac{\delta R - 1}{\delta R(R - \gamma)}$$
$$+ (1 - \gamma)\left(1 - \frac{\gamma}{\delta R^2}\right)\left[1 - \left(\frac{\gamma}{R}\right)(1 - \phi)\right]^{-1} \tag{19.7a}$$
$$\cdot E_{t-1} \sum_{\tau=0}^{\infty} \left(\frac{\gamma}{R}\right)^{\tau} (Y_{t+\tau} - T_{t+\tau}) + \Gamma C_{t-1} + \varepsilon_t,$$

where

$$\Gamma = \left[\frac{\gamma}{\delta R} + \gamma(1 - \phi)\right]\left[1 - \gamma\left(1 + \frac{1}{\delta R^2}\right)\right]\left[1 - \left(\frac{\gamma}{R}\right)(1 - \phi)\right]^{-1},$$

and where Y is gross income and T is the level of taxes (both in per capita terms), and ε_t is a zero mean, finite variance, error term. In order to express the consumption equation in terms of observed consumer purchases, we use recursively the per capita aggregate version of equation (19.2a) applied to aggregate per capita consumption, and substitute it into equation (19.7a). This yields

$$X_t = \gamma\alpha(R - 1)\frac{\delta R - 1}{\delta R(R - \gamma)} + (1 - \gamma)\left(1 - \frac{\gamma}{\delta R^2}\right)$$

$$\cdot \left[1 - \left(\frac{\gamma}{R}\right)(1 - \phi)\right]^{-1} E_{t-1}\sum_{\tau=0}^{\infty}\left(\frac{\gamma}{R}\right)^{\tau}(Y_{t+\tau} - T_{t+\tau}) \quad (19.7b)$$

$$+ (\Gamma - \gamma(1 - \phi))\sum_{\tau=0}^{\infty}\gamma^{\tau}(1 - \phi)^{\tau}X_{t-\tau-1} + \varepsilon_t,$$

where X_t is the aggregate per capita value of consumer purchases.

Equation (19.7b) is the focal relation for our empirical work. It expresses aggregate consumption purchases (per capita) as a function of a constant term, expected human wealth, lagged purchases, and an error term. The present formulation is general enough to encompass both Ricardian and non-Ricardian systems as special cases. The key parameter, in this context, is γ. When $\gamma = 1$ the system possesses Ricardian neutrality, and equation (19.7b) indicates that only lagged consumer purchases can be used to predict current purchases (similar to Hall [1978]). However, when $\gamma < 1$, expected human wealth affects current consumption purchases over and beyond the impact of lagged consumption purchases. For example, a current-period cut in taxes raises expected human wealth and thus results in an increase in consumption. The reason is that the future tax hike, needed in order to balance the intertemporal budget constraint of the government is given a smaller weight, by finite-horizon consumers, than the weight attached by them to the current cut in taxes.

3. Liquidity-Constrained Consumers

The foregoing specifications hold under the assumption that all consumers have free access to the capital market and thus can borrow against future incomes. In that case, Ricardian neutrality breaks down due to finite horizons (as captured by $\gamma < 1$). In this subsection, we extend the model to allow for an additional channel through which nonequivalence results may arise: the existence of liquidity constraints. Accordingly, we allow here for the possibility that while a fraction Π of aggregate consumption is due to consumers that have access to capital markets, a fraction $(1 - \Pi)$ is due to consumers who are liquidity-constrained in their consumption purchases. Formally,

$$X_t = \Pi X_{ut} + (1 - \Pi) X_{ct}, \tag{19.8}$$

where X_{ut} denotes consumption purchases of liquidity-unconstrained individuals, and X_{ct} denotes purchases of those that are subject to liquidity constraints. For X_{ut}, we use the specification in equation (19.7b), and for X_{ct} we use the following simple specification,

$$X_{ct} = Y_{t-1} + v_t, \tag{19.9}$$

That is, consumption purchases under liquidity constraints are modeled as the sum of two components last period's net income and an error term.[6]

It can be easily verified that in this augmented version of the model, Ricardian equivalence holds only under the restriction that $\gamma = 1$ and $\Pi = 1$. This restriction is tested in the next section.

2 Empirical Implementation

Specifications

To implement equation (19.7b) it is necessary to specify, under rational expectations, the stochastic processes that govern the evolution of gross income and taxes. Accordingly, we stipulate simple first-order autoregressive processes for these variables.[7]

$$Y_t - Y_{t-1} = \rho_Y (Y_{t-1} - Y_{t-2}) + \eta_{Yt} \tag{19.10}$$

$$T_t - T_{t-1} = \rho_T (T_{t-1} - T_{t-2}) + \eta_{Tt}, \tag{19.11}$$

where the ρs are time-independent, and the ηs are serially uncorrelated zero-

---

6. We use Y_{t-1} in this formulation because earned income (wages) during period $t - 1$ is typically paid at the beginning of period t. We also allow for a stochastic component of payment, v_1, during period t.

7. On the sensitivity of the empirical results with respect to alternative specifications see note 8.

mean stochastic terms that are orthogonal to variables dated $t - 1$ and previously.[8]

Using equations (19.10) and (19.11) to calculate expected human wealth yields, as shown in the Appendix, the following expression for consumption purchases:

$$X_t = d_0 + \sum_{i=1}^{n} d_{1i} x_{t-i} + d_2 Y_{t-1} + d_3 Y_{t-2}$$
$$+ d_4 T_{t-1} + d_5 T_{t-2} + \eta_{xt}, \quad (19.12)$$

where n is the number of lagged-purchases terms, and the d-coefficients satisfy the following restrictions:

$$d_0 = \frac{\gamma \alpha (R - 1)(\delta R - 1)}{\delta R(R - \gamma)};$$

$$d_{1i} = [\Gamma - \gamma(1 - \phi)]\gamma^{i-1}(1 - \phi)^{i-1}, \quad \text{for } i = 1, \ldots, n;$$

$$d_{1,n+1} = \Gamma \gamma^n (1 - \phi)^n;$$

$$d_2 = (1 - \gamma) 1 - \left(\frac{\gamma}{\delta R^2}\right)\left[1 - \frac{\gamma}{R}(1 - \phi)\right]^{-1}\left[\left(\frac{R}{R - \gamma}\right)(1 + \rho_y)\right.$$
$$+ \frac{\rho_Y^2 \gamma}{R} + \frac{\gamma^2 \rho_Y^2}{R(1 - \rho_Y)(R - \gamma)} - \left.\frac{\rho_Y^4 \gamma^2}{(1 - \rho_Y)R(R - \rho_Y\gamma)}\right];$$

$$d_3 = (1 - \gamma)\left(1 - \frac{\gamma}{\delta R^2}\right)\left[1 - \frac{\gamma}{R}(1 - \phi)\right]^{-1}\left(\frac{R}{R - \gamma}\right) - d_2;$$

$$d_4 = -(1 - \gamma)\left(1 - \frac{\gamma}{\delta R^2}\right)\left[1 - \frac{\gamma}{R}(1 - \phi)\right]^{-1}\left[\left(\frac{R}{R - \gamma}\right)(1 + \rho_T)\right.$$
$$+ \frac{\rho_T^4 \gamma}{R} + \frac{\gamma^2 \rho_T^2}{R(1 - \rho_T)(R - \gamma)} - \left.\frac{\rho_T^4 \gamma^2}{(1 - \rho_T)R(R - \rho_T\gamma)}\right];$$

$$d_5 = (1 - \gamma)\left(1 - \frac{\gamma}{\delta R^2}\right)\left[1 - \frac{\gamma}{R}(1 - \phi)\right]^{-1}\left(\frac{R}{R - \gamma}\right) - d_4.$$

Equations (19.8–19.12) form the system to be empirically analyzed.

8. Experimentation with univariate and multivariate autoregressive processes with longer lag structures for the forcing variables and with constant terms yielded results that do not reject the present first-difference univariate system (with no constants).

Findings

Several versions of the system consisting of equations 19.8–19.12 are estimated using Israeli monthly data covering the period 1980–1985. The use of
monthly data clearly limits our choice of the actual time series that serve as
counterparts for the variables in the model. For consumption purchases, X,
we use an index of purchases within the organized retail trade.[9] Total wage
bill is used for income, Y, and government tax receipts are used for T. The
data source is Bank of Israel's Publication *Main Economic Indicators* (various
issues).

Estimation was performed by nonlinear least squares (from the TSP program) jointly applied to the system. The estimator is based on computing
maximum likelihood, and the estimates are obtained by concentrating variance parameters out of the multivariate likelihood and then maximizing the
negative of the log-determinant of the residual covariance matrix. As is well
known, the estimates are efficient if the disturbances are multivariate normal
and identically distributed. Table 19.1 reports different versions of the estimated model, allowing for seven lags in the estimation of the durability parameter and setting the monthly risk-free real interest factor to 1.002.[10]
Column (1) gives the parameter estimates of the model. The likelihood ratio
test of the model against its unrestricted counterpart yields a χ^2 statistic of
12.3 (with 8 degrees of freedom), which is not significant at the one-percent-
significance level. The statistic for the test equals twice the difference between
the unrestricted values of the log-likelihood function. Estimates of the unrestricted version are given in the Appendix. While this indicates that the data
do not reject the model, some of the parameters obtain somewhat implausible
estimated values. In particular, δ and Π seem to be too high relative to what
is commonly expected. The parameter γ is smaller than but close to unity.
Under Blanchard's formulation, this parameter stands for the survival probability. A monthly $\gamma = 0.989$ implies under this interpretation an expected life
of $\gamma^{12}/[(1 - \gamma^{12})]^{-2} = 58$ years. Although viewed from the time of birth this
is a low life expectancy, it seems more plausible when viewed from the point

9. These monthly measures of consumption are closely correlated with the national-accounts
series for consumption. Using quarterly moving averages of the monthly purchases data we obtain a correlation coefficient of 0.9 between our time series and the national-accounts quarterly
consumption series. (See also Fischer 1986.) In conformity with the theoretical model one should
have used per capita data. However, in view of the small changes in population during the short
sample period and the unavailability of these data on a monthly basis we use aggregate data in
the study.

10. Experimenting with different lags as well as different realistic values of R did not yield
noticeably different results from those reported in table 19.1. We a priori set the value of R in
order to identify the other parameters.

Table 19.1
Estimated Versions of the Model
(Israel: 1980:9–1985:12)

Parameters	Model's Restrictions (1)	As in Column (1) and $\gamma = 1.0$ (2)	As in Column (1) and $\Pi = 1.0$ (3)	As in Columns (2) and (3) (4)
ρ_Y	−0.17	−0.23	−0.23	−0.24
	(0.05)	(0.10)	(0.10)	(0.10)
ρ_T	−0.57	−0.58	−0.58	−0.58
	(0.09)	(0.09)	(0.09)	(0.09)
δ	1.20	1.03	1.04	1.03
	(0.06)	(0.02)	(0.02)	(0.02)
α	104.81	233.19	220.54	301.80
	(105.89)	(112.11)	(110.03)	(62.79)
ϕ	0.24	0.20	0.20	0.21
	(0.04)	(0.06)	(0.06)	(0.06)
γ	0.986	1.00[a]	0.999	1.00[a]
	(0.01)		(0.0002)	
Π	2.09	0.99	1.00[a]	1.00[a]
	(0.45)	(0.02)		
L	−618.94	−622.27	−622.19	−622.45

Note: The basic model consists of equations 19.8–19.12.

Its parameter estimates are reported in Column (1). L denotes the value of the log-likelihood function. Figures in parentheses are estimated standard errors. The values of L for the unrestricted system is 612.79 (free parameters).

[a] Imposed value.

of view of the average horizon for consumption-decision-making of the mature population.

Columns (2) and (3) impose further restrictions on the esimated model. In column (2), we set consumer's time horizon to infinity ($\gamma = 1.0$) and the estimated model is not rejected when compared to the unrestricted model. (The likelihood ratio is 18.96, with 9 degrees of freedom.) Interestingly, more plausible parameter estimates obtain in this column than in the previous one, including an estimated value for the fraction of liquidity-unconstrained consumption close to (and below) unity. Column (3) allows for estimation of γ, but sets of parameter Π equal to unity. Again, this version of the model is not rejected using a likelihood ratio test (whose value is about the same as the one for column [2]). The parameter γ obtains a value of 0.999 which is larger than the one reported in column (1). Notice that in moving from column (1) to the next column the estimated value of δ decline and become closer to unity.

The Ricardian-equivalence proposition implies the $\gamma = \Pi = 1.0$ restriction, which is tested in column (4). The likelihood ratio for testing this restriction against the unrestricted counterpart of the model is 19.32 (with 10 degrees of freedom). This is lower than the one percent chi-square critical value of 23.2. Thus, Ricardian neutrality is not rejected by the data.[11]

Having established this result, we can now discuss the parameter estimates for the specification of the model that embodies the neutrality properties. The parameters generally obtain the hypothesized signs and are significantly different from zero. The estimated first-order autoregressive parameters of the processes for $(Y_t - Y_{t-1})$ and $(T_t - T_{t-1})$ are negative indicating that shocks to these variables tend to be reversed in subsequent months. Shocks to the gross income variable show a larger degree of persistence than shocks to the tax variable. The estimated monthly subjective discount factor is slightly above unity; however, we have tested for $\delta = 1.0$ and the test does not reject this hypothesis.[12] The utility function parameter α is positive and equal to 301.8. An important feature of this value is that it satisfies the assumption that marginal utility of consumption is positive, i.e., $\alpha > c$. Specifically, the maximal value of consumption purchases in the sample implies, using a durability parameter of 0.79, for seven lags, a maximal stock of consumption goods of about 85 (index units) which is smaller than the estimated α. Further, this estimated parameter can be used to calculate the implied degree of relative risk aversion $(C/(\alpha - C))$, which turns out to be equal to 0.3 (at the mean sample value of consumption purchases).[13] The parameter estimate for ϕ implies that 21 percent of the stock of consumer goods depreciates from month to month. Since, due to lack of more refined monthly data, our measure of consumption purchases includes goods with different degree of durability, this parameter ϕ should be interpreted as an average depreciation rate.

3. Substitution between Public and Private Consumption

We now extend the model by allowing direct effects of government spending on private consumption. The model's specification in section 1 can be interpreted as one that incorporates public goods in the utility function in a separable way, implying that public goods have neutral effects on the consumption

11. This result is different from that in our NBER paper (Leiderman and Razin 1986). It turns out that once we allow for some degree of durability in consumption (as in the present paper) the results become more favorable to Ricardian neutrality.

12. Interestingly, Hansen and Singleton (1983) also found that the point estimate of δ (with monthly U.S. data) is close to (and sometimes above) unity.

13. This estimate for the degree of relative risk aversion falls within the range of those reported in studies for the United States.

of private goods. The present extension differs from the foregoing specifications since it allows for substitutability between public and private consumption. When the degree of substitution approaches zero we are back to the original model.

Let the utility function be specified by

$$U(c_t, G_t) = \alpha(c_t + \theta G_t) - \frac{1}{2}(c_t + \theta G_t)^2,$$

$$(19.3a)$$

$$G_t = (1 - \phi)G_{t-1} + g_t,$$

where G denotes the stock of public consumption, g denotes the flow of government purchases, and θ is a parameter that measures the weight of public consumption in total private *effective* consumption, $c_t + \theta G_t$ (see Aschauer 1985). For tractability, the rates of depreciation of the stocks of private and public consumption goods are assumed to be identical and are denoted by ϕ. As shown in the Appendix, in this case, the analogue of equation (19.6), expressing aggregate per capita consumption, is

$$C_t = \beta_0 + \beta_1 \left[E_t \sum_{\tau=0}^{\infty} \left(\frac{\gamma}{R} \right)^{\tau} (y_{1+\tau} + \theta g_{t+\tau}) - RB_{t-1} \right.$$

$$\left. + \gamma(1 - \phi)(C_{t-1} + \theta g_{t-1}) \right] - \theta G_t. \qquad (19.14)$$

Similarly, the analogue of equation (19.7a) of above is

$$C_t = \gamma\alpha(R - 1) \frac{\delta R - 1}{\delta R(R - \gamma)} + (1 - \gamma)\left(1 - \frac{\gamma}{\delta R^2} \right)\left[1 \right.$$

$$\left. - \frac{\gamma}{R}(1 - \phi) \right]^{-1} E_{t-1} \sum_{\tau=0}^{\infty} \left(\frac{\gamma}{R} \right)^{\tau} \left[Y_{t+\tau} - T_{t+\tau} + \theta g_{t+\tau} \right] \qquad (19.15)$$

$$+ \Gamma(C_{t-1} + \theta G_{t-1}) - \theta G_t + \varepsilon_t'.$$

We assume that the expected flow of future public consumption evolves according to the simple process

$$g_t - g_{t-1} = \rho_g(g_{t-1} - g_{t-2}) + \eta_{gt}. \qquad (19.16)$$

Equation (19.15) can then be rewritten as

$$X_t = d_0' + \sum_{i=1}^{n} d_{1i}(X_{t-i} + \theta g_{t-i}) + d_2 Y_{t-1} + d_3 Y_{t-2}$$
$$+ d_4 T_{t-1} + d_5 T_{t-2} + d_6 g_{t-1} + d_7 g_{t-2} + \varepsilon_t', \tag{19.17}$$

where d_1 through d_5 are as in equation (19.12) above, and

$$d_6 = \theta(1 - \gamma)\left(1 - \frac{\gamma}{\delta R^2}\right)\left[1 - \frac{\gamma}{R}(1 - \phi)\right]^{-1}$$
$$\times \left[\frac{R}{R - \gamma}(1 + \rho_g) + \frac{\rho_g^2 \gamma}{R} + \frac{\gamma^2 \rho_g^2}{R(1 - \rho_g)(R - \gamma)}\right.$$
$$\left. - \frac{\rho_g^4 \gamma^2}{(1 - \rho_g)(R(R - \rho_g \gamma))}\right] - \theta(1 + \rho_g),$$
$$d_7 = \theta(1 - \gamma)\left(1 - \frac{\gamma}{\delta R^2}\right)\left[1 - \frac{\gamma}{R}(1 - \phi)\right]^{-1}\left(\frac{R}{R - \gamma}\right)$$
$$+ \theta\rho_g - d_6.$$

Note that equation (19.17) holds for liquidity-unconstrained consumers. As in section 1.3, Liquidity-constrained Consumers, we embed this equation in a more general framework in which aggregate consumption includes also another component which is due to liquidity-constrained individuals. Accordingly, equations constitute the more general system to be implemented in this section.

Table 19.2 reports the results of estimating two versions of the system. To save degrees of freedom under this augmented version of the model, the number of lags used in estimating the durability parameter is set equal to 3. Column (1) gives the parameter estimates under the model's restrictions. These restrictions are not rejected against the unrestricted version of the model; the pertinent likelihood ratio is 14.52 (with 7 degrees of freedom), a value that is below the critical one percent value of 18.5. Column (2) can be used to test Ricardian neutrality which implies the $\gamma = \Pi = 1.0$ restriction. As before, this hypothesis is not rejected by the data. In extending the model and going from table 19.1 to table 19.2 it can be observed that most of the parameter estimates do not change noticeably. However, in contrast to the notion of government consumption yielding positive marginal utility, the estimated value of θ is negative.[14] Thus, although statistically the

14. This may reflect improper measurement of public consumption in our data set. This measure is derived from cash-flow accounts of the Treasury, which partly include transfer payments

Table 19.2
The Model with Public Goods
(Israel: 1980:9–1985:12)

Parameters	Model's Restrictions (1)	As (1) and $\gamma = \Pi = 1.0$ (2)
ρ_Y	−0.23 (0.08)	−0.22 (0.10)
ρ_T	−0.59 (0.07)	−0.59 (0.07)
ρ_g	−0.56 (0.08)	−0.55 (0.07)
δ	1.17 (0.12)	1.04 (0.04)
α	152.66 (218.47)	128.78 (36.64)
ϕ	0.41 (0.08)	0.39 (0.09)
γ	0.989 (0.02)	1.00[a]
Π	1.37 (0.29)	1.00[a]
θ	−0.52 (0.20)	−0.47 (0.26)
L	−781.87	−782.52

Notes: The model consists of equations 19.8–19.11, 19.16–19.17. Its parameter estimates are reported in column (1). L denotes the value of the log-likelihood function. Figures in parentheses are estimated standard errors. The value of L for the unrestricted system is −774.61 (16 free parameters).

[a] Imposed value

specification underlying column (2) is not rejected by the data, the public consumption variable has effects that do not conform with the theoretical model.

4. Conclusions

In this paper, we have developed a stochastic framework in which the intertemporal implications of the Ricardian-equivalence proposition can be tested with aggregate time-series data. The framework allows for two types of deviations from Ricardian neutrality. The first is due to finite consumers' plan-

---

such as consumption subsidies. In a study based on U.S. data, Aschauer (1985) reports estimated value for θ of 0.23.

ning horizons, and is modeled as an extension of Blanchard (1985) to a stochastic environment. The second is due to the existence of liquidity constraints on consumption behavior. In addition, our framework allows for direct substitutability between private and public consumption, and treats explicitly the degree of durability of aggregate consumption.

The model was implemented on monthly data for Israel during the first half of the 1980s, a period of high and volatile government budget deficits. Our main findings are that the restrictions implied by the Ricardian-neutrality hypothesis are not rejected by the sample information, and that the resulting parameter estimates generally conform with the theoretical model. These features held up when the model was extended to allow for public goods consumption, with the exception that the parameter capturing the direct effects of public consumption on private utility turned out to be implausible.

There are several interesting possible extensions of the present research. First, it would be important to allow for additional sources of deviations from Ricardian neutrality, such as the existence of distortionary taxes (e.g., income, value added, and inflation taxes). In this context, it is desirable to decompose taxes into at least two categories: consumption and income taxes.[15] Second, another channel through which government policies can affect private consumption is related to monetary and exchange-rate policies.[16] Third, the model's specifications can be modified to allow for different effects on private consumption of various components of government spending, potentially capturing substitutability as well as complementary with private consumption. Fourth, the model could be extended to allow for a bequest motive. Since negative bequests are not feasible, individuals may become constrained. In such a case Ricardian neutrality breaks down. In this specification the key factor to be tested in the context of Ricardian neutrality is the strength of the bequest motive relative to the path of income growth in the economy. These extensions to the intertemporal framework of consumption determination are necessary before policy recommendations based on the Ricardian neutrality theme are advanced.

Appendix

1. Derivation of the Consumption Function (Equation 19.4))

The maximization problem described in section 1.1 can be expressed in dynamic programming terms by the value function V as

15. As shown by Frenkel and Razin (1986), private spending responds differently to cuts in alternative types of taxes.

16. For a theoretical analysis, see Helpman and Razin (1987).

$$V\left(y_t - \frac{R}{\gamma} b_{t-1}\right) = \underset{x_t}{\text{Max}}\left\{ U(x_t + (1 - \phi)c_{t-1}) \right.$$

$$\left. + \gamma\delta E_t V\left(y_{t+1} + \frac{R}{\gamma}\left(y_t - x_t - \frac{R}{\gamma} b_{t-1}\right)\right)\right\}. \quad (19A.1)$$

Differentiating the right-hand side of (19A.1) and equating to zero yields

$$U'(c_t) - \delta R E_t V'(\cdot) = 0, \quad (19A.2)$$

where prime denotes derivatives.

Totally differentiating (19A.1) yields

$$V'(y_t - \frac{R}{\gamma} b_{t-1}) = [U'(c_t) - \delta R E_t V'(\cdot)] \frac{dx_t}{dy_t}$$
$$+ \delta R E_t V'(\cdot) = \delta R E_t V'(\cdot), \quad (19A.3)$$

where use has been made of (19A.2). Equations (19A.2) and (19A.3) imply

$$U'(c_t) = \delta R E_t U'(c_{t+1}). \quad (19A.4)$$

Using the quadratic utility function specified in equation (19.3), (19A.4) can be expressed as

$$\alpha - c_t = \delta R E_t(\alpha - c_{t+1}) \quad (19A.5)$$

Define expected human wealth by

$$E_t h_t = E_t \sum_{T=0}^{\infty} \left(\frac{\gamma}{R}\right)^\tau y_{t+\tau}. \quad (19A.6)$$

From equation (19A.6) we obtain

$$y_t = E_t h_t - \frac{\gamma}{R} E_t h_{t+1}. \quad (19A.7)$$

Define expected wealth by

$$E_t w_t = E_t h_t - \frac{R}{\gamma} b_{t-1} + (1 - \phi)c_{t-1}. \quad (19A.8)$$

Then, from the constraints (equations (19.2a) and (19.2b)) and from equation (19A.7) we get

$$ac_t = E_t w_t - \left(\frac{\gamma}{R}\right) E_t w_{t+1}. \tag{19A.9}$$

where $a = 1 - (\gamma/R)(1 - \phi)$.

Postulating that the solution to the maximization problem is of the form

$$c_t = \beta_0 + \beta_1 E_t w_t, \tag{19A.10}$$

equations (19A.9) and (19A.10) imply

$$E_t w_{t+1} = \frac{R}{\gamma} [-\beta_0 a + (1 - \beta_1 a) E_t w_t]. \tag{19A.11}$$

Substituting (19A.10) into (19A.5) yields

$$\alpha - (\beta_0 + \beta_1 E_t w_t) = \delta R[\alpha - ((\beta_0 + \beta_1 E_t w_{t+1})]. \tag{19A.12}$$

Substituting (19A.11) into (19A.12) yields

$$\alpha - (\beta_0 + \beta_1 E_t w_t)$$

$$= \delta R\left[\alpha - \left(\beta_0 + \beta_1 \frac{R}{\gamma} \cdot (-\beta_0 a + (1 - \beta_1 a) E_t w_t)\right)\right]. \tag{19A.13}$$

Rearranging terms in equation (19A.13) yields

$$\left[(1 - \delta R)\alpha - \left(1 - \delta R\left(1 - \frac{R}{\gamma}\beta_1 a\right)\right)\beta_0\right]$$
$$+ \left[-1 + \frac{\delta R^2}{\gamma}(1 - \beta_1 a)\right]\beta_1 E_t w_t = 0. \tag{19A.14}$$

The solution specified in equation (19A.10) is confirmed when (19A.14) holds for all $E_t w_t$. This requirement is fulfilled when the bracketed terms in (19A.14) equal zero. Thus,

$$1 - \beta_1 a = \frac{\gamma}{\delta R^2}, \quad \left(\beta_1 = \frac{1}{a}\left(1 - \frac{\gamma}{\delta R^2}\right)\right). \tag{19A.15}$$

$$\beta_0 = \alpha \frac{\gamma(1 - \delta R)}{\delta R(R - \gamma)}. \tag{19A.16}$$

2. *Derviation of Equations (19.7a) and (19.7b)*

Aggregating equation (19.2b) over all cohorts, the per capita flow budget constraint lagged one period is

$$B_{t-1} = X_{t-1} - Y_{t-1} + RB_{t-2}, \qquad (19A.17)$$

where X_t denotes aggregate purchases per capita. Substituting equations (19.2a), (19A.7), and (19.6) into (19A.17) yields

$$B_{t-1} = \beta_0 + (\beta_1 - 1)E_{t-1}h_{t-1} + \frac{\gamma}{R}E_{t-1}h_t \qquad (19A.18)$$
$$+ R(1 - \beta_1)B_{t-2} + \gamma(1 - \phi)(\beta_1 - 1)C_{t-2}.$$

Define

$$E_tW_t = E_th_t - RB_{t-1} + \gamma(1 - \phi)C_{t-1}$$
$$= E_{t-1}h_t - RB_{t-1} + \gamma(1 - \phi)C_{t-1} + \varepsilon_t', \quad (19A.19)$$

where $\varepsilon_t^* = (E_th_t - E_{t-1}h_t)$. Substituting (19A.18) into (19A.19) yields

$$E_tW_t = (1 - \gamma)E_{t-1}h_t - R\beta_0 - R(\beta_1 - 1)E_{t-1}W_{t-1} \quad (19A.20)$$
$$+ \gamma(1 - \phi)C_{t-1} + \varepsilon_t^*.$$

Equation (19.6) in the text is rewritten as

$$C_t = \beta_0 + \beta_1 E_tW_t. \qquad (19A.21)$$

Lagging (19A.21) and rearranging yields

$$E_{t-1}W_{t-1} = \frac{1}{\beta_1}(C_{t-1} - \beta_0). \qquad (19A.22)$$

Substituting (19A.22) into (19A.20) yields

$$E_tW_t = (1 - \gamma)E_{t-1}h_t + \gamma(1 - \phi)C_{t-1} - R\beta_0 \qquad (19A.23)$$
$$- \frac{R(\beta_1 - 1)}{\beta_1}(C_{t-1} - \beta_0) + \varepsilon_t,$$

which can be substituted into (19A.21) to yield

$$C_t = \beta_0(1 - R) + \beta_1(1 - \gamma)E_{t-1}h_t$$
$$+ [\gamma(1 - \phi)\beta_1 - R(\beta_1 - 1)]C_{t-1} + \varepsilon_t, \tag{19A.24}$$

where $\varepsilon_t = \beta_1\varepsilon_t^*$.

Equation (19A.24) corresponds to equation (19.7a) in the text. The solution to the individual maximization problem, therefore, is given by the equation (19.4) in the text.

3. Derivation of the Estimated Consumption Equation (Equation 19.12)

Here we incorporate the stochastic processes governing the evolution of disposable income into equation (19.7b) in the text. For brevity, we illustrate the calculations for the case in which there is a single autoregressive process applicable to Y and T, given by

$$Y_t - Y_{t-1} = \rho(Y_{t-1} - Y_{t-2}) + \eta_t, \qquad E_t\eta_t = 0. \tag{19A.25}$$

Notice that here we allow for a constant term λ, which is dropped later in the empirical analysis. Let $z_t = Y_t - Y_{t-1}$. Equation (19A.25) yields

$$z_{t+i} = \rho^i z_t + \sum_{\tau=0}^{i} \rho^{i-\tau}\eta_{t+\tau}, \qquad i \geq 1. \tag{19A.26}$$

Substituting equation (19A.26) into $E_t h_t$ yields

$$E_{t-1}h_t = E_{t-1}\left[Y_t + \frac{\gamma}{R}(Y_t + \rho(Y_t - Y_{t-1})) \right.$$
$$+ \left(\frac{\gamma}{R}\right)^2(Y_{t+1} + \rho(Y_{t+1} - Y_t)) + \ldots \right]$$
$$= E_{t-1}\left[Y_t + \frac{\gamma}{R}(Y_t + \rho(Y_t - Y_{t-1})) \right. \tag{19A.27}$$
$$+ \left(\frac{\gamma}{R}\right)^2(Y_t + \rho(Y_t - Y_{t-1})$$
$$+ \rho^2(Y_t - Y_{t-1}) + \ldots) \right].$$

Using (19A.26),

$$
\begin{aligned}
E_{t-1}h_t &= E_{t-1}\left[Y_t + \frac{\gamma}{R}(Y_t + \rho z_t) \right. \\
&\quad + \left. \left(\frac{\gamma}{R}\right)^2 (Y_t + (\rho + \rho^2)z_t) + \ldots \right] \\
&= \left(\frac{R}{R - \gamma}\right) z_{t-1} + \rho(z_{t-1} - z_{t-2})) \\
&\quad + \rho \frac{\gamma}{R}\left[1 + \left(\frac{\gamma}{R}\frac{1}{1 - \rho}\right)\left(\frac{R}{R - \gamma}\right) \right. \\
&\quad \left. - \frac{\gamma}{R}\frac{\rho^2}{1 - \rho}\left(\frac{R}{R - \rho\gamma}\right) \right]\rho(z_{t-1} - z_{t-2}).
\end{aligned}
\tag{19A.28}
$$

Finally, noting that $E_{t-1}h_t = E_{t-1}\sum_{\tau=0}^{\infty}(\gamma/R)^\tau(Y_{t+\tau} - T_{t+\tau})$ allowing for separate stochastic processes for Y_t and T_t as in equations (19.8) and (19.9), substituting formulas such as (19A.28) for both expected gross income and taxes into equation (19.7) yields equation (19.12) in the text.

4. Derivation of Equations (19.14) and (19.15)

The solution method applied in section 1 of this appendix is now applied to the extended utility function, equation (19.13a). The analogue of (19A.5) is

$$
\alpha - (c_t + \theta G_t) = \delta RE_t(\alpha - (c_{t+1} + \theta G_{t+1})). \tag{19A.29}
$$

The solution to the maximization problem is of the form

$$
(c_t + \theta G_t) = \beta_0 + \beta_1 E_t \tilde{w}_t, \tag{19A.30}
$$

where

$$
E_t \tilde{w}_t \equiv E_t\left[\sum_{\tau=0}^{\infty}\left(\frac{\gamma}{R}\right)^\tau (Y_{t+\tau} + \theta g)_{t+\tau} - RB_{t-1} \right.
$$
$$
\left. + \gamma(1 - \phi)(C_{t-1} + \theta G_{t-1}) \right].
$$

This gives equation (19.14) of the text.

To see this, one can use equations (19A.9) and (19A.21) to obtain

$$\left[(1 - \delta R)\alpha - \left(1 - \delta R\left(1 - \frac{R}{\gamma}\beta_1 \right) \right)\beta_0 \right]$$

$$+ \left[-1 + \delta\frac{R^2}{\gamma}(1 - \beta_1) \right]\beta_1 E_t\tilde{w}_t = 0, \quad (19A.31)$$

which holds for any values of $\tilde{w}_t$ and G_t when β_0 and β_1 are chosen so that the bracketed terms are zero.

It can be verified that the expressions of β_0 and β_1 which solve (19A.31) are given in equations (19A.15) and (19A.16), respectively. Equation (19.15) of the text is obtained from equation (19A.30) using similar calculations as done in section 1 of the Appendix.

5. Estimates of the Unrestricted Versions of the Model

A. *The Model in Table 19.1.*

$$Y_t - Y_{t-1} = -0.23(Y_{t-1} - Y_{t-2}).$$
$$\qquad\qquad (0.13)$$

$$T_t - T_{t-1} = -0.61(T_{t-1} - T_{t-2}).$$
$$\qquad\qquad (0.08)$$

$$X_t = 4.27 + 0.25X_{t-1} + 0.04X_{t-2} + 0.14X_{t-3}$$
$$\quad (7.70) \quad (0.14) \qquad (0.15) \qquad (0.12)$$

$$+ 0.07X_{t-4} - 0.02X_{t-5} - 0.14X_{t-6} + 0.11X_{t-7}$$
$$\quad (0.10) \qquad (0.11) \qquad (0.12) \qquad (0.12)$$

$$+ 0.31X_{t-8} + 0.03Y_{t-1} - 0.04Y_{t-2} - 0.06T_{t-1}$$
$$\quad (0.17) \qquad (0.03) \qquad (0.03) \qquad (0.27)$$

$$+ 0.65T_{t-2}$$
$$\quad (0.23)$$

B. *The Model in Table 19.2.*

$$Y_t - Y_{t-1} = -0.22(Y_{t-1} - Y_{t-2}).$$
$$(0.14)$$

$$T_t - T_{t-1} = -0.61(T_{t-1} - T_{t-2}).$$
$$(0.08)$$

$$g_t - g_{t-1} = -0.56(g_{t-1} - g_{t-2}).$$
$$(0.10)$$

$$X_t\, p = 11.26 + 0.37X_{t-1} + 0.04X_{t-2} + 0.26X_{t-3}$$
$$(7.85)\quad (0.15)\qquad (0.13)\qquad\quad (0.12)$$

$$+ 0.18X_{t-4} - 0.04g_{t-1} - 0.40g_{t-2} - 0.25g_{t-3}$$
$$(0.13)\qquad\quad (0.20)\qquad (0.26)\qquad\quad (0.20)$$

$$- 0.13g_{t-4} + 0.01Y_{t-1} - 0.02Y_{t-2} - 0.12T_{t-1}$$
$$(0.14)\qquad\quad (0.03)\qquad (0.05)\qquad\quad (0.32)$$

$$+ 0.81T_{t-2}.$$
$$(0.31)$$

(Numbers in parentheses are estimated standard errors. Log-likelihood values for these unrestricted systems are provided in tables 19.1 and 19.2)

References

Aschauer, David A. 1985. Fiscal Policy and Aggregate Demand. *American Economic Review* 75 (March): 117–27.

Barro, Robert J. 1974. Are Government Bonds Net Wealth? *Journal of Political Economy* 82 (November/Decmeber): 1095–1117.

Blanchard, Olivier J. 1985. Debt, Deficits and Finite Horizons. *Journal of Political Economy* 93 (April): 223–47.

Feldstein, Martin. 1982. "Government Deficits and Aggregate Demand. *Journal of Monetary Economics* 9 (January): 1–20.

Fisher, Yaacov. 1986. Economic Indicators in the Israeli Economy. *Bank of Israel Economic Quarterly* 61 (July): 75–103 (Hebrew).

Frenkel, Jacob A., and Assaf Razin. 1986. Fiscal Policies in the World Economy. *Journal of Political Economy* 94 (June): 564–94.

————. 1986. Deficits with Distortionary Taxes: International Dimensions. Paper prepared for the 4th Sapir Conference. Tel Aviv University, December.

Hall, Robert E. 1978. Stochastic Implications of the Life-Cycle Permanent Income Hypothesis: Theory and Evidence. *Journal of Political Economy* 86 (December): 971–88.

Hansen, Lars P., and Kenneth J. Singleton. 1983. Consumption, Risk Aversion and the Temporal Behavior of Asset Returns. *Journal of Political Economy* 91 (April): 1269–86.

Hayashi, Fumio. 1985. Tests for Liquidity Constraints: A Critical Survey. Working Paper 1720. National Bureau of Economic Research, (October).

Helpman, Elhanan, and Assaf Razin, 1987. Exchange Rate Management: Intertemporal Tradeoffs. *American Economic Review* 77 (March): 107–23.

Hubbard, R. Glenn, and Kenneth L. Judd. 1986. Liquidity Constraints, Fiscal Policy, and Consumption. *Brookings Papers on Economic Activity* 1: 1–50.

Kochin, Levis A. 1974. Are Future Taxes Anticipated by Consumers? *Journal of Money, Credit, and Banking* 6 (August): 385–94.

Kormendi, Roger C. 1983. Government Debt, Government Spending and Private Sector Behavior. *American Economic Review* 73 (December): 994–1010.

Leiderman, Leonardo, and Mario Blejer. 1988. Modeling and Testing Ricardian Equivalence: A Survey. *IMF Staff Papers*, 35:1–35.

Leiderman, Leonardo, and Assaf Razin. 1986. Consumption and Government-Budget Finance in a High-deficit Economy. Working Paper 2032. National Bureau of Economic Research, (September).

Lucas, Robert E., Jr. 1976. Econometric Policy Evaluation: A Critique. In *The Phillips Curve and Labor Markets,* Karl Brunner and Allan H. Meltzer, 19–46. Amsterdam: North Holland.

Poterba, James M., and Lawrence H. Summers. 1986. Finite Lifetimes and the Crowding Out Effects of Budget Deficits. Discussion Paper 1255. Harvard Institute of Economic Research, (August).

Reid, Bradford G. 1985. Aggregate Consumption and Deficit Financing: An Attempt to Separate Permanent from Transitory Effects. *Economic Inquiry* 23 (July): 475–86.

Seater, John. 1982. Are Future Taxes Discounted? *Journal of Money, Credit, and Banking* 14 (February): 76–83.

Tanner, J. Ernest. 1979. An Empirical Investigation of Tax Discounting. *Journal of Money, Credit, and Banking* 11 (May): 214–18.

Tobin, James, and Walter Dolde. 1971. Wealth, Liquidity and Consumption. In *Consumer Spending and Monetary Policy: The Linkages,* 99–146. Federal Reserve Bank of Boston.

van Wijnbergen, Sweder. 1985. Interdependence Revisited: A Developing Countries' Perspective on Macroeconomic Management and Trade Policy in the Industrial World. *Economic Policy* 1 (September): 203–48.

Index